# ARCHBISHOP

# ARCHBISHOP

*The Life and Times
of Robert Runcie*

Jonathan Mantle

SINCLAIR-STEVENSON

*First published in Great Britain by*
*Sinclair-Stevenson Limited*
*7/8 Kendrick Mews*
*London SW7 3HG, England*

*Copyright © 1991 by Jonathan Mantle*

*British Library Cataloguing in Publication Data*
*A CIP catalogue for this book is available from the British Library.*
*ISBN: 1 85619 058 7*

*Phototypeset by Rowland Phototypesetting Limited*
*Bury St Edmunds, Suffolk*
*Printed and bound in Great Britain by*
*Clays Limited, St Ives plc.*

# Introit

'*If a man desireth the office of bishop, he desireth a good work.*'
– St Paul, *circa* AD 50

'He's not the Archbishop of Canterbury; he's my Dad. He will retire and live in a two-up, two-down in St Albans. We were a family before and we will be a family afterwards. As soon as he's not the Archbishop of Canterbury, I shall be a normal person again.'
– James Runcie, 1983

'I'm not so sure of that any more.'
– James Runcie, 1990

# Contents

# PROCESSIONAL

LAMBETH PALACE, DECEMBER 1987.

The Archbishop had thought long and hard before he made up his mind. He did so in most things. To some this was his great strength, to others his great weakness.

The telephone rang at the other end and the familiar voice answered. There was no mistaking it: Dr Gareth Bennett. The Archbishop spoke.

Silence followed.

The Archbishop spoke again. A further silence. Neither man spoke another word. Dr Bennett had replaced the receiver.

Afterwards, long afterwards, there were two conversations that stood out in his formidable memory. Two conversations which had never happened, never could have happened, and which he devoutly wished had taken place. The first was with Terry Waite:

*'Terry, would you please step into my office for a moment? And, Terry. I wonder if you would be kind enough to bring your passport?'*

*'Terry, I do not want you to undertake any more journeys abroad without first consulting me. Is that clear? I do not want you to have anything more to do with hostages. Terry, you are NOT going back to the Lebanon.'*

Downstairs in the Crypt, a solitary candle burned in hope, the only evidence for almost a year now.

That conversation, and now this one. What would he have said to Gary Bennett? That he had read the *Crockford's* Preface, guessed who had written it? That there was nothing new in the content, even if the tone had surprised him?

In the Crypt, a big man was reduced to a single candle. Now, with this affair, precisely the opposite had happened. James 3 had it: '*Behold how great a matter a little fire kindleth*.' Though he did not know it, worse was to come.

Who else could he talk to? Bill Vanstone? Sister Jane? They were more than friends. They seemed somehow closer to God, the last calls you could make to Him by conventional, telephonic means. There was prayer. Prayer to the sceptic was just another conversation that had never taken place. But, to the believer, prayer was an altogether different matter. Prayer was harder work than the telephone and there was no certainty of getting through as quickly. But the Archbishop knew that there would at least be an answer.

# 1

# *The Priest*

(The Bishop) 'Do you think that you are truly called, according to the will of our Lord Jesus Christ, and the due order of this Realm, to the Ministry of the Church?'
(Answer) 'I think so.'
— THE ORDERING OF DEACONS IN THE BOOK OF COMMON PRAYER

ROBERT Alexander Kennedy Runcie was born on 2 October 1921, the youngest of four children. Anne 'Nancy' Runcie and Robert Dalziel Runcie lived at 6, Moor Lane, Crosby, Lancashire. They were not a particularly religious family.

Robert Runcie Senior was a draper's son from Kilmarnock, a lowland Scot who worked in Liverpool as an electrical engineer at the Tate & Lyle sugar refinery. He was a good-natured man with a love of football and the turf, and a Presbyterian suspicion of the clergy, whom he called 'black beetles'; he would recite salvoes of Burns on the subject to prove his point.

Nancy Runcie's parents were Irish. She was an adequate if unenthusiastic home-maker, an avid reader of romantic novels and a freelance hairdresser. After she married and before Robert was born, she had worked in this capacity on two Cunard cruises to the Mediterranean: an environment her youngest child was later also to find congenial.

Robert had a brother, Kenneth, aged eight, and two sisters, Marjorie aged nine and Kathleen aged twelve. Shortly after he was born the family moved to 26, Queen's Road, Crosby. When he was two years old his mother departed on the last cruise of her hairdressing career, travelling around the world. A great-aunt came to look after the children with a young woman companion; Nancy returned six months later.

The Runcies were a happy enough family, but the age difference between Robert and the rest soon made itself felt. He never went to the same schools at the same time as his brothers and sisters. He lacked many close friends of his own age. His sister Marjorie doted on him, less as a brother than a baby. He developed the loneliness, then the separate self-sufficiency, of the only child.

He was close to his father, who took him on holiday to Kilmarnock. They followed the fortunes of Kilmarnock FC, and its star centre-forward James 'Bud' Maxwell: 'Pit it doon the gully, Bud!' they would cry with the rest of them on the terraces. He played football and cricket at home and at Coronation Road Primary School.

Kathleen had started attending a Methodist youth club, and, fired by the tales of visiting missionaries, decided to rescue her youngest brother from the dark interior of 26, Queen's Road. After one visit to Sunday School he declined the second invitation, especially when the minister visited the house to try to persuade him. His father did not object.

Although he was a fellow Scot, Dr Cosmo Gordon Lang came in for a battering when he was announced as the next Archbishop of Canterbury: '*One of the most brilliant men of his time, one of the few certainly first-rate minds in England,*' declared *John O'London's Weekly.* 'Unctuous old humbug!' said Robert Senior. Robert Junior was then seven years old and listening to the wireless beside him. Nancy made sure they all stood up when the King delivered his Christmas broadcast.

In the league table of Liverpudlian suburbs, Crosby was above Bootle and below Formby and Southport. There was great competition to enter Merchant Taylors', the distinguished local direct grant school, and great relief when Robert won a scholarship to follow Kenneth there at the age of eleven.

Kathleen and Marjorie had attended Merchant Taylors' Girls' School. Kenneth had not prospered at school and now lived in Manchester. Marjorie worked in a children's home in Prestwick and Kathleen was away in Nottingham as a social worker. By the time he started at Merchant Taylors', Robert was the only one of the four children who lived at home.

Of the four institutions – school, university, army and church – that were to envelop him and shape his life, Merchant Taylors' Crosby was probably the least formative. But it set him on the road to the second of these, and gave him a life uncircumscribed by his family in all except one respect. The exception was religion, and in this again it was Kathleen who took on the missionary role.

Robert Runcie was confirmed by Bishop David of Liverpool when he was fourteen years old. Kathleen, now twenty-six, had nothing to do with this. What drew Robert to confirmation classes and full membership of the Church of England was a sudden and all-consuming interest in the sacred mysteries of a girl called Betty Cooke.

This adolescent crush was unrequited and possibly unknown to the girl in question, who married an insurance administrator called Cecil and was still living in Crosby fifty years later. But it led Robert, who had been baptised as a matter of propriety rather than parental conviction, to confirmation. Even given the talent he later showed for embellishing the early years of his life with amusing and dramatic touches, the occasion was by all accounts one which moved him unexpectedly deeply.

This was more than could be said for the normal services at St Luke's, the resolutely low church where he was christened and confirmed, and where he was expected to make regular attendance at Holy Communion. It was at this point that Kathleen took a hand.

Kathleen, when visiting her family in Crosby, preferred to attend the higher church of St Faith's on the Liverpool Road. At St Faith's the evangelism of St Luke's and the mean spirit of Calvinism which had antagonised Robert Runcie Senior were nowhere evident. Holy Communion was called Mass, and the priest who celebrated it was known emphatically as 'Father' Schofield. St Faith's, an uninspiring church from without, contained the full theatre and props of Anglican Catholic worship.

This meant incense, bells, candles and rich vestments; feast days commemorated with assiduousness; and Mass celebrated daily. Un-ashamedly complicated, eschewing banal statements of literal truth, possibly elitist and all the more alluring for that, this was heady stuff for a fourteen-year-old boy whose confirmation had moved him so unexpectedly and whose first encounter with the Church of England had been synonymous with an adolescent crush.

It was here that Kathleen brought him for his first communion, and it was to Father Schofield that she entrusted Robert's spiritual well-being while she was away in Nottingham. Within a few weeks of her departure, he was serving at the altar; within a few months he was imagining himself in Father Schofield's place. If the child was father to the man, the sister was the mother in Robert Runcie's case.

Merchant Taylors' was dominated by its headmaster, the Reverend Charles Russell. Russell was a former assistant master at Harrow, and an unabashed and energetic elitist, in whose hands the able sensed unlimited prospects and the less able tried to come to terms with their place in the world. At Merchant Taylors' that world was everywhere present in microcosm; there were hierarchies and honours for everything from classics to cricket.

Robert Runcie excelled in both of these. He fitted in, on both the strength of his natural ability and his desire to please his elders, rooted in the circumstances of his childhood. These twin motives were inseparable in him from an early age and became indistinguishable in later life.

But, when he was fifteen years old, two events took place which were to affect him deeply. In more than one sense they were related to each other, although the shock of the latter struck harder at the time.

The first was Kathleen's engagement, in 1937, to Angus Inglis, curate of St Mary's Church, Nottingham. In spite of her father's distaste for 'black beetles' it was almost inevitable that the devout Kathleen should marry a Church of England clergyman. The wedding took place later that year in London, at the church near where she had been a social worker. The Runcie family attended, although not without anxiety where Robert Senior was concerned.

The second event was a catastrophe for what remained of the Runcie family unit. It had nothing to do with his feelings towards clergymen. Robert Senior had been suffering progressively from neuritis, an inflammation of the nerves leading to muscular atrophy, a serious illness for which drastic treatment had been prescribed. The treatment had worked but the after-effects were equally drastic. Only in his mid-fifties and still employed at Tate & Lyle, Robert Runcie Senior had regained the use of his muscles but was rapidly losing his sight.

Robert Runcie now returned each day from Merchant Taylors' to these deteriorating circumstances at home. His father's ill-health soon cost him his job. The former breadwinner who loved football was marooned at home on a reduced pension, dependent on others to take him to football matches and give him a running commentary on the play. This was a role and a situation Nancy Runcie was unable to meet, and his father came to depend on Robert to read him the racing pages and take him to the terraces. The combination of his mother's frequent tearfulness and his father's decline made additional demands on his own resources at a time when his continued ascent at school was of paramount importance.

His parents would survive into old age and would come to terms with Robert Senior's blindness. But the heightened emotions raised by its onset, and the need to resist being overcome by such a disaster, as sometimes seemed to be happening to his mother, led to the formation of a certain amount of scar tissue. This took place in the mind of an adolescent boy already propelled prematurely towards adulthood, and yet who was emotionally still a child in need of parental comfort and a sense of belonging. This was a need that he might now reliably expect to be answered only at St Faith's, in the sanctuary of which he continued to be seen on Sundays, and occasionally on weekdays too.

In 1938 Robert Runcie Senior was not the only listener calling for silence while the latest international news was broadcast on the wireless set. Germany had annexed Austria, the British navy had been mobilised and Neville Chamberlain had participated in the Munich Agreement. This act of appeasement outraged left-wing opinion everywhere, including that of a master at Merchant Taylors', R. F. Parr.

Parr was a classicist and a communist, not an uncommon combination for the period, and his lively mind made him popular among the more intelligent boys. The unlikely alliance of Parr and the headmaster Charles Russell provoked Robert Runcie and his fellow pupils into thinking for themselves, and developing if nothing else a coherent response to Parr's seductive vision of a communist utopia.

In Robert's case this took the form of a heightened awareness of two systems of values now under threat: the Christian gospels and the legacy of the classical world. In pursuit of the latter Angus and Kathleen took him to see the Oxford colleges, where Angus had been an undergraduate, and where he and Kathleen hoped Robert would win a place.

By 1939 his father was completely blind and his sister Marjorie returned from Scotland to stay with Robert and their parents. At the outbreak of the Second World War in September Angus, who had served in the Territorial Army, was called up as a chaplain to the forces. Kathleen and her baby went to live with friends. Kenneth had been working in London and was now commissioned in the Royal Engineers. Marjorie took a job in Liverpool in the post office censorship department and was shortly afterwards posted to Belfast for the rest of the war.

26, Queen's Road was sold and Nancy and Robert Senior moved back to a smaller house in Moor Lane. But the air raids on Liverpool made Kathleen anxious about her parents and she soon persuaded them to sell up and move again, this time to lodgings near where she was living. In September 1940 this left Robert as a boarder at Merchant Taylors', the only one of the family still in Crosby.

Charles Russell was a Cambridge man, and for his bright sixth-former Runcie it was at his old college, Pembroke, that he envisaged a place. Russell was a liberal low churchman and had already tried to insist that as a boarder Robert should attend St Luke's rather than St Faith's. He had withdrawn the suggestion after encountering a steely request to differ in this respect. He was to have no more luck with his choice of university. After winning a small bursary and being offered a place at Pembroke, Robert turned this down in favour of two scholarships, one from Merchant Taylors' and the other from the University, to Brasenose, Oxford.

The reasons were simple: the impression Oxford had made when Angus and Kathleen took him there, and the fact that the two scholarships combined gave him slightly more money. There was still insufficient to cover his costs, but his family would borrow the rest.

Apart from Angus, who was an outsider and a 'black beetle' to boot, no one had ever gone to Oxford University in the Runcie family.

Oxford was the second of the four great institutions that were to shape his life. In the days before the welfare state it represented a major leap forward for a young man from his kind of family. Robert Runcie had already come a long way from Coronation Road Primary School, Crosby – only to see his future become uncertain. This was the autumn of 1940 and he was nineteen years old. The age of conscription – and the uncertainty – was twenty.

Robert arrived at Oxford for the beginning of the Trinity term after Easter 1941. As had been the case with St Faith's, his first proper encounter with Oxford proved an intoxicating experience.

Brasenose had been partly taken over as a military school and instead he was given a set of ground floor rooms in Christ Church, with views across the Meadow to the river. As compensation they could hardly have been equalled. The view of the rest of university life was just as breathtaking.

He found he was not there merely to study the combination of philosophy, classics and history collectively known as Greats, although he did so with enthusiasm and the help of a diverse and exotic collection of tutors. Socially, politically, athletically and spiritually Oxford was a market-place of contacts, ideas, sporting opportunities and church services, from which he was free to take his pick. Truly, here was the proof, promised only to the select among his sixth-formers, of the Reverend Charles Russell's earthly paradise.

He joined the Labour Club, whose Literature Secretary was Kingsley Amis; attended the occasional Communist Party meeting (the influence of R. F. Parr was not yet dead); played cricket, and served at the altars of Christ Church, the University Church of St Mary and at Pusey House. He joined the Senior Training Corps and learned how to map-read.

Above all, he made friends: friends from richer and smarter families than his own, friends from poorer ones, and friends like Derek Waters. Waters was not witty, not socially adept, not upwardly mobile like the attractive and amusing Bob Runcie. Few of Robert's friends ever understood what Robert saw in him. Waters was a shy, introverted only child, a classical scholar reading Greats in preparation for theological college and ordination in the Church of England. Robert was invited home to meet Derek's parents, who treated him as a second son. The answer to the question of what Robert saw in him was probably something, latent and as yet unformed, of himself.

In October 1941 Robert Runcie was twenty years old. His first encounter with the army was arranged through the University Senior Training Corps and took place at the Oxford recruiting office. He inquired after a commission in the King's Own Scottish Borderers. They sounded like the kind of regiment of which his father would have approved.

To his surprise the adjutant, a Coldstreamer, asked him if he had ever considered the Scots Guards. Robert's immediate reply was that he was not sure he possessed either the pedigree or the income for such a regiment. There followed a conversation worthy of Evelyn Waugh, in which the adjutant and his assistant, a Grenadier, discussed whether or not it was possible for a Scots Guards officer to live on his income during wartime.

Yes, they concluded, it probably was. With disarming candour, they added that the Scots Guards had lately been fighting in North Africa and had suffered particularly heavy losses. In the circumstances, would he consider going to London for an interview?

Thus it was that the young man from Coronation Road Primary School and Merchant Taylors', Crosby, found himself at Wellington Barracks, Birdcage Walk, in the presence of Colonel Bill Balfour DSO, OBE, MC. Balfour too seemed unconcerned by the lack of money in Robert's case. Robert was good at games, he was a Scot on his father's side, and he came recommended by two Guards officers at the Oxford STC. Plenty of Scots Guards officers who had fought and died for their country were Oxford men. He even had the 'B' Certificate of basic military proficiency. In the circumstances, would he consider going for a commission? Fired by the prospect, Robert signed on without further delay.

The Scots Guards were an armoured regiment, and he returned to Oxford full of the idea of himself as a future tank commander. His elders and mentors there were approving. His undergraduate friends, however, reacted in one of two ways. Some were outraged, and only half-jokingly told him so. What price his socialist principles now, they asked, among the upper-class public schoolboys, the banquets and the bagpipes, of the Scots Guards?

Others, possibly from the kind of background which would have enabled them to join such a regiment either in peace or war, were simply puzzled. Did he have a family connection with the regiment, they politely enquired? Was that the explanation, after all? He could convince neither party; and without receiving a satisfactory answer both soon stopped asking him about it. He soon stopped trying to explain. Perhaps he suspected that they would have found the truth even more vulgar or shocking. The truth was that he had been made an offer that was too good to refuse.

The motto of the Scots Guard is *Nemo Me Impune Lacessit* – 'Nobody hurts me and remains unhurt themselves'.

The unofficial motto of the Scots Guards might justifiably be described as 'Once you're in, you're in'. Getting in, however, was not just a matter of signing on, as he soon discovered.

Robert arrived in Surrey at Pirbright Camp, which contained the Bisley ranges and was in the army's scrubby training heartland. It was a hot day in June 1942. His arrival alone was enough to antagonise most of his fellow-recruits.

The hard core of these were Etonians whose fathers and grandfathers had served with the regiment. They were unimpressed by the appearance and credentials of the scholarship boy from Liverpool. Their fear that the regimental blood would be polluted by opportunistic social inferiors was near the ideology of the proponents of the National Socialism against which they were supposed to fight. Nor did they feel obliged to conceal this fear from the new recruit, but made it clear to him at every opportunity and in the crudest fashion.

But if they thought the first few weeks would break him (and there were times when he thought they would) they had reckoned without the scar tissue that had formed with the blindness of his father; without the need, established at an early age, to win the approval of his elders and betters; and particularly without his native intellectual and sporting ability. A truly talentless upstart would never have stopped trying to ingratiate himself in a way that would only have damned him ever more irredeemably in their eyes.

But Robert Runcie had already acquired enough outward self-confidence to survive the first few weeks and even play his tormentors at their own game. His own social mobility, far greater than theirs, had given him a gift for mimicry, and this became his talent. He mimicked everybody to order and it was probably this above all his other qualities that redeemed him in the eyes of his fellow guardsmen. After trial by those whom he would have as his peers, he was well and truly 'in'.

Derek Waters, by contrast, was in the Pioneer Corps. While Robert was learning to be an officer and gentleman at Sandhurst, Derek was discovering what it was like to be a private soldier. While Robert learned how to dress, how to speak, how to hold his whisky and how to dance, as well as about tank command, gunnery and radio procedure, Derek was expected to learn how to swear, how to drink beer until he vomited and how to dig one trench after another. As Robert's self-assurance grew, so did Derek's misery. He confided as much on one of Robert's visits to his parents, but apart from offering sympathy there was little Robert could do. As officer-elect and private soldier, they should not even have been seen walking together. Their relationship grew more distant under these pressures.

Second-Lieutenant R. A. K. Runcie passed out of Sandhurst after a three-month course and was posted to the Third Battalion Scots Guards in November 1942. The winter and spring were spent training in the new 40-ton Churchill tanks on Salisbury Plain. The battalion was organised into four squadrons, each of six troops, each troop of three tanks and each tank containing a crew of five. The three tanks in a troop were individually commanded by the troop corporal, the troop sergeant and the troop commander. The last of these was Robert's job.

The training was wet, dirty and arduous. They were training to take over from men who were going to be killed, and other men were training to take over from them for the same reason. Early on, the new Second-Lieutenant distinguished himself by dropping a heavy tank part on his foot. He was taken to hospital, where he was discovered to have broken his toe. He was also discovered a couple of nights later by the matron, drinking whisky and making friends with the night nurse.

In April 1943, the battalion moved to Hawes in Yorkshire for further training. In the Nissen huts that served as officers' messes at Hawes and Bovington he made other new friends: Peter Balfour,

Hugo Charteris, Archie Fletcher, Hector Laing, John Shearer and William Whitelaw. Also in Yorkshire was Derek Waters, and one Sunday they attended evensong in the local church with his parents. It was an uneasy occasion, with Robert the new young officer in the company of an unhappy private soldier, the one contemporary who knew about the religious life he had felt obliged to put aside in himself for the duration of the war.

It was also their last meeting. Not long afterwards Derek was posted to Italy, where he was struck by stray bomb fragments while on sentry duty. After suffering for several weeks he died of his wounds and was buried near Salerno.

Mr and Mrs Waters found the death of their son almost unbearable and kept in closer touch with Robert thereafter. They saw something in Robert that they had seen in Derek, and they prayed for his survival. But he was not just a substitute for the son they had lost. In Robert, this led to the development of that latent and unformed part of himself and the conviction that, if he survived, it would ultimately be because his God had seen him through.

The battalion had moved south by the winter of 1943, but only as far as Nottinghamshire. The training never seemed to end. In April 1944 they again moved south, this time to Kent. The invasion forces were massing, and on 30 May, with battle in the wind, the Scots Guards attended a service in Canterbury Cathedral. The service was conducted by the Church of England's only professed Stalinist, the celebrated 'Red Dean', Hewlett Johnson. The preacher was William Temple, the Archbishop of Canterbury.

Robert had never been to Canterbury Cathedral before. Temple, the son of an Archbishop of Canterbury, had succeeded Robert Runcie Senior's bête noire Dr Cosmo Gordon Lang only two years earlier. Temple's death later that year was an incalculable loss. Yet, when he had appointed him, Winston Churchill had suspected him of socialism and described him as 'the only sixpenny item in a penny bazaar'.

After the service the band of the Scots Guards led the march past of the whole brigade. Six weeks later, they crossed the English Channel.

*

They landed at Arromanches in the aftermath of D-Day. After a further week of false calm behind the lines, they were ordered to advance. Operating in tandem with the infantry as they had been trained to do at Bovington and Hawes, they drove south through Normandy, clearing first one potentially lethal hiding place and then another.

This was nervy, uncomfortable work. Only after a while did they realise that they were killing and in their turn being killed. At Caumont the reality of the slaughter first became plain. 'S' Squadron's second-in-command Major Sidney Cuthbert had borrowed another tank to go forward on reconnaissance; a gun opened up and killed him instantly with his crew. German tanks, hidden in the woods, all but destroyed 'S' Squadron in the barrage that followed. It was a terrible thing, to train for years, to go into action, and suddenly to be wiped out. Later the survivors would be congratulated for pushing forward the front line.

Through August and September the Scots Guards advanced through Normandy into what had been occupied France, experiencing alternately periods of action and lulls for rest and repairs. In September and October they crossed Belgium and the Dutch border. They celebrated Hogmanay at Maastricht and in early 1945, having briefly detoured across the German border, the battalion turned north-east and advanced on the Rhine. It was in Holland that a tank near the one commanded by Lieutenant Runcie was hit and its occupants baled out; all except one, who had been overcome by smoke, whom he rescued.

The next day they were outside the town of Winnekendonk. It was an afternoon in early March, and they were refuelling with petrol and ammunition before going in the following day. They were two squadrons, each of three troops, each troop of three tanks. Before long, however, the squadron commander Lord Cathcart called an 'O' (Orders) Group. This was attended by the commander and sergeant of each troop. They were told that the plan was now to go straight into Winnekendonk.

The official account of what followed played down the chaos, absurdity and horror, and gave a seamless quality to the bravery that won decorations for Lieutenant Runcie and others. He would rarely talk about some of the events of that day; every moment of which he and others who survived would remember for as long as they lived.

The troop commanders and sergeants synchronised watches and went through the plan of attack. Cathcart pointed to 2 Troop, represented by Lieutenant Robert Runcie and Sergeant Jim Alldred, a tough regular soldier who had been in the Scots Guards since 1930: 'Now,' said Cathcart, 'order of march.'

This was always a cause for trepidation at this point in the war, when the likelihood was that just around the next corner was a group of desperate Germans armed with an 88 millimetre anti-tank gun. Nobody ever wanted to lead. 2 Troop, said Cathcart, had led twice already. It was somebody else's turn.

He told another young officer to lead. They moved off and formed up in readiness for the assault on Winnekendonk.

This was to be a two-pronged attack by the usual combination of tanks and infantry. On the right, the lead troop moved out from behind the shelter of some buildings and almost immediately came under heavy fire. It was from an 88.

The lead troop was destroyed within moments. It was Caumont all over again. 2 Troop, led by Lieutenant Runcie, was next to advance.

Alldred was behind him in the second tank: 'Go on!' he shouted over the radio. 'Go!'

But still Runcie did not move. Alldred, however, could see the 88. Frantically he stood up in his turret and waved back the tank behind him so that he had room to manoeuvre. Then they all moved. The radio frequencies were jammed with commands: '400 yards', screamed Alldred to Hollerton, his gunner, who fired and hit the barn. The Germans fired their 88 and missed. 'Up target!' he shouted, and Hollerton fired again. Everybody was firing at once. The 88 stopped firing, as did two 75mm self-propelled guns, and 2 Troop continued its advance.

Later they were in a farmyard, when the German shelling again found its range. The farmer was lying dead across the threshold; instead of moving his body they just stepped over it, fearful of booby-traps. Alldred asked Robert, his troop commander, if this was where they were to spend the night.

'Yes,' he said. There was a large barn, with what looked like a sound concrete cellar. They agreed to reconnoitre it by the light of Runcie's torch.

They were standing by their tanks when the first airburst struck. A

piece of shrapnel the size of a dinner plate missed them by inches.
Robert dived into his tank.

Alldred tugged at his legs and his troop commander re-emerged.

'I thought you were dead,' Robert said.

'I couldn't get in,' said Alldred, 'because of your bloody great feet.'

Then they made for the barn.


The next morning it was a beautiful day. The medical staff came and
sewed up the dead in body bags.

Colonel Dunbar, the battalion CO, told them with the help of the
map: 'It was just like the set piece we practised. We took Jerry on here'
STAB 'and we came on here' STAB 'and we destroyed him.'

'Yes, sir,' said Alldred boldly, 'but there's a difference, though.'

'What's that, Sergeant?'

'Last night we lost twenty-five good men.'

Dunbar glared at him, as if, given the chance, he would have had
him court-martialled and shot. Later, Robert said to his troop sergeant:
'You'll be decorated.'

'No, I won't,' said Alldred. 'You might, but I won't.'

Then they moved on to the Rhine.


That spring the battalion had driven east through Munster and then
turned north-east towards the Baltic. In May, while they were on the
Baltic coast, Colonel Dunbar informed Runcie that he had been
awarded the Military Cross for his part in the action at Winnekendonk.
Hollerton, Sergeant Alldred's gunner, was awarded the Military Medal.
*'There is no doubt,'* read the citation, *'that Lieutenant Runcie's courageous
leadership and the magnificent marksmanship of his troop dealt so effectively
with this strong enemy anti-tank screen that our tanks and infantry were
able to get on into the town.'*

In the officers' mess they chaffed him and nicknamed him 'Killer'.
But Germany had surrendered a few days earlier and the tank battalion's
war was over. The Churchills were loaded up and taken away and their
commanders and crews became foot soldiers. From Cologne, Robert
had his first home leave in three years and was reunited with his
family. In February 1946 he was still in Cologne when the Third

Battalion was dispersed, and he was posted to Trieste as part of the Italo-Yugoslav Boundary Commission. This was a pleasant, cosmopolitan atmosphere in which to socialise and work. Here he was told the news of his father's death from a heart attack, at the age of sixty-seven.

Unable to go home in time for the funeral he remained in Trieste, and was demobilised in August 1946. Within two months he was back in Oxford. His set of ground-floor rooms at Brasenose were of the kind he would normally have been allotted five years earlier. From his windows he could see across the well-kept grass to the porter's lodge and the Radcliffe Camera. He could also see the University Church of St Mary. He had survived.

But, if Oxford had not changed, there was a whole generation of undergraduates there who had. The first post-war generation were older and had nearly all been in the armed services in some capacity. Twenty-five years old, a six-foot-tall, straight-backed, decorated former Scots Guards officer who knew how to drink and dress and dance, Robert Runcie cut an impressive figure on the social scene. The war years had left him with an unpatronising authority in the presence of his juniors and equals, and a natural ability to mix on equal terms with the great and the good.

In Oxford there was no shortage of invitations on his mantelpiece. His replies were eagerly received, always by note as was the established system and with *RAKR* written across the corner of the envelope. He was a willing guest and a popular escort; when Vickie Reynolds of St Hugh's wanted a partner for the St Hugh's dance, not a dizzy social occasion, she asked him and he obliged. She knew that they would have fun, and that he would not be unkind or malicious about it afterwards.

As he acquired further sophistication he dropped more aspects of his pre-war self. In politics, socialism was the first casualty, although he maintained an arm's length contact with it and chatted amicably at Worcester College with the treasurer of the Union, Anthony Wedgwood-Benn. As a member of the Oxford University Conservative Association, however, though its college secretary for a short time, he did not convince either its president or former-president, the serious-minded Grantham grocer's daughter and Somerville under-graduate, Margaret Hilda Roberts.

Although he had perhaps correctly identified OUCA as a social club, they detected in him an 'excessive frivolity'. This was a particularly heinous crime. He was dropped from the Association at Miss Roberts' instigation. When he left Oxford it would be with a First Class Degree, while she would be described by her principal as 'a perfectly good second-class chemist'.

Nor did he convince Norman Sykes, the Yorkshire historian who later became Professor of Ecclesiastical History at Cambridge. Sykes was a passionate Yorkshireman who always entertained the Yorkshire cricket team to dinner when they came to Cambridge to play. As a child he had once crawled under the hessian matting of the latrines to see the match. He had known Robert at Oxford before going to the war.

'Eh, Runcie,' he said, 'you've exchanged your birthright for a mess of Scots Guards pottage.'

This was not a statement of literal fact. There was, however, the unmistakable impression that, as well as his socialism, he had dropped all but a few traces of his Crosby accent. Given the linguistic onslaught of Oxford and the Scots Guards over the preceding five years, this was hardly surprising. It would most likely have gone unnoticed by Sykes and others, had it not been for the curious manner of speaking that Robert had acquired instead. The surviving Crosby vowel sounds now jostled for position with a mixture of aristocratic languor and the deliberate pausing for emphasis of an after-dinner speaker. The effect, though loud and clear, and not without character, was not unlike a strangulated Malcolm Muggeridge.

But there were other changes in him which neither Sykes nor any of his Oxford contemporaries ever noticed. This was partly because in terms of attendance at church he had only resumed his pre-war religious life to a limited extent. But with peace the sense of the reason that he had survived the war had not gone away.

He visited Dr and Mrs Waters regularly and was at ease with their expectations that he should in one sense be the son they had lost. He communicated his feelings to his sister Kathleen and his brother-in-law. Angus wrote about Robert to the Principal of Westcott House, Cambridge, his old theological college, in the spring of 1947. The

Principal, W. D. L. 'Billy' Greer, another Scot, was about to leave for a bishopric, as successful theological college principals were wont to do. But he wrote back telling Angus that he was coming to Oxford in June to preach the University Sermon in St Mary's, within sight of Robert's rooms, and that he would visit Robert. Angus passed this on.

It was an odd encounter, as the circumstances usually are of the first conversation between the principal of a theological college and a possible ordinand. It was Eights Week. Robert had returned from an all-night party and was somewhat the worse for wear. They sat and talked in his rooms and he felt he was giving no clear indication of why he wanted to be ordained to the priesthood. Greer listened; it was a gift he had. He said nothing to discourage. They parted on good terms.


Robert and half a dozen others spent the summer vacation that year at Bonn University, on an exchange visit organised by the Oxford Bonn Committee. This was in a small way in the same spirit of ecumenism and reconciliation that G. K. A. Bell, Bishop of Chichester, had shown in his celebrated speeches in the House of Lords in 1944.

Bell had looked forward to the peace, before the war was even won: 'What have we in common?' he asked. 'What can we build on, after the war?' To Robert Runcie, immersed in the Greats syllabus at Oxford after his experiences in Germany and German-occupied Europe, this was a language he could instinctively understand.

Like Bell, he was being educated in the great tradition of classical humanism, a tradition which was later Christianised and given focus, but which gave to the world such words as 'city' and 'state' and 'society'; ideals which transcended international boundaries and were not mere party-political catch-phrases.

At Oxford they threw Thucydides and Herodotus at him in the original, and made him work through the Greek and Roman history of the whole pre-Christian world. The classical tradition could be overblown, but with the Catholic Anglican in him it produced a high concept of religious faith and a strong classically-inspired liberalism of outlook. Many years later some would suggest he was merely hedging his bets, and that there was a hopeless contradiction between the two. Others would mistake his classical liberalism for a shallow political liberalism which happened not to coincide with the government of the day.

These ideas were developed in his last year at Oxford, the year in which he also attended and passed the three-day selection board of the Central Advisory Council for Training for the Ministry. They were the intellectual basis for his movement towards the priesthood. They were also the basis of the qualities that would eventually commend him to a Prime Minister; and which would all be reportedly held against him by the same Prime Minister, ten years later.

He worked solidly through the remaining terms and most of the vacations. Late in his last year he was visited by Kenneth Carey, 'Billy' Greer's successor as principal of Westcott House. Carey, in his public school way, wanted to know if he was still 'on' for ordination.

Robert did not appear to be bursting with missionary zeal, but nor could he find a reason to say 'No'. Like Greer, Carey departed apparently satisfied. Robert sat his final examinations in the last weeks of 1948. He was awarded a First Class Honours Degree in Greats.

There was a theology college only a few miles away, at Cuddesdon. But Angus was a Westcott man, and ordinands were often advised to do their training in a different place from where they had taken their first degrees. University life meant the accumulation of three years of distracting friendships. So, in the early weeks of 1949, Robert arrived in Cambridge.

Westcott House, Cambridge was a plain, brick building on Jesus Lane. Much of its rather unprepossessing architecture dated from 1926, but the college had been founded in 1881. From 1919 to 1944 its principal had been B. K. Cunningham, and Cunningham's spirit lived on there in the person of his favourite son, Kenneth Carey.

Westcott accommodated around 40 ordinands for four terms a year. The course of study cost £172 per annum and lasted two years. Apart from Mrs Minn, the housekeeper, and one or two other female domestic staff, Westcott House was a resolutely all-male institution, where until recently students had been expected to dress for dinner, and where the few married ordinands were still supposed to sleep away from their wives at least part of the time.

The bursar was a retired bank manager with a proprietorial attitude to the place. When a student claimed to have experienced a vision of the Virgin Mary, he was indignant and said so; that sort of thing simply wasn't on at Westcott.

'I don't use the word "class",' he told the chaplain, Harry Williams, 'let's use the word "grades". Some of these men, like the one in question, belong to a different grade to what is usual here.'

Williams had been curate at All Saints', Margaret Street in London, and in those days he embodied its high Anglo-Catholicism. Always dressed in a black suit, witty in conversation, elegant in his devotions and incisive in his Compline addresses (given last thing at night before silence was supposed to be observed), he taught the New Testament and ministered to the students' doubts with a conviction that captivated everyone.

Robert was no exception, and modelled his own Compline addresses on Williams, in whom he saw the passionate young Anglo-Catholic priest he had first imagined himself becoming at St Faith's fifteen years earlier. But, if Robert saw in Williams his own personal ideal, Williams was beginning to see in himself a very different person. After Williams left Westcott House and became a fellow of Trinity, his spiritual crises and his suppressed homosexuality led to a massive nervous breakdown. He eventually recovered to become one of the best-known spiritual writers in the Church of England. He ended up as a monk of the Community of the Resurrection at Mirfield. '*Religious establishments invariably give me the creeps,*' he wrote in his autobiography *Some Day I'll Find You*, which he prefaced with Martin Buber's remark that '*Nothing is apt to mask the face of God so much as religion*'.

'*If people are silly enough,*' he wrote, '*to allow their conduct to be dictated by a bunch of clergymen, then they deserve whatever comes to them.*'

The vice-principal of Westcott was Alan Webster, who taught church history and was popular with staff and students. Webster would shortly be the first member of the teaching staff to marry and start a family, a move which would end his close working relationship with the principal, Kenneth Carey.

Kenneth Carey was an important and well-loved figure in the lives of many men who achieved eminence in the Church of England. In his own life he was a mass of complex and sensitive feelings; a homosexual of the old-fashioned kind, a 'confirmed bachelor', he was ill at ease with women. As a young curate at Spennymoor he had once been observed running in and out of the French windows, away from an ardent female admirer.

He was a strong influence with an equally strong inferiority complex. He had taken a Third Class Degree in Theology and routinely likened himself to A. A. Milne's 'bear of little brain'. Because of this he taught little, but took prayer and was responsible for pastoralia, or the spiritual care of students. This was a typical exaggeration rooted in insecurity, as was his personal reaction to criticism of any kind. But he was a gifted listener and a sensitive counsellor, and he exerted a strong pull over the individual. Many students made their confession to him, and to some, although far from all, he was a father figure. The brighter and more self-assured the ordinand, the less likely he was to fall completely under the Carey spell.

But, for those who needed a firmer hand, there was always the expectation that they would 'go for a walk' with him in the afternoons to discuss what was on their minds. If a student was shattered by the end of term and found himself in spiritual difficulties during the vacation, Ken Carey was always there. He would write back by return of post, and his letters, though not written for that reason, were objects to keep and treasure. There was a low drop-out rate at Westcott during Carey's happiest years.

It was into this strange environment that Robert Runcie came as an ordinand in the Lent term of 1949. What was he looking for that he felt he might find, in such an institution? Certainly he sought and found the encouragement of self-discipline, the structure and space to develop his prayer life. The intellectual freedom also appealed to him. He was already studying the New and Old Testament, church history, doctrine and liturgy for the General Ordination Examination, and although he did not have a theological qualification he decided not to read theology for a degree. He would concentrate on his personal experience of the Gospels and build on the ideas he had developed at Oxford. Like his classically influenced liberalism, his lack of a theology degree would later be seen as a grave shortcoming in some quarters.

On the social level Westcott was a less attractive place than the officers' mess and the Junior Common Room of BNC. Cosy and patriarchal, often ringing with hearty laughter, it tended towards 'the monstrous merriment of the clergy'. There were coy titles apportioned with individual jobs: the senior student was 'Sheriff'; there was a 'Minstrel' in charge of music in the chapel; there was a 'Bailiff of the Beer'.

But among his fellow-ordinands there were those who were to become friends for life. Simon Phipps, formerly of Eton, Cambridge and the Coldstream Guards, like Robert an MC, was president of the Footlights; a gifted actor who moved in royal circles. Hugh Montefiore, born into a wealthy Jewish family, had converted to Christianity at seventeen after experiencing a vision of Christ, having known nothing of the Gospels. He was and still is a brilliant and provocative thinker. Bill Vanstone, scholar, was one day to be a spiritual writer of the highest order.

There were occasional visitors from the outside world, and from the three years of distracting friendships Robert had accumulated at Oxford. Vickie Reynolds, whom he had escorted to the St Hugh's dance, was one. Jill Turner, also a Commem Ball partner, was another. She lived in Cambridge and her father was a fellow of Trinity Hall. The Turners were a large and powerful Cambridge tribe. Jill was one of six children and it was on a visit to her family home that Robert first met her sixteen-year-old sister Rosalind, a lively, wilful girl known as Lindy. After he left, she had inquired after her sister's friend. 'Oh, he's going to be a celibate priest,' her elder sister replied.

Lindy thought little more of this, although she did look up 'celibate' in the dictionary and found out what it meant. But she preferred her own definition. She thought it 'a waste of a lovely man'.

1949 was a glorious later English summer. A regular feature of the long vacation term at Westcott House was a play produced, written and performed by the students. That year it was an open-air version of *Androcles and the Lion* produced by Simon Phipps. Androcles was played by Bill Vanstone and Robert Runcie played the part of Caesar as an apoplectic Guards officer.

The performance took place on the terrace in front of an audience of eminent academics including Professor Norman Sykes, the radical preacher and religious philosopher Charles Raven (both of whom Runcie and Phipps used to imitate with deadly accuracy), and a historian from Trinity College, the Reverend F. H. Simpson. Simpson nearly fell off his chair laughing when the Emperor and the Lion caught sight of each other peering out of the windows overlooking the terrace.

Once a year each member of staff took a group of Westcott students to a parish for a week. Phipps and Runcie were among a group who went with Harry Williams to Leicester. The young ordinands were much prized socially in such places and one of the parishioners put in a special request: 'Could one of the young gentlemen come along on Sunday afternoon to tea, to bring our Enid out?' Enid, it transpired, was rather a withdrawn girl.

They all voted for Runcie. Robert went along, and Harry Williams and the rest of them departed. In the train on the way back, Williams said: 'I know what will happen. When we get back to Westcott there will be a telegram, saying "Come at once. Cannot get Enid back in again."'

At Easter 1950 Robert was staying with Dr and Mrs Waters when the news came of his mother's death. Nancy Runcie was buried at Cotgrave outside Nottingham next to her husband and, after staying with Angus and Kathleen, Robert returned to Westcott House. He played St Peter to Phipps' Judas Iscariot in another open-air production, this time written by Phipps and entitled *The Garden of Decision*. He played in the annual cricket match between Cuddesdon and Westcott. He discussed, with Kenneth Carey, where he was to be ordained deacon and 'serve his title' as a curate.

Different theological colleges had different links through their past graduates with different parts of the country; but there was a general looking to parishes in the north of England as a training ground for curates. There was perceived to be a virility, a loyalty, a community about northern English Christianity. After the lush pastures of Oxford and Cambridge the thinking was that a man needed to dirty his hands; although some would dirty theirs more than others.

Kenneth Carey had a personal link with Archie Hardy, the vicar at Hexham. Hexham contained an ancient abbey and a beautiful church safely inland from Newcastle. Carey wrote to Hardy and Robert agreed to visit him there. Hugh Montefiore, meanwhile, had already left Westcott for the parish of St George's, Jesmond, near Hexham. Montefiore had only spent six weeks there as a deacon before his vicar

John Ramsbotham left to be bishop of Jarrow. Nobody had bothered to tell Montefiore in time that this was going to happen. As yet unqualified to take services such as Holy Communion or weddings, Montefiore had hurriedly enlisted the help of some of the fully-qualified local clergy.

One of these was John Turnbull, vicar of All Saints', Gosforth. Not long afterwards, Montefiore met him at a bus stop.

Turnbull knew how well Montefiore was doing, and told him he too needed a decent curate: 'But I didn't study anywhere fancy,' he said, 'I'll never get one from Westcott House.'

Montefiore made a mental note. Shortly afterwards a letter from him arrived at Westcott House, addressed to R. A. K. Runcie Esq. In the circumstances, Montefiore wondered, would he consider serving his title at Gosforth?

Runcie put it to Kenneth Carey, who was uncertain, and who suggested he visit both Hexham and Gosforth. He did so, and when he met Turnbull and went into All Saints', Gosforth, he again had a feeling similar to that which he had experienced when he first met Father Schofield and entered St Faith's in Crosby years ago. Turnbull could be a tough man, dour even by north-eastern standards, but he was married with children and had a warmer side. He knew his mind in what he thought mattered. All Saints' was a thriving Anglo-Catholic parish church in the suburbs of Newcastle. Robert returned to Westcott House convinced in himself, and convinced Carey, as he had done the Reverend Charles Russell before him, to allow him his own way in his choice of church. Allan Medforth, another Westcott man, would eventually go as curate to Hexham and Robert would go to Gosforth. He travelled back up to Newcastle shortly before Christmas 1950.

The ordination of a deacon is the first of two steps in the Church of England. The second is the ordination of a priest. Montefiore was about to undergo the latter and Robert the former. Both were confined with other ordinands and the Bishop of Newcastle to a chilly house in Northumberland for the usual pre-ordination retreat. The candidate was supposed to observe a rule of silence and engage in inner contemplation of his impending compact with God. Both men were understandably nervous, but Montefiore's nervousness was of a slightly different kind.

Montefiore's problem, he confided in Robert, was that he could not sing in tune. Since he was shortly due to sing the Preface to Holy Communion for the first time, he desperately needed some last-minute coaching. In spite of the rule of silence, the two men adjourned to the woods some distance from the house.

Montefiore brought with him an altar book, and as he walked along he began singing the Preface. As Montefiore chanted 'Lift up your hearts', he and Runcie were surprised by the equally startled figure of the bishop who was to ordain them the following day. Like them, he had been out for a 'silent' walk in the woods.

On 29 December 1950, the new issue of the *Church Times* reported the following:

*'Advent Ordinations'*

*'By the Bishop of Newcastle, in his Cathedral. Deacons: . . . R. Atkinson (Newcastle Cathedral); G. S. Hoar, Chichester Theol. Coll. (St George's Cullercoats); J. S. Hodgson (Tynemouth Priory); R. A. K. Runcie, MA, Brasenose Coll. Oxford and Westcott House, Cambridge (All Saints' Gosforth). Priests: . . . H. W. Montefiore, MA, St John's Coll. Oxford and Westcott House, Cambridge . . . Gospeller: Rev. R. A. K. Runcie.'*

The Reverend R. A. K. Runcie had done rather more than was suggested in this report. He had prayed for deliverance from evil, mischief, sin, the crafts and assaults of the devil, pride, vain-glory, hypocrisy, fornication, lightning and tempest, plague, battle and murder, sedition, rebellion, false doctrine, heresy, schism and hardness of heart. He had prayed for the blessing and preservation of George the King, Elizabeth the Queen, the Princess Elizabeth and Prince Charles and all the Royal Family. He had declared his belief that he had been inwardly moved by the Holy Ghost. He declared his belief in the Scriptures. He undertook to assist the Priest at Holy Communion, to read from the Scriptures in the Church, to instruct the youth, to baptise infants if the Priest was unable to be present, to search out the sick, the poor and the impotent of the parish, and to make their names and their plight known to the Vicar. He had agreed to obey his Vicar and other superiors. The Bishop had laid his hands on his head and given him a copy of the New Testament. Then, and only then, did he become a Deacon in the Church of England.

All Saints', Gosforth was not as high an Anglo-Catholic church as St Faith's, Crosby, but Robert, who had experienced a profoundly emotional conversion to Anglo-Catholicism as a teenager, was himself older and surer, and now that he was an ordained deacon he did not feel quite the need to model himself on Harry Williams as much as he once had done.

Turnbull's northern Christianity was every bit as virile, loyal and communal as expected. Gosforth was a large and diverse parish; there was the core of the old mining community; new council houses; a sizeable and comfortable middle class, and a mental hospital. Turnbull had been a breath of fresh air in the place. He had introduced the parish communion, educated his parishioners, included music and children. He had introduced parish breakfasts. He was everywhere and yet at the centre of things.

With his curates he was regarded as firm but fair. The Reverend Robert Runcie was not looking for a wife at the time, but another curate who was, and who found one, would be taken on one side for what he thought were a few fatherly words of wisdom.

He had them, but he also had the following:

'I want to make one or two things quite clear,' Turnbull would say. 'You and your fiancée don't hold hands in the street; you will be back in your digs by 10.30 on Saturday night; and that will be after you have played in the parish badminton match and laid the table for Sunday breakfast.'

His curates obeyed. As well as the duties laid down at his ordination, Robert's task was to learn the pastoral and technical skills of parish ministry. Curates were also supposed to keep up their theological studies, which was difficult when they were out visiting most of the day. The moment Turnbull's curates arrived home in the evening, they tended to go to sleep. This led to a problem in Robert's case. The only thing Turnbull could not provide him with was somewhere for him to live.

36, Oakfield Road, Gosforth was one of five houses built in 1926. It was owned and inhabited by Mrs Clara Tiffin. The house was five minutes' walk from All Saints' church, although Robert generally went about by bicycle.

Mrs Tiffin had never had a lodger before. She was many years a widow and happy in her way of life. She did not need the money. But she was a regular and loyal member of John Turnbull's All Saints' congregation. Mrs Tiffin's daughter Audrey had recently married and left home. There was a spare room, and Turnbull asked her if she would accommodate his new curate. They agreed it was a temporary arrangement.

They made an immediate impression on each other. Mrs Tiffin was an instinctive homemaker and an excellent cook. She did not fuss over him and he did not expect her to, but she filled the gap left by the death of Nancy. Although Robert was now nearly thirty years old, this was still a valid comparison. When Kathleen and Angus visited him there they were quick to approve.

Mrs Tiffin kept him in that state of happy dependence that prevented him from learning how to cook or manage money. She also kept a brake on the actor in him. He tended slightly to exaggerate when telling 'true' stories to amuse people.

He had complete freedom to come and go as he wished. He had another small room as his study, and a muddle of papers that was out of bounds to Mrs Gardner, the domestic help. He seemed to know where everything was.

In spite of Kathleen's belief that he was still in need of mothering, to Mrs Tiffin he revealed a mature and perceptive streak. When she was experiencing difficulties with another woman friend, he told her: 'Of course, you know what the problem is, don't you? She's jealous of you.'

Mrs Tiffin did not see how that could possibly be. The other woman had everything that she did not have; money, a husband of her own.

'Yes,' he told her, 'but you have friends, and can make more. She hasn't, and can't.'

There was no sentiment in him, just a precise kind of compassion. He also made her laugh. After visiting a parishioner who disapproved of the Anglo-Catholic style, he stood in the doorway and said: 'I've been visiting Mrs so-and-so. She thinks the services are far too high' . . . (holding his nose) 'Pooh!'

*

He was ordained priest or 'priested' on Christmas Eve, 1951. Once again the *Church Times* recorded the bare facts of the matter:

*'Advent Ordinations'*

*'By the Bishop of Newcastle, in his cathedral. Deacons: G. A. Elcoat, Queen's Coll. Birmingham (Corbridge); A. H. Medforth, BA, Queen's Coll. and Westcott House, Cambridge (Hexham). Priests: J. S. Hodgson, a Literate; R. A. K. Runcie, MA, Brasenose Coll. Oxford, and Westcott House Cambridge. Preacher: Rev. M. H. Bates, Vicar of Jesmond.'*

Again there was the long litany of prayers for deliverance and for blessing, the declaration of belief and the undertaking to apply himself wholly in thought, word and deed. The Bishop and other priests present placed their hands on his head and invoked the Holy Ghost. He was given a Bible and with it the authority to preach and minister the sacraments. The following day, on Christmas Morning, he celebrated Holy Communion to over a hundred parishioners. He was a priest.

What sort of a Church had he entered as a fully-ordained minister? Less than a month before his ordination in Newcastle, the *Church Times* had reported on the 'Revival of Religion at Cambridge'. His old principal Kenneth Carey had joined the Bishop of Peterborough and the Headmaster of Charterhouse on the platform in the Old Library of Pembroke, the college Robert had turned down in favour of Brasenose.

Under the ducks and cherubs on the plaster ceiling, a packed audience had listened to addresses on the state of the ministry. The Bishop had asserted that the urgent need for clergy would not open the door to men 'without true vocations'. Then it had been Carey's turn.

'Many young men,' he said, 'fear isolation from their fellows, caused by a clerical collar. But, in a sense, being Christian is inevitably being separated from the world, for this loneliness was the experience of our Lord. On the other hand if he, like the Lord, is a lover of souls, the joy of friendship with all sorts and conditions of men will transfigure this loneliness.'

The *Church Times* was impressed by this and concluded that the Church been not been so strong in the University since the First World War. This surely augured well for the numbers of future ordinands. But Carey was speaking for men like Robert Runcie and Simon Phipps, former-servicemen who had experienced 'the joy of friendship with all sorts and conditions of men'. They were a unique post-war generation, that had come and gone and would not come again. They were as weak in number as they were strong in their calling. And in material terms they had been called to a ministry in retreat.

In England and Wales there were 8,000 fewer clergy than there had been in 1919 and 10,000 less than in 1900. Only 400 men were ordained a year, out of the 600 needed to fill the gaps caused by death and retirement. The funds of the Central Advisory Council for Training for the Ministry, whose three-day selection board Robert had attended and passed in his last year at Brasenose, stood at £16,500 whereas it was estimated that the sum of over £200,000 was needed annually. Many curacies were vacant. The population, on the other hand, had grown by nearly a third since the beginning of the century.

Added to the shortage of candidates were the financial problems facing ordained clergymen. Nearly half subsisted below the dismal minimum recommended stipend of £500 annually. The church mouse was rich by comparison.

Church attendances, in so far as they were a measure of the Church's influence, told a similar story. One man in four and one woman in five in England had no religious belief. Of those baptised in the Church of England, four out of ten never went to church at all. One out of ten went occasionally. A possible and disturbing explanation for this was that people were put off at an early age; two-thirds of the child population still attended some form of Sunday school.

Against these factors, the Church's chronic inability to manage its financial affairs, and the vicious circle whereby the lack of funds caused by this made good management even less likely, there was no shortage of reasons offered as to why this state of affairs should exist and what the solutions might be.

The Archbishop of York, Dr Garbett, the second most senior churchman in England, was fond of quoting Joel to preface his views: 'Your old men shall dream dreams and your young men shall see visions' ( Joel was not a Westcott man). The Church, he said, was a neglected minority which would triumph in the end. No disaster could prevent this happening; only the failure to learn a new kind of evangelism.

On the subject of falling church attendances he was equally certain. The causes were the shortage of clergy, the widely received idea that science had destroyed the 'plausibility' of Christianity, and the fact that people could see little or no connection between the Church of England and their own lives.

*Crockford's* agreed with him. The 1951–2 edition of *Crockford's* Clerical Directory, to give its full name, contained one of the widely-read and traditionally anonymous prefaces that featured in it from time to time. After the advertisements for communion wine, steeplejacks and choir robes they lent colour and style to a dull but useful work of reference on the names, careers and current whereabouts of the Church of England clergy.

That year's Preface devoted considerable space to the matters raised by Dr Garbett:

*'We think,'* the anonymous author wrote, *'this diagnosis is substantially correct; and would only add that the multiplication of bishops (fewer clergy and smaller congregations apparently needing more oversight on the queer principle that smaller armies need more generals), ceaseless tinkering with ecclesiastical organisation, and strenuous and prolonged archiepiscopal triumphal progresses in the Antipodes (two in little more than a year,) contribute precisely nothing to a remedy.'*

As well as anonymity, it was a tradition of the *Crockford's* Preface that no one, not even an archbishop, was exempt from the judgement of his peers. Geoffrey Fisher was the first Archbishop of Canterbury to enjoy the benefits of intercontinental air travel, and as *primus inter pares* of the Anglican Communion he made a virtue of necessity. If the whip was to be wielded in a *Crockford's* Preface, so be it; but the unspoken rule was that it should be done not in a mean but a forgiving spirit.

The Reverend Robert Runcie continued to throw himself into the duties of his virile northern curacy. He conducted baptisms, confirmation classes, confirmations, preparations for marriages and marriages. He conducted funerals. He took services at St Nicholas' mental hospital, which depressed him at first, and built up relationships with many of the people there. He had a special way with the old, the sick and the lonely.

He dominated the youth club, where some of them knew about his war record. Although he was a clergyman, they respected him as a man who had been to grips with life. If not many of the children in the youth club knew what an MC meant, there were plenty of parents who knew enough of war at first hand to make sure that they did.

He occasionally had difficulty with the Sunday School. The teachers included one or two spinsters who, like Harry Williams' Enid, once brought out could not easily be got in again.


The news of his departure was a shock to his parishioners. Once again, just as Montefiore had been the agent of his arrival, so he was the instrument of his leaving Gosforth.

For the second year or so of his curacy, Robert had been in irregular communication with Kenneth Carey at Westcott House. Montefiore was already back there as chaplain in succession to Harry Williams. Now that Alan Webster's marriage and desire for a parish had finally led to his resignation, Montefiore had moved up to vice-principal. Just as he had recommended Runcie as curate to John Turnbull, so Montefiore now recommended Robert to Carey as the new chaplain. It was an offer Carey passed on to him in the autumn of 1952.

John Turnbull had expected him to stay for three years and was disappointed when Robert told him he wanted to accept. Bishop Hudson, who had ordained him less than a year earlier, was also doubtful. The parishioners of All Saints', Gosforth were particularly dismayed to lose their popular and eligible young curate.

But ultimately none of them was surprised. Precisely the same pastoral gifts he had displayed in his ministry there were now leading him in a different direction. Mrs Tiffin had it right, and told her daughter. She was sad to see him go, but she knew him better than most people. He needed more than Gosforth had to offer.

# 2

# *The Principal*

WESTCOTT House in the early spring of 1953 was little changed from the institution Robert had first entered as a student four years earlier.

Of the theological colleges, Cuddesdon and Westcott still contained by far the largest number of Oxford and Cambridge men. Edward Knapp-Fisher at Cuddesdon and Hugh Montefiore and Robert Runcie at Westcott were also all former-members of the wartime armed forces. By the early 1950s there were fewer former-servicemen among the students, but the class differences euphemistically described as 'grades' by the bursar were still very much in evidence.

A man's material existence at Westcott depended to some extent on his means, and the year before Robert returned there had been prolonged discussion between Carey, Webster and Montefiore about what to do with the last bottle of sherry in college. This, it was felt, unacceptably divided the richer from the poorer students. They eventually put it in the Westcott House museum. There had also been much anxious debate over whether or not they should continue to allow Tim Beaumont's valet to come into college to brush his master's hunting pinks.

Beaumont was one of Westcott's more colourful characters. He was also occasionally to be seen strolling through the courtyard at Westcott with a mallet over his shoulder, in full polo kit. But his sporting interests were clearly circumscribed. When Robert, in his capacity as chaplain, arranged for a group of students to visit a parish in Wigan, a rugby league match was included in the itinerary. The other students were keen spectators, but Beaumont was unimpressed. To their acute embarrassment he committed the sacrilege of sitting down on the terrace, ignoring the match, and studying his Latin textbook.

Kenneth Carey still proclaimed himself a 'bear of little brain' and eschewed academic teaching in favour of prayer and pastoralia. If Carey, as some suspected, knew more theology than he let on, this could hardly have been said of his new vice-principal, Hugh Montefiore.

Montefiore's visible scholarship and extraordinary energy were already distinguishing him from his contemporaries. He seemed to welcome the load he and Robert shared of teaching in groups of four and five the forty-five ordinands. Montefiore's interests lay in doctrine and the New Testament, while Robert taught the Old Testament, liturgy and church history. They recruited as many outside lecturers as they could; as well as Norman Sykes, these included three very different and remarkable men who would be key figures behind the scenes and in the forefront of the Church of England. They were the Dean of Trinity Hall, Owen Chadwick, the Dean of Clare College, John Robinson, and the man who had recommended Robinson for his job, the Regius Professor of Divinity, Michael Ramsey.

But, if Westcott House had not changed greatly during the past few years, there had been a development in the character of the new chaplain. Two years as a curate had accentuated his talents for listening and lowering tension, and made him all the more approachable to students to whom he was closer in age than the Principal. Working alongside the brilliant and sometimes rather tiring Montefiore, there was a welcome lightness of touch about Runcie which Carey might well have predicted would be the case. Because this was rooted in a certainty that was not worn on the sleeve, it passed for mere lightness among some observers. One or two may have found his social graces remarkable for his background; few, however, knew anything of his life before Oxford and the Guards.

In the long vacation term miracle play he played an enthusiastic and realistic Devil. But in him there was also a less synthetic, less borrowed manner and a greater simplicity of seriousness; in the way he talked about prayer to his students, in the way he talked about the parish he had come from and in the way he talked about the Church of England.

In his supervisions he was amusing and yet gave his students the feeling that they were drawing out of the Old Testament important things through which they could see the text in a larger perspective. In the evenings he held forth in his rooms: students were required to bring a poem to read and he would read one himself. In his Compline addresses, a touchstone of the style of a theological college staff member, there was again that deceptive air. The listener was simultaneously engaged by lightness and yet provoked to thought and prayer.

There was authority here, yet also a respect for it, that was not focused in too cramped an ecclesiastical way. He confided in one ordinand, a scholarship boy to Oxford with a First in Greats and a record of war service, who was now a schoolmaster, that he had enormous respect for the schoolmastering profession; the man should not feel obliged to forsake it for a parish. Peter Walker, the student in question, took his advice and would eventually succeed Kenneth Carey as principal of Westcott.

Westcott House was still cosily untouched by an era that elsewhere was showing signs of social and theological disintegration. The social continuity perpetuated by Kenneth Carey and his Oxbridge ordinands belied the first signs of the questioning that would come with the early 1960s. Questioning at Westcott was circumscribed by C. S. Lewis and Barth and Tillich: older men who were read by younger men, who thought they were radical and critical, but in wider terms were no such thing.

But, if the Westcott men were part of the 'establishment' in that they were predominantly middle-class and public school, they were not worried by the fact; and nor in some ways should they have been. Westcott had its limitations, but it also had intellectual and imaginative strength and a positive spiritual entity; three areas of coherence in which a general flourishing of the individual could and did take place.

Robert Runcie was a classically-educated liberal with a clear appreciation of the Anglo-Catholic tradition, and this was the framework within which that liberalism was set. Many of his students had grown up in the liberal, modernist atmosphere of the 1930s and 1940s, had rediscovered the Gospels, and participated in the retreat from liberal modernism and the rediscovery of the Catholic tradition. These men saw in Westcott in general and, in Robert Runcie in particular, a kindred spirit.

The more perceptive of them, who had spotted social graces remarkable in one from what they suspected was his real background, also saw past the Guards officer detachment to the adolescent who had experienced the overwhelming attraction of the Anglo-Catholic tradition. In the depth and capacity he showed for understanding the struggles through which they were going, they strongly sensed that he had himself undergone those struggles in his own life.

But they never drew him out on it; however well they came to know him, on this subject he was always just too reserved.


His confidence as a pastor continued to be counterbalanced by his uncertainty as a theologian. This may have accounted for his refusal to commit himself when other past and present Westcott associates were positively straining at the leash.

The subject was a suitably obscure one to the layman, worthy of the attention of a theological college's best minds and therefore of burning importance at the time. It was the question of the Church of South India.

The Church of South India, or CSI, was made up of four dioceses, Dornakal, Madras, Tinnevelly and Travancore, that had withdrawn from the Anglican Church of India, Burma and Ceylon and formed a new body with the Methodist Church and the South India United Church. Relations between the new CSI and the Church of England were complicated by questions of legitimacy and authority on the one hand, and the need to show fraternal support on the other.

It was into this labyrinth of ecclesiastical subtlety, theological debate and Biblical precedent that Montefiore plunged headlong, followed by others. Not all came out the other end; one participant was rather embarrassingly asked to withdraw his conclusions on the grounds that they did not coincide with those of the rest of the group. But the result was a collection of essays edited by Carey and entitled *The Historic Episcopate in the Fullness of the Church*. The book was widely read and discussed, and became something of a benchmark for future treatment of the issue within intellectual circles of the Church.

The most prominent contributors were Hugh Montefiore, John Robinson and Bill Vanstone. Even Kenneth Carey contributed an essay, although he delegated much of the editorship to Montefiore. But Robert Runcie declined the invitation. Afterwards, this was attributed by some who had committed themselves on the subject as evidence of his reluctance to deviate from the traditional Anglo-Catholicism that had brought him to the Church in the first place. His lack of a theological degree and his intellectual uncertainty were also cited in explanation. Years later, when he echoed the conclusions of *The Historic Episcopate* and proposed that the Church of England and the Church of South India should be in full communion, it went largely unremarked. But it was noted, and remembered, that at the time he would not come off the fence.

Montefiore's appetite for debate was only strengthened by such controversies as CSI, but his enthusiasm for Westcott was waning. Both he and Runcie were overworked, but while Robert could retire to his rooms with his poetry and his students, or simply himself, Montefiore was married with a family to whom he was devoted and yet whom he rarely saw.

Nor was his devotion to his wife and children matched by any particular respect for the celibate ideal. When Westcott House played Cuddesdon in the theological colleges' annual equivalent of the Varsity Match, Montefiore took his wife Eliza along. They showed the courtesy of calling on the principal, Edward Knapp-Fisher.

Knapp-Fisher was so surprised to see a woman in the vicarage, that he did not know what else to say: 'Can I show you the lavatory?' he asked her.

At Westcott the summer holidays were largely taken up by the long vacation term. The strain of bicycling into Westcott House from the outskirts by 7.30 a.m. every day and only returning home after Compline at around 10.30 p.m. was beginning to tell on Montefiore. In the early summer of 1954 he could stand it no longer. He resigned as vice-principal with no other job in sight.

Carey never forgave him his decision and Montefiore never regretted it. A few weeks later, the absence of a Dean at Caius and the influence there of Professor Charles Raven, a familiar figure at Westcott, led to Montefiore being offered the position. He accepted with alacrity, and stayed nine years. There were many aspects to a college Dean's position – social, intellectual and spiritual – that appealed to a man of faith, with a good degree, a gift for the pastoral, and whose experience of the world gave him pleasure in the company of intelligent sceptics.

Robert was now vice-principal of Westcott House and his place as chaplain was taken by a former student and Fellow of All Souls', David Edwards. That summer Robert went to Italy with Dr and Mrs Waters to visit Derek's grave near Salerno. He also travelled to Nice as holiday relief for the Anglican chaplain to the British community on the Riviera.

But with promotion his time was increasingly taken up with new duties in addition to his already heavy workload. He continued to teach and be secretary of the Cambridge Mission to Delhi, founded by Professor Westcott in 1877, which sent Cambridge men to Delhi (and welcomed Delhi men to Cambridge). He continued to have an amicable relationship with Kenneth Carey. David Edwards was a capable chaplain and an able supervisor. But while Edwards and generations of ordinands would come and go, Robert Runcie remained, as did Carey, and so in turn did Westcott House, in its tradition of public school and corporate loyalty.

One long vacation term student who found this style irksome during these years was a clever grammar school boy from Essex who was now an assistant lecturer in History at King's College, London. Dr Gareth Bennett was still only twenty-four and already possessed a caustic touch, the product of his personal insecurity and formidable intellect. He found a sitting target in Kenneth Carey, a wounded soul whose intellectual self-deprecation and public school mannerisms represented to Bennett everything he found most intimidating about the Church of England.

Bennett naturally did not put it quite that way:

*The Principal, Ken Carey, did not know what to make of me at all. I found him very intense and uneasy, and he spent much effort trying to pull me down a peg or two. He kept on about his own Third in History at Oxford as if to reprove me for having got a First; he wholly refused to laugh at my jokes; and kept on asking me if I made my confession. Since he refused to allow me to tell him jokes, I refused to tell him my sins.*

Carey would doubtless have put it differently. Bennett was clearly not a B. K. Cunningham man, and was unlikely ever to be one. Bennett nonetheless received a considerable amount of pastoral help from Carey, a fact which many of his contemporaries remembered and which Bennett seemed conveniently to forget.

If Bennett disliked everything about Carey, he was more generously disposed to Robert Runcie. Yet even this analysis, written many years later, began perceptively, but seems to have been translated with the passage of time into an attitude which said more about Bennett than anyone:

*'He was the one member of the staff who actually seemed to think it was a good thing that I was an academic, and we had a number of humorous conversations . . . He thought that all priests should have a secular side to them, and a false or intense piety was an enemy to real religion. He took a kind of benevolent oversight which was more that of equal to equal than I deserved. He was always cheering me up by asking my advice on this or that theological problem. I became quite devoted to him, and my diary is full of references to his kindness. He had intelligence, wit and style.'*

Then Bennett went on:

*'But I can scarcely have realised that I was laying the foundation of a friendship with a future Archbishop of Canterbury.'*

In 1920 Geoffrey Fisher was headmaster of Repton; in 1935 Michael Ramsey was sub-warden of Lincoln Theological College; in 1948 Donald Coggan was principal of the London College of Divinity. Twenty-six years later in their lives, they all became Archbishops of Canterbury. In 1954 Robert Runcie was vice-principal of Westcott House theological college. Was Bennett seriously suggesting that, unlike them, he should have included the words '(*and future Archbishop of Canterbury*)' in that year's listing in *Crockford's* Clerical Directory?

By the Lent term of 1956 Robert had been back at Westcott for three years. As vice-principal he was unlikely to rise further there in the near future. As a teacher he had probably found his limit at the level of *haute vulgarisation*, as one cleverer student unmaliciously put it. But he continued to underestimate the clarity of his own mind and the range of his scholarship. There was no doubt too that he missed Montefiore's company. It was in this frame of mind that he was visited one evening by Owen Chadwick.

Chadwick was a Cuddesdon man, five years older than Runcie and already one of the most intellectually distinguished figures in the Church of England. He was Dean of Trinity Hall and soon to be Master of Selwyn. He was also shortly to succeed Norman Sykes as Dixie Professor of Ecclesiastical History. These were posts that were not filled by advertisements in the *Church Times*. There was a network in these matters, an unofficial but highly effective appointments board; and Chadwick was a key member.

Chadwick was leaving Trinity Hall shortly to take up his Master's appointment. Given the circumstances, he wondered, would Robert consider coming to dinner?

The news appeared in the *Church Times* of 18 May 1956:

### 'New Cambridge Don'
*'The Rev. R. A. K. Runcie, Vice-Principal of Westcott House, Cambridge, has been elected Fellow and Dean of Trinity Hall, Cambridge.'*

Trinity Hall was one of the smaller and older colleges with gardens that stretched down to the Cam. It was traditionally known for its high proportion of law graduates. The Master was 'Daddy' Dean, who had come into the post before retirement regulations: 'I know I'm a scandal,' he would say, and went on lecturing on pathology well into his nineties. Once he locked himself in his bathroom, and one Dean was deputed to rescue the other.

Other members of staff were comparatively young; among them J. W. Cecil Turner, law don, author, cricketer, winner of the MC during the First World War. Turner had seen such suffering on the Somme that he had become an avowed atheist. Turner was a distinguished and respected man: 'the holiest unbeliever I have ever known' in the words of Trinity Hall's chaplain, Tony Tremlett.

Tremlett was brilliant at spotting and collecting potential ordinands.

Such were his powers that some meaner minds attributed his success to his waiting until they were slightly drunk; whatever the secret, his technique was unsurpassed. Robert knew Tremlett vaguely from his own war when the latter had been chaplain with the fourth battalion Coldstream Guards. He had also met Turner before. He was the patriarch of that large and powerful tribe, one of whose daughters Robert had escorted to a Commem Ball at Oxford, and another of whom he had met as a teenager at their house in Cambridge. Lindy Turner was by all accounts just as lively and wilful now that she was twenty-four years old as she had been as a teenager.

In following Chadwick to Trinity Hall Robert Runcie was entering into a distinguished and highly individualistic tradition. Chadwick's predecessor as dean and chaplain for sixteen years had been the legendary Launcelot Fleming, who had managed to spend several of those years at the South Pole as geologist and chaplain to the British Graham Land Expedition to the Antarctic. During the years when he had been resident in college, evening service was known as 'Fleming-song'.

Fleming was noted for his personal warmth and the honesty of his intellect. At his ordination he told his bishop that he did not accept the doctrine of the Virgin Birth. His opening technique with the young and sceptical was to assure them that Christianity did 'not require them to believe ten impossible things before breakfast'. He was loved and revered as a mentor by the likes of Robert Runcie and Alan Webster, and by generations of ordinands and undergraduates. He was now Bishop of Portsmouth, but remained closely associated with Trinity Hall.

The new Dean was soon established as an approachable figure at an academic but otherwise unclerical institution. He still returned to Westcott House from time to time to lecture on church history, where his place as vice-principal had been taken by a fearsomely bright old Etonian Fellow of King's, John Habgood. He retained the secretaryship of the Cambridge Mission to Delhi. Otherwise he threw himself into the duties and pleasures of life at Trinity Hall.

The former were not particularly onerous. He took charge of the services in chapel. He was available for personal consultation with members of staff and had some pastoral responsibility for undergraduates. But much of the latter was undertaken by Tremlett, who advised him to concentrate on research and channel it into a book that would establish him properly in the college and the Divinity Faculty. He remained interested in reading theology, but shy of reading it for a degree. He learned to polish his already considerable conversational gifts in the common room and at high table.

He made and maintained contact with contemporaries outside Trinity Hall. John Robinson was still Dean of Clare. Eric James, Robinson's close friend whom Robert had first met as a curate at St Stephen's, Rochester Row, where he had taken a party of ordinands, was now chaplain of Trinity. Montefiore was still Dean of Caius. At King's, where the previous Dean had recently hurled himself off the Chapel roof, the new man was the fiery and forthright Alec Vidler.

But above all Robert enjoyed the world of the Fellows of Trinity Hall, an extension of the world in which he had learned to live and come to feel at home during his time in the Scots Guards, at Brasenose and at Westcott. It was a man's world in which there were very few women, and those women who penetrated it were usually connected by family or in some other acceptable way. In that sense they were not so much women as honorary men. One of these, however, became his secretary, his fiancée and his wife in rapid order.

One day he entertained Montefiore to tea. He said he had something to tell him.

'You'll like her,' he told Montefiore, 'she's a lovely girl. I hope,' he added, 'getting married won't interfere with my vocation.'

Montefiore was delighted, but looked at him with some surprise. This was after all the man who had idolised Harry Williams. This was the man whose Anglo-Catholicism had led him to sit on the fence over the Church of South India. Montefiore had not been at all sure that Robert was the marrying kind.


Rosalind 'Lindy' Turner was always less likely to marry a clergyman than a member of the academic world. There was no surprise when she became engaged to a good-looking member of staff of the college in which her father held a position of eminence. Robert Runcie to her was a don who happened to be a priest in the Church of England.

Initially her parents were uncertain about him. Marjorie Turner was obsessive about housework and took in wealthy Swedish girls to 'finish' them in the old-fashioned sense. The money was also useful, but she preferred not to talk about that. She was openly concerned, however, as to how Robert, a poor clergyman, was going to support her daughter.

But there was a curious symmetry about the various relationships in which love would out. To Robert, Cecil Turner was a Senior Fellow for whom he had nothing but respect, and yet was reminiscent of his own father and his dislike of 'black beetles'. To Lindy, her father was someone to rebel against and please at the same time. In Robert, also an MC and Fellow of Trinity Hall, she had fallen for the ideal combination. While, for Turner, Robert's clerical side could be ignored in favour of his Fellowship of Trinity Hall, his good war record and his reputation as a cricketer.

Besides, she swept him off his feet.

The wedding took place in September, less than a year after they had first properly met. Among the hundreds of Scots Guards comrades, Westcott contemporaries and ordinands and Trinity Hall colleagues were Kathleen and Angus Inglis, Kenneth Runcie and his wife, Marjorie and her husband and the Turnbulls from Gosforth.

The University Church of Great St Mary's was divided straight down the middle, between bride and groom, law and church, and, some said, atheist and believer. Lindy, a churchgoer and Robert, a priest, were married by Launcelot Fleming. The reception was held in the Trinity Hall Fellows' Garden.

The couple flew to Nice for their honeymoon, staying where he had worked as a relief chaplain and enjoying the Riviera. Robert sent Mrs Tiffin a postcard. They came home for the Edinburgh Festival. Lindy, a talented pianist and obsessive music teacher, was thrilled to go to a Fischer-Dieskau recital. They sat in the front row, Lindy rapt and Robert half-asleep.

They took up residence in their first home, 20b, King's Parade, previously occupied by Owen Chadwick. Her piano had to be hoisted in via an upstairs window. In the bedroom a cheque from his old landlady and one from friends of Lindy's in Italy paid for what Robert called 'the Tiffin-Turin curtains'. Robert continued to work from his rooms in Trinity Hall. Tremlett continued to advise him to write a book if he wanted to establish himself. And so began the married life of Robert Runcie.

Tremlett was right, of course, and because of this shortage of qualifications there was a corresponding shortage of money. Without a position in the Divinity Faculty there were limitations to Robert's earning power. With no children, and the income from Lindy's piano lessons, the strictures were not as yet severe. But it soon became clear to Lindy that Robert had never been particularly good with money, and as a bursar's daughter she rapidly became expert in that respect.

Robert now had to teach a considerable amount of the ancient history of Greece and Persia. There was no hardship as this was his favourite subject and the income helped supplement his meagre fellow's salary. As Dean he made sure he was visible about the college to staff and students alike. He became known there as he had at Westcott, as a sensitive listener, precise rather than sentimental, encouraging the believer and unintimidating to those who were uncertain or downright suspicious of religion in general and of clergymen in particular.

He was becoming an accomplished preacher. When his former Westcott student Simon Barrington-Ward was due to preach his first sermon at the University Church, he sweated over it and packed in everything he could before taking it to show Robert Runcie. Robert managed to unpack some of it, and the result was greatly improved.

He himself preached in chapel and in 1957 he was Select Preacher at the University Church of Great St Mary's, where he had been married. He also heard many others preach there, among them Pastor Martin Niemoller, the German anti-Nazi theologian who had survived eight years in a concentration camp. Niemoller's sermon made a deep impression on Robert Runcie and he would return to it again and again, most notably at one of the highest points of his life over thirty years later. As a text for the times it cut straight into the cosy, sheltered world of Trinity Hall and Cambridge, and caught the mood of the Church in the uncertain world of the 1950s:

*'As long as the Church lives only for herself, as long as Peter does not leave the boat, she lives safely and undisturbed . . . but when the Church goes*

*forth into the surrounding world and bears witness to the truth, then it becomes clear that her existence is just as impossible as that of her master herself. And yet we are challenged to lead the same impossible sort of life as Christ did, obeying God rather than man and loving our enemy rather than trying to destroy him. That, indeed, means danger rather than security, risk instead of safety . . . [ Jesus] wants his Church to continue his work in the midst of a raging and stormy world, which nevertheless is longing for his reconciliation and peace, and which can be helped only by a Church not afraid of an impossible existence and task, but trusts in the call and promise of her living Lord!'*

Robert Runcie had seen at first hand the ruins of Germany and had heard for himself the call of G. K. A. Bell: 'What can we build on, after the war?' He had read the writings on 'this-worldly Christianity' of Dietrich Bonhoeffer, like Niemoller a German anti-Nazi pastor and theologian, but who unlike Niemoller had not survived the war. He had himself been called to a ministry in the institutions of the Church, but in his heart he was a 'Kingdom' man, who believed in the life and potential of Christianity in this world.

He and many of his generation had been shaped first by war, then by peace, and the post-war ideals of Beveridge and the welfare state. He had felt impelled to put behind himself many things: his background, his socialism, his awe of people in positions of power. But beneath the curious accent and the social savoir-faire, the polished classical liberalism and the ready wit, there remained a strong sense of social justice. He had a stronger vocation than others, perhaps than even he himself, suspected. It was at moments like this that he would have reminded himself that he was a priest first and a don second.

In 1958 Tremlett left Trinity Hall to succeed George Reindorp as vicar of Westminster St Stephen with St John (St Stephen's, Rochester Row), a thriving parish long established as a staging post for those who had achieved notice and were bound for further distinction in the Church of England. His successor as chaplain was Martin Chadwick, younger brother of Sir John Chadwick, Owen Chadwick and Henry Chadwick, and a talented violinist. Robert's teaching load continued to restrict his pastoral contact with undergraduates, but he and Chadwick met regularly to discuss individuals and they formed an effective team.

'Daddy' Dean had died and there was a new Master, Ivor Jennings, a remote and diffident lawyer who wrote the constitution of many of the world's emerging countries. Otherwise life at Trinity Hall continued much as normal. Robert was Select Preacher at Oxford, where among his former students Dr Gareth Bennett had just been elected to New College as Fellow and Chaplain.

In 1959 Robert and Lindy's first child was born. The arrival of James was a source of joy and anxiety. Robert was still not establishing himself by writing a book and seemed less and less likely to do so. His antennae towards possible ordinands, by contrast, were reaching Tremlett-like proportions. David Burgess, a Trinity Hall law undergraduate, for example felt that he did not know Robert as well as Robert seemed to know him, a common sentiment among his ordinands. Burgess was confirmed by Launcelot Fleming the year after Robert had left Trinity Hall, but their paths were to cross again.

It was early in 1960 that the influence of Owen Chadwick again made itself felt in Robert Runcie's life. The Master of Selwyn was also a governor of Cuddesdon, the theological college where he had studied for ordination. The Principal of Cuddesdon, the redoubtable Edward Knapp-Fisher, was leaving to be Bishop of Pretoria. A new man, and in Chadwick's opinion a new broom, was needed there; a committed Anglo-Catholic with proven pastoral skills, committed to academic excellence; but also someone who would humanise the place a little. In Chadwick's opinion, and in Tremlett's too, Runcie was the man to do this. In the circumstances, he wondered, would Robert consider applying for the position?

Cuddesdon College was older than Westcott House, having been founded in 1854 by the Bishop of Oxford, Samuel Wilberforce. Like Westcott House, it was a training college for Anglican clergy. Like Westcott, it drew people from the august and ancient university close to which it was located. Like Westcott, too, it was run by a small number of permanent staff who recruited outside lecturers to help with the teaching of around fifty ordinands who studied there at a cost of £250 per annum, four terms a year, for two years; many of whom would rise as Chadwick had done to positions of prominence in the Church of England.

But there were dissimilarities between Cuddesdon and Westcott which had always existed and which had become more pronounced over the last decade. Westcott was in the middle of Cambridge and Cuddesdon was in a parish that was centred on a small village several miles outside Oxford. The great vicarage was a barn of a place. On cold winter evenings a solitary tractor would be seen crossing the horizon against the sunset. It was an effective environment for a man to contemplate his God and his vocation. Westcott was Anglo-Catholic and unworldly, but Cuddesdon was positively monastic. Westcott, under Kenneth Carey, was an extension of the public school ethic that prided itself on its lack of hard and fast rules. Cuddesdon, under Edward Knapp-Fisher, was an Anglo-Catholic seminary run by a martinet.

The comparison, however, of Cuddesdon with Westcott and Westcott with Cuddesdon only went so far. In one crucial respect they were identical; in their flaws and in their virtues they were dominated by the personality of one man. Nor, though they were the Oxford and Cambridge of the theological colleges, were they exempt from the debate that was taking place over the future of theological colleges everywhere.

The falling numbers of ordinands and shortage of funds to train them had continued unchecked in the nine years since Robert Runcie's ordination. There was disagreement over the way forward within the Theological Colleges and Training Commission, and between the Chairman, the Bishop of Lincoln, Kenneth Riches, and another member, the Bishop of Manchester, W. D. L. 'Billy' Greer. Riches had been Principal of Cuddesdon and Greer Principal of Westcott. The debate would continue, and the crisis would worsen, in the 1960s.

It is not recorded if Robert Runcie was the only person approached as a possible Principal of Cuddesdon early in 1960. Certainly his answer would have been an emphatic 'No' to the idea of his returning as Principal to Westcott House. Montefiore, too, would reject the offer when it was made in 1962. But Cuddesdon in 1960 was a new and challenging proposition. Not only was it an established institution ready for new management, it brought with it a vicarage and a country parish in which the Principal was also Vicar. Robert Runcie was a priest who had never been vicar of a parish before. This thought nagged him more than his lack of a degree in theology.

Preferment too was a secondary but inevitable consideration. Robert was unlikely to be offered anything other than another dean's post if he stayed in the academic world. He knew he did not have either the temperament or the inclination to establish himself as a force in that area. Chadwick and Tremlett knew this too, and shrewdly reminded him of it whenever he appeared to vacillate over his decision. Nor did they have to remind him that both Greer and Knapp-Fisher had gone on to bishoprics. So too, shortly, would Kenneth Carey. Robert could make a success of himself as well as of Cuddesdon.

These were cogent arguments, against which were ranged Robert's innate reluctance to commit himself and Lindy's misgivings about leaving her piano pupils, her family and the place in which she had spent most of her adult life. During the war she had been evacuated at the age of eight with her mother and brothers and sisters to Canada, then moved across the American border to Massachusetts before returning to England while the war was still in progress. Lindy had a strong attachment to Cambridge and tended to see moving anywhere else as a leap into the unknown.

But by the same token she had acquired an adaptability that would enable her to follow her husband beyond the bounds of duty. In the years to come ' Don't worry about Lindy' became a familiar refrain of Robert's, particularly to his rather maternally-minded sister Kathleen, whenever another domestic upheaval was on the horizon.

In the spring of 1960 he set about divesting himself of what few responsibilities he had in Cambridge. One of these was the secretaryship of the Cambridge Mission to Delhi. He handed this over to Peter Walker, the former schoolmaster who had been one of his long vacation ordinands at Westcott House and was now Dean of Corpus Christi College. The Chairman was Owen Chadwick and Robert took his responsibilities seriously. Walker was only entrusted with the files after Robert had taken him through them with a thoroughness that left his successor with a similar sense of his task.

Two years later Walker would himself pass on the files and the secretaryship when he succeeded Kenneth Carey as Principal of Westcott House. But he was struck by Robert's mood at the time:

'You see, I *believe* in Cuddesdon,' he told Walker, and reminded him to send him his promising ordinands, since Walker was still at that time at Corpus Christi. In the long run, and for reasons he had gone over a hundred times in his own mind, he believed in Cuddesdon in a way that he did not believe in Westcott. He had convinced himself, and that was the only way he would ever convince anyone else. He accepted Chadwick's offer:

### 'New Principal at Cuddesdon'

'The Reverend R. A. K. Runcie, MA, former Vice-Principal of Westcott House and Dean of Trinity Hall, Cambridge, is to be Principal of Cuddesdon College . . .'

'For many years,' the Church Times went on, 'there has been a tradition at Westcott House that the Vice-Principal or Chaplain should be a Cuddesdon man. Now it is considered that justice has been done by the appointment of a Westcott House man as Principal of Cuddesdon.'

Tim Beaumont, who had once graced the courtyard of Westcott in his polo gear and hunting pinks, was now honorary curate of Westminster St Stephen with St John and editor of the radical Christian magazine Prism. It was in the latter capacity that he now wrote to his old vice-principal on his new appointment:

The Church (he wrote) was 'so bogged down in the Establishment (in all senses of the word) that not only is it almost impossible for a priest to do his job well, but he is himself rapidly spoiled by the system.

'Can you give your young men an overall vision of the Church as it should be? . . . If you summon them back in twenty years' time – not just those who will come to a reunion, but all of them – you will find it hard to recognise in them the same people who left you.'

They would have deteriorated, Beaumont went on, through loneliness, the demands of the system and the pervading atmosphere of inertia and despair. Beaumont himself would resign his orders in 1973, almost exactly twenty years after he was ordained, but would resume them eleven years later.

Neither he nor Robert was the kind of the priest he was talking about, but both knew that among the ordinands at Cuddesdon there might be those who were. Failure – failure to see them through to ordination, failure to spot the warning signs in advance – was a frightening prospect. To Robert it was one which could best be alleviated by equating success with higher standards of intellectual excellence.

Some criticism would be voiced later of his tendency to equate the latter too closely with men from Oxford and Cambridge. But it was for this reason that he made his need for intellectually able ordinands known to Peter Walker and others, in the months before he was due to take up his new appointment in October 1960.

The vicarage at Cuddesdon was something of a contrast to their flat at 20b, King's Parade. It was built in the same Gothic style as the college which it faced only a few yards away across the gravel. There were twenty-six rooms.

The previous occupant, Edward Knapp-Fisher, was also a contrast in style. Knapp-Fisher was a remarkable man in many ways, not least for the influence he wielded over the college, the ordinands and even the inhabitants of the village. He was a former wartime RNVR chaplain and a strict disciplinarian who led by example and expected others to follow. No one ever got into Chapel in the morning before Knapp-Fisher.

He and his two staff were unmarried and vigorous proponents of priestly celibacy. There were no facilities for women. Wives and fiancées were theoretically permitted, but in practice had to live at least two miles away, which would have placed them in the middle of a ploughed field. Their husbands had to eat every meal in college except Saturday lunch. The wives or girlfriends of those few students who were married or engaged lived lonely lives which were closely monitored, beginning with a squint at their ring fingers: 'Are you a *fiancée*?' became the catch-phrase, 'or an *accredited fiancée*?'

The villagers had nearly all been confirmed by him regardless of whether or not they came regularly to church. He once persuaded two elderly ladies who lived in separate houses to live together on the grounds that this was a waste of space, and provided his students as furniture removers. His parishioners and students greatly respected him, and regarded him with admiration and awe.

The routine at Cuddesdon was far more tightly circumscribed than it had been at Westcott House. The day began at 7 a.m. with Matins followed by a period of meditation and the Eucharist at 8 a.m. Breakfast took place in college for everyone, followed by work, Midday Intercessions, lunch, work, Evensong, work, supper and Compline at

9.30 p.m. followed by silence until breakfast the following morning. On Saturday nights Compline was half an hour later.

Into this way of life came Robert, Lindy and James Runcie in October 1960. As well as a new intake of ordinands, he inherited a generation of students who had arrived under Knapp-Fisher, and two remaining members of staff, the vice-principal John Brooks and the curate of the parish John Ruston. The chaplain, Anthony Bird, was another new arrival.

For the first term or two they shared the teaching load between themselves and with the help of outside lecturers: Professor Henry Chadwick on Guilt and Sin, the Reverend A. J. W. Pritchard on Christian Morals, and David Jenkins, the impassioned and loquacious Chaplain of The Queen's College, Oxford and Lecturer in Theology there, on the Atonement. During these awkward first months Robert demonstrated a pragmatic willingness to fit in with the existing system, and a technique of avoiding confrontation at almost any cost. Unless and until he was solely in charge of boat-rocking, he was almost pathologically reluctant to rock the boat.

In 1961 the first differences began to show between the new and old regimes. Some manifested themselves in comical ways. On one occasion Robert went with John Brooks and various Cuddesdon ordinands on an expedition back to Gosforth, where one of his Westcott students, Tony Meakin, was curate. One night they all went out to the cinema. Afterwards, Meakin and the Cuddesdon men were enthusiastic. But Brooks had a dark face: 'The theology of love,' he said, 'was all wrong,' and he meant it. The film was *South Pacific*.

A few months later Brooks left Cuddesdon for a parish in Zambia. He was followed at Christmas by John Ruston, who went to join Bishop Knapp-Fisher in South Africa.

In the same year, another Cuddesdon man, Michael Ramsey, became the 100th Archbishop of Canterbury. The Reverend Hassan Barnabe Dehqani-Tafti became the fourth bishop in Iran and the first Persian to be consecrated a bishop in the Anglican Communion. '*Signs of change*', as the *Church Times* put it, were detected by the Anglican Group for the Ordination of Women.

At Cuddesdon Robert Runcie proceeded with caution, putting consolidation before change. He had no intention of throwing away the heritage with the personal style of the Knapp-Fisher era. As *Princeps* he was open to the way things were moving, but as a man firmly of the Anglo-Catholic tradition.

He spent the days with the staff and students in college, through Matins, breakfast, lunch, Evensong and Compline. Only then did he return to the vicarage and its twenty-six rooms. There was no nostalgia for Westcott House, only the embracing of a more explicit invocation of shared discipline, order and prayer. In time he would introduce new staff to carry Cuddesdon forward with the aim of fulfilling the expectations of Chadwick and others. But it would take time, and Lindy's organisational and social instincts, to bring the women in from the cold.

The first new face he appointed to the staff was that of Lionel Wickham, who arrived as tutor in philosophical theology. Wickham had already been offered several teaching posts and been an outstanding student of Robert Runcie and Hugh Montefiore at Westcott House. As tutor his stipend was £900 a year, compared with the £500 he had previously received as a country curate.

Wickham was unmarried and had nowhere else to live but his room in college. He had no car and there was little or no public transport to Oxford. Under the previous regime the telephones had been removed from the clergy rooms on the grounds of expense. The place was in poor structural and decorative condition. When Wickham asked if he might have a television set to help lighten his darkness, Robert was in favour and the tutor's prayer was eventually answered. But there was much objection and fuss from other quarters on the grounds that a television aerial would disfigure the college's roof.

The new chaplain was Peter Cornwell, a friend of Anthony Bird. Bird and Cornwell were also unmarried and both had been students under Knapp-Fisher. Runcie, Bird, Cornwell and Wickham, and the growing band of visiting lecturers, were now in charge of the first ordinands of the post-Knapp-Fisher era.

Among these was David Burgess, the Trinity Hall man whom Robert had befriended and whom Launcelot Fleming had ordained the year before. Burgess had changed from law to theology and had resolved to be ordained, although he also wanted to go on voluntary service overseas. Robert had offered him a place on condition that he stayed at Cuddesdon for at least a year. Burgess arrived at Cuddesdon in the late summer of 1962. He was surprised and relieved to be offered a room not in college, but in the vicarage. Burgess was the kind of amusing and presentable young man Lindy liked to have around, and upon whom she could prevail to help with the washing up. He and Malcolm Harper, another Trinity Hall man, lived in what had been the maids' rooms over the kitchen. Another condition of living there was helping tend the coal-fired Aga last thing at night. This was after Compline, when silence was supposed to be the rule, but Burgess and *Princeps* often found themselves pausing amidst the coal dust for a quiet little chat.

Lindy had just given birth to the Runcies' second child Rebecca. *Princeps* had neither the time nor the temperament for changing nappies, and with very little money, and a lot of work in the house and the vegetable garden, there were always other people around. Her women friends, students' fiancées and wives, and a succession of German *au pair* girls were drafted in to help. The presence of one *au pair* eventually put an end to the celibacy of Peter Cornwell, while a particularly attractive and strong-minded German girl became engaged to Anthony Bird.

But the process of introducing women was a slow one, with Robert's innate caution vying with his awareness that life had to be made more humane for married ordinands. When Jim Thompson wanted to marry his girl-friend Sally, he had to go to the Principal for permission. Robert listened while Thompson extolled all the wifely virtues in her that a woman was supposed to have according to the ordering of deacons and priests in the Common Prayerbook.

'Sounds like a good line,' he said, and gave his permission; but Thompson still had to wait until the end of his first year as a student.

Michael Scott-Joynt expected to have to wait a similar period, but received a different response. His intended wife's parents had recently died within six months of each other. Robert surprised him by saying: 'You had better come to Cuddesdon as a married man.'

The Scott-Joynts arrived the year after Jim Thompson and the two couples lived close to each other in the village. But it was still a near-spartan regime in many respects. Women were allowed no further than the college common room and still only showed themselves there on infrequent and specifically-designated occasions, such as Saturday afternoon tea. Two or three married couples lived in houses without hot running water and with chemical lavatories in the back gardens, a chilly process requiring wellington boots in winter.

There were extraordinary discussions: should the wives of students living in houses without bathrooms be allowed to use the bathrooms in college while their husbands and the other students were at Evensong? The Bishop of Oxford, Harry Carpenter, gave Mrs Scott-Joynt and Mrs Thompson a key to the back door of his house opposite the theological college so that they could use his bathroom.

Lionel Wickham, too, would leave to get married. But while he was still engaged his 'accredited fiancée' cut her head at an unscheduled time and had to go to his room to have it bathed, sending a shock wave round the place. The spirit of Knapp-Fisher, and the tradition embodied in the many sermons on celibacy that had been taken to heart by generations of ordinands, was still abroad.

But it would be unfair and misleading to look back on the Knapp-Fisher era at Cuddesdon except in the wider context of customs of clerical life and a relationship between church and society that simply no longer exist. Knapp-Fisher was not a misogynist nor was he opposed to marriage, as he himself would demonstrate again by example. The dismal stipends of parish clergy meant there were compelling economic arguments for priestly celibacy. It was also difficult to run an all-male association whose integrity depended on its members meeting strictly together, if some of them were absent with their wives. Mrs Thompson, Mrs Scott-Joynt and Mrs Runcie, the young mother of young children and wife of an often absent husband, could also vouch for that.

The theological event of 1962 had been the publication of *Soundings*, a collection of essays largely by Cambridge theologians in the tradition of *The Historic Episcopate in the Fullness of the Church*, edited by Alec Vidler. Hugh Montefiore, Harry Williams and John Habgood were among the contributors.

But, unlike *The Historic Episcopate*, *Soundings*, albeit in the language of the theologian, asked questions of wider and more pressing concern.

What was the relationship between science and religion? Was Christian virtue really a form of moral cowardice in the face of a frighteningly incomprehensible world? How should Christians think of God?

These were big questions for which there were no easy big answers, but they were asked by Montefiore as much as anything in response to the answers being given to the same questions by another Cambridge theologian of the time. This was John Robinson, former Dean of Clare and now Bishop of Woolwich. Robinson had already achieved notoriety as a defence witness in the trial of *Lady Chatterley's Lover* and he exerted a magnetic hold over his students. His ideas, although not new to theologians, seemed to dominate the field of theology and were rumoured soon to be appearing in a book. *Soundings* was an attempt to ask some of the same questions in what its contributors felt was a deeper and more detailed way.

Robert Runcie had read *Soundings* and seen a copy of Robinson's manuscript, but it was not until after its publication that the latter was widely discussed at Cuddesdon. Before that, in the autumn of 1962, Robert had an opportunity to show off his own theological scholarship.

The occasion for this was the Teape Lectures at St Stephen's College in Delhi, which he was invited to give in appreciation of his past secretaryship of the Cambridge Mission there. Leaving Cuddesdon in the hands of Anthony Bird, he departed on an itinerary that would take him via Rome, Beirut and Jerusalem.

The trip was an exciting one, and a little more eventful than planned. In Rome he saw the leaders of the Catholic Church assemble for the conference that became known as Vatican 2. In Beirut, a city that was to bedevil him later in life, he was relieved of nearly all his money. In Jerusalem he managed to borrow some, and to see the holy places: the Church of the Holy Sepulchre and, in Bethlehem, the basilica and the cave where Jesus was said to have been born. Then he travelled on to Delhi and gave his six lectures.

His theme was the nature of authority, and the difference between *auctoritas* and *magisterium*. As arranged, he also gave roughly the same six lectures at Bishop's College, Calcutta and the United Theological College, Bangalore. Soon after he returned to Cuddesdon, Lionel Wickham found him lying exhausted in bed.

Lindy was downstairs, complaining about how he had never been good with money and the lengths to which he sometimes went to remind her of the fact. Wickham handed him a cup of tea and asked him how his lectures had gone.

To his surprise, Robert told him that they had been torn up on the aeroplane on the flight home. He told Wickham why he had done this. They were not badly received, he said, in Delhi, Calcutta or Bangalore. In fact they had gone down rather well in all three places. They were quite good, in fact; good enough for one lecture, but not six, on the subject. He did not feel able to leave them as a permanent contribution. That was why he had decided they should not be available for publication.

Wickham respected him for this decision and attributed it as much to modesty as lack of self-confidence on Robert's part. But it reminded him of something else about Robert he had already observed. Wickham had never met anyone in his life, ever, as clever at determining the 'common mind' of a meeting. Robert seemed to know, almost to a preternatural degree, how the other members were and were not going to vote. Then, and only then, did he declare which way he was going to vote, too.

What was more, he usually got away with it. The same was true in the village church, where village and college met on Sundays. Wickham dreaded going into the pulpit to preach after Robert had given the notices; Robert managed to make even the notices more interesting than anything the preacher had to say. In spite of his modesty and his lack of self-confidence, Wickham concluded, Robert had star quality. What was interesting, too, was that it was a strong enough quality to carry him through a series of lectures which on paper might not have withstood rigorous analysis.

John Robinson's book *Honest to God* was published on 19 March 1963. Its opening lines perfectly summed up the simplicity and directness of its message:

*'The Bible speaks of a God "up there". No doubt its picture of a three-decker universe, of "the heaven above, the earth beneath and the waters under the earth", was once taken quite literally . . .'*

Seven months later it had sold 350,000 copies and been translated into seven languages. Graham Leonard, the Archdeacon of Hampstead and a keen gardener, read an article by Robinson in the *Observer* and was so enraged that he spent the rest of the morning with a spade savaging his herbaceous borders. The *Church Times* declared on its front page that it was

*'not every day that a bishop goes on public record as apparently denying almost every fundamental doctrine of the Church in which he holds office'.*

Even SCM, the book's publishers, whose editor was David Edwards, Robert Runcie's former chaplain at Westcott, had only printed a first run of 6,000 copies. In the first few months, Robinson received almost as many letters about the book.

Theological colleges everywhere were facing the same sort of radical questions that were asked in *Honest to God*, but as *Soundings* had shown they were not necessarily coming up with the same answers. Robinson was merely re-emphasising and expanding on the 'this-worldly Christianity' of G. K. A. Bell and Dietrich Bonhoeffer. What was remarkable about *Honest to God* was not the content, which was nothing new, nor the fact that the author was a theologian; nobody took any notice of theologians in England. It was the fact, as the *Church Times* rather uncomfortably pointed out, that the author was a bishop:

*'Unfortunately,'* the *Church Times* went on, *'the Bishop's three heroes are Bonhoeffer, Bultmann and Tillich, the three theologians of the modern galaxy who are admittedly the most difficult to understand. Indeed a good proportion of the theological world is engaged in a wordy battle as to what they do mean . . .'*

If bishops spoke publicly, the inference was that they were expected to speak to the faithful for the faith, and not raise difficult and uncomfortable questions before an impressionable and uneducated flock. Like judges, when they spoke out of turn, people felt that the foundations of their world were being shaken. Robinson was charged by many with fostering agnosticism. What he had in fact done was foster among intelligent and sceptical people a renewed interest in the Church.

While the Archbishop of Canterbury Michael Ramsey would be personally called to account in some sections of the popular press for his bishop's behaviour, the second worst thing the Principal of Cuddesdon could expect from his ordinands would be an energetic discussion of the subject; the worst would have been no discussion at all. But, among his visiting lecturers, there was one for whose own behaviour as a very public bishop, twenty years later, Robert would in turn be called to account.

In that summer of 1963 Robert became a member of 'The Cell', the small, little-known, private support group of senior figures in the Church of England. The Cell met at least once a year for a weekend of prayer, discussion, meditation and meals in a retreat house somewhere in England. The other members were older: Eric Abbott, the Dean of Westminster and close friend of Michael Ramsey, was one; so was Christopher Pepys, Bishop of Buckingham; and the Bishop of St Albans, Michael Gresford-Jones.

The Runcies had a much-needed holiday in Nice. That September *The Honest to God Debate* was published and the debate continued for some time thereafter. Lionel Wickham departed for marriage and a parish in Wakefield and was succeeded as tutor at Cuddesdon by Mark Santer. Santer was a Queen's College, Cambridge and Westcott man with Firsts in both Classics and Theology. He was also married, and lived with his wife in the village.

The 1964 *Crockford's* Clerical Directory was published, and with it another eagerly-awaited and anonymous Preface:

*'There is in the Church of England,'* it said, *'a deliberate cult of amateurishness which is responsible for the futility of much that it tries to do.'*

The Paul Report, *The Payment & Deployment of the Clergy*, was published and also suggested that this was at the root of the problem and quoted a lot of statistics. In 1962 there were 20,247 clergymen in the Church of England (686 more than the previous year). 4,630 were in charge of parishes of 1,500 population or less, while almost as few (4,794) were in parishes of 5,000 to 20,000 people. The average age of a parish priest had gone up (from 49 in 1901 to 54 in 1962) and the number of curates had gone down. The average salary of a clergyman was £850 a year, but many subsisted on as little as £600 (and were married with children).

Paul's solutions to the 'amateurishness' described in *Crockford's* included the creation of a professional caste of clergymen deployed in what he believed to be a more businesslike manner. This was not a view that found favour in the Principal of Cuddesdon's 1964 Lent Letter:

*'For those who sit on recruitment committees and CACTM selection boards, such a way forward seems simplicity itself beside Mr Paul's demand for a vastly increased army of professional clergymen all pushed through the general purposes training. That could only lead to a lowering of standards in our colleges. I am inclined,'* he wrote, *'to believe that we need to produce less men earmarked for the exacting work of a parish priest, but they would need to be surrounded and supported by other kinds of ministry. Which should be called "supplementary" would remain an academic question. The shortage of clergy is not so serious as their misuse.'*

This was a theme to which he would return again and again, and he would demonstrate the success of it as he began to stamp his ideas on Cuddesdon in the middle years. The telephones went back in, but the pattern of worship and study remained. The married quarters were paid for with funds raised from former ordinands, and the college was restored. The ordinands were sent to visit mental hospitals and to conduct sociological surveys; but they were also part of the congregation in the parish church; and, if they were late into chapel in the morning, they felt the coldness of *Princeps'* eyes.

New arrivals at this time sensed that something was happening at Cuddesdon which would not easily be found elsewhere. Jim Thompson had been a Cambridge undergraduate when the main course of lectures at the Divinity Faculty had been *The Objections to Christian Belief*. Thompson was attracted by the wholeheartedness of Cuddesdon; he felt it was a place where he could safely take apart his prayer life and put it back together again. He had once been commissioned in the Third Royal Tank Regiment, which further commended him to his Principal.

Thompson and his contemporaries believed they were following in the tradition of Michael Ramsey; of holiness, scholarship and the willingness to take on board advances in the material world. They believed in being prayerful, committed, eucharistic priests. Yet, only twenty years later, the Church of England would be so bitterly confused in some quarters that Robert Runcie, Jim Thompson and others would be accused of spreading a virulent strain of theologically woolly liberalism.

David Burgess, the wandering ordinand from Trinity Hall, had also returned to live in the vicarage, this time to join another student, Nigel McCulloch. On the occasions when Lindy wanted to entertain important guests to dinner she would draft in Burgess and McCulloch as waiters. Burgess had beaten an erratic path back to Robert Runcie's door; abroad on a scholarship to study the Eastern Orthodox Churches (a burgeoning interest of the Principal's since his visit to Jerusalem), Burgess had literally been on the road to Damascus when he had decided once and for all to be ordained. In his second year at Cuddesdon he was encouraged by Robert to read widely in poetry and philosophy as well as theology. He did research with Frederick Dillistone, Fellow and Chaplain of Oriel. He was neither neurotic, nor inadequate, nor hopelessly confused as to the certainties of faith; but nor could he cope with crass generalisations, clichés or stock expositions. This might have made him a difficult student at some theological colleges, and an easy one at others; but at Cuddesdon Robert Runcie seems to have regarded him as a challenge within the call of duty.

Robert spent a lot of time trying to work out to which parishes his ordinands should go to serve their titles. Burgess had been seriously ill and was not suitable for a virile northern curacy. Westminster St Stephen with St John occurred to him as a possibility. This had been built up by George Reindorp and was now presided over by Tony Tremlett; once again, the answer seemed to lie in the Trinity Hall connection.

Burgess went to visit Tremlett and they took to each other. Then Tremlett was made Bishop of Dover. His successor, a near-contemporary of Robert Runcie at Westcott, did not take to Burgess at all. Nor did the Bishop of Kensington, who thought he should see a psychiatrist. Robert and Burgess did not agree.

Robert then dispatched Burgess to another Cuddesdon-linked parish in Birmingham. Like a boomerang his ordinand was soon back again.

Robert did not say as much, but Burgess felt he was becoming a trial to him. He tried to make himself useful around the vicarage, washing up and helping with the Aga. They continued to break the silence after Compline with the occasional chat.

Burgess' next trip was to a conference about the Orthodox Churches in Geneva. On his way back the boat arrived late at Dover and he stayed at Maidstone with Donald Reeves, a contemporary from his first year at Cuddesdon. Reeves had just been appointed chaplain to Mervyn Stockwood, the Bishop of Southwark. His vicar was looking for a new curate. The two men took to each other and Burgess went home to Cuddesdon with the good news for Robert:

'You should be all right,' Robert said. 'Are you sure?' he added nervously.

Maidstone was in the diocese of Canterbury, and the Archbishop of Canterbury, Michael Ramsey, liked to take a close interest in diocesan affairs. Burgess' next stop was Lambeth Palace, the ramshackle London headquarters and home of the Primate of All England and *primus inter pares* of the 64 million-strong Anglican Communion. He entered through the Tudor gate of Morton's Tower and went through the Outer Courtyard and up the stairs, past the shrewd and intimidating figure of Ramsey's chaplain, John Andrew.

Ramsey was in his study. Burgess entered and told him exactly what he had told the Bishop of Kensington. He poured out his heart, and the Archbishop said nothing and nodded in his inimitable way.

Later, Burgess was to look back on it as the most illuminating moment of his life.

Ramsey at last spoke: 'I would remind you as I remind myself. Faith is the substance of things hoped for. Kneel down, and I will give you my blessing.'

Burgess was ordained in Canterbury Cathedral and went to Maidstone to serve his title. It was not to be the last time that he was helped by Robert Runcie.


In 1964 Anthony Bird left and Peter Cornwell became vice-principal. Robert needed a new chaplain. Through another theological college principal he learned of a curate at Hexham, where he himself had once been bound, called Jeremy Saville.

Saville received a letter from Runcie asking him if he would like to come for an interview. Somewhat surprised, and still recovering from a broken engagement, Saville agreed. At the interview, he told Robert about his recent unhappiness.

'Don't worry' Robert said, 'I'll give you a term before you have to do any real work.'

Saville arrived for work in February 1965. Chichester, his old theological college, had been far more mixed in terms of class and educational background. Runcie, Cornwell and Santer were married and the atmosphere here seemed at once sophisticated and down to earth. 'I've got the cleanest lavatory floors in the Oxford diocese,' Lindy liked to say.

Apart from his duties as chaplain, Saville's area of interest was the New Testament, and he became noted at Cuddesdon for the strength with which he passed on his love of the text to his students. One of the first of these was Nicholas Coulton. Coulton had been attracted by the two communities of which Cuddesdon formed part, the rural village and the industrial suburbs of Cowley over the hill. He had talked about this to Robert at their initial interview, which took place on a walk around the tennis courts.

He also disclosed one or two other matters of concern.

'Are there any other questions you want to ask?' Robert had said.

'Yes,' said Coulton, 'are there any opportunities of going to parties here?'

They had had a good laugh about this. At half term in his first term there, Coulton borrowed the bursar's horse and set off. Robert was the only person around on his return.

'Ah, Nicholas,' he said, 'are you finding many opportunities to go to parties?'


In 1965 Robert Runcie was Chairman of the Cell. The third meeting was in the retreat house of Michael Gresford-Jones' diocese of St Alban's, the martyr who had sheltered a hunted priest, then taken his place and been decapitated for his pains.

The discussions of the Cell reflected his concern with giving his students a strong enough intellectual base from which to face a sceptical and materialistic world. Nicholas Coulton, who had not been to university, was alarmed when Robert insisted that he learnt enough Greek to read a chunk of Gospel and answer a General Ordination Examination question on the subject. 'These days,' he told Coulton, 'when other things are so loose, it's good to have a very tight discipline in this respect.' Coulton did as he was told and did not regret it.

But to others the Principal sometimes seemed blinded by the notion of Oxford and Cambridge men dealing with the world's intellectual and spiritual ills. The men with theological degrees were exempt from the New Testament papers of the GOE because they had theoretically 'done' the Bible. The Cambridge Theology Tripos, however, was not as Bible-orientated as Oxford's; a Cambridge man could arrive at Cuddesdon having spent only a term and a half on the Bible, and then go through Cuddesdon without really grappling with it again. A lot of ordinands went through with relatively little Biblical knowledge.

If they were bright, they coped; but some were brighter than others. To one or two of the more evangelically-minded, it was almost as if it was less important to kneel at the foot of the Cross than it was to have a theology degree.

But even his critics loved Robert, and only later did they ask themselves if the famous Runcie charm was not fortified by a toughness of the kind of which even they had not dreamed at the time: 'Robert would murder his grandmother, provided he had gloves on,' said one. On the other hand, he continued to go out of his way to avoid confrontation, and, unless he was absolutely and solely in charge of boat-rocking, to avoid rocking the boat. Some saw this as his essential enigma; others saw it as the insecurity of a man growing in stature, who felt that he somehow had an Achilles heel in the shape of his origins in the world. Twenty years later, the former would still be trying to puzzle it out and the latter would still be maintaining that they had the answer.

Outside the college at Cuddesdon, the real world began only a few yards away at the vicarage, where James and Rebecca were growing up. Robert saw relatively little of them at this time, a fact of life for which Lindy and the young ordinands who lived in the house tried to make up. James was a strong-willed child, who took after his mother but grew up to have as good a relationship with his father as Robert had had with Robert Senior, and in which football played a similarly important part.

The debate caused by *Honest to God* continued, but other bishops and clergy behaved in a more traditional, if eccentric, fashion. The Reverend Cyril Shufflebotham of Stanton, Shropshire, was using a ventriloquist's doll as a visual aid in his Sunday School. If the doll gave the wrong answer, the children corrected it. Graham Leonard, the Suffragan Bishop of Willesden who as Archdeacon of Hampstead had taken such violent exception to John Robinson's book, suggested that no person should be appointed as principal of a theological college who had not first been a parish priest; although he was Vicar of the parish, this might have debarred Robert Runcie from Cuddesdon, Peter Walker from Westcott House, and various others. Bishop Cuthbert Bardsley of Coventry warned of an 'atheistic onslaught' and declared that Christmas was in danger of becoming 'a holiday orgy'. In South Africa the Bishop of Pretoria and former Principal of Cuddesdon, Edward Knapp-Fisher, surprised many of his old students by getting married.

A photograph of the Bishop and the new Mrs Knapp-Fisher duly appeared in the *Rand Daily Mail*. Next to it was a photograph of the winner of the big event in the racing calendar, the Rand Gold Cup. A copy of this was circulated among a number of his former students in samizdat form, with a certain amount of good-natured amusement. This was because, due to an unfortunate error of typesetting, the newspaper had transposed the two captions. Under the picture of the Bishop and his bride, the legend now read: *Jockey Smith and his winning mount.'*

In 1966, the year that one of his old ordinands again came back to haunt him, the Principal of Cuddesdon made his thoughts on the training of ordinands known at length in the *Church Times*:

*'Training for the Ministry – 1: Intellectual'*
*'Presenting the Age-Old Faith in Modern Terms'*
*'By R. A. K. Runcie'*
*'Theological colleges have been painfully discovering the need for a much more rigorous mental training than they held out to students in the past.*

*A comparative study of GOE papers, library accessions, the size and in many cases the theological qualifications of the staff reveal that the pace has quickened and the scope enlarged. Furthermore, it is arguable that those who live in them are healthily engaged with just those fundamental questions of belief, behaviour, spirituality and ministry which few others in the Church can face for the clutter of secondary issues. No-one in the theological colleges is much concerned with redundant churches, the date of Easter or the parson's freehold, but the Church Assembly has to be.*

*There are, of course, the frightened conservatives with their tenacious insistence on some ancient system, and on the other hand the cocksure pioneer with his sweeping denunciation of the rest of the Church. The stiff and the woolly are to be found in the colleges as elsewhere in the Church; but you have to be up-to-date with your impressions if you are going to generalise about the ordinands of the mid-sixties, and my impression is that there is now more attention given to fundamental theological questions than ever before.*

*The intellectual task of the theological college might be summarised thus – to think through a theological problem, relating it to the documents of the Christian faith and to the coherent totality of Christian doctrine and thus aiming at some relevant formulation in modern terms. The procedure in our study of ethics is first to awaken an awareness of the moral problems of men and women today and the situations which give rise to them; then to consider the tools which the Christian tradition has made available for handling ethical problems; and finally to use the tools in such a way that a piece of teaching or counselling or direction can be given which has been not only assimilated as "the truth" but as the truth for the teacher or counsellor, as part of the basis of his own personal life.*

*Viewed externally, these may seem obvious steps, but they mark something of a revolution in method. They spring from a growing recognition that solemnly intoning "The Bible says" or "The Church teaches" is no substitute for hard thinking.*

*When a college with a resident teaching staff of three is asked to deal with fifty men, some with degrees in theology, some in arts or science and some with no degrees at all, with an age-span from twenty-one to fifty-five, often joining at different times of the year for a variety of programmes extending one, two or three years, it is being asked to do an impossible job.*

*It is time,'* he concluded, *'that the colleges, for their own good and that of the Church and society they exist to serve, submitted themselves to a thorough, professional and independent reappraisal of their function and purpose.'*

Robert agonised over writing this, as he agonised over the agenda of a meeting of the Cuddesdon Parish Council or a sermon delivered to an audience of six villagers in the local church. He expected the same standards of his staff as he did in himself; nor did he confine his attentions to the latest generation of his students. His previous ones were travelling representatives of his ideas, and in some cases required regular pastoral check-ups. David Burgess, after his year in Maidstone, was a case in point.

His vice-principal Peter Cornwell had passed on the latest news. Burgess had worked too hard in the first year of his curacy, drinking too much instant black coffee in too many council flats and finally crashing his car in the middle of the night. A friend travelling behind him had dusted him off and deposited him with Cornwell's mother, who lived nearby and nursed him for a week. Now he was feeling better.

Robert listened with a familiar feeling, and telephoned his former student:

'David,' he told him, 'I think we should meet to talk about your future.'

Robert was already due to travel by train to Canterbury. He arranged to meet Burgess en route so that they could travel together the rest of the way: 'I suspect,' he told Burgess, 'we should be thinking of something different for you. I'll have to think about it. But I have always thought of you as being in the university world. At least,' he added, 'you would be well fed and watered.'

The train travelled on to Canterbury where the two men parted company. Archbishop Ramsey was normally inflexible about his curates serving three years in a parish, but Robert persuaded him to think about it.

Shortly afterwards, Ramsey was approached by the Master of University College, Oxford at a meeting of 'Nobody's Friends', the Lambeth Palace dining club for people in such high places that they had nobody apart from their own kind for company. The Master was looking for an Assistant Chaplain (and had mentioned this to Robert Runcie). He understood that there was an extremely able young fellow named David Burgess, a Cuddesdon man whom the Archbishop had personally ordained, and who might fit the bill.

Precise as clockwork, the machinery whirred into action and the hand moved on to the required position. The bell rang (of the telephone in Burgess' house) and he was duly appointed. Burgess was to spend eleven happy, well-fed and watered years at University College, Oxford as Chaplain, Junior Research Fellow and Bursar, before his telephone rang again in a similar fashion.

Cuddesdon continued to recycle its ordinands as members of staff; sometimes there was only a short interval between the two roles. Michael Scott-Joynt succeeded Mark Santer as curate and tutor in 1967, like Santer serving his title in the parish immediately after finishing his two years at Cuddesdon as an ordinand. Santer took him round, muttering how theological colleges were run by a man and three boys.

As Robert's curate Scott-Joynt not only taught Biblical and Old Testament studies in the mornings, but also shared with him the parish visits in the afternoons. As Robert had done with John Turnbull in Gosforth, Scott-Joynt learned a good deal about parish ministry, including how much it meant to his Principal.

The new vice-principal was Ken Jennings, a Cuddesdon man of the Knapp-Fisher era who married Jim Thompson's sister-in-law. John Garton also arrived as a student and lived in the vicarage. Like Jim Thompson, Garton had been commissioned as an officer in the Royal Tank Regiment and would go on to serve his title with the Scots Guards. He then served as a Chaplain to the Forces before returning to Cuddesdon as Principal less than ten years later.

Thompson himself had served his title as curate in London's poor area of East Ham. He would shortly return to Cuddesdon as chaplain: 'I am so much better at calming things down than I am at stirring them up,' Robert told him, 'I want someone who will put a bomb under the place.'

But in his sense of the Liturgy he remained firmly down to earth. When Thompson first celebrated the Eucharist at Cuddesdon as chaplain, he used to hold up both arms and then drop one to turn the page. After a while Robert called him into his study, and said rather apologetically: 'Jim, you know when you do that' (the Principal made the same hand signals), 'you look like . . . you look . . . like a policeman.'

Early in 1968 the Bunsen Report, *Theological Colleges for Tomorrow*, was published to considerable interest and unease.

The Report recommended drastic surgery in the form of amputation, if the rest of the theological colleges were to enjoy a healthy future. The four-man working party consisted of Sir Bernard de Bunsen, Principal of Chester College of Education, Kenneth Haworth, Dean of Salisbury, Henry Chadwick, Regius Professor of Divinity at the University of Oxford, and Basil Moss, Chief Secretary of the Advisory Council for the Church's Ministry. They described the existing system as 'uneconomic and wasteful'. While the principals of the various colleges singled out for closure or merger sweated it out, the Principal of Cuddesdon was called upon by the *Church Times* to give his opinion:

*'Theological Colleges: the Right Solution?'*

*'Robert Runcie, Principal of Cuddesdon, considers the new report* Theological Colleges for Tomorrow.

*'The Commission,'* he wrote, *'seems to confuse pre-ordination and post-graduate studies. Surely, given a man who has attained a decent academic standard, especially a man who has read theology for an honours degree, it is infinitely more important that he should be sent to learn the life of discipline and devotion in a seminary in the wilds of rural England than that he should hang about in a theological college on the periphery of a university . . .'*

But, after examining the Report in detail, he concluded in favour: *'there is a clarity of direction in its findings and, I believe, a wide measure of goodwill for its proposals among all the parties concerned – and not least among the students at present in training.'*

The Principal of Cuddesdon was contemplating his own future after nine strenuous years amid constantly changing generations of students and staff. He had already turned down offers of the deanery of Guildford and the bishopric of Western Australia; the latter of which was accompanied by a request that he should enclose a urine sample if his answer was in the affirmative. God moved in mysterious ways, but married clergymen did so after consulting their families.

One job he did accept recalled the strange professional life led by Nancy Runcie forty years earlier. This was as a lecturer with Swan Hellenic Cruises, a luxury which he and Lindy could not otherwise have afforded and in which capacity they sailed to the Aegean that summer.

Much agonising took place over drafts and redrafts of lectures, and the results were a series of shipboard and onshore performances that brought out the scholar, the soldier and the priest in him, delivered with maximum dramatic effect. Peter Balfour, late of the Third Battalion Scots Guards and shortly to be Chairman and Chief Executive, Scottish and Newcastle Breweries, would never forget the sight of the man he had known as 'Killer' Runcie standing and delivering the words of St Paul to the Ephesians, at Ephesus: *'who has made the two into one and broken down the barrier which used to keep them apart . . .'*

Another job was to hold together the Conference of Theological College Principals, whose Chairman he was appointed late in 1968. In the aftermath of the Bunsen Report this meant presiding over a nervous and highly individualistic group of men, united not least by degrees of antagonism towards change in direct proportion to how seriously their own colleges were going to be affected. As he had told Jim Thompson, he was so much better (or happier) at calming things down than he was at stirring them up. Yet within two years he would have become gamekeeper turned poacher, having retired as a college principal and chaired the commission that settled the fates of his former colleagues and the colleges, Cuddesdon included.

Early in 1969, after he had chaired his first conference in his new role, he was installed as a canon and prebendary of Lincoln Cathedral, which enabled him to be known as the Reverend Canon R. A. K. Runcie. It was a largely honorary post conferred on him by the Bishop of Lincoln, Kenneth Riches, who had preceded Edward Knapp-Fisher as Principal of Cuddesdon.

At about the same time, in February 1969, and only a few miles from Cuddesdon, the Oxford University Sermon was preached by the Chaplain of New College, Dr Gareth Bennett. The theme was 'The Grace of Humility', a traditional one for the Sermon and in this case was based on Galatians 5.26: *'We must stop being conceited, provocative and envious.'*

Robert's student from the Westcott days had been at New College for ten years now, and had his own views on the subject:

*'Animals kill for food,'* he told his packed and distinguished congregation, *'and they do so without hatred; they practically never kill animals of their own kind. Only man does this: kill his own kind unnecessarily and with hatred. This is our dilemma. How shall we reconcile our natural creative drive with the need that we shall not be perverted into hatred and self-destruction? . . .*

*'It is a fact which you may have noticed that the life of groups which make heavy moral demands on their members is marked by internal disputes, schisms and persecutions, the Christian Church not least among them. A church historian may be permitted the reflection that much of what has passed as dispute on high moral principle has, in fact, been only a desire in disguise to impose oneself on others . . .*

*'But how do we accept ourselves? . . . So much of our harshness and uncharity to others stems from our inner insecurity. Usually it is that some aspect of their character or conduct seems to represent a threat to our own personalities and position . . . if by grace I can admit all the things I am, and perceive God's acceptance of me, then perhaps I shall be able to . . . look upon other people in a new and compassionate light, knowing that both they and I are in the same boat: we both depend upon the mercy which God wills to have upon all men . . .'*

Ten years later Bennett would still be at New College, an established figure and a respected historian of the Church of England. But Bennett would resign his post as chaplain and enter a personal wilderness of thwarted ambitions, real and imaginary, in which the grace of humility gave way to a perverted sense of injustice. The mysterious ways of priestly preferment, of earthly promotion in a heavenly cause, would come to obsess Bennett and ultimately destroy him; and would obscure a proper appreciation by both his critics and his supporters of his academic work.

Eight months later, in October 1969, Robert Runcie was at Cuddesdon when he received a letter from the Prime Minister.

Harold Wilson was not especially noted for his grasp of theology or his interest in the history of the Church of England. He had known Michael Ramsey as a forceful opponent in the House of Lords of the 1968 Immigration Bill. As Prime Minister, he ranked after the Archbishop of Canterbury in the official social pecking order that was part of the traditional fabric of English society. But as another part of that traditional fabric, and of very much more significance in practical terms, he was keenly aware of the wider historical context.

Since Henry VIII, the Sovereign had been Supreme Governor of the Church of England. Since the Restoration, that Sovereign had operated with significantly reduced executive powers. Wilson was the latest beneficiary of those powers, and in that capacity he was now exercising them. He did so with the aid of his own Appointments Secretary and particularly the aid of the Archbishop's Appointments Secretary, William Saumarez-Smith.

Saumarez-Smith, formerly of the Indian Civil Service and a committed churchman, had the job of sifting for the likely candidates for bishoprics (and noting the unlikely ones) and conferring on the matter with his opposite number at the Prime Minister's office. They would then produce not one name but two, which would be forwarded by the Prime Minister to the Queen for her selection. In reality, however, the Queen always ticked the first name on the list. Saumarez-Smith, who happened to live in Cuddesdon, telephoned Robert to inform him that he would be calling at the vicarage later.

In this atmosphere of secrecy and gentlemanly protocol, Harold Wilson was informing Robert Runcie of what he already knew; that Michael Gresford-Jones, his colleague in the Cell, was shortly to retire. Furthermore, Wilson was politely asking Robert's permission to forward his name to the Queen as the next Bishop of St Albans. The mysterious processes of priestly preferment, of earthly promotion, had well and truly begun.


At Cuddesdon the remaining college staff of Jennings, Thompson and Scott-Joynt contemplated the logistical problems facing them until Robert's successor arrived as Principal. Leslie Houlden, chaplain of Trinity College, Oxford and himself a Cuddesdon man of the Knapp-Fisher vintage, was announced as the new incumbent. In the vicarage, as there had been at 20b, King's Parade, there was consternation at the thought of being uprooted from friends and piano pupils, and the cry 'Don't worry about Lindy' could again be heard. In the diocese of St Albans the appointment was made more comprehensible to the common reader by trivial descriptions of the everyday life of the Runcie family in the *Hertfordshire Advertiser*. Letters of congratulation arrived from bishops, mayors, past colleagues and students and parishioners, and people he had never met.

The Archbishop of Canterbury, Michael Ramsey, came to visit. This was not Ramsey's first visit, nor his last, for he retained a special affection for Cuddesdon and had bought the Old Vicarage with the idea of retiring there. The arrangement would not work well; Ramsey was a welcome visitor to his old college, but it was not the place he had known as a student in 1928 and he eventually moved on to Durham where he was happier. He paid tribute to Robert's time as Principal and as was the custom invited the Runcies to stay at Lambeth Palace the night before Robert was consecrated in Westminster Abbey.

In late December 1969 and early January 1970 he chaired his last Conference of College Principals. In early January five honorary canons of St Albans Abbey objected to the outmoded procedure of episcopal 'election' and said so (there were nineteen others who did not and this had nothing to do with the personality of the incoming bishop). In mid-February his staff, past and present students, parishioners and governors gave him a farewell party.

With this came gifts. The Bishop of Oxford presented him with a pair of candlesticks for use in his private chapel; the Chaplain of Trinity College, Cambridge, a former curate of Gosforth, gave him a copy of the modern abstract crucifix that hung in the college common room; the assistant curate of St Helier gave him a cheque, two copes and a mitre on behalf of his students; the villagers gave him a cope and mitre; and Mark Santer, formerly his curate and now Dean of Clare College, Cambridge, on behalf of the Cuddesdon staff gave him his episcopal ring.

He now possessed some of the personal trappings if not yet the authority of a bishop of the Church of England. The latter was vested in him at a series of arcane ceremonies, each more splendid and intimidating than its predecessor.

On 23 February he was confirmed in his election in an ancient legal ceremony at St Margaret's, Westminster, between the House of Commons and Westminster Abbey. His sister-in-law Jill Turner, whom he had once escorted at Oxford and who was now a barrister, accompanied him as his Advocate. That night the Runcies stayed for the first time at Lambeth Palace.

On 24 February he was consecrated bishop in Westminster Abbey. He undertook to show reverence and obedience to his Archbishop; that he believed in the Scriptures and the power of prayer; that he would drive out erroneous doctrine, deny ungodliness and worldly lust, practise sobriety and punish the unquiet and disobedient in his diocese. Harry Williams preached the sermon. Ramsey laid his hands on Runcie's head and all forty-one bishops present did the same. The Archbishop gave him a bible, and he left the Abbey to be greeted by his family and friends. On 25 February he went to Buckingham Palace to do homage to the Queen.

On 14 March he was enthroned in St Albans Abbey. He arrived in full regalia at the ancient door and knocked three times with his crozier. The Dean admitted him and he was taken through further complicated legal ceremonies. He was led to his throne with a fanfare of trumpets of the Royal Horse Guards and 1st Dragoons, partly arranged by Archie Fletcher, a friend from the Third Battalion Scots Guards. He took his place on the throne occupied by six previous bishops, latterly by Gresford-Jones.

There were 2,500 people present: mayors, aldermen, councillors, leaders of other churches, citizens from every parish in the diocese. The new bishop preached his first sermon.

*'Parts of this service,'* he told them, *'owe more to the age of Wolsey than Alban, let alone the age of St Paul or Martin Luther King . . . The feudal lord battering for admission on the door of his cathedral – then the drawing up of a legal agreement.*

*'I confess that there have been times in the past few weeks when I have wondered whether I was being made a baron or a bishop, and there have been times when I wondered whether an inspired misprint in a local paper which referred to my "enthornement" did not do more justice to the prickly seat on which a bishop must sit these days.*

*'It would be easy to deplore lack of faith. It might be more helpful to recognise that our times require a different sort of evengelism, a preaching of the gospel which gives more space to the social context of Christianity and takes more account of honest intellectual difficulties.*

*'It would be easy to deplore the collapse of the authorities. It may be more helpful to explore a new style of leadership geared at helping people to do things for themselves, to lead their community and transform and renew it not from outside but within.*

*'It would be easy to deplore the Church's diminished influence in areas such as education and social welfare, where in the past it has been a pioneer and sometimes exercised a controlling power. It would be more helpful to recognise that the church is a servant and not a rival to society.*

*'It is the capacity to inspire which matters.'*

He was now Robert St Albans, bishop, and brother to the diocesans Ian Dunelm, Ronald Leicester and Edward Bath & Wells; to the suffragans, Graham Willesden and John Knaresborough; and, in the wider Anglican Communion, to Keith Wangaratta, John Matabeleland and Donald the Arctic.

But he was still Robert Runcie. At the more intimate celebrations afterwards, he recited a limerick to prove it:

'At a party arranged by the Dean
The Bishop created a scene.
He stood on a chair
And sang songs out of "Hair"
When he should have been toasting the Queen.'

# 3

# *The Bishop*

IN many ways the Right Reverend R. A. K. Runcie MA, MC was ideally equipped to be a bishop.

As curate of Gosforth he had learned the worth of a good training vicar. As vicar of Cuddesdon he had learned to put that training into practice. He had also learned to understand the mysteries of parish life; of dilapidations boards, rural deaneries and archiediaconal affairs. As Principal of Cuddesdon he had learned the importance of the role of experts from different walks of life in the training of men for the ministry. He also knew that ministry would be more effective if that training continued after they had been ordained.

The diocese of St Albans was rich in possibilities where these accumulated experiences were concerned. Instead of a few hundred souls dominated by a theological college, there were one and a half million people spread over nearly a thousand square miles of which St Albans occupied only a tiny part. Cuddesdon was synonymous with training for the ministry; most people lived in the diocese of St Albans unaware that the Bishop lived in Abbey Gate House.

They were used to seeing the Archbishop of Canterbury more frequently on their television screens than their own Bishop in the flesh. Michael Ramsey came across to them as a remote and holy-looking man. The new Bishop of St Albans had won the MC in a tank battle and reputedly supported Luton Town Football Club. Both were misleading descriptions. But they mattered, and this was why Robert Runcie was ideally equipped to be a bishop. Bishops, in comparison with the theological college principals they might once have been, now had to appear to be worldly as well as holy men.

1970 was not only a year of change for the Runcies but for the Church of England. Until that year there had been two sets of governing bodies: the Convocations of Canterbury and York (composed entirely of clergymen) and the Church Assembly, a combination of the Convocations and a House of Laity elected by the dioceses. The old system was inefficient, time-consuming, unwieldy and unrepresentative. The new one would come to be described in exactly the same terms.

The new system of government was called the General Synod (synod from the Greek meaning roughly 'two into one') of the Church of England, which met two or three times a year in York or at Church House, Great Smith Street in London, the headquarters of the permanent civil service of the Church of England. The General Synod was composed of three Houses: the House of Bishops, the House of Clergy and the House of Laity. The intention was that it would be efficient, considered, flexible and representative.

The new system meant a greater involvement of clergy and lay people in the consultative processes of the Church. This coincided closely with the ideas of the new Bishop of St Albans who attended its first session in November 1970.

First, however, he had had to get to know his diocese. In 1970, apart from one and a half million people spread over nearly a thousand square miles, it also contained over three hundred clergy, including two suffragan bishops, two hundred benefices, three hundred parishes and nearly four hundred churches. Earlier that autumn the inhabitants had left their clergy houses, their vicarages and their deaneries and assembled at Keble College, Oxford, for the triennial diocesan clergy conference. Here Robert had managed to meet most of the relatively few people he had not yet visited. This was a fortunate coincidence in a new bishop's first year.

But, interspersed with the new routine of triennial diocesan clergy conferences, sessions of the General Synod, the diocesan synod, the deanery synod, bi-weekly diocesan staff conferences, ordinations, confirmations, pastoral committees, pilgrimages and preaching in different parishes, there was an unfinished piece of work. This was his chairmanship of the three-man Archbishop's Commission into Theological College Reorganisation, or 'Runcie Commission'. The other members were Kenneth Woollcombe, a Westcott House contemporary and principal of Edinburgh Theological College, and D.R. Wigram, former headmaster of Monkton Combe School and a vice-president of the Church Missionary Society.

Since early 1970 the three men had been visiting the theological colleges and compiling the Runcie Report. By the time of the first session of the General Synod the work was done. The House of Bishops had read it and made its amendments. The Archbishop of Canterbury, Michael Ramsey, was due to introduce the Runcie Report to the second session of the new General Synod in February 1971. The details, at the request of the principals, would never be published. The conclusions were already known.

It was known for example that the bishops wanted one monastic college, Kelham, not merely to reduce its numbers as the Report had suggested, but to close altogether. This and other changes had provoked considerable resentment at a report which unearthed a number of recherché statistics concerning the number and type of ordinands in training in the Church of England. In 1965, twenty-five colleges had provided 1,369 places. By 1970 that number had fallen to twenty-one colleges and 1,141 places. As of October 1970, the bishops and the Runcie Commission found that there were 834 ordinands resident in twenty-one theological colleges, 280 of whom were 'Evangelicals', 223 'Tractarians' and 331 were 'Other'.

By January 1971 the House of Bishops had ratified their findings and the Archbishop had signed the result. Robert Runcie, as Chairman, held a press conference at Church House a week before the General Synod was due to start.

Flanked by Sir John Guillum Scott, Secretary-General of the General Synod and one of the Church of England's most influential laymen, and Canon Basil Moss of ACCM (the Advisory Council for the Church's Ministry) he answered questions about his work. Four of the twenty-one colleges should be closed altogether. Three others, Westcott House, Ridley Hall and Wesley, the Methodist college, should form a federation. He was aware that it was a 'painful' document. On the other hand it made sense. He saw no need to be depressed.

The Archbishop of Canterbury introduced the Report to the General Synod in melancholy terms. He was followed by the new Bishop of St Albans, who repeated the performance he had given at the press conference. He enlarged upon the rich diversity of the colleges and the need to maintain that diversity in leaner, fitter form. He added that it was a 'working document for decisions'; he did not need to say that the decisions had to be taken sooner rather than later.

The Runcie Report was debated, or 'taken note of', in the euphemistic terms of the Synod's standing orders, and its conclusions in large measure implemented. The new bishop was praised for his sensitive, precise, but unsentimental handling of a tricky issue. He had made a good impression on Synod and in the House of Bishops of which he was a new and relatively youthful member. He was also complimented on the way he had handled the press. The words 'star quality' were even mentioned.

At St Albans he did his job with new as well as existing staff. At senior level these still consisted of no more than half a dozen people: John Trillo, Suffragan Bishop of Hertford, John Hare, Suffragan Bishop of Bedford (who was also an archdeacon), the Dean, Noel Kennaby, B. C. Snell, another archdeacon; and the ubiquitous Dennis Yates, Diocesan Secretary, and Secretary of the Diocesan Conference, the Dilapidations Board, the Pastoral Committee, the Board of Patronage and the Education Committee, as well as Press Officer and Editor of the Diocesan Year Book.

To this number he now added a domestic chaplain, far from a luxury, but a figure his elderly predecessor had seen fit to do without. This was clearly a job for a Cuddesdon man. But who among the many able and personable young ordinands of his past acquaintance was available or fitted the bill?

Nicholas Coulton had spent four years as a curate at Pershore in Worcestershire, and was known to be looking for a change. He was on the shortlist for a chaplaincy at Oxford; he had been interviewed for a job at All Saints, Margaret Street. Coulton did not even know where St Albans was, but the story of the saint's martyrdom was familiar. He knew Robert as a man whose handwritten note he had tucked into his cassock pocket before being priested; as a man with a sense of humour and deep devotion, who had charmed him into learning Greek.

Robert made him the offer and Coulton accepted the job. He was the first of many Cuddesdon men to beat a trail to their former principal's door, a move which few could resist and which became something of a standing joke in the Church of England. He was not so much a traditional 'crozier-carrier' as an ADC; companion, personal assistant, communications expert and liaison officer for the bishop with clergy throughout the diocese. He was 'earthed' in the parish of St Saviour's and preached on most Sundays. He was present in what passed as the private chapel at Abbey Gate House at the beginning of the day. They said Matins together in the spare bedroom. Evensong was usually said separately; the timetable did not allow otherwise.

Coulton was unmarried and took up residence in another of Abbey Gate House's bedrooms, a temporary arrangement that lasted several years. Robert, Lindy, James, Rebecca and Coulton were soon at home in the beautiful house with views across the green to the Abbey. Downstairs at the front was the office, and Jill Jackson, his senior secretary. Next door was the coach house, which the Church Commissioners preferred to call the garage flat. Down the lane with his family was John Trillo's successor as Suffragan Bishop of Hertford, the Right Reverend Hubert Victor Whitsey, known as 'Our Vic'.

Whitsey had occasionally preached at Cuddesdon and been another contemporary of Robert's at Westcott House. But a man less like Kenneth Carey would have been hard to imagine. Whitsey wore a beret and was a bluff, plain-speaking northerner, something that St Albans had not quite been used to before.

'Had a man in,' he would say, 'he's had difficulty managing his money. Hasn't come clean about it. I'm going to break him down and build him up.' This was Whitsey's catchphrase, 'I'm going to break him down and build him up.' '"You will come here," I told him, "every Wednesday morning at 9.15 a.m. and we'll work through your accounts,"' and the man did as he was told.

Coulton was in charge of *See Round*, the new, expanded, media-conscious diocesan newsletter. When he asked Whitsey for a contribution, it would come back within half an hour, 'ready, finished, take it or leave it'. This was somewhat in contrast with Robert's style, already familiar to his chaplain and generations of staff and ordinands. After scratching his head and inspecting the piece of blank paper on his desk for several days, he would give birth to his own contribution after a long and protracted labour.

Other, non-resident associates were recruited in line with the need for the ministry to embrace the knowledge of specialist lay people that Robert had first pointed out in his response to the Paul Report nearly ten years earlier. Lady Helen Oppenheimer, a distinguished theologian, was engaged to work with the bishop's examining chaplains. These would shortly include another Cuddesdon man, Mark Santer, to train and test junior clergy.

Jenny Boyd-Carpenter was another new member of Robert's lay think tank. She was a lay member of the General Synod and a stylish figure, with two distinctive hobbies. She was an accomplished seamstress, and at her home at Wyddial Hall she kept black Berkshire pigs.

Robert visited her and developed an Emsworthian desire for a half share in a litter of the latter. Mrs Boyd-Carpenter agreed and he charmed her into looking after them, doubtless with a suitably Gadarene comparison. Robert would soon be photographed by *Farmer's Weekly* dressed for the part, for all the world giving the impression that he visited twice a day to help with the mucking out. Along with the truer imagery of the wartime MC and football fan, the notion of 'the pig-keeping bishop' swiftly became part of the popular mythology surrounding him.

At Abbey Gate House Lindy continued to refine the highly-organised domestic regime of bulk-buying and delegation which had enabled her to survive the years at Cuddesdon. There were garden parties for the rural deaneries and evening receptions for visitors. There were tea parties. One visitor to one of these was a sixteen-year-old St Albans schoolboy called John Witheridge.

Witheridge had been confirmed by Bishop Gresford-Jones and although he found most clergymen 'wet' in the extreme he was enormously impressed by his tall, straight-backed successor. The meeting with Robert Runcie and the legend of the Military Cross and the Scots Guards, and Robert's academic ability, remained with Witheridge as he struggled with his own faith and vocation at university during the next few years.

The reward for Lindy lay not least in the fact that she was doing the same job in new surroundings that were pleasanter in every respect. Robert was as busy as ever and there was never any question that his family came second; but the house was less dominated by the nearness of the Abbey than the Cuddesdon vicarage had been by the college, and more a part of the town and the normal world. She found new piano pupils and made new friends. She wrote about music for the local newspaper. Like Robert, she delighted in the company of intelligent sceptics, and there were plenty of these to hand.

There were also a number of people who cultivated her acquaintance because of whose wife she was, rather than who she was; and the more transparent of these were soon shocked out of their complacency. Lindy liked nothing better than to disabuse people of the notion that her husband was anything other than a human being, and a bookish one at that. 'Watch him,' she once told James when they were all crossing the road, 'he's thinking about Herodotus.' 'Life can be Hell,' she said in a memorable interview in the diocesan newsletter, 'working for God.'

The same policy would be pursued by James as a means of successfully growing up in spite of the unusual life led by his father. But, if Robert and James would come to know each other as men on equal terms, there was a childlike quality to Lindy's loyalty, which Robert appreciated and indulged, and which sometimes blinded her to the perils of the more devious kind of sycophant. Later this blind spot, and her own visible reluctance to fawn upon the clergy, would enable others to attack her, as well as the pig-keeping football fan and war hero, in the popular press.


The bishop's wife acclimatised herself and the bishop learned to delegate and to take on duties outside his diocese.

He voted in favour of union with the Methodists at the General Synod; soon, in accordance with the rules of age and seniority, he would be one of the twenty-six bishops and archbishops entitled to sit in the House of Lords.

He took over the Chairmanship of the Central Religious Advisory Committee (CRAC), a high-profile job suited to a man who was better at calming things down than stirring them up. His predecessor, Ian Ramsey, Bishop of Durham, had died suddenly, of a heart attack, at Broadcasting House. Ramsey had been a brilliant and popular man. beloved of those who met him, and the worst that was said of him was that he did not possess the ways with committees and paperwork that should be possessed by the next Archbishop of Canterbury, an office to which he had likely been bound.

Others departed, through removal or retirement, and a diverse collection of individuals took their place. Inez Luckcraft was a clergy widow living in Exeter, one of whose children was at a Church of England 'orphans' school in the St Albans diocese. Robert heard through the school that there was a trained secretary looking for a job with a roof over her head. Mrs Luckcraft received a letter from him offering both. She and her children took up residence in the coach house and she began work as an assistant secretary in the front office of Abbey Gate House in 1972.

Allan Medforth, the Westcott House contemporary who had been ordained deacon on the same day and in the same place as Robert had been priested in 1952, became vicar of St Albans St Peter, and a rural dean. John Simpson had been brought up in an Anglo-Catholic church and had then taught in an evangelical college, a combination of experiences which had caused him a great deal of self-questioning over the years. Simpson met Robert at theological college staff conferences and discovered Robert's extraordinary capacity for listening and making the other person feel that he knew their doubts and suffering. Simpson became incumbent of Ridge, where he began his own way back into the world.

But Eric James was probably the riskiest and most rewarding appointment of these years. Robert had met and become good friends with him in Cambridge, an environment in which, unlike Robert, James had been something of an anomaly. James was a stormy petrel of the Church of England, a man whose deep personal generosity and strong convictions would ensure the admiration of his peers and a lack of promotion from his elders. He was a close friend of John Robinson, whose biographer he became, and with whose stubborn if not naive side he had much in common. James had been Canon Missioner in Southwark. Mervyn Stockwood, his Bishop had fallen out with James, to the extent that the latter was out of a job.

Robert was willing to take a calculated risk. 'I believe in you,' he told James, in what was as much a command as a statement of faith, 'you can be archdeacon, canon missioner, or whatever you want.'

James would remain in St Albans for ten years. Although never a member of the Cell he would exercise a considerable influence over Robert thereafter. Nor would he always, or ever, tell Robert what he wanted to hear.

There were others who heard the call to St Albans during these early years and there were very few who resisted. One who did was Robert's last curate and tutor at Cuddesdon, Michael Scott-Joynt.

Scott-Joynt consulted him when he made up his mind to leave Cuddesdon in 1972. Robert's reaction was to offer him a job. This was an attractive proposition but Scott-Joynt rejected it. As Robert's student and curate, he had already enjoyed a close relationship with him. They remained on good terms, and Scott-Joynt became a team vicar in Newbury. When he eventually went to a job in the St Albans diocese, succeeding John Simpson as canon residentiary and director of ordinands, it was two years after Robert had left. Most people still assumed however that Robert had given him the job.

In 1973 the Bishop of St Albans spoke at length in the General Synod on the Church of South India (CSI). This was the same subject that had caused him to remain on the fence and not contribute to *The Historic Episcopate in the Fullness of the Church* twenty years earlier. At one point, the abstruse and at times confusing debate in which Robert was trying to clarify certain points was enlivened by the Archbishop of Canterbury, who referred to him as 'the Bishop of Runcie'.

He told his diocesan synod that, if Christians were to be more effective, they had to clear away the lumber the Church had acquired over the centuries. 'If we are to represent Christ in the world we have to ensure our claim to be his body is credible,' he said. Over the centuries the Church had acquired a good deal of luggage and jumble, some of it valuable but unused, some of it of no value but expensive to keep.

But there was one item or organisation some might have called lumber, which he valued highly. This was the Anglican-Orthodox Joint Doctrinal Commission, which had begun in 1931 and in the membership of which he was to find the fullest expression of the different strands in his life. It was through the offices of Harry Carpenter, the Bishop of Oxford, that he was invited to join.

This was not a politically important activity for a bishop like the Chairmanship of CRAC. But it was more exotic, more absorbing and far more demanding of his conciliatory powers. The love of classics begun at school and continued at Oxford, the insistence on Greek at Cuddesdon and the fondness for lecturing on Swan Hellenic Cruises were all combined. So were a strong sense of ecumenism and an ability to feel at home in the officers' mess and the senior fellows' parlour.

This was an all-male world in the old, classical sense; the grey-bearded patriarchs of the Orthodox Churches who invited him and Lindy to Greece, Romania and the Soviet Union became a familiar sight on the Abbey Gate House lawns in their black robes and coal scuttle hats. They vigorously opposed a role for women in the priesthood, an issue which was to tax all Robert's conciliatory powers and on which he himself would chart an idiosyncratic personal course.

The Orthodox Churches stood for a clear and strong sense of order both within and beyond this world. They engaged the world with gusto (and certain restrictions) while practising a transcendant, luminous spirituality. They went beyond the traditional Western notions of the 'otherness' of God and the transfiguration of life. They were emotionally seductive, intellectually majestic, liturgically magnificent; their survival was heroic; their dissensions were ancient and obscure; and their politics were of unmatched viciousness and complexity. Robert Runcie was Anglican Chairman within a year of membership.

This was a marriage of opposites. The Orthodox liked and respected him, but were sometimes bewildered by the power structure in the relationship between the Bishop and Mrs Runcie. 'The Bishop *dixit*,' one Orthodox divine was heard to murmur, 'Mrs Runcie contradicts it.' In the same way, from the outside, the power structure in the relationship between Robert Runcie and the Orthodox Churches would be subject to a certain amount of puzzlement, even suspicion, on the part of his brothers in the Church of England; and of his sisters, as the long years of their struggle went slowly by.

\*

Peter Moore arrived as new Dean of St Albans Abbey, a man to whom Nicholas Coulton had gone from Cuddesdon as curate at Pershore, and who had himself then become a Canon of Ely Cathedral. Moore was something of a specialist in the reinvigoration of cathedrals and abbeys. Robert had known him for many years and invited him to St Albans specifically in this last capacity.

The Suffragan Bishop, John Hare of Bedford, stood in for the bishop when he was away, as he was for a short time on Orthodox business in Romania in 1974. Hare was a greatly-loved pastoral bishop, a hard worker who spent many hours on the road from Bedford to St Albans for the good of the diocese, and too many for his own health.

Robert himself spent many hours on the road, once being stopped for speeding down the M1. On another occasion he was being driven when they passed a pork butcher, which the part-time pigkeeper in him had an urge to visit. His driver told him they would be late for a confirmation and had no time to do so; they stopped on the way home instead.

The bishop went in and asked the butcher if he had any nice bits of pork. The butcher said that he had.

'And do you have a particularly nice one I can buy?' Robert asked him.

'Aye, my lord, I do,' said the butcher, 'and if you get rid of our vicar, you can have the whole bloody pig.'

He went on a tour of the outlying deaneries, staying for weekends, familiarising himself. He did not want to become what he described as a 'talking ornament' who came to institute a new vicar, take a confirmation, and be driven away again. He expanded on his theme in the diocesan newsletter, and the diocesan newsletter was in turn quoted in the *Church Times*. More and more, the St Albans diocesan newsletter featured in its pages. When the Bishop of St Albans had something to say, the *Church Times* was ready to listen.

In May 1974 the Archbishop of Canterbury, Michael Ramsey, announced he would retire immediately after his seventieth birthday in November. The press amused themselves with speculation while the arcane and secretive processes ground into action to choose his successor. There was never much doubt as to who this would be. But after Donald Coggan, the Archbishop of York, it was necessary to tack on a couple of names to that of the hot favourite. Kenneth Woollcombe, his colleague from the Runcie Report who had succeeded Harry Carpenter as Bishop of Oxford, was one. Robert Runcie was another.

Coggan's name was at the top of the list compiled by Prime Minister Harold Wilson's office and placed before the Queen. At the age of sixty-five he was perceived by some as unlikely to step out of Ramsey's giant shadow and as a caretaker appointment. Robert Runcie's inclusion as a possible candidate did not mean that he would necessarily be considered with equal or greater likelihood of appointment in the future. Many men had been mentioned as possible Archbishops of Canterbury once and once only, their names never to reappear through their own desire or that of others. Others had been mentioned more than once and turned it down for their own reasons. What this did mean was that Bishopthorpe, the barnlike, echoing palace of the Archbishop of York, was now empty; and Bishopthorpe was a notoriously difficult place to fill.

Lindy was aghast at the thought of moving there. Apart from the unwelcoming character of Bishopthorpe, she had many reasons to stay in St Albans. Just as she had hated the idea of leaving Cambridge for Cuddesdon, so she had hated the idea of leaving Cuddeston for St Albans, and she hated the idea of leaving St Albans for anywhere. Although York was a common route to Canterbury (or perhaps because of it) bishops and their wives from Wakefield to Truro tended to feel a sudden attachment for their dioceses whenever Bishopthorpe beckoned. Fortunately the Bishop of Liverpool, Stuart Blanch, was an exception.

The Runcies remained in St Albans. Robert was deeply involved in the current thinking about marriage and remarriage, a matter which he had already raised once in the General Synod and in which the Orthodox churches, to whom the label 'liberal' would have been anathema, were surprisingly flexible. He was formulating his own ideas in the wake of the 1969 Divorce Reform Act and particularly the recent Root Report, *Marriage, Divorce and the Church.*

He spoke at length in the General Synod on the need for greater compassion on the part of the Church of England towards divorce and remarriage. His full proposal requested them to consider whether *'an alteration in the present marriage discipline of the Church, in order to permit remarriage of divorced persons in church and under appropriate conditions and with due safeguards, is theologically defensible and pastorally desirable'.*

'Are we wishing to say,' he asked, 'that those married in register offices are not in the deepest sense married? If it is felt that we might arrive at a point where those married through civil process alone could have a second marriage in church on the ground that their previous civil marriage was not a proper marriage, I believe we are set on a very dangerous road of double thinking and bad theology . . .

'It is possible to devise means by which the ceremony and/or its preliminaries give public witness to forgiveness and renewal as well as the life-long commitment which the parties intend. But the first step is to determine as a Church whether we want to try . . .'

John Habgood, then Bishop of Durham, supported him in the motion. So did Alan Webster, then Dean of Norwich. Those against it included Graham Leonard, a fellow member of the Anglican-Orthodox Joint Doctrinal Discussion Commission and then Bishop of Truro, and Donald Coggan, the outgoing Archbishop of York.

The House of Bishops approved the motion by fifteen votes to twelve. The House of Clergy approved the motion by ninety-four votes to seventy-nine. But the House of Laity rejected the motion by ninety-two votes to seventy. The motion was defeated by one hundred and eighty-three votes to one hundred and seventy-nine. The General Synod approved a more conservative motion put forward by the Bishop of Truro. This noted

*'with concern the change in the understanding of the nature of marriage expressed in the Divorce Reform Act, 1969, and is therefore of the opinion that further consideration of proposals for the remarriage of divorced persons in church should be deferred until there has been a fresh examination of the Christian doctrine of marriage discipline in the Church of England'.*

The Synod referred the matter back to the diocesan synods for their consideration.

Robert wrote to his diocese:

*'Christians are called both to witness to the ideals of Christ and to share his sensitive compassion for individual cases. I believe that indissolubility, life-long commitment to the marriage relationship, is not only an ideal, it is of the very nature of marriage. But it is not something automatic, nor is it the creation of law. Divorce is unnatural. It is surgery, not rearrangement, but we are involved in the "cure of souls". That is the background from which I am trying to help the church make its contribution in a field where we have no monopoly of understanding and love.'*

Robert delegated certain duties in order to juggle diocesan and episcopal responsibilities, CRAC obligations and his interest in the Orthodox Churches. He and Coulton were closely involved in ordination retreat prayers and intercessions, and Robert always carried out the Bishop's charge to the ordinands on the Saturday night before he ordained them in St Albans Abbey. This process was not always without incident, as he knew from his own experience in the chilly Northumberland woods with Hugh Montefiore and the Bishop of Newcastle over twenty years earlier.

In 1974, the year that he spoke on divorce and remarriage in the General Synod, he conferred with a colleague over the progress of the latest ordination retreat.

'Everyone's fine,' said the other man, 'except one person.'

'Richard Chartres,' said Robert.

'How did you know?'

Robert knew enough about Chartres to trust his instincts. He listened while his colleague told him what had happened.

Chartres had been one of Robert's last and brightest Cuddesdon ordinands. He had a highly individualistic, often high-handed intellect that marked him out either for disaster or for great things in the Church of England. His vocation had survived his early departure from Cuddesdon and a year drifting about in Spain. He had eventually finished his basic theological training and was a curate at Bedford St Andrew's. Like many a better man before and after him, his ordination retreat had stripped away his intellectually tough veneer and left him standing naked before his Maker.

'We were walking in the garden,' the other man told Robert, 'and he couldn't even speak. His teeth were chattering. Eventually he just walked off into the house.'

Robert thought about this.

'I am sure,' he said, 'Richard is one of those cases where he has to be ordained and then he will be all right. I am going to ordain him. I am going to get him over the hurdle.'

His colleague listened and agreed. The next day Bishop Runcie ordained Chartres in St Albans Abbey.

A year later, the same man saw Chartres and the others again at the St Albans retreat house. Somewhat against the rules, he invited them across the road to the pub.

Chartres was the first across.

The man did not refer directly to the events of a year earlier, but said: 'Richard, are you thinking the same as me?'

Chartres said that he was. Chartres was a man whose father had lived a sad life, whose brother had died young, who had been so unhappy a year earlier. He was happier now.

'What's the difference?' said the other man.

'The difference,' said Chartres, 'is that for most of my life I have had to be a father and a husband and an only child all rolled into one. Now, every day at 4 p.m., I can go and visit an old lady and feel real love for the first time in my life. That is the difference.'


The Bishop's round of engagements continued to grow. In March 1975 he presided over a CRAC meeting at Addington Palace in Croydon, a former country residence of the Archbishops of Canterbury. He attended the General Synod and the diocesan synod and countless other meetings. He ordained many more deacons and priests, including Bezalerei Ndahura, a Luton curate from what was to become the Church of the Province of Burundi, Rwanda and Zaire. He preached throughout the diocese, and at Cambridge and Marlborough College, where James was a pupil. He played tennis once a week with the chaplain of Napsbury Mental Hospital.

He welcomed the representatives of the Orthodox Churches to St Albans Abbey, and gave a garden party for them at Abbey Gate House. Metropolitan John of Helsinki, Archbishop Basil of Brussels and All Belgium and Archbishop Athenagoras of Thyateira made a splendid sight on the lawn as they and the Bishop of St Albans posed for photographs. In the Abbey, Bishop Runcie, the Bishop of Hertford,

Peter Mumford, who had succeeded 'Our Vic', the Dean, Peter Moore, and their Orthodox guests were resplendent in glittering copes, as the blessings were dispensed to the sound of tinkling bells and clouds of incense filled the air.

Mumford had been Archdeacon of St Albans and was not the only familiar friend to change jobs. Nicholas Coulton went from four years as Robert's domestic chaplain to be priest-in-charge at Bedford St Paul. His successor was the Cuddesdon man whom Robert had helped over the hurdle of ordination, Richard Chartres.

The training of ordinands in the St Albans diocese had been under close review for the past year by two more of Robert's many Cuddesdon men: Michael Bourke, the curate-in-charge of Panshanger, and the priest-in-charge of Aspley Guise, Robert Hardy. Bourke and Hardy became Course Directors of the St Albans Ministerial Training Scheme.

This pioneering venture was based on an idea of Eric James'. With John Simpson as Director of Ordinands and Post-Ordination Training in the diocese, and a former Cambridge don and Chairman of the Conference of Theology College Principals as Bishop, this meant a high combined emphasis on organised activity as a means of raising the standards of the clergy.

The course lasted for three years, two nights a week, with five residential weekends a year, usually at the Diocesan House or Mading-ley College, and a ten-day summer school at the latter. One of the first entrants was Robert's secretary, Inez Luckcraft. As a woman, she had to write her external essay on seven subjects instead of five for the men, and spend an extra fortnight a year at Queen's College, Birming-ham. With a full-time job and her children to look after this was a tall order but Mrs Luckcraft persevered.

Robert continued to chart an idiosyncratic if not transparently inconclusive course on the ordination of women to the priesthood. This was in part temperamental (it was an increasingly contentious area in which he was visibly not in charge of boat-rocking), part intellectual (on a pragmatic level the precedents were not promising) and political (the Orthodox and the Roman Catholics, with both of whom he sought closer communion, were totally against it), part marital (unlike Margaret, the wife of his contemporary Alan Webster, Lindy was not in favour) and wholly characteristic of him.

But in Inez Luckcraft he had attracted just one of many people to a scheme for which they applied from all over the country. Mrs Luckcraft had been a clergy wife and had endured the full loneliness of that kind of widowhood which accompanies rather than follows a clergy marriage. Lindy was no such person, and in the case of the young ordinands and would-be ordinands who now came to St Albans she had a releasing effect.

The following year, in 1976, John Hare died of overwork at the age of sixty-four and was succeeded as Suffragan Bishop of Bedford by the Warden of Lincoln Theological College, Alec Graham. The Bishop of St Albans opened Church House's first broadcasting studio and went to Moscow.

This was the occasion of the Anglican-Orthodox Joint Doctrinal Commission's Moscow Agreed Statement, which tried to map out areas of agreement between the members. At the top of the list was the question of the validity of the '*Filioque* Clause' and its relation to the Nicene Creed.

This statement, to the effect that the Holy Spirit proceeded both from the Father and the Son, had been added to the Creed over two hundred and fifty years after the Council of Nicea. The matter had been exercising the best minds of the Orthodox for almost as long. The fact that they had now agreed to accept its doctrinal merits without needing to assign it a place in the Creed was regarded as a major breakthrough.

Among the thirty-six delegates from eleven Orthodox and seven Anglican Churches were the Archbishop of Canterbury, Donald Coggan, and his assistant chaplain for foreign relations, Michael Moore. Both Coggan and Moore were accomplished linguists. Coggan's talent lay in the Semitic tongues and Moore specialised in Eastern European languages. Moore had been a key figure for ten years in the tiny administration at Lambeth, and it was to his office that Robert frequently turned for advice on Orthodox matters in his capacity as Anglican Chairman.

Nowhere on the list of areas of agreement, of course, was there any mention of the ordination of women to any part of the ministry. Robert was only too aware of this omission, and skirted the issue with his usual blend of pragmatism and acute sense of which way the meeting was going: 'We are making slow but substantial progress,' he told the *Church Times* on his return from Kiev and Moscow, 'we are building real bridges across a very big divide.

'This meeting,' he went on, 'between two worldwide Christian families from many nations and speaking many languages, and from such widely different cultural backgrounds, cannot easily be compared with other dialogues such as the Anglican-Roman Catholic conversations.

'We have learned to talk to each other with respect. Perhaps we are not yet ready to talk to our Churches at large, but it is essential that we begin by creating conditions of trust.

'To put it crudely, if Anglicans sometimes look on the Orthodox as a case of arrested development, they are inclined to look on us as hopelessly at the mercy of social change and the latest trend, all too often ready to shed those traditions which have stood them in good stead in dark times.'

There was precious little social change and no mercy shown towards the Orthodox Church in Russia at the time. Patriarch Pimen of Moscow and All Russia survived in an atmosphere of oppression and persecution that had endured for decades. The style of absolutism was contagious. The Orthodox Church controlled the Journal of the Russian Patriarch; they could not understand why the Bishop of St Albans could not simply tell the *Church Times* what it could and could not say.

Shortly after his return, the question became more vexed with the decision to admit women to the priesthood of the General Convention of the Episcopal Church in the USA (ECUSA). The House of Bishops in Minneapolis had voted in favour by ninety-five to sixty-one. The Convention's House of Deputies and the lay delegations had followed suit. The motion would possibly be implemented by January 1 of the following year.

The likes of Metropolitan Stylianos of Australia and Metropolitan Juvenaly of Moscow, with whom Robert had only recently toasted the *Filioque* Clause agreement in Moscow, were appalled. They were unimpressed by the fact that, like them, the Americans were only acting in accordance with their own historical schedule.

Supporters of women's ordination within the Church of England applauded the American move. In his unique and hitherto rewarding role as Anglican-Orthodox go-between, Robert now found himself uncomfortably under fire from both sides; from the Orthodox for belonging to a Church which was in Communion with the ungodly Americans, and from the Anglican supporters of women's ordination for representing a reactionary and obstructionist wing of the Church of England.

This was suddenly an uncomfortable fence upon which he had chosen to sit. The Archbishop of Canterbury, Donald Coggan, made soothing noises about tensions being 'sources of power and beauty and music', as well as threatening division; but it was the latter that was clearly playing on the mind of the Bishop of St Albans. 'I regret the American decision,' he told the *Church Times*, 'I wish it had gone the other way.'

Pressed on the ordination of women, he said he was 'agnostic' on the subject. He added that he thought women's ordination was less important than Christian unity. To others it was becoming an article of faith that there was a connection between the two.

The matter rumbled on, as did preparations for the Lambeth Conference in two years' time. There it would surely receive a measured and balanced airing.

He turned his mind to diocesan matters. He was nearing the end of his three-year programme of eight weekend visits a year to rural deaneries. There was as much a fear in him of being a 'talking ornament' as there was of the confrontation, schism, irreconciliation he dreaded in the wider world:

*'The nightmare of the Bishop is that he gets the worst of both worlds,'* he wrote, in one of his many articles for See Round. *'He has to keep in touch with all the committees and all the paper, and yet the parishes still take their failures, their quarrels and their complaints to him as if he were still the old-style monarch.*

*'I hope that in my visits I have helped to give the diocese a human face,'* he went on, *'I happen to think that there is a style of listening leadership which is not only appropriate to the present day but rooted in the Incarnation. Christianity shares many truths with other religions but in one regard it is unique. It testifies to a God who makes himself available to men – and at the same time speaks strangely of God's need of them.*

*'I have discovered in villages, suburbs, housing estates and city centres small congregations being renewed as they come together week by week for*

*worship and as they go out in service to their neighbourhood and the world*
*. . . I am sure the weakness of the Church can be exaggerated by critics who*
*do not know enough about its life today, or by Christians who are too*
*romantic about its past as compared with the present.'*

He despised what he called 'megaphone morality'. He dreaded becoming 'a platitude machine'. He proclaimed the need to build bridges, and dreamed of the results; but if he wanted to cross chasms he was also aware of the dangers of homogenising the parties joined on either side.

Opening the new office of the World Association for Christian Communication (WACC) in London, he said it was a bridge-builder between 'powerful but sometimes rather tired Christian communities in the emerging nations'.

He drew strength from both his public person and his aloneness as a priest. Even on Christmas Day at Abbey Gate House he would emerge from his study and read Dickens to whoever was there. Then they would have lunch. After lunch they would go for a walk around the lake. Robert always walked ahead. Lindy and the guests and the children followed.

On more than one occasion, a guest would ask her: 'Is he all right?'

'Yes,' she said, 'he likes walking ahead.'

A few minutes later she would say: 'You go and walk with him now. He's actually enjoying this very much.'

The guest would do as she suggested. He and Robert would walk together for a while. Then Robert would walk ahead again, alone. When they returned to Abbey Gate House he would disappear behind his study door.

By coincidence, the unofficial body which was supposed to foster friendship between Western and Eastern Orthodox Christians was called the Fellowship of St Alban and St Sergius. In 1977, with the Lambeth Conference still a year away, the Orthodox problem again reared its head. It continued inconveniently to do so throughout the diocese of St Albans' centenary year.

The problem was no longer just the issue of the ordination of women. Not only had the American Episcopal Church, with whom the Church of England was in communion, voted in favour; they had also voted to restore the 'Filioque Clause' to the Nicean Creed, although it had previously been dropped by the American Liturgical Commission.

The Orthodox Church were predictably outraged by this latest proof of the unreliability of their brothers – they would not even speak of sisters – in the Anglican Communion. They had been due to celebrate the Moscow Agreement with an official statement and come to Cambridge for the next round of meetings. Now they were delaying the publication of the former and threatening to boycott the latter. It was in the middle of this crisis, and after the Easter pilgrimage to mark the centenary celebrations of his own diocese, that Robert flew to Istanbul in May.

Already in Istanbul was the Archbishop of Canterbury, Donald Coggan, on a tour of religious centres. Jean Coggan and Rosalind Runcie could not have been more dissimilar; their husbands too were a contrast in style. One was a devoted Semitic linguist and scholar, ill at ease in the shadow of Ramsey amidst the faded grandeur of Canterbury and Lambeth; a man of schoolmasterly demeanour and evangelical inclination. The other was now emerging at home and abroad as a consummate ecclesiastical diplomat, a more accessible and less austere figure, whose charm and clarity of thought tended to obscure from others the doubts he harboured about his own intellectual and spiritual qualifications for the Church's highest offices: offices which he still privately regarded in awed and worldly terms.

This combination of qualities helped the Archbishop of Canterbury and the Bishop of St Albans ensure the publication of the Moscow Agreement and prevent the collapse of the forthcoming talks between the Anglican and Orthodox representatives of the Joint Doctrinal Commission. Coggan and Runcie managed to calm the Orthodox side by explaining clearly and in detail the complicated synodical process by which decisions were taken by the Church of England and other members of the Anglican Communion. They assured them that the American decisions over the ordination of women and the 'Filioque Clause' did not mean that either the Church of England or the Anglican Communion was insincere in what it said. They looked forward to seeing the Orthodox representatives at the next talks in Cambridge in July. Coggan continued on his tour of religious centres and Runcie flew back to St Albans.

The Archbishop of Canterbury acknowledged the centenary celebrations there when he preached at the evening Eucharist in St Albans
Abbey on 22 June, St Alban's Day. Over a thousand people were
present there and at the garden party at Abbey Gate House. The
Archbishop was guest of honour. The Dean of St Albans presented
him with the first copy of a special commemorative plate; Dr Elsie
Toms, a local historian, gave him a copy of her latest offering, *The
New Book of St Albans*. The Archbishop presented various prizes,
including one to the diocesan missioner Eric James, whose hymn 'Sing
We of St Albans' was sung that evening. On 3 July the Abbey was
the scene of the 'Thanksgiving for Music' organ festival and the
Dean of Winchester came to preach. On 24 July, the Anglican and
Orthodox delegates sat down in Cambridge for the latest round of
talks.

On his return from Istanbul Robert had described the rescue of
the talks as 'quite a triumph, really'. The Orthodox co-chairman,
Archbishop Athenagoras of Thyateira, was fond of Robert but had no
inhibitions about stating his position. 'If the Lambeth Conference
agrees to the ordination of women,' he said, 'then ninety-five per cent
of Orthodox delegates will say to their Churches: "What is the point
of continuing the discussions?"' Robert was still trying to calm things
down rather than stir them up. 'We are really undergirding the life of
the Church,' he said, 'providing materials by which people will look
at things more responsibly. We do take note of the Orthodox views.
There is a danger,' he added in tones which recalled his attitude to
boat-rocking, 'of being blown off course, by being asked to settle
contentious issues immediately.'

Things could hardly have happened otherwise with an agenda which
included the ordination of women, the communion of saints, ikons,
the Virgin Mary and the recent publication of a controversial book
entitled *The Myth of God Incarnate*. The Orthodox members seemed
more and more nervous about the first item as the 1978 Lambeth
Conference approached. Within a short time some were standing up
and walking out, and could barely be consoled by hasty modifications
to the agenda. The repair work effected in Istanbul seemed in danger
of coming undone. 'The talks were conducted in a friendly and
Christian spirit,' Robert told the *Church Times* afterwards, 'but they
were not tranquil.'

But, if theatrically expressed disagreement was one prominent feature of Anglican-Orthodox conferences, the desire to go on holding them was another. Pendeli, a pleasant spot outside Athens, was agreed as the venue for the next meeting, immediately before the Lambeth Conference the following year.

In August the round of garden parties and diocesan centenary celebrations continued, and the Anglican Chairman of the Orthodox Joint Doctrinal Commission went in to bat against his own clergy as Captain of the Bishop of St Albans' XI.

This was a sport at which he had excelled as a Merchant Taylors', Crosby schoolboy, but age and experience seemed to have tempered his technique. It was something Jim Thompson, by now a team rector in Thamesmead and fellow member of the Cell, had noticed when he was chaplain at Cuddesdon. Robert would go in to bat, take up his stance and play the first ball straight back down the pitch.

He was a versatile stroke player, but he would continue in this vein to the end of the match. The scorecard would read: 'R. A. K. Runcie *2 not out*' . . . and it was the '*not out*' above all else that mattered.

In September a Liturgical Mass was celebrated in St Albans under the Diocesan Catholic Action Council. The Fraternity of the Friends of St Albans Abbey held a flower festival. Over one hundred parishes combined for the occasion, under the direction of Mrs Grizelda Maurice of Flamstead. A six-foot petal collage triptych depicted scenes from the life and death of St Alban; there was a display on the same theme by the Borough of Luton Parks Department; and the shrine was decorated with the St Alban rose, bred by Harkness of Hitchin.

In October there was *The Play of Alban* by James Forsyth. Robert went to Lambeth Palace where he and Archbishop Athenagoras held a press conference to mark the publication of *Anglican-Orthodox Dialogue*, the fruit of the Anglican-Orthodox Moscow Agreement. The two men talked about relations between their Churches and agreed that the talks should continue. 'But the ordination of women is an invention,' Archbishop Athenagoras declared, 'and every invention causes trouble.'

In November the final thanksgiving service in the St Albans centenary celebrations was held at the Abbey in the presence of Queen

Elizabeth the Queen Mother. Shortly afterwards Robert was offered and turned down the bishopric of Oxford. There were many associations in favour of and against his taking the job. Lindy's reaction to the prospect of moving was as full and frank as ever. There were some jobs a diocesan bishop with seven years' experience and a seat in the Lords could either take or in all conscience turn down; one was the bishopric of Oxford. The job went to a Westcott near-contemporary, the Bishop of Manchester, Patrick Rodger.

The Bishop of St Albans revealed some of his recent thinking on the presence of different faiths in one world in his diocesan newsletter:

*'I don't believe,'* he wrote, *'our choice lies between doing battle or reaching soft compromise with other faiths. There is a way of listening to them which might be God's way of stimulating us to a richer and deeper discipleship.*

*'We will of course have to abandon the idea that other religions are evils to be destroyed. That has not worked and will never work because it is simply not true.*

*'They are not all darkness, they are full of light of which we believe that Jesus Christ is the author and fulfilment, and we need to approach them with a great reverence as well as our belief in Jesus as himself the Word and the Light.'*

In *Cathedral and City*, a book he edited to commemorate the nine hundredth anniversary of St Albans Abbey, he included the text of a sermon he had preached earlier that year at the height of the centenary celebrations. He had revealed his thinking on the relationship between what some might have seen as two different faiths, the Church and the State. 'I hope that St Albans diocese,' he wrote, 'will be part of a disestablished Church.'

He rejected the idea that the 'establishment' of the Church as part of the State constituted proof of the latent religiosity of the English people:

*'We are frequently told that nobody can do a royal wedding or a Churchill funeral like the good old C. of E.; but honestly I do not think that such arguments can sustain the case for establishment. 'The clergy have got above themselves,'* he went on, and declared that there was a popular notion that as Christians the clergy were the professionals and laity were the

amateurs, '*and that if you are really serious about the faith you become a clergyman.*

'*I think the Church will be disestablished . . . and that my successors will no longer sit as of right in the House of Lords.*'

These were sentiments worthy of Harry Williams' favoured saying of Martin Buber: '*Nothing obscures the face of God like religion.*' They also recalled the burgeoning style of Robert's own domestic chaplain.

Richard Chartres was a highly individualistic character, a man possessed of certain disarming eccentricities and great originality of mind. He was full of psychological insights and pithy statments which he was willing to share: 'Synod,' he liked to say, was 'the dull echo of a liberal consensus'. Of another priest, he once said: 'he has eight languages and nothing to say in any of them.'

Ordination seemed to have released inhibitions in him as well as having brought him happiness. Over six feet tall, never backward in coming forward, he was even more of a contrast to Nicholas Coulton than Donald Coggan was to Robert Runcie. Some felt Chartres served his God, his Bishop and himself in equal measure. Others took time to warm to his powerful presence at Abbey Gate House. But no one would have denied either his growing influence or his exceptional ability.

In his capacity as a bishop in the House of Lords, Robert St Albans questioned the exclusion of the Church from the Wolfenden Report on the future of voluntary organisations. Graham Leonard, the Bishop of Truro and Chairman of the General Synod's Board for Social Responsibility, also spoke in his maiden speech.

At the General Synod early in 1978, Bishop Runcie described his disappointment at the report of the Church Information Committee, *The Responsibility of the Church in Communication*. As Chairman of CRAC he knew the power of television, a medium the authors of the report did not in his view fully appreciate. 'We are battered by words,' he told the Synod, 'words which have become threadbare. Words don't have the power they had at the Reformation.'

He praised recent television programmes on religious themes and pursued his comparison. 'At the Reformation,' he added, 'the Church emancipated itself from Latin. It now needs a new Reformation to free itself from its addiction to words.'

But his main task at this session of Synod was to open the debate on a report by the Board of Mission and Unity on Anglican-Orthodox relations. He ran through the familiar list of stumbling blocks: the '*Filioque* Clause' and the ordination of women. In Synod he was careful to wear his 'Anglican' hat. He told them that there was a desire for the talks to continue on both sides but that the future of them was in the balance. They were too valuable, in his opinion, to be allowed to die.

He reassured them that the Orthodox Churches understood that the Lambeth Conference had no power to decide these questions once and for all. 'However,' he told them, 'they are unable to believe that we are so far removed from apostolic order that a gathering of all our diocesan bishops from all over the world would not be of some significance in determining the mind of our Church on this subject – and personally I believe they are right.'

The Synod welcomed the report and commended it for further study. In six months he was due to fly to Pendeli to meet the Orthodox; the Lambeth Conference was less than seven months away.


Robert was also involved in less public but powerful institutions such as St George's House, Windsor, where he was a member of the organising committee. This had been founded in 1966 in redundant premises within the Castle at the instigation of Robert Woods, Dean of Windsor and Domestic Chaplain to the Queen, and of the Duke of Edinburgh. The Duke had the idea of a 'staff college' or discussion centre for the laity and clergy, funded by making its conference resources available to industry. St George's House was an important network for the great and the good. Robert was looking for a new Canon of Windsor who would be a council member.

Once again the answer lay in the Cuddesdon connection. David Burgess, after his turbulent career as ordinand and curate, had spent eleven happy years at University College, Oxford. He sensed it was time to move on, but did not know where. When he voiced this to the Master, the latter had replied: 'Oh, don't worry, I've put you on the list.'

This was the list of Crown Appointments, compiled through energetic networking for the Prime Minister's and Archbishop's Appointments Secretaries, and consulted by them in the choice of substantial appointments. Much mystery – or mystique – surrounded it, and Burgess had been told that his name had been included. He was part of the establishment. He was 'in'.

Burgess was in bed on a wet Oxford morning when the telephone rang. It was Robert Runcie.

Robert told him about the job; about Prince Philip; the Knights of the Garter; the members of the Lords and the Commons; the captains of industry; the multi-party, multi-religious range of membership.

'If you are officially asked,' he told Burgess, 'you have no opportunity to say no. It's a royal appointment.'

Burgess thought about this.

Robert said: 'I need to know now.'

They talked about it in greater detail for twenty minutes. Burgess said yes. Then he told his wife. The following weekend they went to Windsor. They attended Matins, and were interviewed at the Deanery by the Queen, Prince Philip, Princess Margaret, the Dean and the Dean's wife. Burgess had the job.


The Pendeli meeting with the Orthodox took place in the middle of July. Robert was annoyed by the timing of the debate on marriage in the second session of the 1978 General Synod. This was a matter on which he had spoken at length and he had been instrumental in setting up the Commission on the subject. Now the Commission was due to report and he was flying to Athens the same day.

Derek Pattinson was the General Synod Secretary-General who had succeeded Sir John Guillum Scott. Pattinson was a former senior civil servant in the Treasury and had served as Guillum Scott's deputy until 1972. He was a devout man and an accomplished operator for whom the Synod was his life. He epitomised bureaucratic discretion and was building a reputation as a 'pin-striped *éminence grise*'.

He reassured Robert in his familiar tones. The planning of the agenda was a very complicated matter . . . dates of debates were fixed long in advance . . . not least, long before those of the Anglican-Orthodox meeting.

Sunday, he said, may have been suitable for Robert. But it was no use as a day for debating controversial matters. Some members took a strongly sabbatarian view. Only a few did, but their feelings had to be considered.

Pattinson had his way and Robert flew to Athens as planned. The Orthodox representatives gave him a message to take back to the Lambeth Conference. Predictably, it expressed their grave misgivings about the effect the ordination of women would have on relations between the Anglican and Orthodox Communions.

Robert delivered this message at the Lambeth Conference of 1978. This was the eleventh session of a conference that had met roughly once a decade since the first session at Lambeth Palace in 1867. In that year seventy-six bishops had been guests of Archbishop Longley in the Lambeth Palace Guard Room. There had been clear differences between High Church and Evangelicals.

The Lambeth Conferences were a touchstone of the Archbishop of Canterbury's authority over the scattered and disparate dioceses of the worldwide Anglican Communion. Archbishop Tait, the first Scotsman to hold the office and a man whose domestic life was marked by tragedy, presided over the second conference at Lambeth in 1878. Over one hundred bishops attended and the agenda had included 'Modern forms of Infidelity.'

Of the agenda, Tait had remarked: 'It must be remembered that it is a serious matter to gather the Bishops together from all parts of the globe, unless there is some distinct object for their so gathering. I therefore am disposed, by the advice of my brethren, to request that our brethren at home, and also those at a distance, will state to me as explicitly as possible what the objects are that it is desirable to discuss at such a meeting. They are of a somewhat limited character.'

At the seventh conference in 1930, three hundred and seven bishops had crowded into the Lambeth Palace Library. Archbishop Lang, the 'unctuous old humbug' of Robert Runcie Senior's era, had stood at St Augustine's seat and welcomed them to Canterbury Cathedral. 'It was indeed moving to see this great company of Bishops from every part of the world,' he recalled, 'slowly and with ordered dignity passing before me as I stood at that Chair.'

Fisher and Ramsey had both touched their conferences with their personalities in the post-war years. The 1978 Conference had met residentially for the first time in the University of Kent at Canterbury. Donald Coggan took a low-key, almost reticent approach. He seemed reluctant to acknowledge the enormous dramatic potential of St Augustine's seat, and when delivering his powerful sermons avoided the pulpits altogether.

At one point he moved from the platform to the piano and struck up the hymn 'Blest are the pure in heart'. This was the first time at a Lambeth Conference that the Archbishop of Canterbury had played the piano for Evensong.

The 1978 Lambeth Conference would be assessed both at the time and later, by people who had been there and people who had not, both favourably and unfavourably, as had been the case with its predecessors. There was a strong emphasis on worship as well as an agenda which included the ordination of women to the priesthood, homosexuality, the training of bishops, human rights and communications between different dioceses of the Anglican Communion.

Over a hundred American bishops made up the largest visiting delegation. The relationship between the Anglican and the Orthodox Churches, in that perspective, was not likely to carry a great deal of weight. 'When the Anglican Church,' said Robert, 'embraces such a fundamental change as to the nature and character of the ordained ministry without sufficient regard for those with whom we proudly aim to share the apostolic ministry, it registers itself as a different sort of church.'

This was an Anglo-Catholic convert speaking as an Anglican bishop on behalf of the Orthodox Churches to an audience including African Anglicans and American Episcopalians. There was little surprise in the plurality of the Anglican Communion being upheld as an article of faith at the Lambeth Conference. There was little surprise in the discussion of the possibility of consecrating women bishops. There was no surprise at all for the Orthodox Churches. They had feared the worst; now they heard it.

Archbishop Athenagoras repeated even more vehemently his response in these circumstances, that there was no future to the Anglican-Orthodox talks, that he and his fellow patriarchs would not even grace the talks with their presence in future, that they would send their humblest underlings instead.

This faith in an appeal to an 'authoritarian' side of the Anglican Communion was as misconceived before the conference as it was afterwards. But, unless he was to come off the fence altogether, there was nothing else Robert could do except continue in his best efforts to build a bridge between the two sides.

The chasm under him was widening daily. By the November session of the General Synod, when his secretary Mrs Luckcraft was well into the St Albans Ministerial Training Scheme and would shortly be ordained deaconess, he was speaking in opposition to the debate on whether or not legislation should be introduced for the ordination of women to the priesthood.

'It is the Orthodox,' he told the General Synod, 'who have talked in the past about a special relationship with the Anglicans, and that has not been hollow, and it has been particularly concentrated on the history of the Church of England. That is why today is so important to them. They know that from the seventeenth century onwards the Anglicans, through this country, have particularly maintained the bridge between East and West.

'They are now coming out of their geographical isolation and winning the respect of many seekers for their witness to serious religion, particularly in Eastern Europe, along with Roman Catholics and Baptists. They believe that stand depends upon being rooted in tradition. They have even said to me: "We only came into the ecumenical movement because we thought you were our friends," and it seems that we are letting them down.'

The General Synod rejected the motion. The House of Bishops was in favour, but not the House of Clergy. The matter was deferred and the Orthodox Churches were partly mollified. Robert had long planned to take the sabbatical in early 1979 to which he was entitled. He still cherished the Anglican-Orthodox dream. Now he had the idea of combining the two.

*

As well as the ordination of women to the priesthood, there was a further issue which many felt was more sensitive, more divisive and less likely to be settled by a prolonged public airing in the General Synod or anywhere else. This was the issue of the ordination of practising homosexuals to the priesthood, something which had long taken place and which, were it to cease, would have resulted in a sudden falling off in the numbers of newly-ordained clergy.

But, if it was one thing tacitly to acknowledge its existence, to try to control it by talking euphemistically about homosexuals as 'celibates' in the heterosexual sense, it was quite another to legislate openly and positively in its favour. Yet there were those who sought this, and who did so with a quasi-missionary fervour and all the hysteria and indignation of those who, they claimed, were ranged against them.

Richard Kirker was a Hitchin curate whom Robert had ordained deacon. Kirker was a practising homosexual who made no secret of the fact. When it came to the possibility of his ordination as a priest, his bishop Robert was undecided in the matter. He took advice from various colleagues, including priests in the Hitchin team ministry of which Kirker was a part. 'Look,' he told them, 'I need your advice. I may not abide by it, but I need it.'

The advice was duly forthcoming and Robert took it. Kirker would not be ordained a priest.

Kirker left Hitchin and the St Albans diocese and became Secretary of the Lesbian and Gay Christian Movement. Ten years later he was still Secretary and still unpriested. He would still not actively discourage the notion that Robert Runcie had personally refused to ordain him to the priesthood. But he was leaving out two pieces of information in this respect. First, Robert had not acted unilaterally out of some deep-seated homophobia, but had consulted various colleagues in the matter. Second, at least two of the colleagues he had consulted were themselves 'gay'.

Robert spent three weeks reading and relaxing in Cambridge before embarking on the first, foreign, leg of his sabbatical.

In the middle of February 1979 he flew to Istanbul, where he had gone to see the Orthodox representatives with Archbishop Coggan two years earlier. Here he met the Ecumenical Patriarch and members of the Holy Synod. In Jerusalem too he met the Patriarch and others. In Damascus he was welcomed by the Patriarch of Antioch; in Alexandria he was greeted by Metropolitan Methodius of Aksum. In Cyprus he was looked after by Archbishop Makarios, who also knew a thing or two about less orthodox, military matters. In Athens he met the Archbishop and left with Lindy, who accompanied him on a lecture cruise in the Mediterranean. They returned to St Albans before he embarked on the second leg of his sabbatical.

This took him to Hungary, Yugoslavia, Bulgaria, Romania and Russia, where he toured churches and parishes in Moscow and Leningrad. The Orthodox Church was a highly independent living entity that could not be easily captured in talks in St Albans or Cambridge or Lambeth. The differences between the Orthodox and Anglican Churches could be bridged, but the chasm was far greater than that between the Orthodox and the Roman Catholic Church, in which patriarch and pontiff could more easily find a common notion of authority. He said as much and more to the Archbishop of Canterbury, Donald Coggan, in his report.

Coggan himself embarked on a two-week tour of Eastern Europe and returned early in June to give a press conference at Church House. He spoke for half an hour and gave a number of television interviews before driving himself off in his blue Morris Minor; he was a keen motorist and this was his official car.

Only after he had gone did John Miles, who was based at Church House but acted as Coggan's press officer, make the surprise announcement that the Archbishop of Canterbury was to resign the following January. The reason, he said, was 'to make way for a younger man'.

The suddenness of the announcement caused something of a sensation. This was in spite of the fact that under new Church policy future Archbishops would have to retire at seventy, and Coggan himself would be seventy later that year. The new policy on retirement meant that the odds were now considerably lengthened against Stuart Blanch, the Archbishop of York being his successor.

The religious and national press too had been taken by surprise and in the absence of hard information wasted neither time nor ingenuity in hypothesising about Coggan's possible successors. These were in three categories: those outside the Church of England and active in the wider Anglican Communion; those inside the Church of England and non-episcopal candidates; and those inside the Church of England who were diocesan bishops.

Archbishop Ted Scott, leader of the Canadian Anglicans, and Bishop John Howe, Secretary-General of the Anglican Consultative Council, were in the first category. Scott would have highlighted the international and ecumenical side of the primacy, but there was much distaste at the prospect of a foreigner at Canterbury.

In the second category were Owen and Henry Chadwick, Master of Selwyn College and Regius Professor of Modern History at Cambridge and Dean of Christ Church and Regius Professor-elect of Divinity at Oxford respectively. But Owen Chadwick, although immensely capable and highly respected, was sixty-three and an established church historian, and his brother too was thought unlikely to go back on his new academic appointment.

In the third category, and in order of age, were the Archbishop of York, Stuart Blanch, the Bishop of Truro, Graham Leonard, the Bishop of St Albans, Robert Runcie, the Bishop of Newcastle, Ronald Bowlby, the Bishop of Durham, John Habgood, and the Bishop of Liverpool, David Sheppard.

Apart from his age, Blanch was thought temperamentally unsuited to the prospect of going to Lambeth. Leonard was a stronger candidate, but a strongly conservative 'party man'. Runcie was strongly tipped as an Anglo-Catholic, modernist and bridge-builder, but thought 'unsound' on the ordination of women. Bowlby on the other hand was possibly a little too dedicated to the latter. Habgood was always described in terms of his outstanding intellect as 'the best brain on the bench', and of his formidable and sometimes off-putting manner. Sheppard was a former top-ranking cricketer and outspoken champion of the inner-city underdog, qualities which made him popular in his diocese, but which were less likely to endear him to the new Conservative Prime Minister, Margaret Thatcher.

As had been the case with the elections of Donald Coggan and Michael Ramsey, for many of these men this would be the first and the last time they were mentioned. Apart from the exhortation to pray for divine guidance by clergy everywhere, the actual process of selection would be carried out by the new Crown Appointments Commission.

They would involve wide and secretive consultations between bishops, clergy and laity, under the Chairmanship of the Head of the Manpower Services Commission, Richard O'Brien DSO, MC and Bar.

The process of selection ground on, and so did the wild surmises in the press. The *Church Times* tried to introduce a note of sanity into the debate, and in so doing perhaps inadvertently reflected the shifts in awareness that were simultaneously going on among the members of the Commission:

*'Never before,'* it said, *'in its history will the Church have had so much say in the appointment of its own leader. Many are bound to ask: would that it could go to the far-flung corners of the Anglican Communion in search of the new man! For in his hands lies much of the future credibility of the Church at a time of peculiar stress.*

*'Perhaps it would be better not to bandy names but to ask rather: will the Church of England be able to move away from the predictable, follow the lead of the Roman Catholic Church, and pluck from the unknown someone to set the world on fire – an Anglican Karol Wojtyla?'*

But only two weeks later, in its editorial entitled 'The next Primate', the *Church Times* had tempered its idealism:

*'It is natural that Anglicans should envy (we trust in a gentlemanly way) the personal triumphs already won by Pope John Paul II. The question is inevitable: is there no hope that the next Archbishop of Canterbury will be, by his own charismatic gifts as well as the prestige of his office, a great, creative figure in the life of this country and of the whole of Christendom? However, it is not an unmitigated tragedy that there does not appear to be any Anglican of the stature of the present Pope available for appointment. In these days an Archbishop of Canterbury would probably be doomed to frustration if he adopted the lifestyle of an ecclesiastical superstar. He is expected to be, and to be seen to be, a diocesan bishop among diocesan bishops, a chairman among chairmen, a preacher among preachers; not another Pope, not even another William Temple.'*

The second Synod of the year sat in session with as much normality as could be mustered in the circumstances. The question of the ordination of women to the priesthood was again on the agenda.

Robert was privately unable to forget that he was being mentioned as a strong candidate for Canterbury. He spoke in public, however, as a man whose enduring concern for the Orthodox Churches seemed to some to override his approach to the ordination of women; and, to these listeners, he seemed to be damaging his chances of going to Lambeth.

But there were many others to whom his caution was welcome, and they were not afraid to speak out.

*'We can only pray,'* declared the Church Union, *'that the Commission will have the courage to appoint a man who has the spiritual stature and clear commitment to ecumenism which will conquer the greatest scandal of English Christianity – the breach between Canterbury and Rome.'*

As the time taken by the Commission to reach a decision was passing, the latent disagreements between the different factions of the Church of England were heating up. Who was to be the man on whom all their fears and expectations could be focused?

Michael Ramsey had been an academic. He had published learned works, he had been half in this world, half in the next; and many had loved him for this. Donald Coggan too had been a holy and a learned man, whose wife had been greatly respected, and whose effectiveness had not always been appreciated because of his low-key style.

But Ramsey had also been quite capable of stuffing important correspondence in the pocket of his dressing gown and forgetting about it. Coggan's primacy had been marked by his age and lack of sophistication and donnish preference for what some saw as obscure Oriental languages.

Nor was there any use hearkening back to what might have been if Ian Ramsey were still alive. A man of great energy, holiness and goodness, he might have made a great Archbishop of Canterbury. But there had been so much inside him that he might also have talked himself out of the job. What was needed now was a man with a proven aptitude for bureaucracy, to whom English was his favourite tongue; who could preach well in it, with a spirituality that was accessible, but rooted in deep certainty; who had a quick brain and a visible awareness of the world.

This combination of qualities was uppermost in the minds of the

Crown Appointments Commission in July 1979. At this time the rumours of Robert Runcie's suitability were reaching their height. There had already been comic side-effects of this. Most bishops' wives were indifferent newspaper copy. But, when a St Albans newspaper asked Lindy for her comments, she was only too happy to oblige. 'The only way I ever want to leave St Albans is feet first, in a coffin,' she told the reporter. 'We love it here. I don't know what on earth we should do if he was offered the job. I don't know much about these things,' Lindy went on cheerfully, 'I'm only a humble pianist. But I should think the Archbishop of York ... he is used to being an Archbishop and would probably be very good ...'

There was plenty more where this came from; the reporter kept a straight face and wrote it all down. Shortly afterwards the article appeared in the *St Albans Review*: 'Mrs Runcie Puts Her Foot Down.' When the story was picked up by both the religious and the national press, Bishop Runcie felt impelled to issue a corrective. 'It was an expression,' he told reporters, 'of our deep affection for St Albans.'

Later that same July Eric James received a telephone call from Robert Runcie. James had spent several years in St Albans and was one of Robert's closest friends and most trusted advisers.

(Once, returning from a lunch at the Reform Club with Jeremy Thorpe, they had had a disagreement about the Ministerial Training Scheme. At St Albans station Robert and James had got into the car which had come to collect them. Robert had turned and said to the driver: 'Eric's had too much to drink.'

James had been hurt by the means Robert had used to win his point. An hour later he was at home when he heard the click of the letterbox. He went downstairs and found a note on the door-mat: *'I should never have said what I said. It wasn't true. Love, Robert.'*)

On that July day in question James was at Cranfield College of Technology helping at the annual school for junior clergy. He did not drive. When the telephone rang Robert said: 'How are you getting back to St Albans tonight?'

James said he had not thought about it. Robert told him he was himself driving down shortly to meet the clergy and celebrate communion. 'I'll drive you back to St Albans,' he told James, 'I want to talk to you about something.'

Robert duly arrived and the two men left together as arranged. Halfway back to St Albans Robert pulled over into the car park of a service station. They sat there among the refuelling cars and families stopping for food. James did not know what was happening.

Robert turned to him.

'Eric,' he said, 'what would you say if I were asked to be Archbishop of Canterbury?'


The following six weeks were stressful and faintly ludicrous because the identity of the Archbishop-elect, the name at the top of the Crown Appointment Commission's list, was still a closely-guarded secret. But after reputedly expressing doubts about his 'soundness', the seeds of which had been sown at the Oxford University Conservative Association thirty years earlier, the Prime Minister had made up her mind. She may or may not have been assisted in this by a discreet meeting with Bishop Runcie in the London flat of her close friend Sir Hector Laing. Laing was 1979 'Businessman of the Year', Chairman of United Biscuits and late of the Third Battalion Scots Guards.

This secrecy was mainly at the request of the successful candidate, who wanted to have one last peaceful and normal holiday with his family. Robert now seemed at ease with his decision, even fortified by having climbed the hurdle over which he had dreaded passing. For Lindy this was a period akin to the phoney war, in which they continued to give interviews which studiously avoided the subject and yet for which there was no other obvious pretext. She dreaded the idea of leaving St Albans, just as she had dreaded the idea of moving there, and was depressed by the isolated and gloomy palace at Lambeth. But Rebecca was now seventeen and on the verge of leaving school; James was twenty and an undergraduate where his father and maternal grandfather had both been fellows, Trinity Hall, Cambridge. Both were able to see a life for themselves above and beyond that which was now beckoning their mother and father.

For Richard Chartres and Inez Luckcraft, his chaplain and secretary, the knowledge that Robert was going to Lambeth was charged with the certainty that they were going too. Coggan's secretary was retiring and, although Mrs Luckcraft had been due to go as a deaconess to a parish in Hertfordshire, Robert had persuaded her she was needed at

Lambeth. Chartres too had become an invaluable aide and support. He was unmarried and Mrs Luckcraft was a widow with children; there was accommodation available for them both within the Palace. The fact that there was little or no continuity there between one Archbishop and the next was but one example of the ramshackle and amateurish nature of an administration to which its few permanent staff had become inured; and which Robert found a terrifying prospect.

The announcement that the Right Reverend R. A. K. Runcie MA, MC, would be the 102nd Archbishop of Canterbury and Primate of All England was made on 7 September 1979. The reaction was swift and widespread.

In America, one Washington newspaper headline read: '*Easy-going, over six feet tall, husky, pig-keeping war veteran gets top job.*' In Britain, the headlines included '*New Primate will bring openness to office*', '*War hero named as new Archbishop*', '*A warm welcome for new Primate of All England*' and '*Robert Runcie: the man for the hour*'.

There were favourable reactions from the clergy of all churches. Cardinal Basil Hume paid tribute to the Archbishop-elect's pastoral experience, scholarship and ecumenical spirit. The Archbishop-elect in return challenged him to a squash match. Archbishop Athenagoras of Thyateira and Britain, his old friend and sparring partner from the Anglican-Orthodox Joint Doctrinal Commission, rejoiced at the prospect. Robert in turn could only express his condolences; the Greek Orthodox Patriarch died two days later from a heart attack. Dr Kenneth Greet, the Secretary of the Methodist Conference, paid tribute to Robert's openness and stature as a diocesan bishop. The Church Union welcomed his knowledge of Orthodoxy and lack of small-mindedness.

The Secretary of the Protestant Reformation Society was, however, disappointed at the prospect of closer relations with Rome under the new Archbishop. The General Secretary of the Evangelical Alliance suspected the new Archbishop's support for them was less than enthusiastic. Another leading Evangelical described him as 'a very human sort of person'. Miss Christian Howard of the General Synod, a leading supporter of the ordination of women to the priesthood, predicted that 'we shall have a most interesting time with him as Archbishop'.

Among the Church of England clergy there were predictably mixed reactions. Canon Trevor Beeson of Westminster Abbey described him as 'the best of a mediocre bunch'. Bishop Leonard of Truro had to be sat down and given a strong drink. Hugh Montefiore, then Bishop 'Montefurore' of Birmingham, thought him the best of a reasonable bunch, but was told by another senior colleague: 'You won't believe it, Hugh, but I would rather have had you.' Simon Phipps, then Bishop of Lincoln, his old friend from Westcott House who had written the play in which Robert had played St Peter and Phipps had played Judas Iscariot, wrote him a letter promising he would not play Judas Iscariot to his St Peter. Letters and telephone calls of congratulation poured in from Cambridge contemporaries and students, Gosforth parishioners, Cuddesdon students and colleagues and colleagues and parishioners at St Albans.

A few days after the announcement the Bishop of St Albans presided over the St Albans clergy conference at Kent University. After Compline one night, everyone went into the great cathedral. The cathedral was dark, and they processed holding candles up the stone steps to the choir. Ahead and above them was St Augustine's Chair, the seat that Robert had first seen as a young army officer over thirty-five years before. It was visible now, in the flickering candlelight, the seat he had been chosen to occupy.

It was an extraordinary moment. Robert said: 'Now I feel I can say goodbye properly to St Albans.'

Then they processed back again, down the steps, through the choir and the great dark cathedral, and parted at the door.


Outside the cathedral, in 1979, he was Archbishop-elect in a less than majestic world.

In London, a Church of England Board of Social Responsibility report entitled *Homosexual Relations* was published, and although he was not involved in its compilation his opinion was sought and printed before anybody else's in the matter. He found it no better than a rough guideline for further debate. *Gay News*, however, declared he had knowingly ordained practising homosexuals to the priesthood, and were loudly supported in this claim by the Secretary of the Lesbian and Gay Christian Movement, Richard Kirker.

Kirker, who was still not a priest, declared Robert would 'not be able to delay making public the commitment he has so far made in private to many homosexual clergy without losing credibility'. Robert retorted that he was manufacturing his claim on the basis of one confidential and complex incident. Given that this was true, there was nothing more, as Kirker knew perfectly well, that Robert could say.

In Rome, Archbishop Coggan's Adviser on Foreign Relations Michael Moore had been attending a meeting of the Council of the Anglican Centre. During his visit Moore had a chance encounter with another Englishman, a former Church Army captain and lay reader, who was employed by the Vatican as a roving troubleshooter. His name was Terry Waite.

Moore was closely involved with the preparations for Robert Runcie's enthronement at Canterbury the following March. It was a wet evening as the two men walked back through the Roman streets. Moore immediately took to Waite, as did most people.

'I've got a job for you,' Moore said, 'something I have wanted to have at Lambeth for so long. Someone to do for the Archbishop on the Anglican side internationally what I have tried to do on the ecumenical side.'

Waite was immediately interested. He was addicted to travelling, but his wife and children were based in London rather than Rome. This sounded like the ideal arrangement.

He asked Moore how he thought it might be engineered.

'Contact Bishop Runcie,' Moore told him, 'I'm sure you'll like him. See how you get on.'

Before the two men parted, Waite had agreed to give it a try.

In Iran, the first Persian to be Anglican Bishop there miraculously survived an attempt to kill him at his home in Isfahan. Bishop Dehqani-Tafti was in bed with his wife Margaret, the daughter of his English predecessor in this tiny and little-known outpost of the Anglican Communion. His assailants fired four shots at his head and fled pursued by his wife, whom they shot in the hand. She returned expecting to find her husband's corpse, still unaware that she had been wounded, and he was staring in disbelief at the grouping of four bullet holes in the pillowcase, shaped like a halo around the outline of his head.

His senior Persian priest in Shiraz had already been murdered; worse was to come. Bishop Dehqani-Tafti had met Bishop Runcie briefly at the 1978 Lambeth Conference, which he had attended in his capacity as presiding Bishop of the Middle East. Now the paths of the three men, Dehqani-Tafti, Runcie and Waite, were shortly to cross for the first time.

This conversation in a Roman street, and the shootings in Shiraz and Isfahan, would bring Terry Waite and Robert Runcie together and send Waite plunging off on some of the most extraordinary and unorthodox diplomatic adventures of the 1980s.

In St Albans, the last batch of men and women were ordained deaconesses, deacons and priests under his episcopate. Among them was John Witheridge, who as a St Albans schoolboy had visited Abbey Gate House and been so impressed by Bishop Runcie a few years earlier. Witheridge was also among the many ordinands encouraged by Richard Chartres, whom Robert himself had helped over the ordination hurdle.

Chartres had in turn observed the effectiveness of deep-seated faith communicated via a lightness of touch. 'The great thing about being a curate,' he told them, echoing what he had told a colleague five years earlier, 'is that you are there to be loved. I will always remember the first day I moved into my house in Bedford. There was a little knock at the door and this little old lady was standing there: "Father Richard," she said, "I know you're going to be very busy and you haven't got a wife. Would you mind if I helped you? Would you mind if I left you a tart on your doorstep every Friday?"'

After the laughter had subsided, Chartres said: 'And can Christian charity go deeper than that?'


Michael Moore had chosen the date for the new Archbishop's enthronement in Canterbury Cathedral. 25 March 1980 was sufficiently long after Christmas and fell during the University of Kent vacation, so that accommodation could be commandeered locally. The enthronement was less than three months away.

In January, the date of the Budget was announced for the same day as the enthronement of the Archbishop of Canterbury, a coincidence which led to much speculation about the Church–State relationship. After appeals from MPs of all parties, Sir Geoffrey Howe, the

Chancellor of the Exchequer, wrote to Bishop Runcie telling him that
the government had changed the date:

*Dear Geoffrey* wrote Robert,

*I am delighted that it has been possible to transfer the date of the Budget
to March 26 and I am grateful to you and the Prime Minister for taking
the matter so seriously and for acting so swiftly.*

*I so much appreciate your good wishes for the enthronement. The occasion
will certainly be enhanced by the presence of friends from all parties, who,
thanks to your decision, will now be able to attend.*

*There is one further happy consequence for me of the change of date. I
shall not have to miss the television coverage of your Budget on the 26th.*

*Yours ever,*

*Robert St Albans*

The Archbishop-elect was made a Freeman of the City of St Albans
and continued his round of farewell functions in the diocese. He gave
a series of major interviews in the national press. He cancelled a Swan
Hellenic lecture cruise booked for that summer.

His last duty as Bishop of St Albans was to confirm forty people
in St Michael's Church, Bishops Stortford. Afterwards parishioners
queued for his autograph. On 25 January Donald and Jean Coggan
left Lambeth Palace for a converted public house in Sissinghurst. On
25 February, in a ceremony in the crypt of St Paul's Cathedral recalling
that by which he was elected bishop, Robert Runcie was 'confirmed'
as Archbishop of Canterbury. On 13 March, he was the first Primate
of All England to be guest of honour of the Board of Deputies of
British Jews. He told them that, of all the comments he had read about
himself on his own appointment, he preferred 'Radical conservative
with a self-effacing charisma'. He also liked a notice he had once seen
in the Middle East: 'Double crossing is only permitted for diplomats
and certain bishops.' Religion, he told them, meant building wholesome communities.

On 25 March 1980, he was enthroned in Canterbury Cathedral.
The congregation had processed in its hundreds to be in place at the
appointed time. This included the Prince of Wales, Princess Margaret,
the Prime Minister, the Chancellor of the Exchequer, the Leader of
the Opposition and other political parties; the former Archbishops of

Canterbury, Lord Ramsey and Lord Coggan; the House of Bishops of the Church of England and Bishops from all over the Anglican Communion; the Dean of Canterbury and clergy of the diocese; the heads of other churches; people from Crosby, Gosforth, Cambridge, Cuddesdon, St Albans and Lambeth.

The Dean, Victor de Waal, opened the ceremony. 'Brethren of the Chapter,' he said, 'we have elected our Archbishop and his election has been confirmed. Let the mandate for his enthronement now be read.'

The Principal Registrar, David Carey, did as de Waal requested. There were three knocks at the Cathedral's great west door. The door swung open and the congregation welcomed the new Archbishop of Canterbury. He entered the Cathedral to a stirring fanfare, in a magnificent cope of wild white silk made by Jenny Boyd-Carpenter and embroidered with gold thread he had bought in a market in Istanbul. Preceding him, carrying the cross, was Richard Chartres.

He stood before the nave altar and declared his assent to the scriptures, the creeds and historic formularies of the Church. He swore an oath on the Canterbury Gospels, given to St Augustine by St Gregory the Great 1,400 years earlier, to observe the cathedral's customs, and to defend its rights and liberties.

Dr Philip Potter, General Secretary of the World Council of Churches, read from the Old Testament. Cardinal Basil Hume, Roman Catholic Archbishop of Westminster, read from the epistle to the Ephesians. The Orthodox Archbishop Methodius, the Moderator of the Free Church Frederal Council and the Moderator of the General Assembly of the Church of Scotland offered prayers, as did the first women to take part in an archiepiscopal enthronement, the Third Church Estates Commissioner, Dame Betty Ridley.

The Dean gave thanks in the name of the saints and martyrs, including Oscar Romero, Archbishop of San Salvador, murdered while taking a funeral the day before. The new Archbishop was then enthroned twice, first on the Quire throne as Bishop of the See, then as Primate of All England on St Augustine's marble chair. The Archbishop of West Africa, Moses Scott, pronounced a blessing. After the fanfare the choir and then the rest of the congregation burst into spontaneous applause.

The Archbishop preached his sermon. He knew this would be seen as the touchstone of his primacy, in the same way as his style as a young Westcott House chaplain had been set by his Compline addresses thirty years earlier. His theme, as it had been in many variations and on many occasions before, was authority:

*'And the angel said to Mary, "Jesus shall be great and shall be called the Son of the Highest, and the Lord God shall give him the throne of his father David."' (St Luke i, 32)*

'Jesus was given a throne. That means he was given authority. But authority of what kind, and how did he come by it?

'On the day of his own enthronement an archbishop does well to ponder such matters, which touch not only him but the whole Christian community. The Church exists as an embodiment of Jesus Christ. It exists to express God's love for men, and to draw men to an ever deeper love of God.

We are doing this work as we become more like Jesus Christ. Our proper authority comes by being like him, and our way to a throne must be like his way.'

*Halfway back to St Albans Robert had pulled over into the car park of a service station. They sat there among the refuelling cars and families stopping for food. James did not know what was happening.*

*Robert had turned to him.*

*'Eric,' he said, 'what would you say if I were asked to be Archbishop of Canterbury?'*

'Of course the Church has often tried to take short-cuts to authority, enforcing respect and obedience by worldly means and so obscuring the face of God. I have inherited a substantial supply of weapons which once equipped the Archbishop's private army. Men of power sat in that chair, and their pikes now decorate the walls of Lambeth Palace. Museum pieces?'

'I had a dream of a maze. There were some people very close to the centre: only a single hedge separated them from the very heart of the maze, but they could not find a way through. They had taken a wrong turn right at the very beginning, and would have to return to the gate if they were going to make any further progress.'

*'I think you should do it,' said James.*

*'I can't,' said Robert, and leaned his head forward on his hands, which were still holding the steering wheel. He stayed like that for a minute or so. 'Of course you can,' said James.*

*Robert said: 'I can't. I'm a child.'*

*James knew he meant it. He said: 'It's beyond all of us, but you are the best person to do it. I will never respect you if you refuse. You are telling other people all the time to follow their vocations, to go here and there to be priests. Now you are being called.'*

*Robert sat there. He said: 'You know I can't do it.'*

*'I don't know that,' said James.*

*'Well, I know it,' said Robert.*

*James said: 'That's not for me to say.'*

*They sat there talking for another half hour. Then they drove on up the road.*

'But just outside the gate, others were standing. They were further away from the heart of the maze, but they would be there sooner than the party that fretted and fumed inside.

'I long to be able to speak while Archbishop with men and women who stand outside the Christian Church. I would say to them: "You can teach us so much if together we could look for the secret of the maze-like muddle in which the world finds itself." I ask for your prayers, that I may be given the grace to speak like that and listen.'

*The next day Robert was driven north to see John Turnbull, his old vicar at Gosforth. Turnbull was dying of cancer.*

*'What shall I do?' Robert asked him.*

*'Say "Yes",' said Turnbull, 'and get on with it.'*

'That is why this is a service of glorious celebration. But the personal dedication around which it revolves is a dedication to the way of Jesus Christ; and the support of all who share with me in this day will find no better expression than in the personal dedication of all who can follow with me in that way.'

'But, if you would seek to put the world to rights, do you begin with some other person or with yourself? It is a day to remember that the confrontation of God with man calls out not the interest of the spectator but the fresh and renewed response of the seeker. "Here am I, send me. I am the Lord's servant. As you have spoken – so be it."'

After the sermon the Nicean Creed was said, without the *Filioque* Clause. A number of the Orthodox Church representatives had nonetheless stayed away from the enthronement in protest at the boycott by Britain of the Olympic Games in Moscow, of which Robert had spoken in favour.

Robert gave his first blessings as Archbishop of Canterbury, first from the high altar and then from the nave. He walked out of the Cathedral to meet the people. A pale sun shone as he stooped to kiss a child. The newspapers called it 'a bright signal for a new age'.

# ARCHBISHOP

# 4

# *First Among Equals*

'Cupitt is much cleverer than I am, but I'm the Archbishop of Canterbury.'
ARCHBISHOP ROBERT RUNCIE

THE ramshackle physical condition of Lambeth Palace when the Runcies moved there in the spring of 1980 was matched only by the primitive state of its administration.

Hardly anybody passing the Palace walls realised that people lived here. Lambeth was an area of offices and warehouses; with its tower under scaffolding and plastic sheeting flapping about on dark and windy nights, the badly-lit Palace looked more like a derelict prison than the headquarters of the 102nd Archbishop of Canterbury and *primus inter pares* of the sixty-four million-strong Anglican Communion.

Children climbed over the walls for horse chestnuts by day and by night tramps slept in the gardens. Security was a constant headache to Christopher Fox, the gatekeeper, and the bursar, the retired naval lieutenant-commander Michael Winn. Winn was also in charge of giving the very infrequent guided tours granted to church groups who had applied a year in advance. Gaining entrance to Lambeth Palace, even in 1980, was officially more difficult than gaining entry to the Kremlin. It was easier to visit Tibet.

Once inside the great wooden door of Morton's Tower and Gate, the visitor was confronted by the Outer Courtyard, the Great Hall and Cardinal Pole's fig tree. Behind them was the Lollard's Tower, with its own prison where Wycliffe's followers were chained to the wall. To the right and behind the Cardinal's fig tree was the Guard Room, which once housed the Archbishop's bodyguard and now served as an official dining room. As well as a number of splendid portraits of previous archbishops it also housed the shell of Archbishop Laud's tortoise. Next door were the State Rooms, above which was the Archbishop's apartment. These were reached by the main staircase, which was lined with pikes and at the head of which was a bell marked 'Footman'. Neither bell nor footman worked here any more.

Apart from Michael Winn, there were a number of other permanent inhabitants of this bizarre enclave in the middle of one of the world's busiest capital cities. They included the gardener, the two gatekeepers, the handyman, the cook and a number of clergy. The clergy and lay staff, housed on either a daytime or permanent basis, apart from the Archbishop, included two chaplains, a lay assistant, Michael Kinchin-Smith, and five secretaries, who worked in the residential wing. There was also the Palace Librarian, Geoffrey Bill, and the Archbishop's Councillors on Foreign Relations, Michael Moore and Christopher Hill.

There were even a number of lodgers who did not work here at all; two were employed by the Church Commissioners and three by St Thomas's Hospital. There was no Palace press office and no Palace press officer. This role was filled by John Miles at Church House on the other side of the river in Westminster. Miles had previously worked for the BBC as press officer for *The Goon Show*; he saw no contradiction in his present position.

Lambeth was underfunded, understaffed, overworked and isolated from the world of which it had to be a part. The situation was every bit as bad as Robert Runcie had feared as Archbishop-elect at Abbey Gate House. Now that he was Robert Cantuar, Archbishop at Lambeth, there was a permanent call on his time from a public whose expectations of him were wildly misleading and yet who were barred from visiting his official residence. Too few people were employed effectively to enforce this privacy and nobody had been detailed either to review it or to consider the proposition that greater accessibility should be given to the public.

This was neither the fault of the staff whom Robert Runcie inherited, nor of the outgoing Archbishop, Donald Coggan. The shortage of funds had become the self-fulfilling rationale for the Church Commissioners' refusal to do anything about it. Coggan, a man of simple tastes whom nobody could have accused of laziness, had warned him that life at Lambeth was one way to a martyr's death from overwork. He had survived by writing agendas on the back of an envelope; but had still opened letters himself before handing them out to the various members of staff.

Michael Ramsey had frequently smeared letters with marmalade and 'lost' them, or thrown them away if they carried the dreaded Trent postmark which indicated yet another piece of unwanted advice from his predecessor, Geoffrey Fisher. As Bishop of Durham, Ramsey had allowed copies of correspondence to pile up on a table outside the butler's pantry. The butler had read all the copies and was consequently better-informed than anyone else about what went on there.

Ramsey's flamboyant chaplain John Andrew was a priest and therefore one up from a butler, but in the eyes of some bishops he too had enjoyed a disproportionate influence at Lambeth. Andrew had gone to be Rector of St Thomas's, Fifth Avenue in New York, a position in which he was enormously successful (and where his discretionary allowance was rumoured to exceed the Archbishop's salary). A new post had been created at Lambeth of senior chaplain to which a bishop was appointed, in the theory that he would be more acceptable to his brothers on the bench. Although Robert would also shortly bring in a bishop of his own, the shortage of staff and volume of work were such that Richard Chartres, as his domestic chaplain, retained a considerable amount of autonomy.

Richard Chartres and Inez Luckraft were the two new staff members who took up residence in Lambeth Palace in the spring of 1980. Chartres was unmarried and took easily to the medieval bachelor lifestyle. Mrs Luckcraft moved in with her son, who brought his motorcycle. They had a flat beside the Archbishop's lodgings and her son and his friends performed motorcycle stunts around the Outer Courtyard; nobody seemed to mind.

The Archbishop camped in the Palace while his apartment was being renovated. Lindy made horrified visits from the temporary refuge of a friend's house in Earls Court. James and Rebecca, now twenty-one and eighteen, had the use of modest rented apartments within the Palace grounds. But, beyond the immediate renovation of their personal quarters, it became clear that if the same process were to be applied to the Palace's official rooms then a more substantial injection of funds would be required. Needless to say this was not forthcoming from the Church Commissioners. This situation gave rise to the phenomenon at Lambeth of Sir Hector Laing, or, as he became known there, 'Uncle Biscuit'.

Laing was one of the first close friends to visit Robert and Lindy at Lambeth and he was appalled by what he found. The State Drawing Room overlooking the gardens, which served as a reception room for official visitors and functions, had had its fireplace sealed up with cement and cork tiles stuck on the floor. Laing took one look and asked Lindy what she had in mind. She told him and he paid for the redecoration out of his own pocket.

But Laing and the Runcies knew that his personal largesse was not the solution to the shortage of funds from the Church Commissioners and Lambeth's image problem. Laing in particular had strong feelings about Britain's meanness towards its public servants. To him it was a matter of personal dishonour that his close friend the Prime Minister travelled in less comfortable style than the French President.

Laing was a churchgoer. He believed in God and the Church of England. He believed that the Church was one of the foundations of English life. He believed that, if the Church were weak, the country would decline. He did not share Robert's views on disestablishment. He knew Robert was the leader and that he would have to make the decisions. He also knew Robert sometimes needed a certain amount of support where decision-making was concerned.

Decision-making was Laing's speciality. He had decided there was no contradiction between the Archbishop of Canterbury's humility before God and his friend Bob Runcie's need to travel in earthly comfort. Captains of industry, he reminded Robert, had helicopters at their disposal.

They decided to resurrect the Lambeth Fund. This had existed for some time to help service the maintenance of the Palace and gardens and still contained a modest amount of money. Laing and Lindy now embarked on a long-term fundraising drive to enlarge it.

The success of this combination of two such strong-willed individuals was never in doubt. But the means they used would be held against Lindy in particular by those who did not hold to the view: 'And because thou art virtuous, are there to be no more cakes and ale?'

To some, the presence of even one cake and half a glass of ale would be evidence of the absence of virtue on Mrs Runcie's part. But it was an excess of virtue, in the shape of Lindy's own over-trusting nature, well-placed though it was in Laing's case, that would enable such unkind allegations to be fed by less scrupulous 'friends' at court.

The day began early in Chapel. Robert's appetite for work, developed at Cuddesdon and rewarded at St Albans, was now to meet its severest test.

His office was at the top of the main staircase. To the right, and connected with it, was the office of Richard Chartres. Mrs Luckcraft initially occupied a large room to the right overlooking the Outer Courtyard, but shortly moved to where she could see who was coming down the corridor. Her old room was taken over by another new arrival, though non-resident, the Archbishop's Assistant for Anglican Communion Affairs, Terry Waite.

There was no kitchen in which to make coffee and no lavatory for the secretaries; the only one was next to Terry Waite's office. There were no word processors or electric typewriters. There was no effective internal telephone system. There was no Tipp-Ex: 'Oh, no,' the older secretaries told Mrs Luckcraft, 'they won't let us have it.'

There were hundreds of letters, for which, as he had done at Abbey Gate House, Robert insisted on same-day service. Mrs Luckcraft strove valiantly to oblige.

She listed the subjects on one day alone:

*Abortion*
*Animals*
*Brain damage*
*Chicken's Liberation*
*Church administration*
*The Death penalty*
*Homosexuality*
*The Moonies*
*Nuclear Warfare*
*Overseas Aid*

All these were addressed to the Archbishop in person and had to be marked in various ways: Archbishop's Immediate Attention, Archbishop's Attention, Archbishop to Pass on to Staff, Archbishop to See. There were letters from autograph-hunters, letters from children's projects, letters from people wanting recipes, funny stories, embarrassing stories, letters from lunatics, letters from cranks, and letters of obscene abuse; the worst one she opened contained a piece of used lavatory paper.

One package arrived looking suspicious in second-hand brown wrapping. Mrs Luckcraft pulled gently at it, and tissue paper and oozing brown substance came away in her hand, looking, she thought, like explosive. She carried it out of her office, down the corridor, past the Archbishop's office, down the main staircase to the Outer Courtyard.

Christopher Fox the gatekeeper was within earshot. 'I'll look at it,' he said. 'No, on second thoughts, I'll send for someone else.'

Mrs Luckcraft returned to her office. Later, Fox admitted to her that he had opened the package himself. It had turned out to be a gingerbread archbishop, sent in by a child; what Mrs Luckcraft had seen was the feet.

Not only had all letters to be given the Archbishop's same-day service, but no platitudes were permitted. Mrs Luckcraft had to weigh the replies for postage; but, whereas the stamps worked in grams, the scales at the Palace only worked in the old imperial measurements. 'Why do you want another one?' was the Church Commissioners' reaction.

One reason was that, in order to prepare a reply, the same letter had to be taken to four different parts of the office. Mrs Luckcraft persevered and managed to obtain both a new set of scales and large quantities of Tipp-Ex. The older secretaries' gratitude was matched by their disbelief. 'Can we have them?' they asked her. 'Can we really? Oh, *thank you* . . .'

In her worst moments she thought of herself not as Robert's secretary but as a paper processing machine. She would look out of her bathroom window at 1 a.m. and see the light still on in the Archbishop's study. At 8.30 the next morning he would be pacing the corridor, having already been to Chapel and dictated the tapes which he would be clutching in his hand.

'Where have you been, Inez?' he would say.

He began to look exhausted. Their personal relationship began to suffer. At Abbey Gate House she had been less of a secretary than a trusted confidante. At Lambeth she was not only less than a secretary, at the staff meetings she attended nobody seemed interested in what she had to say. This was not like running a diocese, she told herself, this was simply being run off her feet. Unlike the others, however, she was no longer in a position to do anything except keep on running, as long and as fast as she could.

Mrs Luckcraft continued valiantly to try to cope with the flood of correspondence. Richard Chartres was Robert's domestic chaplain and ADC, a role he had performed at St Albans and which was enlarged by the transition. Michael Kinchin-Smith, the lay assistant whom Robert had inherited from Donald Coggan, continued to liaise with the government and the Home Office. He briefed Robert when the Archbishop's opinion was required on secular matters and liaised with the bishops in the House of Lords. Christopher Hill and Michael Moore continued in their role as Councillors on Foreign Relations to advise the Archbishop on liaison with other churches. But Moore was exhausted and would shortly leave after ten years at Lambeth. By contrast, down the corridor from the Archbishop's office, Moore's new recruit was already making his considerable presence felt.

Terry Waite's appointment as Archbishop's Assistant for Anglican Affairs was a reflection of the emphasis placed on this area by the new Primacy. He was already busy planning the Archbishop's visit to Ghana and the new Anglican province of Burundi, Rwanda and Zaire. Waite was never happier than when he was travelling. Behind a desk he looked distinctly uncomfortable and his major weakness was paperwork. His strengths lay in his sheer size – he towered over both Chartres and Runcie – his stamina, his personal commitment and the force of his personality.

His contacts were priceless and his work for the Roman Catholic Church meant that they extended far beyond the Anglican Communion. That April, Waite and Christopher Hill travelled to Rome to negotiate arrangements for Robert's first meeting with the Pope. The Pope was to be in Accra at the same time as the Archbishop and this was seen as a suitable prelude to the first official Papal visit to Britain.

Robert preached his first Easter sermon in Canterbury Cathedral and addressed a youth pilgrimage there, familiarising himself with Canterbury. Canterbury, and what to do with the diocese, were questions on a par with how to survive life at Lambeth in Robert Runcie's mind. Both Donald Coggan and Michael Ramsey had tried to run the diocese with the Bishops of Maidstone and Dover as their clear suffragans and juniors. In his latter years Coggan had tried to create an area bishop scheme, but still kept his finger on the pulse. The diocese consequently missed out, in many people's opinion; the Archbishop of Canterbury was simply too busy being President of the Anglican Communion and Primate of All England.

In order to rectify this situation and yet maintain his links with Canterbury itself, Robert decided to separate the cathedral from the diocese. This was a bold move calling for diplomacy on his part, in which he was helped by the imminent retirement of his Trinity Hall colleague Tony Tremlett as Bishop of Dover, and his choice of Richard Third as Tremlett's successor.

Third was designated as Robert's deputy for the diocese, and all diocesan enquiries were henceforth to be addressed to him. Robert delegated his authority, but retained a general pastoral relationship with the clergy. In his first two years he visited more parishes than his predecessors.

He maintained Canterbury as his cathedral. The Bishop of Dover had no cathedral of his own, and a lesser man than Third might have taken umbrage at this. But Third persevered and won over the clergy, while Robert tried to stay at the Old Palace for half the weekends of the year. This meant that Richard Chartres in turn needed a surrogate in the diocese, and one was found in a local priest called David Maple. This arrangement suited Robert and Chartres, and Third and Maple. But it did not find favour with Lindy, whose patience was exhausted by Lambeth and who had a dislike for the cavernous Old Palace at Canterbury. A steward and his wife were appointed to welcome the Archbishop after he was driven down from Lambeth on Friday nights, and to look after him during his solitary working weekends.

In late April, the Archbishop was visited at Lambeth by Louisa Kennedy, wife of one of the American hostages held in Iran. Mrs

Kennedy brought with her a letter from the Episcopalian Bishop of Washington; she was in London seeking British support. Robert could only reassure her of his, but other events in that country were now conspiring to involve him on a much closer basis.

Shortly after his meeting with Mrs Kennedy, Jean Waddell, secretary to Bishop Dehqani-Tafti, was shot and seriously wounded in Tehran. A few days later the Bishop's only son was shot and killed. The Bishop was unable to return to Tehran and the remainder of his family were trying to leave the country. Jean Waddell and other missionaries, however, would not be allowed to leave. The hostages in Iran would shortly consist therefore not just of American Episcopalians, but also of missionaries and clergy of the Anglican Communion.

In May Runcie, Chartres, Hill and Waite flew to Accra where they stayed with the British High Commissioner. The next morning they were driven to the Papal Nuncio's house, where they were introduced to numerous senior Roman Catholic clergy in the garden. A few minutes later the Pope appeared from the house. After pleasantries he led the Archbishop of Canterbury inside.

They talked for forty-five minutes, during which Robert extended the invitation for him to become the first Pope to visit England. He stressed that the focus for this would be the cathedral at Canterbury. They re-emerged smiling like elder statesmen, and the Archbishop and his party went on their way.

The Accra meeting was one such between many people: a Pope and an Archbishop of Canterbury, a Pontiff and a Primate, Karol Wojtyla and Robert Runcie. Millions of words and thousands of pictures were printed and through their meeting the new Archbishop became a world figure. Karol Wojtyla's fame was at its height. Their encounter was private and brief. They issued communiqués placing the usual stress on the need for common action to spread the modern faith rather than squabble over ancient differences.

But the long-term effect on relations between Roman Catholics and Anglicans could not be measured by either the public fact of such an event or the brevity of a private meeting. What distinguished this and the others that followed was that the mere fact of the contact transcended profound doctrinal disagreements. To the new Archbishop of Canterbury, himself an Anglo-Catholic and a committed ecumenist abroad in the first year of his primacy, this was a major personal inspiration that lasted long after the publicity, and the Papal honeymoon, was over.

Runcie and Waite flew on via Nairobi to Zaire, where the official purpose of his African visit was to inaugurate the new Anglican province of Burundi, Rwanda and Zaire, and attend the enthronement of the Archbishop Bezalerei Ndahura. Ndahura, who was to die only eighteen months later on Christmas Day 1981, was the Luton curate whom he had ordained priest at St Albans five years earlier. The venue was a football pitch at Bukavu and his acquaintance with Ndahura gave Robert the opportunity to stress the importance of Anglican Communion through a personal connection, a technique for which he became famous as 'the man from everywhere'.

The following Sunday he was able to do this again at a massive outdoor Eucharist celebrating the thirteen hundreth anniversary of the founding of the diocese of Worcester. This time the excuse was the venue, Worcester Cricket Ground: 'This sacred spot,' he told the crowd, 'was where my father-in-law J. W. C. Turner was captain of the county team.'

In Edinburgh, at the General Assembly of the Church of Scotland, he declared that he was proud to bear a Scottish name and to have been brought up in a Scottish household. This impressed most of his audience, but not Pastor Jack Glass, chairman of the Twentieth Century Reformation Movement. Glass accused the Archbishop of closet Popery and pointed to his recent meeting with John Paul II in Africa. The Archbishop repeated the message of his Accra communiqué to the effect that the search for unity in faith was more important than old rivalries.

In Walsingham, on Whit Monday, he became the first Archbishop of Canterbury in modern times to lead the fifteen thousand-strong annual pilgrimage to the shrine to the Virgin Mary in Norfolk. The traditional high Anglo-Catholicism of the shrine provoked demonstrations of unease at his presence but the event passed off peacefully, not least because he was so much better at calming things down than he was at stirring them up.

The Protestant Truth Society was in evidence and an Ellesmere Port taxi driver, Mr Robert Phoenix, thrust a pamphlet through the

Archbishop's car window which read: 'Christ is the only mediator between God and Man.'

'I know,' the Archbishop replied, and was driven on.

At the shrine, one reporter began counting clerical toupees, convinced that the presence of so many signified a new addition to the High Church wardrobe. Another reporter observed the plaques left by grateful pilgrims inside the door: 'Daisy returns thanks for cure of abscess in her left ear after pilgrimage here, 1937'; 'Thanks for the gift of a child'; 'For the safety of one at Dunkirk.'

David Samuel, Rector of Ravendale, Grimsby, headed the Protestant Reformation Society demonstrators with banners proclaiming: 'Walsingham no place for Archbishop' and 'Walsingham Way not Anglican Way'. Another man held a banner which read: 'Howl Ye Shepherds And Cry and Wallow Ye Principal of the Flock.' The Duchess of Kent walked among the pilgrims, contrary to press reports that lack of security had forced her to withdraw. The Archbishop was only one of many diverse celebrants in the grounds of the priory ruined during the Reformation. He quoted his predecessor Augustine, that unity in faith transcended differences in custom. The audience applauded and the dazed reporters adjourned to the pub.

In London, the Church of England Report *Towards Visible Unity: Proposals for a Covenant* was published, revealing considerable disunity among those who had compiled it. Lindy wrote in *The Times* about her first six months at Lambeth:

*'Now, after nearly five months, and in spite of many set-backs, we are getting used to it. At Lambeth, my husband still wanders from room to room searching for his socks or shirts, because the decorating is not yet finished, and our clothes are scattered all over the place, or left at Canterbury by mistake, but it is beginning to feel like home.*

*'. . . I hope that during our time at Lambeth we may open up this historic building to more people, so that what hitherto has only been shown to a select few, may be seen by others who do not necessarily carry a church membership card.'*

The fee for this article and many others like it went to the Lambeth Fund. Lindy had no illusions about why the press wanted her to write about life at Lambeth. She was the Archbishop's wife, and she knew it was for the same reason that she was booked to play piano recitals, when her hands were too small to enable her to join the ranks of Brendel, Pollini *et al.* Why else had she been booked to appear at Southwark Cathedral, or at St Peter's, Eaton Square, the parish church of Buckingham Palace, on the same bill as Esther Rantzen, Alan Price, Mr Ian Hall and his Caribbean Combo and the Asante Drummers?

At Chichester Cathedral she had been playing to raise funds for its restoration when her page-turner had whispered: 'There's a man sleeping so soundly he's going to hit his head on the pew.'

She had stood up and announced she would play two pieces by Rachmaninov. 'Those who wish to continue sleeping,' she added, 'will be able to do so during the first piece, but not during the second, as it is rather noisy.'

She still taught piano at St Albans School, commuting and staying with friends. She missed St Albans, in a way she had not missed Cuddesdon or even Cambridge. Her children were grown up, or growing up, and her husband was busier than ever. Lindy was not overawed by anyone however distinguished, and came from too powerful a tribe ever to be so. She needed a cause, and she found one in the Lambeth Fund. But she also needed a social outlet; and it was to St Albans that she increasingly looked, to the place where she and Robert had spent their golden years.


In July of that year he preached at the Queen Mother's eightieth birthday service of thanksgiving in St Paul's Cathedral. The Royal School of Church Music elected him President, as it had Coggan, Ramsey, Fisher and Lang. Oxford University awarded him an honorary Doctorate of Divinity, enabling him to be known not merely as 'The Most Reverend and Right Honourable Robert Runcie' but also as plain 'Dr Runcie'.

This proliferation of roles was accompanied by a modest expansion of the Lambeth staff. Among these, as his new title suggested, was the Bishop of Bradford, Ross Hook, who became Chief of Staff.

Hook had spent the Second World War as a chaplain with the Royal Marine Commandos, and like the Archbishop had won the MC. He had first met Robert Runcie when the latter arrived at Cuddesdon and Hook had been secretary of a body that monitored theological colleges.

Hook was a bluff, approachable man with a high reputation among his fellow bishops. He was sixty-three, four years older than Robert and had a genuinely patrician confidence of manner that the Archbishop lacked. Ruth Hook demonstrated a pastoral care for the staff and their families that made her a much-loved figure at Lambeth.

Hook's job, in military parlance, was to hold the fort while the Archbishop was travelling. Robert planned to do a great deal of this, and he wanted someone to take the decisions while he was away and prevent the paperwork from piling up on his desk. 'You're to be the head of the household,' Robert told Hook.

He did not know what title to give him. They wanted to depart from the old idea of senior chaplain; Richard Chartres was now officially designated 'Archbishop's Chaplain'. Eventually Hook suggested 'Chief of Staff'.

Robert trusted Hook implicitly and supported him in everything he did. One of his first moves was to find a way to make the household of which he was *de facto* head run properly. Another was to understand how it had ever run in the first place. These questions alone, apart from his other duties, kept Hook occupied during his first months at Lambeth.


In Iran, Bishop Dehqani-Tafti's wife and daughters had finally secured exit visas and flown to England and exile. The Bishop himself had arrived the same day from Cyprus.

'God asked Abraham to sacrifice his son,' he told reporters at Heathrow Airport. 'I was saved but my son was not. I do not understand why. In a way it would have been much easier if I had gone.'

Jean Waddell and a Persian Anglican priest were still in Evin prison. The Bishop's administrator, Dimitri Bellos, and John and Audrey Coleman, another missionary couple, were under house arrest. According to Tehran radio, the entire Anglican diocese in Iran was in the pay of the CIA.

Bishop Dehqani-Tafti appealed to the Archbishop of Canterbury, as *primus inter pares* of the Anglican Communion. Robert liked to describe the Anglican Communion as the most widely dispersed church on earth. He could not ignore this cry from one of its remotest and smallest outposts, least of all now that it had reached his own front door.

He had already written to the Ayatollah Khomeini politely appealing as one man of God to another. There had been no reply. He wrote again, this time asking permission to send Terry Waite, his Assistant for Anglican Communion Affairs, on a goodwill visit to the Anglicans held in Tehran. Neither Runcie nor Waite had heard from Tehran. Waite was busy organising the Archbishop's visit to America; but ever keen to travel, he had applied for a visa and booked an open ticket to Tehran.

The Archbishop was much preoccupied at this time with the publication of the Alternative Service Book, the fruit of fifteen years' work and the first of its kind since the Book of Common Prayer of 1662. Controversy surrounded the plain and sometimes banal language of the new publication, and there was confusion over whether or not it was intended as a direct replacement for its much-loved predecessor.

The Archbishop himself celebrated the new order of Holy Communion in Westminster Abbey that November, at the start of the General Synod. The Queen was among the communicants. The following Sunday he and the Archbishop of York issued a rare pastoral letter to be read in all churches of the Church of England. It supported the modern language of the Alternative Service Book but assured congregations that it was intended to complement rather than replace the 1662 version.

On Christmas Eve, Waite was finally granted a fifteen-day visa to enter Iran. He was exultant. Bishop Dehqani-Tafti, however, was nervous. 'I wish you were ordained,' he told Waite, 'then at least you could go as a priest, in a cassock.'

'I am a lay reader,' Waite replied, 'I can wear one.'

Waite flew out to Tehran on Christmas Day amid enormous publicity. Nobody had ever heard of this six foot seven inch bearded figure before. For several days he was kept waiting before his bravery and persistence paid off; he was taken first to see the Colemans and then Jean Waddell. At the latter meeting he tape-recorded a special message from the Persian Anglican priest held with her, to give to Bishop Dehqani-Tafti.

The Anglicans remained captive but Waite returned to London full of optimism. In late January the American hostages in Iran were freed.

Waite applied for another visa and set off for the second time for Tehran.

The Archbishop was deeply involved in the General Synod, which was debating among other things *Homosexual relationships: a Contribution to Discussion*, a report by the Board of Social Responsibility under the chairmanship of the Bishop of Truro, Graham Leonard. Leonard himself was being strongly tipped to succeed Gerald Ellison as Bishop of London.

This was the Archbishop's third session of the Synod as Primate, but the first at which he had a number of important statements to make. In the debate on marriage, remarriage and divorce he reaffirmed the relatively liberal views he had made known as Bishop of St Albans. In the debate on homosexuality he was more cautious. But he offered as an example of his views a rebuff to the Secretary of the Lesbian and Gay Christian Movement, Richard Kirker. 'One of my rule of thumb tests for ordination,' he told Synod, 'would be if a man was so obsessive a campaigner on this subject that it made his ministry unavailable to the majority of church people. Then I would see no justification in ordaining him.'

The debate on unity between the Church of England and the Free Churches, inspired by the recent report, was a complex theological matter of the kind in which he excelled at giving a lucid exposition while at the same time managing to present an ambivalent personal point of view.

The uncanny way in which he had been observed to be able to gauge the mood of a meeting at Cuddesdon again came to his rescue, and the Synod eventually reflected his own ambivalence by voting for the motion in barely sufficient numbers. It may or may not have been the case that the eventual failure of the motion was caused by his reluctance to take a strong lead; this was certainly the view of those who had voted unreservedly for it.

He announced the news of the Pope's first visit to England and the news of the engagement of the Prince of Wales and Lady Diana Spencer. But the great event of the first session of the General Synod of 1981 was his announcement of the news of the departure from Tehran of the aircraft carrying Jean Waddell, John and Audrey Coleman and Terry Waite.

The scenes at Heathrow Airport were televised all over the world. The Archbishop and his Assistant for Anglican Communion Affairs were the heroes of the hour. A joyful party for the freed missionaries followed at Lambeth. The vital factor in the distinction between American and British hostages being made by the Iranians had undoubtedly been the visible integrity and priestly bearing of Terry Waite.

But even Waite's title was now changed to fit more appropriately the legend that had been born. The press found 'the Archbishop of Canterbury's Assistant for Anglican Communion Affairs' difficult to digest, and rapidly translated it into 'the Archbishop of Canterbury's Special Envoy', as befitted Waite's new Scarlet Pimpernel-like status. This misleading and portentous title rapidly became received wisdom. It was one which even Waite himself was unable and eventually unwilling to correct.

Bishop Dehqani-Tafti, whose persecution had first brought to public notice the fact that there was an Anglican dimension to the Iranian revolution, would remain in exile in Britain. Cut off from the diocese in which he had been a Christian among Moslems, he now found himself a Persian among the English; a stranger in both worlds. While Jean Waddell and the others were still in captivity he had written *The Hard Awakening*, a moving and powerful book about his experiences, which both Waite and the Foreign Office feared would jeopardise their release.

Nobody at Lambeth Palace seemed to know what to do with him now that the Anglican hostages were free. Bishop Hook made the well-meaning suggestion that he minister to the numerous Pakistanis and Moslems in his own former diocese of Bradford. Bishop Dehqani-Tafti politely pointed out that as a Persian his knowledge of Urdu was limited; he was still needed to help the beleaguered Church in Iran. He continued to do this quietly and successfully over the years that followed. He did not wish to embarrass Archbishop Runcie.

He became an assistant bishop in the diocese of Winchester, which gave him a house. His salary was paid by the Church Missionary Society. Jean Waddell became his secretary. He published a number of books from his small house in Basingstoke. In the hall hung a picture of his murdered son, Bahram. On the wall of one room, in a frame, hung the pillow-case marked with the four bullet holes from that night in Isfahan.

He never received the tape-recorded message from his Persian priest made for him by Terry Waite. He had gone to listen to it in Waite's office at Lambeth. The message was long and Waite was busy. Waite said he would send him a copy, but the copy never came.

Years later, his Persian priest would be free and Bishop Dehqani would pray daily for Terry Waite. He had not forgotten how much the message had meant to him at the time. But, when he thought back and remembered it, it was only one of a number of things that had filled him with a growing sense of foreboding, whenever he looked at his television and saw the familiar features of the tall, bearded figure of 'the Archbishop's Special Envoy' flashed on the screen.


Mary Cryer joined the Lambeth Palace staff that spring after twenty-five years as secretary to Mervyn Stockwood, recently retired as Bishop of Southwark. Like Ross Hook, Miss Cryer was at something of a loss as to the exact boundaries of her job. Like Hook, she could see that she was far from alone in this.

She arrived with the title of Second Secretary to the Archbishop to help the hard-pressed Inez Luckcraft. When the Archbishop was in residence he handed out tapes all day to be transcribed, and Mrs Luckcraft could not keep up. She now passed some of these on to Miss Cryer, who did not know the Archbishop's style, had no address book, and discovered that he did not always hand out the letter he thought he was answering.

One of the older secretaries objected loudly to her title on the grounds that she had been there longer. For the first year she shared the general office with the telephonist. Miss Cryer would also look after the accounts, the domestic staff, the Palace treasures, order new equipment, plan and give guided tours, and work with Lindy to raise money for the Lambeth Fund. By this time Miss Cryer's title would have been changed to Palace Secretary, and then, on the retirement of Gordon Winn and the elevation of Christopher Fox as Steward, to Bursar, in which capacities she would play a stabilising role at Lambeth for nearly a decade.

Bishop Leonard of Truro also took up his new appointment. As widely predicted he became Bishop of London, the third most powerful bishopric in the Church of England and head of a diocese of 473 parishes and three million people. He would reveal a very different temperament both to the Archbishop and to the man Robert Runcie had hoped would fill the position, the Bishop of Durham, John Habgood.

The Archbishop of Canterbury travelled with Richard Chartres to America on the three-week visit arranged for him by Terry Waite. In Sewanee he was awarded an honorary Doctorate in Divinity by the University of the South. In Washington DC he preached live on television in Washington Cathedral and presided at the five-day Conference of Anglican Primates. He discussed the Brandt Report with the President of the World Bank, Robert McNamara. In Los Angeles he was joined by Lindy who gave a charity concert.

In Iowa he was presented with Martha, a Berkshire pig, who was taken through customs with difficulty and was the latest product of the legend of the 'pig-keeping archbishop', which also brought him pig cushions, pig-headed writing paper, pig-ended pencils, silver pigs, china pigs, glass pigs and volumes on pig husbandry.

In Chicago he was confronted by a single demonstrator bearing a placard that read 'Runcie is a Government agent for the promotion of God-fantasy.'

In New York he visited Harlem and Lindy gave another charity concert.

In Ireland, shortly afterwards, he consecrated the new north transept of the Anglican cathedral in Belfast and addressed the Presbyterian General Assembly. He told them Protestants and Catholics had to build bridges between each other. He said he was quite prepared to meet the Reverend Ian Paisley, who being an MP at Westminster had only to 'walk across the water' to Lambeth.

In England, he entertained the Prince of Wales and Lady Diana Spencer at a private lunch at Lambeth Palace. Tremendous secrecy surrounded the visit, which was for the purpose of a pre-nuptial 'chat'. Even the permanent staff were urged to stay out of sight. Miss Cryer managed a blurred photograph from the window of the Guard Room. Mrs Luckcraft, who was typing draft after draft of the Archbishop's wedding sermon, met them in the corridor. Terry Waite, who by some mysterious process had also become *de facto* Press Officer, was furious when he only found out about the visit later. This was in spite of the fact that Robert had given strict instructions about the secrecy of it to Bishop Hook.

Afterwards, too, the tabloid press deliberately misinterpreted re-marks the Archbishop made at a press conference: '*What I told Di and Charles*' and '*Archbishop's sex advice*' were two examples of how a standard conversation of which the Archbishop had revealed no specific details beyond the mere fact that it had happened, could be presented with impunity by the best-selling newspapers in Fleet Street.

The Dalai Lama came to tea. James took a First from Cambridge and joined the Bristol Old Vic as a trainee theatre director. His father, once a keen participant in amateur theatricals, spoke in the Lords against the Nationality Bill and in Synod in favour of the principle of the remarriage in church of certain kinds of divorcee. He officiated at his first marriage for some time, that of the Prince of Wales and Lady Diana Spencer.

Richard Chartres had shown himself to be highly effective in his liaison with Buckingham Palace and St Paul's Cathedral over the form of the service. The Moderator of the Church of Scotland and Cardinal Hume were both given parts to play. The Speaker of the House of Commons, the Welshman George Thomas, was to read the lesson. Harry Williams, who had known Prince Charles as an undergraduate at Trinity, had written a special prayer. After the worldwide spectacle of the fairytale couple, the sermon of the Archbishop of Canterbury attracted most attention.

Chartres and Robert came back to Mrs Luckcraft with draft after draft for typing. What trivial matter had they overlooked that could make the whole thing go desperately wrong? Would there be a lectern for his notes? She bought special lecture cards and a new daisy wheel. She typed a paragraph on each card. All he had to do was drop his eyes to pick up the first line.

Both Prince Charles and Lady Diana made mistakes under the pressure of the occasion. When she faltered over the order of her husband's various Christian names, the Archbishop steered her for-ward, leaving the error and the nervousness behind.

Only afterwards was this pronounced more remarkable than the sermon itself, which in turn was less remarkable than some of the press reactions.

'Here is the stuff of which fairy tales are made,' he told the congre-gation, and a hundred million viewers on television, 'the Prince and Princess on their wedding day . . .

'A marriage which really works is one which works for others. Marriage has both a private face and a public importance. If we solved all our economic problems and failed to build loving families, it would profit us nothing, because the family is the place where the future is created good and full of love – or deformed.'

'Drivel,' wrote Clive James in the 'Observer', 'adding further fuel to the theory that he's the man to hire if what you want at your wedding is platitudes served up like peeled walnuts in chocolate syrup: he's an anodyne divine who'll put unction in your function.'

Given that Robert Runcie had only been in the job for just over a year, during which time he had already managed to offend both American Catholics and Irish Protestants, it was not clear to which theory James was alluding. It was even possible that the sophisticated James was inadvertently revealing his position in the ranks of those who thought the Archbishop of Canterbury could somehow save them from something; as did the hundreds of people who each day wrote to him at Lambeth.

In Canterbury, he blessed and 'baptised' fourteen new bells cast by the Whitechapel bell foundry and subsequently installed in the south-west tower of the cathedral in a steel frame donated by the Woolwich Equitable Building Society. The bells had names (the Extra Treble was 'Simon', the Sixth 'Anselm' and the Eleventh 'Augustine') and the donors included the Friends of Canterbury Cathedral and the Kent Association of Change Ringers.

The Dean of Canterbury, Victor de Waal, had officiated at Robert's enthronement. John Simpson, Robert's Director of Ordinands at St Albans, had been just one of many guests on that occasion. But de Waal suffered from nervous debilitation which would eventually lead to a breakdown and his departure from Canterbury in sad circumstances for both the Cathedral and the Church of England. Although he would not officially succeed de Waal as Dean until five years later, Simpson came to Canterbury as Archdeacon in 1981 and was shortly afterwards invited to take responsibility for all worship there.

The Archbishop himself was feeling the strain after a busy year and departed on a cruise around the Greek islands with Lindy. This time there were no lecture duties. While Lindy returned to see a play James had directed at the Fringe Festival in Edinburgh, her husband travelled on to Malta. A friend had offered him the use of a villa. One night they were having a quiet drink at a local taverna. The Archbishop was dressed in sweat shirt. 'Oh,' said a woman across the bar, 'you're the one who married Lady Di . . .'

The honours continued to accumulate. He was a Freeman of the City of London, honorary Doctor of Literature at Keele, honorary Doctor of Divinity at Cambridge. He went as *ex officio* President to the fifth meeting of the Anglican Consultative Council at Newcastle.

He revealed a near-photographic memory by greeting Gosforth clergy and parishioners with a hug and the right names as if they had met only yesterday. Some, fearful of appearing sycophantic, held back from greeting him there.

Audrey Carey, née Tiffin, was the daughter of his old Gosforth landlady. Robert had written to her on Mrs Tiffin's death some years earlier. When he had been translated from St Albans to Canterbury, Mrs Tiffin's daughter had written to congratulate him. 'Gosforth,' he wrote back to her, 'was such a memorable and happy chapter, and not least because of your marvellous Mum.'

The Careys had heard the conference was shortly to happen. After some hesitation, Audrey wrote a note to him at St Mary's College of the Sacred Heart, where she knew it was taking place. She welcomed him back to the north of England.

Afterwards, she felt a little foolish at having done so. One evening her telephone rang. It was Robert Runcie.

They talked for twenty minutes in spite of the media coverage that had built him into a seemingly inaccessible public figure. He had been back to look at the house where he once lived with her mother in Oakfield Road. He was busy and tired. He said his brother-in-law had advised him and Lindy to buy a house.

She asked after Lindy. He said it was difficult, seeing so little of each other.

'Well,' she found herself saying, 'you must be careful. It's terribly important you know, it's you and Lindy who matter in the end. Look after yourselves,' and she went on in this way.

Afterwards, her husband said: 'Do you realise who you were talking to? That was the Archbishop of Canterbury.'

But, as far as Mrs Carey was concerned, she had been talking to a friend; and he had talked to her in the same vein.


The small house the Runcies purchased was in St Albans and it was their first home after twenty-four years of marriage. As well as an investment, it was an expression of Lindy's deep dislike of feeling beholden to what she called the 'tied cottage' at Lambeth.

Lindy still taught piano at St Albans and had many friends there. Her passion for the next piano lesson had only intensified with her husband's immersion in his work. At Lambeth she would develop a trust in one woman member of staff, confiding in her and telling her her problems, before transferring her affections to another. She may have acted in this way out of the fear that her confidences would reach the wrong ears. In any event this was precisely the result.

The work Lindy and Laing undertook on behalf of Lambeth Fund also caused some resentment among the Church Commissioners, who suspected Laing of appropriating responsibilities for his own advancement. This was not the case, but as word travelled so it inevitably became exaggerated of the 'biscuit king's' power and influence at Lambeth.

This suspicion on the part of the Church Commissioners would change as time went by, not least through the soothing influence of Ross Hook, who had himself served in that capacity. Ten years later, the Lambeth Fund would be seen as a triumph, Lindy would be hailed as a selfless and charitable helpmate and the Church of England would be consulting advertising agencies about its image problem. But in 1981 no one had ever seen the likes of Laing and Lindy at Lambeth before.

Just as Laing had proclaimed the right of the Archbishop to live in comfort and reached into his own pocket as an example, so he used the simile of the Prime Minister's Cabinet Office to point out the inadequacy of the Archbishop's staff to deal with the affairs of sixty-four million Anglicans.

A management consultancy was hired and made various recommendations. One was that Mrs Luckcraft, an able speaker presently gagged by a mountain of paperwork, should be given a role more suited to her abilities. Another was that a research assistant should be hired to build a database of material on the myriad subjects, great and small, which were raised in the press, parliament and the letters Mrs Luckcraft opened daily, and on which the Archbishop of Canterbury was expected to have an expert opinion.

The first recommendation was not implemented and Mrs Luckcraft remained as pressed as ever. The second position was created, initially at Sir Hector Laing's expense. Andrew Acland arrived at Lambeth Palace for an interview in the summer of 1981.

Acland had read Russian at university and worked as the historian Hugh Thomas's assistant at the Centre for Policy Studies. He and his family were steeped in political research and international affairs, in a vision of the world as seen by Foreign Office and Chatham House.

Acland had a confession to make. 'Archbishop,' he said, 'there is one thing I think I should tell you. I do have . . . doubts.'

'Don't you think,' Robert replied, 'an Archbishop has them too?'

Acland became researcher, speechwriter and at certain functions acted as the Archbishop's representative. He built up a huge filing system of issues on which the Archbishop and the Church of England might be expected to comment. He prepared material for the Archbishop's speech in the General Synod debate on disarmament that November. He spent much of his time trying to convince the Church Commissioners of the virtue of word processors. He helped Rebecca with her homework. He was also conscripted to help with the correspondence. One letter came from an elderly woman who had recently suffered the loss of her pet goat. She wanted to know if the Archbishop thought they would be reunited in Heaven.

This was the kind of letter Richard Chartres enjoyed dropping on Acland's desk. 'Now get out of that one,' he would say with a chuckle.

Acland would set about drafting a suitable reply, only to be visited as often as not by Terry Waite, who could not look at a piece of paper for more than a few seconds before adopting a glazed expression. His solution was to forsake his own desk and office for those of others, where he would stand about, an irrepressible presence, making jokes while they were trying to wade through their own paperwork.

Acland shared Chartres's opinion of the General Synod as 'the dull echo of a liberal consensus', and the opinion voiced by others of it as a body excessively influenced by an old-fashioned homosexual freemasonry and by ecclesiastical lawyers labouring over abstruse points of procedure.

Robert was loyal to Synod, but had a similarly robust, though necessarily veiled, opinion. 'That place is a nest of queers,' he said to Acland in a stage whisper, as they came out of one committee meeting.

Acland formed a lasting affection for Robert Runcie. He was charmed by him but he also respected the Archbishop's insistence that he learn to see both sides of a question. The Archbishop encouraged him to play devil's advocate and to abhor platitudes. Acland sometimes felt the cost was too high. The Archbishop's only serious defect, in his eyes, was that at times a positively platitudinous, black and white statement was what was needed, and it was not forthcoming from him.


This was the team of people, assembled from new and existing staff, from a multiplicity of backgrounds and funded in both conventional and less orthodox ways, that the Archbishop of Canterbury had gathered round him by the end of 1981.

Ross Hook, as Chief of Staff, had established himself as a solid and reliable presence and was unintimidated by taking charge in the Archbishop's frequent absences. Richard Chartres, the Archbishop's Chaplain, was the closest and greatest single influence on him. Robert was happy that this should be so. Cynical, seductive, intellectually impressive, an original thinker with a brilliant turn of phrase, Chartres was a key element in the Archbishop's public utterances. He kept the diary, arranged and accompanied him on visits, organised research, attended daily service and various other services, carried the primatial cross on ceremonial occasions and made sure people bowed to it and not to the Archbishop.

In Terry Waite, too, the Archbishop had absolute trust and was never heard to utter a word of criticism about him.

Although Waite's whereabouts were not always known, he was believed presently to he hard at work organising the Archbishop's forthcoming visit to the Far East and China.

Christopher Hill, his Counsellor on Foreign Affairs, was organising the reception for the Pope's imminent visit to Britain. Michael Moore was shortly to leave Lambeth for the chaplaincy of a quieter palace at Hampton Court. As Lay Assistant, Michael Kinchin-Smith was a successful inheritance from the previous administration. Andrew Acland had established himself in spite of being referred to by Sir Hector Laing as 'that Bolshevik Acland'; an odd remark to make about a former researcher at a right-wing think tank. Mrs Luckcraft, Miss Cryer and the secretaries struggled on. Faith, and a sense of humour, united them; two factors that even the best management consultancies tended to ignore.

In Rangoon in January 1982, Robert visited a beleaguered and brave Anglican community and was impressed by a question a Buddhist priest put to a teenager: 'What ethical effect does a belief in the after-life have on our actions?' In Hong Kong, he found a larger Anglican community. In Nanking, he celebrated Communion in private with Bishop Ding, leader of China's one million Protestants, and denounced the profiteers from the Bible-smuggling into the country which was rampant. In Sri Lanka, he witnessed the exotic hybrid Catholicism of the Church of Ceylon.

In London, Elizabeth Canham, an Englishwoman who had been ordained deaconess by the Bishop of Southwark, Mervyn Stockwood, and had gone to America and been ordained priest by Bishop John 'Jack' Spong of Newark, celebrated a clandestine Eucharist in St Paul's Deanery. This was at the invitation of the Dean, Alan Webster, whose wife was executive secretary of the Movement for the Ordination of Women. The action appalled the newly-enthroned Bishop of London, Graham Leonard.

Robert Runcie was closer to Graham Leonard than he was to Jack Spong, but he was no longer as beholden to the Orthodox Churches over the issue. He and Leonard subscribed to very different types of Anglo-Catholicism. The two men also had different personal styles. Although both had married dons' daughters, Priscilla Leonard was far more in the traditional image of a clergy wife, making church curtains, embroidering her husband's vestments and forming a congregation of one when her husband said Mass daily in his private oratory.

Leonard was the leader of conservative traditionalists in the Church of England, a label with which he was not always comfortable but which he did little to discourage. As well as the issue of the ordination of women, there were complicated questions involved of episcopal authority and diocesan jurisdiction between different members of the Anglican Communion.

Alan Webster was prepared to overlook these questions. So was Webster's supporter Jim Thompson, Robert's former chaplain at Cuddesdon and now 'Bishop Jim', the Suffragan Bishop of Stepney. Thompson, Like Mark Santer and Peter Cornwell, was a member of the Cell, the meetings of which occupied a sacred spot in Robert Runcie's diary. But Leonard was not prepared to overlook these questions, and raised them in defence of his own opposition to the ordination of women to the priesthood. He issued a statement criticising Elizabeth Canham's actions and sent copies of it to Bishop Spong and the Archbishop of Canterbury. Robert criticised Elizabeth Canham, but this was the habitual reaction of one who was better at calming things down than stirring them up.

At the first session of the General Synod in 1982 he announced details of the Pope's forthcoming visit to Britain. The focus of the visit would be a service at Canterbury.

This visit and in particular this service were events of momentous importance for British Roman Catholics and for the Church of England. Canterbury Cathedral had existed for nearly five hundred years before the Reformation. Nearly five hundred years after it, there could have been no better setting than the Cathedral for the symbolic and public affirmation of the commitment that had led to the private meeting between Robert Runcie and Karol Wojtyla in Accra two years earlier.

To Robert Runcie, a committed Anglican who liked to describe himself as a 'radical Catholic', there were profound connections between the future of the Church of England, the presence of the head of the Church of Rome and the past separation, out of which the Church of England had been so violently and traumatically born. No faction of the Church of England, evangelical or Anglo-Catholic, priest or would-be priest, could entirely avoid reference to the history of the English Catholic Church before and since the break with Rome in their defence of or opposition to any argument whatsoever. There was no important liturgical, doctrinal or social issue, be it the order of service, the use of vestments, marriage, divorce, remarriage, the ordination of women and the relationship between Church and State, that could be discussed without in some way taking into account the long heritage of the English Catholic Church.

But, if the Archbishop was a connoisseur of the beauties and a sophisticated practitioner of the complexities of English Catholicism, there were many who had not enjoyed the benefits of a subtle ecclesiastical schooling and had no desire to do so. Anglicanism had long been enshrined in what people liked to think of as the rich fabric of English life, and the Queen was at its head; a distrust of Popery was an ancient and equally potent thread.

In Edinburgh, the opposition of Pastor Jack Glass had been conducted within a civilised debate. At Walsingham, the anti-Popery protesters had been present in greater numbers, but were good-natured and even something of a joke. In Liverpool, however, the Archbishop was to have a less pleasant experience.

The occasion was the Lenten Service and address at St Nicholas's Parish Church at the Pier Head. This was the culmination of a two-day visit to the city, already made memorable for him by celebrating the Eucharist at St Faith's, where he had first come to the Church as a teenager forty-five years earlier.

But St Nicholas's offered a very different reception from that offered by Father Schofield and his incense to an impressionable adolescent whose father maintained a basically benevolent anti-clericism. Runcie, Chartres and Miles, the press officer, had to make their way into the church through a hostile crowd waving placards that read 'Rome Loves Runcie', 'Revive Reformation' and 'Not One Inch to Rome'. The congregation were loyal in the pews, but the aisles were packed with Liverpool Irish and Ulster Protestants demonstrating against the Pope's visit. They had already unfurled their banners, and the air was thick with obscenities and catcalls the moment he began to speak.

After only a few sentences he was forced to abandon his address and turned instead to the Bible. He began to read from the Beatitudes in St Matthew's Gospel. When he reached the words 'Blessed are they who are persecuted for righteousness' sake' a woman shouted 'That's us'. When he read 'for great is their reward in heaven', a voice said: 'You'll never make it.' 'Read your Bible,' another screamed. 'You are a traitor and a Judas.'

When he invited them to be silent, the demonstrators began to sing the anti-Roman Catholic hymn: 'Brave like Daniel, Dare to stand alone, Dare to see and believe the truth, Down with the Church of Rome.' He encouraged the rest of the congregation to sing another one, and the organist struck up 'City of God, How Broad and Far'. When he began the Lord's Prayer, the interruptions returned with renewed ferocity.

'All that I am concerned about,' he told them, 'is that this place should not be desecrated by disobedience to the Lord's will.'

He left the pulpit and, after praying at the altar, walked down the aisle, accompanied by abuse on one side and members of the congregation reaching out to shake his hand on the other.

The Protestant 'Loyalists' were exultant. The Mayoress of Liverpool was in tears. David Sheppard, the Bishop of Liverpool, suggested they say a prayer together in the vestry. The Archbishop was driven away at high speed, having answered just one question from one of the many reporters present.

'I am trying my best to find forgiveness for them,' he said, 'but it is very upsetting.'

On the train from Liverpool he felt sick and fell asleep. At Euston Chartres and Miles could not find the car and the three men took a taxi back to Lambeth. An hour later, he had to leave Lambeth for his next engagement. It was a lecture on Anglican-Roman Catholic relations.


The Pope's imminent visit also gave prominence that spring to the appearance of such abstruse publications as the Agreed Statement of the Anglican-Roman Catholic International Commission (ARCIC). This posited the Pope as 'universal primate' in any union of the two churches, hardly a surprising conclusion, and accompanied by so many qualifying clauses that it was received no more than politely at both Lambeth Palace and the Vatican. But the conclusion drawn by those who opposed the Papal visit and were prepared to desecrate churches if necessary, was that the ARCIC report was one more piece of evidence in the conspiracy against England and the Queen.

On 2 April the armed forces of Argentina, a large Catholic country, invaded one of Her Majesty's last and smallest imperial outposts. The Falkland Islands were also an extra-provincial diocese of the Anglican Communion under the episcopal jurisdiction of the Archbishop of Canterbury. A British Task Force sailed for the South Atlantic.

At Canterbury that Easter, the Archbishop said two prayers composed for the British servicemen and the people of the Falklands. He addressed a youth pilgrimage and received a deputation of fifteen hundred demonstrators against nuclear weapons. The assembled multitudes were friendly on this occasion but after Liverpool he was noticeably nervous in the presence of large unpoliced bodies of strangers. With the prospect of non-nuclear but nonetheless bloody high technology warfare breaking out in the South Atlantic, both he and the Pope were making soothing noises against the rising political hubbub.

While the Task Force steamed south, the Pope's aide and bodyguard Archbishop Paul Marcinkus travelled to Canterbury, where he proceeded to make a nuisance of himself over the Pope's security arrangements. The Archbishop of Canterbury flew out on a visit to another part of the Anglican Communion.

The Province of Nigeria had been formed by the division of the Province of West Africa three years earlier. This consisted of over thirty dioceses ranging from the urban development of Lagos to the more up-country areas of Benin, Egba-Egbado and the eighteen political divisions of the Rivers State.

At Jos, the headquarters of the area covered by Plateau, Benue and Gongola States, the Archbishop stood next to Bishop Timothy in front of yet another huge outdoor gathering. The Nigerian bishop had for some minutes been studying a large black cloud over the audience's heads. Suddenly he nudged the Archbishop sharply in the ribs, and hissed: 'Get your hands up!'

'What?'

'Get your hands up!'

The Archbishop was puzzled but did so; and at that moment the heavens opened. The Nigerian congregation, animists to a soul, burst into rapturous applause.

*

In the House of Lords he spoke of the need to remember international law as the basis of world peace. The first losses of shipping occurred in action in the South Atlantic. At Wesley's Chapel, as the first Archbishop of Canterbury publicly to take communion in a Methodist Church, he repeated the words of a prayer composed for the funeral of the dead of HMS *Sheffield* by a Task Force sailor.

The hostilities between Britain and Argentina now threatened to postpone or cancel the arrival of the Pope, although his visit was as likely to symbolise reconciliation as it was to cause further division. As casualties mounted, the point of view at Lambeth, and at the Cathedral of Westminster, and in thousands of Anglican and Roman Catholic households across the country, was that the visit should go ahead. On Thursday 27 May, after intensive shuttle diplomacy by Cardinal Hume and the Roman Catholic Archbishops of Glasgow and Liverpool, Pope John Paul II arrived in Britain. On Friday 28 May he met the Queen. On Saturday 29 May he flew by helicopter to Canterbury.

He landed at a recreation ground. The Archbishop welcomed him and the two men were driven in the Popemobile through the packed streets to the Cathedral. They were greeted by the Dean and Chapter, five Cardinals and the Prince of Wales. In spite of the doubts of English and Vatican security men the visitor insisted on walking around the crowded precincts of the Cathedral before going inside.

The congregation were already in place as the Pope and the Archbishop of Canterbury approached the West Door. As they entered the Cathedral the Pope looked nervous while the Archbishop was visibly delighted. The choir began a glorious anthem of which hardly a note was audible; the congregation burst into spontaneous applause, and many into tears. Ulster Unionists had demonstrated at the Cathedral only a week earlier. This was neither an Anglican nor an Anglican-Catholic service, but an ecumenical service in the first cathedral of the Church of England. The Pope had had little idea of how he would be received. But here were the descendants of Gregory and Augustine walking up the aisle together.

The order of the service had been written by the Archdeacon, John Simpson. The theme was recognition and reaffirmation of each other's baptism. The Pope had inspected an earlier draft and himself suggested the addition of a prayer from one of the Roman baptismal masses. For Runcie, Simpson, Hill, de Waal, Chartres and all those who had been involved in the planning, this was an extraordinary personal experience.

The Archbishop helped the Pope to his feet after they had knelt at the nave altar in prayer. They embraced amid further applause. 'I rejoice,' said Robert, 'that the sucessors of Gregory and Augustine stand here today in this great church. But our unity is not in the past only, but also in the future.'

Dean de Waal brought the Canterbury Gospels and held them for the Pope and Archbishop to kiss. The Pope spoke of the Anglican Communion 'whom I love and long for' and called the heterogeneous congregation to witness the commitment he and the Archbishop were making. The Archbishop in his address cited the suffering in the South Atlantic and in the Pope's own country of Poland. The bishops of the Church of England, the Primates of the Anglican Communion, the leaders of the Roman Catholic and Free Churches gathered around the altar while the choir sang the *Te Deum*. The Pope, the Archbishop, the African Cardinal Nsubuga and several others lit candles for the martyrs and prayed together at the stone in the north-west transept where Thomas Becket was martyred.

The Pope and the Archbishop blessed the congregation and left the Cathedral as they had arrived, together, but deep in conversation. The congregation were transfixed, as were several million viewers on television.

After the Pope and Archbishop had disappeared from view the congregation poured out of the cathedral in a state of high excitement. Among then were the former Archbishops, Coggan and Ramsey, both of whom had actively encouraged links between Lambeth and the Vatican. Ramsey had been instrumental in the diplomacy of the past few months and had visited the Pope at Castelgandolfo as he convalesced from a bullet in his stomach. 'I got nine kisses during the service!' Ramsey told a friend excitedly afterwards. 'Did you notice how many Bob Runcie got? He only got two!'

After lunch, the Archbishop was able to encourage the Pope to rest.

'In Canterbury, a Pope obeys,' the latter replied with a glint in his eye.

They had walked in the Cathedral Cloisters. The Pope had turned and taken Robert's hands in his own.

'Next time in Rome,' he said.

# 5

# 'The Boss Is Livid'

THE Pope's visit to Britain and the triumph of the Canterbury service made a deep impression on those who witnessed and participated in them. They also pushed the Archbishop of Canterbury to the forefront of public awareness as never before.

Robert Runcie was no different in one sense from Coggan, Ramsey and Fisher. All his predecessors had had to endure both the beginning and the ending of the honeymoon with the public. There was no doubt, either, that the medium of that public awareness was the popular press. By comparison with the fates of earlier Archbishops such as Cranmer and Laud, who were executed, and Sancroft, who was exiled, Fisher, Ramsey and Coggan had escaped lightly.

But in June 1982 the Pope had barely departed when the Falklands War ended, and with it the overt need for reconciliation affirmed by his presence. The most widely read newspapers in Britain now vied with each other in an orgy of triumphalism. In spite of continuous campaigns in the imperial twilight in Malaya, Suez and Borneo in the 1950s and 1960s, and the bloody mess in Ulster since then, Britain had not experienced an armed conflict of such emotive power since the Second World War.

Robert Runcie, Ross Hook, Simon Phipps, Hugh Montefiore, Peter Walker, Edward Knapp-Fisher, Tony Tremlett, Hector Laing and many of their generation inside and outside the Church of England had served and in some cases fought in that war. They knew that a person who had heard a shot fired in anger could never call war glorious. Their religious beliefs and social values had to varying degrees been forged by the experience. The vast majority of readers of the *Sun* newspaper – and certain persons close to the Prime Minister, or wishing to been seen to be close to her – had not.

The service of thanksgiving for the end of the Falklands War was to be held in St Paul's Cathedral on Monday 26 July, 1982. The Royal Family, one member of which had spent the Falklands War on active service, the Prime Minister, senior representatives of the Opposition and other political parties, leaders of many different Churches, members of the armed forces and members of families of the British dead, were to be present.

As had been the case with his own enthronement, with the Royal Wedding and with the service with the Pope at Canterbury, the Archbishop was to take part in a widely-reported event of great public interest. The order of this service was to be ecumenical and was supervised in this case by the Dean of St Paul's, Alan Webster. Webster had already been at odds over the issue of the ordination of women to the priesthood with the Bishop of London, Graham Leonard.

The ecumenical and political nature of the service provoked a modest amount of clerical anxiety. Cardinal Hume of Westminster and Dr Kenneth Greet, Moderator of the Free Church Council, were only willing to participate on condition that the service was not triumphalist in content. There was objection on the same grounds to the idea of the Prime Minister reading a lesson from the scriptures. By the same token, it was also agreed that there was to be no weighting in favour of the armed services among the principal participants.

The Prime Minister ranked below the Archbishop of Canterbury in the official hierarchy of public life, but was consulted about the order of the service. She expressed dismay at the suggestion that the Lord's Prayer should be recited in Spanish as well as English, and that the Pope's recent sermon about nuclear weapons preached in Coventry should be included. Both suggestions were dropped in deference to her wishes.

One Conservative backbencher, Sir John Biggs-Davison, a wartime Marine Commando, right-winger and Roman Catholic, objected to the order of service in advance so much that he declined to attend and communicated his decision to the *Daily Telegraph*. Neither the Prime Minister nor anybody else in government had advance sight of the sermon to be preached by the Archbishop of Canterbury.

The Archbishop and the Prime Minister had enjoyed cordial relations since they had met in Sir Hector Laing's London flat nearly three years earlier. They had also continued to have as little in common with each other as they had when they first met at the Oxford University Conservative Association thirty years before.

There was no evidence that either disliked the fact of the other's position. There was no evidence that the temperamental, intellectual and social differences between them had either widened or narrowed or would do so as the years went by. There was no evidence to suppose that this mattered at all to the Archbishop, and any more than slightly to the Prime Minister. There was evidence, however, observed by Sir Hector Laing and others, that by July 1982 the Prime Minister's Churchillian public bravado had worn rather thin and that she could no longer conceal a sense of personal trauma at the scale of the British losses.

Amidst these private events and during a mood of national uncertainty over whether to mourn or be triumphant, the man whose duty many regarded as being to tell the nation what to think in these matters set to work on his sermon with his aides at Lambeth. Robert Runcie, Richard Chartres, Andrew Acland, probably Eric James, possibly his colleagues in the Cell such as Jim Thompson, Peter Cornwell and Mark Santer, would all have to greater or lesser degrees been influential in its making. There would have been no question that the final word was that of the Archbishop.

As more than one onlooker noted, the note and tone of the organ set the mood of the service from the start.

In a minor key, and clouded as if by painful memories, the organ accompanied the procession of the Archbishop and clergy into the packed Cathedral. The Dean, Alan Webster, said the Bidding Prayer. 'We thank God,' he declared, 'for the cessation of hostilities, for the courage of those who took part and for the safe return of so many.'

Prayers were said for the wounded by the Moderator of the General Assembly of the Church of Scotland. Cardinal Hume said prayers for the bereaved and the dead. The Moderator of the Council of Free Churches said prayers for reconciliation and peace. A sailor, a soldier and an airman introduced the hymns with short verses from the Bible. These were 'Praise My Soul the King of Heaven', 'All my Hope in

God is Founded', the Scottish version of Psalm 23 and the National Anthem.

The Archbishop entered the pulpit to speak.

'The first note in this service,' he said, 'is thanksgiving. We begin with particular thanksgiving for the courage and endurance of those who fought in the South Atlantic, and that is also the starting point for my sermon.

'What I have heard about the conduct of the British forces in and around the Falkland Islands has moved and heartened me. I have experienced battle myself . . .'

*That spring the battalion had driven east through Munster and then turned north-east towards the Baltic. In May, while they were on the Baltic coast, Colonel Dunbar informed him that he had been awarded the Military Cross.*

*In the officers' mess they chaffed him, and nicknamed him 'Killer' . . .*

'While giving thanks, however, we also mourn for grievous losses. Thank God so many returned, but there are many in this cathedral who mourn the loss of someone they love, and our hearts go out to them.

'They remind us that we possess a terrifying power for destruction. War has always been detestable, but since 1945 we have lived with the capacity to destroy the whole of mankind. It is impossible to be a Christian and not to long for peace.'

*They were standing by their tanks when the first airburst struck. A piece of shrapnel the size of a dinner plate missed them by inches. Robert dived into his tank.*

*Alldred tugged at his legs and his troop commander re-emerged:*

*'I thought you were dead,' Robert said.*

*'I couldn't get in,' said Alldred, 'because of your bloody great feet.'*

*Then they made for the barn.*

'"Blessed are the peace-makers for they shall be called the Sons of God." This is one of the themes to which the Pope repeatedly returned during his visit to this country. His speech at Coventry was particularly memorable, when he said: "War should belong to the tragic past, to history. It should find no place on humanity's agenda for the future."

'I do not believe that there would be many people, if any, who would not say amen to that. War is a sign of human failure and everything we say and do in this service must be in that context.'

*Alldred went through the door of the darkened barn and started striking matches. He went down the stone steps. There were several big rooms. In the first room there were about thirty Germans.*

*'Kamerad, kamerad!' they said. All he had was matches.*

*Robert came down the steps behind him with his torch.*

*'Have you got your pistol?' said Alldred.*

*'No. What do I need a pistol for?'*

*'It's lousy with Germans down here.'*

*'Oh,' he said, 'will you be all right?'*

*'Yes,' said Alldred wearily, 'I've got my matches . . .'*

*Robert went away and came back with his revolver. The Germans were standing and sitting on the straw. In the next room was their kit. There were two or three officers, a Feldwebel and assorted other ranks.*

*'Oh, my God,' he said.*

*Under the straw there were rifles and other assorted small arms.*

*'What are we going to do?' he asked Alldred.*

*'We're going to chase their arses out of here,' his troop sergeant told him, 'this is our bed for the night. Right, raus!' he yelled at them.*

*Alldred gave his troop commander two German pistols and kept one for himself. The men used to sell them to the Americans.*

*Robert went back up the steps and summoned the others. The German packs contained luxuries they had bought in Paris. Some of the men went on looting until two or three o'clock the next morning.*

'Even in the failure of war there are springs of hope. In that great war play by Shakespeare, Henry V says: *"There is some soul of goodness in things evil, would men observingly distil it out."* People are mourning on both sides of this conflict. In our prayers we shall quite rightly remember those who are bereaved in our own country and the relations of the young Argentinian soldiers who were killed. Common sorrow could do something to reunite those who were engaged in this struggle. A shared anguish can be a bridge of reconciliation. Our neighbours are indeed like us.'

*When they were down in the cellar of the barn Robert had shone his torch, back and forth, back and forth, over the German soldiers.*

*Alldred had looked at him.*

*'Your top lip's quivering, sir,' he said.*

*'Yes,' he said, 'I can't stop it.'*

'Cathedrals and churches are always places into which we bring our human experiences – birth, marriage, death, our flickering communion with God, our fragile relationships with each other, so that we may be deepened and directed by the spirit of Christ.

'Today we bring our mixture of thanksgiving, sorrows and aspiration for a better ordering of the world.

'Pray God that he may purify, enlarge and redirect these in the ways of His kingdom of love and peace. Amen.'

*The next morning it was a beautiful day. The medical staff came and sewed up the dead in body bags.*

The Prime Minister thanked him at the end of the service. Shortly afterwards, Denis Thatcher had a relaxing lunch on the terrace of the Palace of Westminster.

In a moment of jocularity and in a phrase he often used of her in the company of like-minded souls among the Tory back-benchers, he referred to the form of the service and the objections that had preceded it:

'The boss was livid,' he said.

This was music to certain ears.

The next morning the following version of events appeared on the front page of the *Daily Telegraph*:

### DR RUNCIE ANGERS TORIES
*St Paul's peace sermon resented*
*Falklands service 'failed to honour armed forces'*

*The Prime Minister was privately unhappy and senior Conservative MPs were openly critical last night of the Falklands Islands service in St Paul's Cathedral . . .*

*'Mr Edward Du Cann, MP for Taunton and Chairman of the Tory*

*backbench 1922 Committee, said he would be writing a letter of complaint to Dr Runcie . . .*

*'Mr Du Cann added: "I was sad and disappointed that there was no mention during the service that the Falklands crisis was an example of Britain standing alone for international law, freedom and democracy . . ."*

*'Mr Julian Amery, Tory MP for Brighton Pavilion and a former Minister, said: "I was very shocked by the Order of Service. There were no martial hymns like 'Fight the Good Fight' and 'Onward Christian Soldiers'". . .*

*'I thought it was a deliberate counter-attack against the mass of opinion in this country on the part of the pacifist, liberal wet establishment who were shocked when we went to war and more shocked when we won . . .*

*'A campaign which, according to Christian theology, could not have been more just . . .*

*'Revolting . . .*

*'Cringing clergy . . .*

*'The sacrifices of our fighting men . . .'*

The following day the *Daily Telegraph*'s downmarket equivalent, the *Sun*, launched an even more bizarre attack:

### WAR HERO WHO HATES WAR
Sun *profile on Archbishop in row over Falklands*

*'ARCHBISHOP Robert Runcie is the war hero who hates war.*

*He won the Military Cross in 1945, when he was was only 24 . . .*

*So what turned this daring soldier into the man who made the Falklands Remembrance Service at St Paul's an apology for victory?*

*How did Dr Runcie, the Archbishop of Canterbury, so sadly misjudge the mood of the nation over the war dead?*

*Basically, he fell under the spell of fashionable liberal intellectuals after the war . . . and has never shaken off their influence.*

*At first Dr Runcie, the son of a working-class Scottish engineer, rejoiced in his richly-deserved military success . . .*

*After Dr Runcie took a degree at Oxford he studied theology at Cambridge.*

*The only time he came face to face with his working-class background was as a curate in the early 1950s on industrial Tyneside.*

*There he pulled in the crowds and mesmerised local congregations.*

*But he was drawn back to Cambridge like a magnet – to teach theology.*

### TASTES

*After marrying the daughter of another don at Trinity Hall, he began to acquire the kind of tastes which later made a good wine cellar a must.*

*He continued to listen to his friends who felt nothing could be done about Britain's decline. Many thought we were just a second-class nation.*

*Dr Runcie, now 61, became Archbishop in 1980.*

*He is now best known for his diplomacy and his contribution to the first visit of a Pope to Britain.*

*But maybe it is time to read the Bible again.*

*The New Testament makes it plain that Christianity is a battle against the kind of evil perpetrated by ex-President Galtieri.*

*That the very things which make a nation great – the belief in freedom – need at times to be fought for.*

### NOVELS

*Perhaps the brave young officer has become the kind of Christian soldier best left at home in the barracks.*

*To do what he likes best – read novels and feed his pigs.'*

After the Pope's visit, the letters of congratulation and support had poured in to Lambeth Palace. One or two others were addressed to 'Traitor Runcie' but the Post Office prided itself on delivering all the mail. One item even contained thirty little halfpenny pieces wrapped in silver foil.

After the Falklands Service, 99 per cent of the thousands of letters received were similarly in favour. Dozens were from past and serving members of the armed forces. Others in support were from the parents of sons who had been killed.

There were letters of support from men who had been severely injured in the campaign. More than one senior serving officer wrote in support of the Falklands Service to say that he personally had attended funerals of both British and Argentine dead. Again, there were only a few letters addressed to 'Traitor Runcie'; unsigned, of course, and revealing the kind of moral cowardice of which they were accusing him.

The Archbishop was reassured by the letters of support and sanguine about the press coverage. He knew a more triumphalist march past in salute of the Task Force had been arranged for that October. He knew that twenty times as many people read the *Sun* every day as went to church once a week. He knew too that, in spite of the *Daily Telegraph*'s insinuations to the contrary, the Church of England was not, and as far as he was concerned never should be, the Tory Party at prayer; or any other party, for that matter.

But he was hurt by the letters from the lunatic fringe. In spite of his willingness in public to speak his own mind (and that of other people, if it happened to coincide with his own), in private and in personal encounters he always wanted to please people.

He would materialise, a thin lanky figure, during organised tours of the Palace and gardens at Lambeth. The Archbishop would invariably be in a hurry and on his way somewhere else. In his mind would be the question of how he could make his getaway without giving offence to the group of visitors. But he would always approach them first:

'Toronto? Ah,' on being informed of where they had come from, he would speak with the authentic voice of 'the man from everywhere', 'I was in Canada two years ago, and I went to Toronto, to your fine civic offices, and on the third floor . . .'

He would take their hands for a moment, and look into their eyes, and smile. Then he would be gone. The entire process took a matter of seconds. They would remember it for longer.

'Oh,' they would turn to each other, 'Oh . . .'

As the pressure mounted, he found it increasingly difficult to say no.

'You'll kill yourself,' Ross Hook would tell him.

'I want to do it,' he would say, and he would accept yet another request for a public appearance, an *ex officio* presidency, a visitorship or honorary membership of a body to which he had been asked to lend his name and authority.

He had few friends, and no apparent decompression chamber between his private prayer life as a priest and his demanding public persona. He seemed to have shed any unlikely acquaintances of the kind that most people accumulate and carry with them through life, and whom they re-encounter from time to time. He was a regular attender at 'Nobody's Friends', the strange Lambeth dining club.

The growing pressure of work touched on and reinforced these aspects of his character. He remained as charming to strangers, as committed a workaholic, as able a speaker, as charismatic in person as ever. But he was beginning to learn now to survive as the 102nd Archbishop of Canterbury in spite of his fundamental uncertainty about his ability always to do the right things.

In the same way that he was unable to say no to people, and was constitutionally able to bear the burdens he placed on himself as a result, so he was not always able to give credit either to himself or to the few close aides on whom he relied to see his commitments carried out. He appeared not to need the occasional word of appreciation, perhaps because he thought he did not deserve it. They thought he did, and could not always understand why he appeared unable to offer the occasional word of encouragement to them in return.

This aloneness, this need of the priest in him to be alone, this humility bordering on painful self-knowledge, was only properly comprehensible to the ordained members of his staff and was central to his dependence on the Cell. For years they had been inspired by his deep faith and regaled by his hilarious anecdotes. He had been revived and sustained by the spiritual energy of this diverse and far from homogeneous group.

Although the Cuddesdon connection was dominant, there was no conformity of ideas or deference to his membership. Jim Thompson, the 'Mayor of the East End' and Bishop of Stepney, held more radical political views than either Mrs Thatcher or Robert Runcie. Mark Santer, then Suffragan Bishop of Kensington, was if anything more of a radical than Thompson, a fact of which the Prime Minister seemed unaware when she chose him over Thompson as Bishop of Birmingham. Peter Cornwell was Rector of the University Church of St Mary the Virgin, Oxford. Two years later he would cause a sensation by announcing from the pulpit there his intention to become a Roman Catholic and leave the Church of England.

These were the key if barely visible figures in the spiritual life of the Archbishop of Canterbury who had been brought to greater public prominence by the summer of 1982. The next, more visible layer of his circle consisted of his closest personal staff. A separate but pervasive influence was his family.

James was away working and Rebecca was at university. Lindy was often left alone with her friends. As she began her own rise to greater public prominence, some of these proved a mixed blessing:

'Clergy wives are people, too,' read her latest article in *The Times*. She briskly debunked the dated but enduring image of the clergy wife as doormat, divine inspiration and general purpose do-gooder:

*At the age of eight, my daughter failed a scripture exam because she could not draw nomads. As I taught music at the same school I had to apologise to the teacher for this terrible crime because she was more upset than my daughter. I am sure there would not have been a fuss if her father had not been a bishop.*

*When my son worked in a factory in the holidays, the first words that greeted him were:*

*'How about a quick Communion service?' His reply: '1662 or ASB?' floored them.*

*So next time you meet one of us, do us a favour and treat us as individuals in our own right, will you?*

Unfortunately, as well as standing up for clergy wives in *The Times*, Lindy also decided to lie down for them in the tabloid press. Supine on top of her grand piano in a bright red evening dress, she stared mistily up into the camera. 'Oh dear' was the first reaction of John Miles, the head of information at Church House, but who had known nothing of the photographic session, 'that looks like the Bechstein in the Drawing Room.'

Other photographs showed Lindy leaping over a tennis net and posing dreamily on the roof of Lambeth Palace wearing a one-piece swimsuit. They were printed in part in *Private Eye* and in *Hola!*, a Spanish magazine, before being made available, with a more restrained text, to several million readers of *Sunday* magazine.

If it was impossible to imagine Lady Coggan or Lady Ramsey posing in this manner, it was difficult for most people to imagine why Lindy should have done so either:

*Meet the incredible Rosalind Runcie*

blared the headline:

*'I'm more than just the Archbishop's wife'*

and, in case the photograph of the incredible Rosalind had not yet sunk in, the biggest headline of all declared:

## *THE LADY LOVES TO PLAY*

The coy double entendre and accompanying photograph gave if anything an impression of innocence rather than eroticism. Robert had long indulged Lindy in the mercurial side of her character. But the effect of these and other such articles was to plant a series of images in the public mind.

These showed the Archbishop as a bleating clergyman and hapless husband, rather than Christian soldier and master in his own house. They showed the Archbishop as victim of two powerful women, of a wife who wandered scantily clad around Lambeth Palace and a wrathful Prime Minister at Downing Street. They showed him as victim of the thugs who shouted him down in a church in Liverpool; victim of a clique of unpatriotic left-wing intellectuals who manipulated him as their puppet; victim of a charismatic and untrustworthy Pope. None of these images was true; all were mirages; but all were potent inspiration for further stories.

Neither Lindy nor Robert Runcie, with all his experience of the media, seemed to have understood a fundamental truth about the popular press. There was an inexorability about them, whereby they required an ever greater degree of exposure of their subjects. A mixture of goodwill and perhaps a hint of vanity could lead those subjects to further exposure, but of their weaknesses, and a diminished recognition of their actual worth.

Thus it was that these false images became holy writ in certain quarters of the popular press, which themselves closely reflected the contempt for liberalism and the crude ethos of 'them and us' of the Thatcher government. By these criteria and in those quarters, the facts that Lindy had already raised £60,000 for charity, that her engagements included piano recitals in aid of the blind, disabled and women's refuges, and that Robert would set up a major commission to examine the problems of urban life in Britain, were not and would not be considered worthy of note. The Archbishop's 'wet' public image – and that of his wayward wife – were declared dogma in certain quarters of Westminster and Fleet Street.


On becoming Archbishop Robert had resigned the Anglican Chairmanship of the Anglican-Orthodox Joint Doctrinal Commission. But in his present role he maintained a close friendship with the various patriarchs who under the late Archbishop Athenagoras had driven him to delight and despair in equal measure. In the autumn of 1982, a few weeks after his and Lindy's twenty-fifth wedding anniversary, he travelled to Romania as guest of the Orthodox Church.

The ordination of women to the priesthood, the issue on which he continued to be cautious and over which Anglican-Orthodox relations had been strained to breaking point, was uppermost in debates at the General Synod's third session that November 1982. Among the speakers was the Fellow of New College and respected church historian, Dr Gareth Bennett. Bennett in no way conformed to Richard Chartres' image of 'the dull echo of a liberal consensus'.

Bennett was opposed to the ordination of women by both religious disposition and personal temperament. He had resigned as New College Chaplain to make way for a younger man but remained as History Tutor. Among his own students were small but growing numbers of women. Bennett's arrival for a tutorial would invariably begin with his casting his gaze over the assembled participants including a female undergraduate, and commencing proceedings with a pointed 'Good morning, gentlemen'.

In Synod that November, he argued strongly for a conservative reassessment of the diaconate. The Synod, he warned, had 'a way of formulating changes before working out theologically or pastorally what those changes ought to be'.

Like Robert Runcie, whom he had known for thirty years. Gareth Bennett was an able speaker and academic with a deep affiliation to the English Catholic tradition. Unlike Robert Runcie, he was the representative of an increasingly introverted and marginalised body within the Church.

But the public statements of the Archbishop, and of the Church of

England, were not circumscribed by the complex and often legalistic procedures of the General Synod. This was a blessing. He could use statements he made outside Synod to draw public attention to important issues.

A Church of England working party report advocating unilateral nuclear disarmament had already been leaked to the press. The Archbishop had taken a characteristic stance. He promoted consideration of the issue as being of major importance. He welcomed the report as a useful working document. He reserved the right to his own opinion in the matter.

The distinctions here were by no means fine, but they were nonetheless beyond the comprehension of the popular press:

*The Pulpit and the Bomb*
*Dr Runcie in storm after*
*sermon backs Greenham protest*

To the popular press, whose cuttings libraries contained the facts that he was a decorated former serving officer who had spoken out against unilateralism in Synod in November 1981 and acknowledged the role of the armed forces in the Falklands, the Archbishop's 1982 Christmas Day sermon in Canterbury Cathedral contained a contradiction. This was in his declaration of respect for the ideals of the women of Greenham Common, and his commitment to multilateral rather than unilateral nuclear disarmament. It was impossible for them to accommodate the two points of view.

This was perhaps expecting too much of the press, but it was a sad reflection on a Tory back-bencher such as Julian Amery, who charged over the top in the same way as others had done after Robert's Falklands sermon a few months earlier. Amery's statement ignored what the Archbishop had actually said, and revealed a lamentable degree of trust in the *Daily Express*:

'Everybody wants disarmament,' the former Parliamentary Under Secretary of State for the Colonial Office told them, 'but to do it unilaterally is an open invitation to be taken over.

'Peace on earth and goodwill to all is a fine sentiment – but to go from there to unilateral disarmament is very dangerous ground for someone who is not conversant with strategy.

'Perhaps he should talk to Mrs Thatcher and Mr Nott before he takes up these issues.'

Meanwhile, the debate rumbled on.

In January at Chatham House, the Archbishop addressed the Royal Institute of International Affairs on the theme of 'Just and Unjust Wars'. He continued to reject the naïveté of the unilateralist posture. Until relations improved between Eastern and Western Europe, he acknowledged the role of nuclear deterrence as an unpleasant reality.

'I do not like talking about nuclear weapons as morally acceptable,' he said, 'on the other hand, I do recognise that we are in a situation where, in order to get from where we are to where we want to be, we have to recognise both the possession of nuclear weapons and the stability that may be maintained by the nuclear deterrent.

'Once the doctrine of deterrence has broken down, we are in a different world. I cannot see myself if I were ever asked to advise a government, giving advice of a return nuclear exchange.

'I am convinced that full-scale nuclear war cannot possibly qualify as a just war.'

He rejected the Cold War doctrine which presented the Soviet Union as a coherent and threatening entity, capable of inflicting more damage on others than on itself:

'When disarmament initiatives are produced by whatever government, it is frightening to hear the immediate dismissive responses. It is becoming incredible to write off every Soviet suggestion as a propaganda ploy.

'To do so underestimates the extent to which everyone has an interest in seeing the present questions relaxed.'

In this context he was prepared to applaud *The Church and the Bomb*, the report produced by the Church of England working party chaired by the Bishop of Salisbury, John Baker.

*The Church and the Bomb* was debated at the first session of the 1983 General Synod. Hugh Montefiore had his own brilliantly reasoned and probably unworkable version of Christian deterrence. The outgoing Chairman of the Board of Social Responsibility, Bishop Leonard of London, was in full cry.

'Nuclear weapons,' he told Synod, 'have introduced a new dimension into nuclear relations. The principles underlying the Just War are not altered, however . . .

'As a Christian, I believe that negotiating disarmament from a balance of power is the best way of preserving peace, because that process is based on valuing human life above mere survival.'

The Prime Minister, as Clifford Longley pointed out in *The Times*, was a long way out of touch with the predominant mood of institutional Christianity in Britain:

*'That mood,'* Longley went on, *'exists equally in the other major denominations, and is not peculiar to British Christianity, either. It is a deep movement, an almost universal desire to purify Christianity of its corrupting relationship with political power . . .*

*'The Church of England is part of this world-wide inter-denominational phenomenon, and did not invent it, neither does it lead it. But it knows that the Roman Catholic bishops of the United States have made a serious challenge to the nuclear policies of the Reagan administration, for instance, which, with countless lesser examples, shows the trend.*

*'Abuse from certain right-wing Conservative MPs is far more likely to harden the General Synod's determination than to weaken it. And in this mood, politicians are not likely to be hailed as arbiters of national morality.'*

As an arbiter of national morality, the Prime Minister probably did not even regard herself as a mere politician. Certainly she no longer regarded Graham Leonard as a mere bishop. Henceforth she reserved the right, wholeheartedly and without prior consultation, to misunderstand and misappropriate his views. With the Bishop of London 'on her side', the challenge the Prime Minister would be perceived as making to the Runcie 'administration' would be more serious than that which the Roman Catholic bishops had made to Ronald Reagan.

The departure took place of Inez Luckcraft after over a decade at St Albans and Lambeth.

Mrs Luckcraft had survived three years of processing paper without help from the Church Commissioners in the form of an assistant. She had seen others take on the responsibility in the archiepiscopate she had once enjoyed in the diocese. She had lost her close personal relationship with the Archbishop, but retained her respect for him. She was succeeded as his Private Secretary by Anne Shirwill, who had experience of industry and managed to make her mark in spite of the fact that there was no effective training for her in her new capacity.

The Archbishop marked the departure of Mrs Luckcraft with a party for her in the Guard Room and made a warm and witty speech. It was now forty years since the day when, as a young Second Lieutenant in the Third Battalion Scots Guards, he had dropped a heavy tank part on his toe. The injury had long ceased to hurt, but he was compelled every three years or so to attend hospital for the removal of an ingrowing toenail. He spent most of the party seated and resting his foot.

Deaconess Luckcraft had been ordained under the St Albans Ministerial Training Scheme and went to the parishes of Preston with Sutton Poyntz and Osmington with Poxwell in the diocese of Salisbury. There she flourished in her ministry and remarried.

She was a loyal and discreet guardian of the Archbishop's reputation. In this last capacity she would be put to the test on at least one occasion. This was the result of the activities of another woman busy making a niche for herself at Lambeth, with whom Inez Luckcraft, Mary Cryer and Lindy were all familiar; and who would display no such scruples about trying to market her own less loyal version of life there.


The Archbishop went as usual to Canterbury for Easter and preached his sermon in his Cathedral. His theme was the Resurrection, and the folly of regimes such as those in Eastern Europe which propounded the notion that God could be replaced by Man.

'Tragically, man's progress towards god-like management of his fellows and of nature itself has in our own day culminated in the unleashing of seemingly unmanageable forces,' he said, recalling his statements on nuclear weapons.

But he conspicuously avoided giving the Eastern Bloc what certain Conservative MPs would have regarded as the benefit of the doubt.

'The tragedy,' he went on, 'can also be seen in the capacity of totalitarian states to subject their citizens to previously undreamed of manipulation and social engineering.'

Yet repression led not to godlessness, but to faith: 'The reality of the Resurrection has blazed up in the darkness created by the lie that man is a god, with no dependence upon the will and word of the Creator.'

He travelled to Hawaii, to meet clergy and laity of the Episcopal Church; to New Zealand, to commemorate Anzac Day with the Anglican Church; and to Vauxhall, and to a polling station. The 1983 British General Election was taking place, and R. A. K. Runcie of Lambeth Palace on the electoral register wanted to vote.

This last action provoked a certain amount of speculation about the nature and legitimacy of his vote. While there was little doubt that the local Social Democratic candidate was the recipient, there was uncertainty over whether or not as Archbishop of Canterbury he should have voted at all.

There was much legal argument in the matter. Peers of the realm were debarred from voting because they had their own assembly. Bishops, however, were not peers of the realm, but 'lords spiritual of Parliament', and it was argued therefore that they could vote in the same way as everyone else. The Archbishop had already voted as Bishop of St Albans. However, after discussion with the Archbishop of York and the other bishops who sat in the House of Lords, he agreed that they would all refrain from voting in this way in future.

He also travelled to Cambridge, to visit a fellow bishop whom he had known for many years and whom he knew he would not see there again.

John Robinson remained faithful to his principles to the end:

'Alas,' he wrote in his diary, 'my absence from voting would have made no difference at all . . . The most appalling revelation of the Election is the total unfairness of the electoral system. However . . . I am delighted that Jack Straw [the Labour candidate] got in at Blackburn with an increased majority.'

He was only sixty-four, two years older than Robert, and close to death from inoperable cancer. But he enjoyed repeating to him the words of Bishop Lakshman Wickremesinghe, who had visited him recently: 'Robert Runcie has the gift of saying the right thing at the right time: I shall be even more impressed when he says the right thing at the wrong time.'

Robinson died as he had lived, honestly, selflessly and with great moral courage. As Dean of Clare, Bishop of Woolwich and Dean of Trinity, his path had frequently crossed Robert's although they were very different men and prime examples of the extraordinary diversity of the Church of England. As author of *Honest to God* he had influenced generations of Robert's Cuddesdon ordinands. Eric James, Robert's close friend and adviser, was also close to Robinson and would write his biography. James, Ruth Robinson and Robert later discussed establishing a permanent place for Robinson's books and papers at Lambeth.

Eric James had had the idea of persuading a group of like-minded bishops who met informally to discuss and compare the problems of their urban dioceses, to turn themselves into an official commission with the blessing of the Archbishop of Canterbury. James had little trouble in persuading either them or the Archbishop to agree.

The commission was chaired by Sir Richard O'Brien, who had chaired the new Crown Appointments Commission which had selected Robert as Archbishop of Canterbury. Among the members were Jim Thompson of Stepney, Hugh Montefiore of Birmingham, David Sheppard of Liverpool, Stanley Booth-Clibborn of Manchester, David Young of Ripon, Kenneth Skelton and his successor Keith Sutton of Lichfield, David Lunn of Sheffield, Tom Butler of Willesden and Ronald Bowlby of Southwark.

The result was the establishment of the Archbishop of Canterbury's Commission on Urban Priority Areas. Their findings would take two years to conduct and compile, and constitute a landmark in the work of the Church in England in the 1980s. The report would bring controversy and criticism to those who researched and compiled it; and above all to the Archbishop in whose name it was published. They would call it *Faith In the City*.

As Bishop of St Albans he had welcomed the remote prospect of the disestablishment of the Church of England from the State. As Archbishop of Canterbury he had preached against men who would behave as gods over their fellow men. In lending his name to the Commission on Urban Priority Areas he had reasserted the Church of England's right to remain active on the moral, social and economic ground that was being invaded by a re-elected Conservative government. In the second session of that year's General Synod, he allowed a debate on a motion opposing the reintroduction of another traditional right of the State, namely capital punishment in Britain.

The motion was moved by Brother Michael, the Suffragan Bishop of St Germans, Cornwall. Robert Runcie, Graham Leonard and John Habgood, shortly to succeed Stuart Blanch as Archbishop of York, all spoke against the reintroduction of the death penalty and in favour of the motion.

'If I really believed,' the Archbishop told Synod, 'that the restoration of the death penalty would give added protection to our policemen and to those who are especially vulnerable, then I might take a very different attitude to this question.

'I certainly do not hold the pacifist position that it is wrong to take life in all circumstances.

'But, having studied evidence of commissions of inquiries over the past few years, I am forced to agree with the conclusion that appears in the excellent British Council of Churches statement that "there is substantial doubt that capital punishment has any significant deterrent effect".'

Even terrorists, he said, faced the possibility of death in a clash with security forces, and this did 'not seem to deter them from their barbarous strategy'.

The General Synod overwhelmingly agreed with him and voted in favour of the motion by 407 to 36 with ten abstentions.

The next day in Parliament, MPs also voted against the reintroduction of the death penalty, albeit by a less substantial majority.


On 14 July 1833, John Keble had given his celebrated Assize sermon in Oxford at the University Church of St Mary the Virgin, denouncing the 'National Apostasy' practised by the government and reclaiming the Church of England's Catholic tradition. In Oxford, on 16 July 1983, the Archbishop preached at a Pilgrimage Eucharist Service in the University Park to mark the 150th anniversary of the Oxford Movement. In Manchester, two days earlier, the preacher in Manchester Cathedral on the same subject was Dr Gareth Bennett.

Bennett was an Oxford don and an Oxford Movement man. He was a governor of Pusey House and close friend of its Principal, Philip Ursell. His former Assistant Chaplain at New College, Geoffrey

Rowell, was now Chaplain of Keble College. Rowell had been among Robert Runcie's last Cuddesdon ordinands.

Bennett was a central figure to Ursell, Rowell and the Librarian of Pusey House, Dr William Oddie. His sermon was an eloquent hymn to the Oxford Movement of Keble, Newman and Pusey, and an apologia for the relevance of the contemporary Oxford Catholic tradition:

'The Church of God has an extraordinary power to renew itself. Just when it seems that all vision has failed, the springs of spirituality have run dry and mission has ceased, then there is a sudden surge of new life and expectancy. Certainly in 1833 the Church of England seemed almost dead . . .

'Nothing can diminish Keble's spiritual stature,' Bennett continued, 'He was academically brilliant yet a man of deep humility, simplicity of heart and transparent goodness. He had no greater ambition than to be a parish priest, and the greater part of his ministry was to be spent at Hursley, near Winchester. What was perhaps characteristic of him was that he was a poet, and in his poet's way he could look at the Church and see through all its dullness, cynicism, careerism and lack of real faith, to what was within, to what it could be; he could understand what riches of prayer and worship and overflowing grace it had in store, if only he could bring them out of its treasury . . .'

At first, Bennett declared, Keble's sermon seemed primarily to be an attack on the Whig government of the day.

'But as you read on,' he said, 'you see that it is more than that. He is asking a critical question: "What is the real nature of the Church? In what does its very being consist: its inner glory, freshness and power? What makes it different from being part of the English constitution, or a historical museum, or an agency for social welfare or the agitation of moral causes?" Keble's answer was clear. The Church had one end: to make Christ, the Crucified and Risen Lord, known . . .'

Given the knowledge that catastrophe was to engulf Bennett and threaten both the heterogeneity of the Church and the integrity of the Archbishop, it is perhaps worth comparing what both men said on the same subject and on more or less the same day.

In the two sermons there were profound spiritual similarities and differences only of emphasis and circumstance. Bennett's was written and preached in Manchester by an Oxford man about a movement to which he had a deep devotion. Runcie's was written by himself and most likely by Richard Chartres, and preached in Oxford by a self-styled 'radical Catholic' who as Archbishop of Canterbury was concerned to place the Oxford Movement in the context of a broader Church.

The Archbishop started lightly, but he too soon paid tribute to Keble's vision of the Catholic Church of England; and in language similar to that of Bennett:

'That great disciple of the Oxford Movement, William Gladstone, recalled travelling as a young man on the outside of a stage coach where he overheard a snatch of conversation between two of his fellow travellers: "Well," said one, "what is the Church of England?" "The Church of England," said the other, "is a damn big building with an organ inside." When Keble and his friends had done their work, such a utilitarian definition was not possible . . .

'Keble himself lived with a profound awareness of God's presence in the Church, and by his preaching, poetry and person reminded some of the best of his contemporaries that it was not sufficient to think of her as a merely useful institution; a department of state; an educational or welfare agency, or a society for the improvement of morals.'

But, whereas Runcie saw the Oxford Movement in the context of a broader Church, Bennett presented the Oxford Movement as a broader church than it might have seemed to some to be.

'One thing the Oxford Movement Fathers were not afraid of was change,' he declared. 'Because they had a vision of what the Church could be, they longed to reform it and make it more effective. Though men like Keble and Pusey loved the Church of England, they were well aware of her faults. We sometimes forget just how innovative they were . . .

'Looking today at Pusey's writings, one sees how much of the modern ecumenical movement he had anticipated. And it was Newman, who went to Rome, who took into the thinking of that great communion many of the distinctive ideas of the movement he had left behind . . .'

Runcie too made the historical parallels, but for different purposes:

'Keble . . . protested against the subordination of the Church to a system of belief reared on different foundations from those we find in

The Archbishop-elect welcomes you to Canterbury, 1979

The Archbishop of York, John Habgood – "the best brain on the bench"

*Terry Waite before his fourth trip to Libya, where he negotiated the release of Britons held hostage, 1985*

*At the height of the first controversy over Church and State, the Archbishop visits Bishop Jim Thompson's inner-city diocese of Stepney, 1984*

*The Bishop of Durham listens as the Archbishop tells him off, 1985*

*Lindy conducts
the band of the Scots Guards,
her husband's old regiment, 1985*

*Divine intervention ruled out – after the York Minster fire, 1984*

*A precise kind of compassion – visiting a home for the elderly, 1986*

*Terry Waite, the Archbishop, John Witheridge and Desmond Tutu at the Crossroads squatter camp, South Africa, 1986*

*The Bishop of London listens
as the Archbishop tells him off, 1986*

*"My job is full of
adventures – I
have to do this."
Terry Waite leaves
the Riviera Hotel,
Beirut, with his
Druze bodyguard
on 20 January,
1987 – the last
known photograph*

*The Reverend Tony Higton and the Reverend Richard Kirker – two turbulent clerics with very different callings, 1987*

*"Mr Synod" – the man who commissioned the 1987 Crockford's Preface, Derek Pattinson*

*"They will never know for certain that I wrote it" – but Dr Gareth Bennett was the Crockford affair's first and most tragic victim*

*Mark Santer, Sam Van Culin, the Archbishop, the Pope and Christopher Hill at the Vatican, 1989*

*The Archbishop's finest hour – with some of the 525 bishops at the Lambeth Conference, 1988*

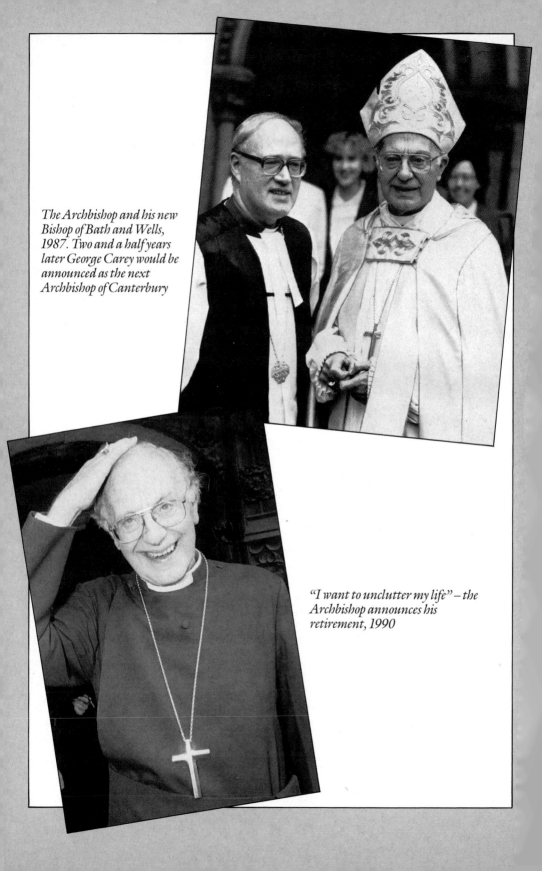

The Archbishop and his new Bishop of Bath and Wells, 1987. Two and a half years later George Carey would be announced as the next Archbishop of Canterbury

"I want to unclutter my life" – the Archbishop announces his retirement, 1990

the Bible and the apostles. He rejected the idea that the Church should merely be a useful agency in the service of the state.

'We are not faced with precisely the same problems . . . We are, however, faced with the danger of the Church becoming just a Friendly Society in a culture whose public structure of truth and meaning excludes God and centres on the autonomous individual. There is, for us, a danger that Christian doctrine could become so attenuated that the divine reality will be diluted' – and here was the voice of Chartres – 'into a dull echo of the liberal consensus.'

Above all, where Bennett was for traditionalism, Runcie was for tradition:

'In its own day, the Oxford Movement stimulated a great missionary effort to our own country and culture. We need to do this now – it is the best way of celebrating 150 years of Tractarian influence . . .

'So be of good courage. We are meant to praise a movement that goes on, not to bury it. Be hopeful. Be loyal to your Church . . .'


As well as to Oxford, he travelled to Germany, to preach on Remembrance Day at the Kreuzkirche in Dresden; to China again, to celebrate the reopening of relations at Mo-en church in Shanghai; and to Canterbury.

In a powerful and tender Christmas night sermon broadcast on BBC Radio 3, he invoked the Gospel of St Matthew and drew attention to the debates over the Virgin Birth and the Resurrection. He illustrated both their lack of novelty in theological terms and the need to see past debate to the profounder experiences and rewards of faith.

'We do not read these stories out of idle curiosity,' he concluded, 'in quest of mere information about the biography of some celebrated historical character. We read to the end that Christ himself can enter into us, be born and grow inside us, transforming us into lights in the darkness. We pray that under the inspiration of the child of Bethlehem, we may shine in a way which will lead others to the true source of peace and joy. May God bless you this Christmas time – you and all those whom you love.'

*Windows onto God* was the title of the selection of sermons and addresses published from the first three years of his primacy. At

Lambeth Palace, where the end was near of the partnership that had produced them, they were known as 'The Thoughts of Chairman Richard'.

Richard Chartres had been the favourite son of the clerical household at Abbey Gate House and a key figure in the transition to Lambeth. He had laid many of the foundations of the Lambeth administration. Chartres had recently married, and in spite of the Archbishop's dependence on him he was determined to move on in his ministry.

He found this process more difficult than expected: 'I've got my job,' he would say, 'no thanks to anyone at Lambeth.'

He alerted his successor to the demanding nature of a chaplain's job and warned him to maintain his contacts outside the Palace. Chartres knew that the temperamental inability of the Archbishop to have confidence in himself was behind his corresponding inability to show his appreciation of others. He also knew better than anyone else the absurd pressures to which the Archbishop was subjected.

He remained on good terms with Robert Runcie, taking over from him as a Swan Hellenic cruise lecturer and becoming Priest-in-Charge and then Vicar of Westminster St Stephen with St John, following in the footsteps of George Reindorp and Tony Tremlett.

Chartres' years of intimacy with the Archbishop and his great contribution made him a hard act to follow at Lambeth. But there were substantial differences between the management of a diocese and an archiepiscopate. It was time to break this particular link with St Albans.


Chartres's departure was accompanied by that of the Archbishop's long-serving Lay Assistant Michael Kinchin-Smith, whom he had inherited from Donald Coggan and who now crossed the river to become Archbishop's Appointments Secretary in Westminster. Kinchin-Smith was succeeded at Lambeth by Wilfred Grenville-Grey. Eve Keatley was another new arrival to the newly-created post of Lay Assistant (Communications) or Press Officer, the hitherto ill-defined position occupied between his many other commitments by Terry Waite.

The third arrival was Richard Chartres' successor. John Witheridge had been the St Albans schoolboy so impressed with Robert Runcie at Abbey Gate House in the early 1970s and who was known to Eric James and Richard Chartres. After ordination he had returned to the St Albans diocese as Curate of Luton St Mary, before becoming Assistant Chaplain of Marlborough College, whose pupils had included James Runcie. Witheridge was married with young children and the Witheridge family took up residence within the walls of the Palace of Lambeth.

He was a straight-backed, straightforward and straight-talking young priest, with a strong faith and equally strong ideas. When he first read the letter offering him the job as Chaplain to the Archbishop of Canterbury, he thought it was a practical joke. But he soon demonstrated the seriousness with which he took the job of writing and drafting the Archbishop's addresses and sermons and of 'Runcifying' those written by outside advisers.

Like other close aides, he would learn to understand the Archbishop's temperamental inability to show the appreciation for others that he denied himself. But, if he had been star-struck as a schoolboy at Abbey Gate House, he swiftly came to appreciate and adapt to the enormous pressures of the archiepiscopate. Wilfred Grenville-Grey described the Chaplain's job as that of a 'lightning conductor'.

John Witheridge, Wilfred Grenville-Grey, Eve Keatley, Ross Hook, Terry Waite, Christopher Hill (now redesignated Archbishop's Assistant for Ecumenical Affairs), Mary Cryer and Andrew Acland were the key personal staff responsible to the Archbishop and on whom he depended as he entered his fifth year at Lambeth. At Canterbury, he continued to identify himself nationally and internationally with the Cathedral while still devolving the running of the diocese to his Suffragan Bishop of Dover.

In late January 1984, the Archbishop, Waite and Witheridge flew on their first overseas trip together, to Uganda. For Waite it was a return visit.

Waite's extraordinary career even before Rome and Lambeth included three years from 1968–71 as adviser to the first African Archbishop of Uganda, Rwanda and Burundi. In 1977 the Ugandan Archbishop Janani Luwum was murdered by agents of Idi Amin. Luwum, with Oscar Romero and others, had been one of the latter-day martyrs especially honoured by the Archbishop of

Canterbury, the Pope and the Ugandan Cardinal Nsubuga at the service to mark the Pope's visit to Canterbury Cathedral eighteen months earlier.

Uganda covered nearly one hundred thousand square miles and numbered over two million Anglicans among its population of fifteen million people. The first Anglican Bishop of what was then known as East Equatorial Africa, James 'One-Thumb White Boss' Hannington, was speared to death by tribesmen in 1885. Missionaries and martyrs were inseparable from Uganda's turbulent history.

The purpose of the Archbishop of Canterbury was to bring encouragement and support to this beautiful and tragically afflicted part of the Anglican Communion and to preach at the enthronement of the new Archbishop Yona Okoth near Kampala. In his sermon he stressed the common ground of the Anglican and Roman Catholic Churches, the confusion between which had compounded the religious and social turmoil there.

The previous day he had attended an ecumenical service at the invitation of leaders of the Ugandan Roman Catholic Church. Cardinal Nsubuga had presented him with a portrait of himself. The painter was also presented.

'My word, that's magnificent,' the Archbishop told him, 'but how did you get it done so quickly? I've only just arrived.'

'No problem, Your Grace,' the painter replied. 'When the Pope came here I painted a picture of the Cardinal saying hello to him. Then I painted another one, because the first one wasn't good enough. So this morning I took the first one and painted out the Pope's head. Then I put on your head. So it is still the Pope's body but it is your head, Your Grace . . .'

The African Anglicans loved the Archbishop and could never understand the way he was treated by certain sections of the press in his own country. His infinite curiosity about other people made him the ideal traveller from Lambeth around the worldwide Anglican Communion. He had sworn to visit as many parts of it as possible before the Lambeth Conference in four years' time.

He was now sixty-three years old, but his stamina remained remarkable, outstripping the physically imposing Waite and even the wiry Witheridge, by far the youngest of the three. He seemed to thrive on gruelling schedules, and on anxiety: 'I'm worried about the next thing,' he would say, so often that it eventually became a catch-phrase. Waite in particular would bide his time until they had fulfilled a particularly undemanding commitment, and were moving on to another equally mundane duty. Then he would turn to the Archbishop with a straight face: 'Well, Archbishop,' he would say, 'I'm worried about the next thing . . .'

Runcie, Waite and Witheridge also travelled that spring to the West Indies where they carried out an equally punishing programme. The Archbishop gave fifty addresses in one month and travelled 2,000 miles, beginning in Belize and hopping down twelve islands. There was no central secretariat for each of these outposts of Anglicanism and the demand for his attendance in every one of eight scattered dioceses meant an exhausting round of sermons and speeches. At many landfalls the three men who made up the Archbishop of Canterbury's little party would be met by a Governor-General, the wife of the Governor-General and a large crowd of excited schoolchildren:

'Where is Mrs Runcie?' the local mothers' union would ask, and occasionally the press is Britain would inflate the question to suggest there was something untoward in her absence. The fact that funds were not forthcoming to pay for her would not be considered newsworthy.

In Belize he visited the British troops who supplemented the local defence force and echoed the local disquiet about the recent American invasion of Grenada. In Guyana he visited what he called 'the most remote and original theological college in the Anglican Communion', the Alan Knight Training Centre on the Brazilian border, whose students supported themselves by hunting.

The travel arrangements for this and other tours were made by Waite and his overworked secretary. One of the chief glories of the Church of England to the Archbishop, Waite and Witheridge was that it did business on a personal basis. The expressions on the faces of the children and adults waiting at each little airstrip and quayside were testimony to that. But occasionally, when the fatigue set in and he had been asked to draft yet another speech or sermon half an hour before an extra engagement arranged after they had left Lambeth, Witheridge's mind did start to run along ths same lines as Sir Hector Laing's. Nobody seemed to dispute the validity of the Pope's doctrinal statements in spite of the fact that he travelled in his own aircraft with his clergy, valet and cook.

In the West Indies, however, the three men were saved at the last moment from having to shuttle backwards and forwards to and from each island via Miami. Their unlikely saviour came in the form of John Shearer, once of the Third Battalion, Scots Guards. Shearer had made a fortune in insurance and had a private aeroplane and pilot, both of which he placed at the Archbishop's disposal. He came along for the ride, adding a rather different flavour to the experience.

Waite still liked nothing less than paperwork and nothing more than travelling, even in this extraordinarily amateurish if gentlemanly fashion. He was always working on half a dozen schemes. His success in negotiating the release of the Anglican missionaries from Iran had brought him the MBE and a huge postbag of letters pleading for his intervention in 'similar cases'.

In fact, there were and would be very few cases similar to that of Jean Waddell and the Colemans in Tehran. But there was no shortage of Britons in trouble abroad, of anxious relatives at home being fobbed off by a seemingly indifferent Foreign Office, and of powerful and dangerous Moslem leaders in the public mind.

Among the Britons abroad whose relatives had appealed to Lambeth were a group of British expatriate workers held on trumped-up charges in Tripoli. Britain had severed diplomatic relations with Libya after the murder of WPC Yvonne Fletcher in London that April, and the Anglican Chaplain there had been among those forced to return to Britain. None of the men still held was a missionary, or priest, or worker for Anglicanism. Two were English teachers, one was an oil engineer and one a telephone engineer. One of the English teachers occasionally played the organ in the English church in Tripoli. The humanitarian implications of their incarceration were not in doubt. The Anglican connection was tenuous, to say the least.

In the early summer of 1984, Waite and Acland selected the release of these men as the next challenge to be faced by the 'special envoy' of the Archbishop of Canterbury. In the role previously occupied by the Ayatollah Khomeini was the man widely seen by the West as Public Enemy Number Two in the Middle East. He was Colonel Muammar Ghaddafi.

\*

The Archbishop trusted Terry Waite and was well aware of the greater degree of prominence his aide brought to his own primacy. If the price of that prominence was sometimes a hurtful letter or a deliberate misrepresentation in the press, so be it.

There was an opposition and yet a symmetry to their roles. Waite was larger than life, certainly larger than the title of Assistant for Anglican Communion Affairs. Robert Runcie, on the other hand, could never be bigger than the Archbishop of Canterbury. They were also both loners. This aloneness, this powerful personal drive at work behind an equally powerful affability of manner, was an essential factor in any understanding of their relationship.

The first session of the 1984 General Synod addressed the Church of England report *Marriage and Divorce* presented by the Church of England Board for Social Responsibility of which the Chairman was Hugh Montefiore. The previous Chairman, the Bishop of London, Graham Leonard, was again in full cry:

'I believe that there are many in the country,' he declared, 'who are now looking for a bold affirmation by the Church of the meaning of true marriage . . . At this very moment, we are being told that within one year you can tell whether a marriage is going to work or not. What a travesty of love that is.'

Leonard's dignity and efficiency as Chairman had brought him the respect of his opponents in debate, Montefiore included. The Archbishop was concerned to preserve the collegiality of such diverse minds. But, as Gareth Bennett attempted to do in debates on the diaconate and the ordination of women, Leonard's lucid delivery, his emotive invocation of 'the hungry sheep' and his nostalgia for a style of authority that was more Roman than Anglican scorned the notion of a 'common mind' and exposed the limitations of the Archbishop's strategy.

The Archbishop meanwhile continued to broadcast elsewhere his feelings on issues that were dealt with in Synod. He addressed the National Confederation of Parent-Teacher Associations on 'Morality in Education' and he wrote on 'Fighting divorce with faith' in an article in *The Times*.

The latter recalled the side of him that combined firmness with charity, and resisted the urge to reassert the moral absolutes of the past as if they too had not been found seriously wanting:

*'It is a lot to ask that two young people marrying in their twenties should vow to be faithful to each other for their whole lives, when they may easily live into their eighties; and when they have learnt to mean by "faithful" not just docile and well-behaved, but romantic and companionable. Furthermore, women are seeking an identity which is not solely dependent on the family.*

*'Society and our children desperately need good marriages. The law deals with fairness and with people's rights. The Church has to communicate a message about what Austin Farrar called "the union of duty with delight". We cannot expect the lawyers to do our job for us.'*

The Archbishop and Bishop Leonard would continue for the time being to avoid confrontation over issues which privately saw them on either side of a widening chasm. Both men were temperate and considered, however, compared with the personal style of the Professor of Theology at Leeds University, David Jenkins. That spring, Jenkins was announced as the next Bishop of Durham.

Jenkins was a distinguished theologian and author of a number of books and papers that dealt lucidly with questions of doctrine and belief. He was personally liked by a great number of bishops and it was in recognition of his intellectual and personal qualities that he had been chosen as 92nd bishop of the fourth most senior diocese in the Church of England. He had lectured to Robert Runcie's students at Cuddesdon in the 1960s. He had had very little pastoral experience, and at the age of 59 had a desire to bring his considerable energy as quickly as possible to bear.

Dr Gareth Bennett was rumoured to be disappointed not to have been chosen for the appointment. Jenkins soon revealed he had no inhibitions about making his feelings plain on any subject. In a series of television interviews he spoke about the Virgin Birth, the Resurrection and a host of other doctrinal matters with the sophistication and depth for which he was already known and respected at clergy conferences and in theological colleges. He also displayed a breathtaking lack of understanding of the media.

'The Church of England is so insignificant and unimportant – it doesn't matter,' he said, and appeared not to realise that a newspaper was likely to print this kind of remark in letters an inch high and out of its theological context. This in itself mattered less than the misleading impression it gave of contemporary theological debate. Jenkins was in fact saying nothing about the Virgin Birth or the Resurrection that had not been widely said in theological colleges and the writings of theologians for thirty years or more. Nor, had he been pronouncing these views as a theologian rather than a bishop, would even the *Church Times* have seen anything remotely newsworthy in him.

This was not at first understood even at Lambeth Palace. After the first flood of stories about 'the Bishop who doesn't believe in God' in the popular press, Andrew Acland suggested that Jenkins' consecration be delayed until the Archbishop had had the chance to issue a statement explaining what was going on. 'Go away, Andrew,' the Archbishop said, 'and read some theology.'

Acland did so, and like many others came to the same conclusion. What Jenkins was saying and the manner in which he said it were far less significant to the intelligent sceptic than what John Robinson had said in *Honest to God* twenty years earlier.

But Jenkins' torrents of words on television did lend themselves to distortion and misinterpretation, and unlike the case of *Honest to God* (a debate to which Jenkins himself had made a major contribution) there was no specific book or manifesto to which the confused and interested listener could go for clarification. This damaging state of affairs was reflected in the increased postbag at the Palaces of Durham, Bishopthorpe and Lambeth.

After a few weeks this decreased, as did the hysteria generated by Jenkins' well-intentioned if occasionally injudicious statements. There was unease in Durham but a willingness to give the bishop the benefit of the doubt. Eleven clergy members of the General Synod asked the Archbishop of York to delay Jenkins' consecration until it could be debated at the second session of that year's General Synod, due to open on 7 July.

John Habgood, Archbishop of York, would do no such thing and kept the consecration in perspective. He told his own diocesan Synod that the Jenkins affair was 'a huge opportunity for Christian education'. He acknowledged the objections of a small number of clergy only in so far as they reflected a worrying assumption that people somehow needed to be protected from questions 'which in their heart of hearts they do ask'. Habgood, the second most senior clergyman in the Church of England and probably its most brilliant essayist, also asked why the clergy assumed such a feeble faith in people that it could be threatened by 'the most ordinary kind of questioning'.

David Jenkins was consecrated Bishop of Durham at York Minster on 6 July 1984. The Durham clergy made no secret of their strong support. The first interruption from other quarters came just before the sermon. As the preacher was about to begin, a person who would disclose only that his name was 'Barry' yelled: 'You want to stop this. Let no more denigration be brought on Jesus Christ. This is invalid.' Barry was escorted by two vergers to the north-west door.

A total breakdown in the Minster's public address system rendered inaudible both the protests and the sermon which followed. A steward later described this as 'divine intervention'. The Reverend John Mowll, Vicar of Congleton, Cheshire, seized the lectern just before the reading of the Royal Mandate. He began to read from a prepared speech. 'Shame!' cried the congregation, which included thirty-five bishops. 'Remove him!' And this protester too was led away struggling.

Professor Denis Nineham, an eminent theologian, preached an inaudible sermon that included a sober and sensible examination of the early creeds. This also contained a number of ambivalent pieces of advice to the congregation, had they been able to hear.

'You will have drawn your own conclusions,' he told Jenkins, 'from the controversy of the past few weeks. Certainly a bishop cannot speak quite as a professional scholar may do, but he speaks in a representative capacity; and that imposes certain restraints.

'But I hope – and I am sure – that you will not mistake those constraints for any sort of muzzling. We shall all need all the help your courage and energy and learning and clear-sightedness can give us.'

Only a single protester bearing a placard yelled 'Heretic' as the new Bishop of Durham and the Archbishop of York emerged smiling from the Cathedral. The sigh of relief was audible in Lambeth and elsewhere. Two days later, on the second day of the second session of Synod, a bolt of lightning struck York Minster.

Some followed the steward's line and took this as a sign of divine displeasure at the new episcopal appointment. Others even saw a sign of satanic approval. 'Durham' and 'Devil' after all began with the same letter. The Archbishop of Canterbury rejected these suggestions as he clambered through the blackened wreckage. Some of the best minds of the Church of England nonetheless immediately set to work pondering these problems. These included the new Bishop, who seemed undaunted and continued to make known the same views as he had expressed before.

If anything, the York Minster fire gave Bishop Jenkins a certain extra mystique, a powerful magic, as he widened his concern from the questions of whether or not Mary was a Virgin and the Tomb was Empty. Henceforth, he would also question the literal truth of some of the political creeds and orthodoxies of the day.

Two years after the largely manufactured controversy over the Archbishop's Falkland Islands sermon, relations were cordial between the Prime Minister and the Archbishop of Canterbury. The Prime Minister had even spoken fulsomely of the Archbishop at a private dinner at Lambeth. But the Bishop of Durham was about to shake the temple again. The Archbishop of Canterbury and the Church of England were about to be more firmly and flagrantly confused with the forces of political opposition and social disorder than ever before.

# 6

# *The Miners, the Missionaries and the Monstrous Regiment*

AT that second session of Synod in 1984 in York the Archbishop spoke in favour of the proposed new Marriage Regulation. The present point-blank refusal to allow remarriage in church did 'sound like the refusal to heal on the sabbath,' he said, 'upholding our good tradition in a way that does not uphold it but makes people feel rejected.'

Nine bishops, led by the Bishop of London and including John Baker, Bishop of Salisbury, a Cuddesdon man from the Knapp-Fisher era, had tried to persuade the majority in favour to reconsider their decision. They were supported in Synod by the Vicar of Holy Trinity, Reading, Brian Brindley. The Archbishop said he respected their misgivings and agreed with their argument that the Church would be misunderstood, if it voted in favour of the measures.

'We shall be taken to have changed our doctrine,' he told them, 'however much we may say this is untrue; and this is very serious. But,' he went on, 'we are being misunderstood at the moment. It is partly what is perceived as legalism, a slowness to understand people's real lives, that has made our teaching incomprehensible and inaccessible to some.'

In the debate on the recognition of overseas women priests, he had to speak as *primus inter pares* of the Anglican Communion. He seemed to have come to terms with the idea in his own mind.

'What was once inopportune may become timely,' he said. 'It is clearer now that the ordination of women to the priesthood – like it or like it not – is almost certainly a permanent development in the ministry of at least some Anglican Churches . . . There can hardly be a way back as long as there are women priests in the Communion. They are here to stay.'

He did not believe that the draft Measure was phrased in such a way as to antagonise the Roman Catholic and Orthodox Churches. But, as if in concession to the Bishop of London, there was a whiff of Catholic authoritarianism about his final words on the matter: 'No doubt there will be a temptation to fly in ordained protagonists of women's priest-hood. But, if we pass the Measure, I hope those in favour of the ordi-nation of women will respect the spirit as well as the letter of the law – PCCs, parish priests and bishops – so that it is not used as an instrument for the forced conversion,' he concluded, 'of the contumacious.'

The measure was overwhelmingly carried. The supporters of the ordi-nation of women to the priesthood were exultant; the Archbishop, it seemed, had finally made up his mind.

The Archbishop, Waite and Witheridge then flew to Lagos, for the sixth Meeting of the Anglican Consultative Council of which he was ex-officio President. He preached at the opening service in Archbishop Timothy's Lagos Cathedral.

'In my home at Lambeth,' he told the congregation, 'there is a photo-graph of the Lambeth Conference of Bishops taken in 1887. As you look along the rows of bishops you soon notice that there is only one African face – just one. Next to that picture hangs a photograph of 1978. What a difference!

'Now the truth that the Anglican Church is numerically stronger in Africa than in any other part of the world begins to be seen. No longer can it be said that the Anglican Church is the Church of England. Rather the Church of England is a member of the Anglican Communion. Though,' he added, 'I have to spend much time preaching to the Angli-can Communion that it includes the Church of England, and to the Church of England that it is part of the Anglican Communion.'

If the Nigerian animists would have understood the burning down of York Minster, they would not have appreciated the subtleties of the Bishop of Durham. While the Archbishop was in Lagos, the Bishop was in a London radio studio expounding on the Empty Tomb.

The Bishop had a spirited exchange in a phone-in programme with a Religious Education and Sunday School teacher from New Malden. The Bishop interrupted him so often that the latter was having trouble making his point. 'I don't think it's fair to keep chipping in like that,' the teacher reprimanded him; his pupils, he said, were 'totally disgusted' with denials of the Resurrection.

'I *do* believe in the Resurrection,' the Bishop asserted, 'I've said it again and again. You've misunderstood what I said,' he went on testily. The point, he said, was that Christ's Resurrection body was 'spiritual' . . . 'that's why it could go through doors and things.'

The presenter eventually restored order, and the Bishop carried on. 'There's one explanation in Matthew,' he said, 'that the disciples came and pinched the body. People could give all sorts of explanations. We can't be sure about it,' he added, 'can we?'

Early that August, a few days after the Archbishop and Terry Waite had written their first epistle to the Libyans, a demonstrator invaded the pulpit of Durham Cathedral. It happened between the *Te Deum* and the second lesson. The first had just been read by Canon Ronald Coppin.

'I couldn't hear what he was saying,' Canon Coppin explained, 'because I was at the lectern, but his general points were that he felt very strongly that the Churches are worldly and corrupt, and that David Jenkins doesn't believe all that should be believed.'

Bishop Peter Walker of Ely had known Robert Runcie since Westcott House and had succeeded Kenneth Carey as its Principal. He had also been devoting a good deal of time to trying to understand the fire at York Minster.

*'I have been asking myself,'* Bishop Walker wrote in the Ely diocesan *Contact, 'about any lessons to be learnt from it all . . .*

*'In the first place, I cannot begin to see the fire as God making himself felt. That would not be, for me, the God who showed himself to us in Jesus Christ crucified and risen as the God of infinite compassion and love. He is also the God of truth and truthfulness; and the two things, truth and love, go together.'*

Walker commended to his readers the wise words of Robert Runcie's predecessor, William Temple; that to admit acrimony in theological discussion was more fundamentally heretical than any erroneous opinions upheld or condemned in the course of discussion.

This was an opinion shared by David Jenkins and Robert Runcie.

It also applied favourably to Robert Runcie's former student at Trinity Hall and Peter Walker's vice-principal at Westcott House, Don Cupitt. He was the controversial Dean of Emmanuel College, Cambridge whose *Sea of Faith* series on BBC Television that autumn made the Bishop of Durham appear to some like a pillar of orthodoxy. But Temple's wisdom would not, it seemed, be shared by all those who chose or were chosen to express their views of the Runcie primacy.

On a diocesan visit to Derby the Archbishop had asked that a striking miners' village be included in his itinerary. In his sermon in Derby Cathedral he warned of the 'bitter harvest' of the dispute: 'That is the task of the Church – not to provide amateur advice from on high, but to stand with all those who are locked into this dispute in their local communities. I know places in your diocese where daily that unspectacular ministry is being fulfilled . . .'

In Cresswell, a village which had seen violent picketing, he listened to the villagers and the local vicar, whose stories of the divisions caused by the strike were the stuff of the Archbishop's worst nightmares. One young wife of a working miner whose child had met with an accident had telephoned her parents for help; her striking miner father had put the telephone down without a word.

There was a time to speak, and a time to keep silence, said the Archbishop: 'and this afternoon is a time for me to learn'.

On the Friday of the following week he was driven to Canterbury, among other things to meet the members of his Commission on Urban Priority Areas for an informal assessment of their work. That same day, St Matthew's Day, Bishop Jenkins was enthroned at a majestic ceremony in one of Europe's most magnificent cathedrals. As Robert Runcie had done at Canterbury and St Albans, as Michael Ramsey had done at Canterbury and in this same Cathedral, as Ian Ramsey and John Habgood had done here, the new Bishop knocked on the door. The Dean welcomed him and the Bishop took the oaths on the 1,200 year-old Durham Gospels. The enthronement completed, the Dean presented the new Bishop to the people, who broke into spontaneous and prolonged applause.

The Bishop of Durham then preached his enthronement sermon. This was a lengthy and detailed theological argument and a passionate reaffirmation of personal faith. In the last few minutes of his sermon he illustrated how he believed the power of God could bring reconciliation in the present miners' strike. He criticised the government and called upon both Arthur Scargill, the National Union of Miners leader, and Ian MacGregor, Chairman of the National Coal Board, to climb down. He referred to MacGregor as 'an elderly imported American' – an unnecessary and incorrect description which drew attention away from the substance of his sermon and landed the Bishop of Durham in more trouble. At the end of his sermon the congregation broke into renewed applause.

Jenkins' remarks about MacGregor provoked furious criticism from Conservative politicians and the more conservative members of the Church. The Bishop of Peterborough, Douglas Feaver, said 'the man had no sense of time or place'. The Chairman of the Conservative Party John Selwyn Gummer MP, a clergyman's son and a member of the General Synod, regretted them. Even Peter Walker, the Energy Secretary, accused Jenkins of preaching about fiction rather than facts.

Various Conservative backbenchers, their worst fears doubtless confirmed by the publication of an interview with Bishop Jenkins in the October issue of *Marxism Today*, attacked him for 'gutter politics' and for being a 'walking disaster area'. They called upon the Archbishop of Canterbury to rid them of 'this turbulent priest'.

The Archbishop stood by him. 'The Bishop of Durham,' he said, 'must say what he believes the gospel requires him to say, speaking from his particular position in the North-East. The Bishop's sermon,' he added, 'was a robust statement about reconciliation, which all would agree is central to the gospel message.'

John Habgood of York too stood firm, while hinting that it was perhaps unwise to have criticised individuals by name. The letters of complaint and support poured into Bishop Auckland, Bishopthorpe and Lambeth Palace. At Lambeth they had to draft in extra staff to deal with them. But the biggest irritation to the Archbishop, Andrew Acland and others was the ammunition, via newspapers such as the *Daily Mail*, that Jenkins' remarks gave to those reactionary members of the Tory party, whose share of the public platform was out of all proportion to their understanding of Christianity and their importance to society.

The *Daily Mail* in particular muddied the pool without mercy or mindfulness of the truth. The Archbishop wrote a brief private note to Ian MacGregor saying that he 'sympathised for any hurt that had been caused to him or his family by personal remarks made in the sermon'. He did not apologise for the Bishop of Durham or in any way modify the statement of support he had already made for him. The *Mail* obtained a copy of the letter:

## RUNCIE REPENTS

declared the *Daily Mail*

*He tells MacGregor: Bishop was wrong*
*and I was wrong to back him*

The Archbishop now had to spend a good deal of time rejecting this deliberate misinterpretation (worthy of the 'fiction' charge levelled at Jenkins by Peter Walker) and assuring Jenkins of his continued support. He also represented the Synod in a delegation to the Home Office to protest to the Home Secretary about the British Nationality Act. In an interview in *The Times*, he spoke at length about Parliament and the moral law, the present political unrest and the role of the Church in public life:

'The undoubted increase in the general living standard of the ma-jority of the country is taking place at a time when the number of young unemployed, and the sense of helplessness about future plans for communities, are becoming really acute. This of course means that you are faced with the question of how you achieve efficiency in order to make us competitive in world markets, which is a justifiable aim of a government.

'How do you achieve these objectives without losing the mutual respect which you need in society, in order to achieve the efficiency? It is the efficiency versus compassion argument. Now that is the stage where I am at, asking serious questions about justifiable aims, undoubted achievements of social betterment, at the expense of real breakdowns in human relations and a sense of common purpose and hope.

'I think there is a crisis,' he went on, 'which springs from fear, puzzlement and deep changes taking place in our society . . .

'We live in a society in which the majority are better off, but nevertheless there is growing poverty and despair and a sense of powerlessness. People will say if this can be shown to be the case, this is not a decent society in which to live. They won't accept that greed and self-interest are the driving dynamic of our society. And that is why I think that people will say, we can't allow this state of affairs to continue.

'It is not an easy position; sometimes it is more comfortable to be on the wings than to be clobbered on both sides in the middle, but that's of course where the Church of England with its public position lies. I believe there is an opportunity at the present time in a highly polarised society to explore much more the middle ground.'

He spoke of his ideal of national leadership:

'We need leadership in our national life which will unite and not divide the nation. That's not an attack on the Government . . .

'The Church must be concerned with public affairs, but this does not entail pronouncing on all public issues. Much public concern can be expressed in ways which are deliberately low-profile, bringing people together, or sticking with communities. The most admirable people so far as I have found in the Church in this strike, have not been the "speakers", but people who have stuck with the situation in mining communities. I would like that underlined if possible.

'Problems will be solved by those who have the management of power. We must pray for those who have responsibility for the management of power. But we can't leave our future simply in the hands of the brokers of power.

'We live in a highly competitive international world, and you can't deny the worry about that. At the same time you feel as a Christian that you have got to speak for those who are suffering most. That is the middle ground, that is where we must resist simplistic statements and restate certain principles.'

### WHAT AN UNHOLY ROW
#### declared the *Daily Mail*
*Archbishop's conflict with Maggie angers top Tories*

*The Church of England and the Prime Minister were at war last night over the Archbishop of Canterbury's controversial intervention in the unemployment crisis.*

*The first senior Minister to hit back at the Primate's attack on Mrs Thatcher's policy was Industry Minister Norman Tebbit.*

*He spoke of 'a little woolly' thinking about what the Government was trying to achieve.*

*The onslaught on Dr Runcie . . .*

*Consternation at Downing Street . . .*

The Archbishop had not of course declared war on the Prime Minister, nor intervened in the unemployment crisis. He had simply given an important interview on the eve of the Annual Conference of the Conservative Party.

Its Chairman John Selwyn Gummer, apparently oblivious to the irony of what he was saying, said the time was nigh to 'confront the truth'. The backwoodsmen came out of their woods, lobbed their all-purpose insults and ran back into the woods. The Conservative MP for Taunton, Edward du Cann, called his words 'naïve and foolish'. The Conservative MP for Birmingham Anthony Beaumont-Dark said the interview was 'mindless'. The Conservative MP for Northampton, Tony Marlow, said there was no hope for the Church of England as long as it was led 'by muddled old men'. The Bishop of Peterborough said that mobs were attempting to overthrow the constitution of the realm.

The Archbishop said no more, telling his Chaplain John Witheridge he wanted his words 'to sink in'. Then he went off to the East End, to play pool with black unemployed men at a community centre in the blighted inner-city diocese of his comrade in the Cell, 'Bishop Jim' Thompson.

Needless to say a picture of him doing so appeared in the Conservative *Daily Telegraph*. 'It is not an easy position; sometimes it is more comfortable to be on the wings than to be clobbered on both sides . . .'

The Archbishop was in relaxed and witty form when he spoke after dinner about these matters to the Coningsby Club in London on 24 October 1984. As a distillation of the thinking of a classically-educated liberal and a man of deep private faith in high public office at a troubled time, this was one of the keynote addresses of his primacy:

'When you first invited me to accept your kind invitation to offer you some thought on the subject of Church and State,' he told them, 'I expected that the national mood on the matter would, more or less as usual, be one of a rather disinterested complacency, punctuated by occasional rumblings of discontent and irritation. How wrong I was!

'Suddenly a storm blew up. Judging by my postbag and the media, the leadership of the Church has suddenly become the focus of excessive vituperation or extravagant praise. I find myself expected to give quick definitive answers to complex problems and to take on tasks, such as being an alternative ACAS, quite outside my competence. These are totally unrealistic expectations of the Archbishop of Canterbury.

'Tonight, I do not mean to dodge your questions. I will do my best with all of them. But, first, for a few minutes, I would like to step back from this turbulence and to seek a longer perspective on these events by looking for inspiration and insight from the presiding genius of your Club – Benjamin Disraeli.'

The Archbishop referred them to *Tancred*, the novel in which the Victorian Prime Minister wrote about relations between the Church of England and the State. He found some inspiration there, but insufficient for the problems of today. He referred them to Burke, in whom he found excess of romanticism. He referred them to Anthony Sampson's *Changing Anatomy of Britain*: 'He could not tell me much about the Church, for the only reference to it I could find concerned disestablishment. We have obviously become an unmentionable part of the nation's anatomy.'

He rejected this view without immediately referring them back to the recent public furore. As he had said in his *Times* interview, the strengths and weaknesses of the Church were not easily measurable in terms of topicality:

'I think the weaknesses of the Church can be exaggerated by those with a romantic view of its past or ignorance of its present life. Diminished in numbers and distanced from Westminster, it is still the largest network of voluntary associations for social wellbeing in this country. Time and again it is this network, mostly staffed by the laity, that nudges the government . . . Above all the Churches still provide a nationwide meeting place for people of otherwise differing opinions to seek and find divine inspiration.'

He spoke of the attitude of Church to State as one of 'critical solidarity' and cited numerous recent examples of this. He looked beneath the secular, political interpretation of the events which would come to be termed this era's history. He suggested that in doing so he was touching a particularly raw nerve:

'Sometimes one might think that in the present climate the demonstration of compassion for the weakest in our society is some dangerous and subversive instinct. It is not. The protection of the weak is the first charge on a government's responsibilities.'

He reasserted the great virtue of Anglicanism: its ability to 'marry together religious experience and faith in rational processes'. This might at times seem like a vice to a Conservative government; a government with which his fellow-diners would be in broad sympathy.

'I should like to finish by giving you three assurances about Church and State in the future. The first is that the Church of England will continue by the grace of God to be faithful to the gospel we preach, and to be its defence in a questioning age. The second is that we shall continue in spiritual and human sympathy with those who have the arduous responsibility of the government of our nation. The third is that we shall continue to provoke the complacent and unsettle the somnolent. We may occasionally be turbulent priests,' he told them, 'but we shall be turbulent because sometimes loyalty to Church and State makes silence impossible and criticism imperative. If we do this the caravan of Church and State will keep moving forward towards a future in which, by being faithful to our Church, we shall also bring enduring benefits to the State.'


But other events of that autumn were not relevant to relations between Church and State, or susceptible to the kind of analysis possible before a sympathetic audience at the Coningsby Club. They concerned the more turbulent outposts of the Anglican Communion, the Church of England's continued divisions over the ordination of women, and relations between the Archbishop of Canterbury and the Pope.

In late October the Archbishop and his Assistant for Anglican Affairs were to be seen at Heathrow Airport towering over the diminutive and dynamic Bishop Tutu, recently announced as winner of the Nobel Peace Prize. The Tutus had arrived by Concorde en route from New York to Johannesburg, and the Archbishop introduced him as 'one of the world's great peacemakers' to the assembled press.

Waite himself undertook a series of major international air journeys, but under less public circumstances. In November he flew to Tripoli at the invitation of the Libyan Foreign Bureau, after an exchange of correspondence between the Archbishop and Colonel Ghaddafi.

As he had done in Tehran nearly four years earlier, he worked day and night to build an atmosphere of trust under difficult conditions between himself and the Libyans. Again, his unusual combination of visible integrity uncompromised by Western political interests, and his streetwise shrewdness, won him the respect of a chaotic, suspicious and volatile Moslem administration.

On his return to Lambeth, he was disarmingly modest about it all. 'It's a man's life,' he would say, 'in the modern Church of England,' and repeated this over and over again until his colleagues begged him to stop. He was laying the foundations for his next visit. He was quietly optimistic about having the detained Britons home for Christmas.


The Archbishop travelled to the less exotic environment of Church House, Westminster. Here, among other matters, the third session of that year's General Synod was to debate the continuing motion of the priestly ordination of women.

The background paper for the debate had been prepared by Miss (later Dame) Christian Howard, whose distinguished contribution to the matter was often overlooked by her opponents, who simply described her as a member of MOW (the Movement for the Ordination of Women).

Bishop Leonard had already made his feelings known immediately before the debate. In an article in the *Guardian* entitled '*Why Women Priests would be Divisive*' he claimed that if carried the motion would split the Church, at a time when


*'the Church should be looking for renewal in faith and life to commend the Gospel to a nation which so desperately needs it'.*

The full title of the motion was: 'That this Synod asks the standing committee to bring forward legislation to permit the ordination of women to the priesthood in the provinces of Canterbury and York.' The house and galleries were packed for the debate.

Oswald Clark, a prominent Synod lay member, said that if passed the motion would 'set member against member so that the Church tears itself apart'.

Dr Gareth Bennett declared: 'I do not say that in Scripture there can never be any changes. There can be discovery and development within a tradition. The problem is to distinguish true development from what is merely contemporary fashion. In Church history the popular majorities have a way of being consistently wrong. We have not yet reached the consensus that will make this what it has to be – a clear pastoral good.'

Ronald Bowlby, Bishop of Southwark, said that divisiveness was 'not an argument for indefinite delay'. Wilberforce had persistently represented his motion for the abolition of the slave trade: 'Once in six years for this issue does not seem excessive by comparison.'

John Habgood, Archbishop of York, declared this was the wrong debate at the wrong time, and then went on to explain why he would vote for the motion. Defeat, he said, would be 'a crushing blow to a cause in which I believe'.

Authority in the Church was already divided, Habgood maintained, by a deliberate dispersal of authority 'as part of our theological understanding of the nature of the Church. We have demonstrated,' he said, 'that ecumenical fellowship can survive quite radical action in pursuit of what we believe to be God's will.'

The Archbishop of Canterbury rose to speak.

'I can't conceal my conviction,' he said, 'that we have a duty not to be seen to be acting in abrasive and unfraternal disregard of very large Catholic bodies with whom we share the very fundamentals of the faith.'

He had come to accept the presence of ordained women priests within the Anglican Communion.

'I have become convinced that the arguments for the ordination of women now tip the balance favourably.

'But a decision by the Church of England depends upon more than archiepiscopal theological opinion. Against what all admit to be a radical change must be balanced both ecumenical reticence and the internal unity of the Church of England. I therefore urge the Synod to adopt a doctrine of gradualism as an argument of principle, not expediency.

'To grow towards the ordination of women we must first take steps towards a wider experience of women's ministry . . . We also need to encourage some interplay between the various points of view, and I welcome what has recently begun. I promise to do all I can to promote such dialogue myself.

'But these are necessary preliminary steps. Until we have both achieved and experienced women deacons, women priests from abroad and a real internal Church of England dialogue, I do not believe we can move with integrity to the following stage of legislating for the ordination of women in the Church of England.'

The Houses of the Synod voted overwhelmingly for the motion, and so began the long legislative process for admitting women to the priesthood. The Movement for the Ordination of Women were exultant but maintained their lack of desire to cause pain in others. The conservative Church Union declared it had lost the battle but not the war.

The Archbishop had spoken in what he saw was the only way on a measure of which he was now more certain of his own approval, but in which he was not in charge of rocking the boat. In spite of his recent highly publicised statements on the affairs of Church and State, he was and would remain better at calming things down than stirring them up. He was most likely aware of the mood of the meeting in spite of his negative vote.

In the immortal words of Frank Field, Labour MP and General Synod member, he had 'nailed his colours to the fence'. This gave ammunition to his opponents, including the Conservative back-benchers, the Bishop of London and later to Dr Gareth Bennett. But the Archbishop knew better than any of them that the fence was sometimes a necessary though highly uncomfortable place for him to be.

At Lambeth in early December the Archbishop was to be seen in the grounds of the Palace holding on to the running board of a red London Transport double decker bus. Lindy, who was at the wheel, was dressed as a bus driver for the occasion. Afterwards he helped her down from the cab, and the vehicle was driven on to Canterbury as part of a convoy in aid of the 'Crisis at Christmas' homelessness appeal.

In France, he was the first Archbishop of Canterbury to address the congregation in the Cathedral of Nôtre Dame. His theme was 'Evangelisation in secular Europe'. A packed cathedral first heard the Canterbury Cathedral choir sing at Anglican Evensong there. After his address, the reply was given by the Roman Catholic Archbishop of Paris, Cardinal Jean-Marie Lustiger.

Archbishop Lustiger welcomed him warmly and agreed with the Archbishop's basing his comparison of the churches in France and Britain on 'a similar degree of marginalisation' in their respective societies. The Roman Catholic Archbishop, however, expressed alarm over the recent decision of the General Synod of the Church of England concerning the possibility of the ordination of women to the priesthood. He said this would create 'a perhaps irreparable division' with the Roman Catholic Church, the Orthodox Churches and within the Anglican Communion.

This was a portent of things to come. Shortly after the Archbishop's return to England he received a letter on similar lines.

This letter was from the Pope.

*'To the Most Reverend Robert Runcie Archbishop of Canterbury.*

*'The long but necessary task of evaluating the final report of the First Anglican/Roman Catholic International Commission, in which both our Communions are now engaged, is a vital part of that journey of faith on which we have embarked together in our efforts to establish full ecclesial communion. It has been a joy to learn how seriously this task is being taken in so many countries, and how this study is frequently associated with joint action and common witness which express, as far as possible, the degree of communion which has already been brought about between us by the grace of God.*

*'This degree of communion, indeed God's very call for us to be one, also bids us face frankly the differences which still separate us. While the Catholic Church must always be sensitive to the heritage which she has in common with other Christians, she must nevertheless base frank and constructive dialogue upon clarity regarding her own position.'*

This was only two and a half years after the Pope's visit to Canterbury, and only four weeks after the General Synod's latest debate on the ordination of women to the priesthood.

*'It was in this spirit that, in an important exchange of letters in 1975-6, Pope Paul VI affirmed to Archbishop Coggan the position of the Catholic Church concerning the admission of women to priestly ordination, a step at that time being considered by several Churches of the Anglican Communion. The reasons that he then stated briefly for the Catholic Church's adherence to the long tradition on this matter were set out at length by the Sacred Congregation for the Doctrine "Inter Insigniores" of 15 October 1976. This same position was again stated clearly by observers from the Secretariat for Promoting Christian Unity during the hearing on this subject at the Lambeth Conference of 1978.*

*'I know that Your Grace is well aware of the position of the Catholic Church and of the theological grounds which lead her to maintain it. Indeed I am grateful that, in the recent debate in the General Synod of the Church of England, you referred to the implications of this question for Anglican relations with the Catholic and Orthodox Churches. But the outcome of that debate prompts me to reaffirm with all brotherly frankness the continuing adherence of the Catholic Church to the practice and principles so clearly stated by Pope Paul VI.*

*'With his well-known affection for the Anglican Communion and his deep desire for Christian unity, it was with profound sadness that Pope Paul VI contemplated a step which he saw as introducing into our dialogue "an element of grave difficulty", even "a threat". Since that time we have celebrated together the progress towards reconciliation between our two Communions. But in those same years the increase in the number of Anglican Churches which admit, or are preparing to admit, women to priestly ordination constitutes, in the eyes of the Catholic Church, an increasingly serious obstacle to that progress.*

*'Pope Paul VI stated that "obstacles do not destroy mutual commitment to a search for reconciliation". We too were "encouraged by our reliance on the grace of God and by all that we have seen of the power of that grace in the ecumenical movement of our time" when we set up the new Commission, whose task includes study of "all that hinders the mutual recognition of the ministries of our two Communions" (Common Declaration, 29 May 1982, No. 3).*

*'It is in that same hope, in the charity that "hopes all things" (1 Cor.*

13:7) *but which seeks the unity of Christ's Body by "speaking the truth in love" (Eph. 4:15), that I write these words to you, my dear Brother, as we celebrate the Birth of the Lord who came in "the fullness of time to unite all things" (Eph. 1:10).'*

> *'From the Vatican,*
> *'20 December 1984.*
> *'Joannes Paulus II'*

The Archbishop's good personal relationship with the Pope made such frankness possible, but it also revealed to him the theological distance between Rome and Lambeth. The text of this letter would not be released for nearly two years. The contents were much on his mind as he addressed himself to other matters.

In his Christmas message to the Anglican Communion, he made oblique reference to the doctrinal questions which had been publicised in distorted form in the mass media.

'However,' he went on, 'when all is said and done, at the heart of our faith there lies the mystery which is just as accessible to the simple as to the sophisticated. Provided we are ready to let it master and mould us all, we can be united in one body. We shall never be able to understand mystery with the language of logic and reason, but we can share in mystery and be caught up in it, and it will change our lives and renew our Church.'

In a long interview with the *Sunday Telegraph*, he expanded on this theme. The trouble with Don Cupitt, he said, was that he had moved from natural science to the philosophy of religion, without pausing to study much Church history.

'Cupitt is much cleverer than I am,' he added, 'but I'm the Archbishop of Canterbury.'

The Archbishop of York, he said, was a much abler theologian than he. The Bishop of Durham had lectured excellently in his time. But he had perhaps failed to distinguish between the job of a bishop and an academic theologian.

'Jenkinses come and Jenkinses go,' he added, 'it's just that TV gives them much wider coverage.'

In a letter after the interview, he wrote at the bottom: 'Spare a prayer for me, that I may speak with simplicity and wisdom at Christmas.' To his credit the journalist recorded the fact.

That Christmas he preached as usual in Canterbury Cathedral. Four days later, in the dining room of the Deanery, the first meeting took place of the Canterbury Committee of the 1988 Lambeth Conference, then three and a half years away. It was St Thomas's Day; 29 December 1984.

The Archbishop was in the chair. Also present were the Archdeacon of Canterbury, John Simpson, who was to chair the Committee thereafter, and Canon Sam Van Culin, Secretary General of the Anglican Consultative Council. One person was absent when, at 10.30 a.m., the Committee sat down to business.

At 11.15 a.m. the door of the dining room opened, and the missing member of the meeting walked in. But no apologies were required from the latecomer, nor were words of reproach forthcoming from the assembled. Such was his stature that, the moment he appeared, everyone including the Archbishop stood up to welcome back Terry Waite from his latest journey to Libya.


Bishop Hook retired and was succeeded by Ronald Gordon, who was to be known as Head of Staff and Bishop at Lambeth. Bishop Gordon was a man of the Knapp-Fisher era at Cuddesdon, where he had also served as chaplain. He had spent nine years as Bishop of Portsmouth. He was unmarried. Ruth Hook was missed for her care and concern among the staff and families at Lambeth.

Terry Waite and the Archbishop posed outside the Palace with a copy of the Koran: a Christmas present from Colonel Ghaddafi. The Libyan leader had witten in it: 'My greetings and congratulations for the new year, hoping it will be a year of blessing for humanity.'

Waite had presented him with a copy of a book entitled *Aristotle and the Arabs*. They had spent part of Christmas Day discussing theology in Colonel Ghaddafi's Bedouin tent inside his heavily fortified headquarters in Tripoli. Waite had promised that the British Churches would help Libyan students detained in Britain, who he assured the Colonel were not being tortured. He also managed to hold a carol service for the British detainees, praying with them and distributing presents sent by their families. They were still detained when he returned to Britain, but he remained optimistic about their release.

Waite almost immediately flew back to Tripoli. He addressed a

2,000-strong 'people's congress' in a circus tent. In a speech broadcast live on Libyan television, he told them: 'Politics is made by men. Mercy, compassion and justice come from God. The way to deal with the enemy is not by the gun or the bullet. The way to deal with the enemy is by superior moral and spiritual strength.'

He told them he had met Libyan students in Britain, and that he would meet their families in Tripoli: 'I want to give them further assurances. Why do I do it? It is my duty to God and to you.'

His speech was enthusiastically received in Libya. Although he returned empty-handed for the third time he was again invited back by the Libyan Foreign Bureau, this time to address the Libyan General Congress. On 8 February 1985, after more delays and delicate negotiations, Waite and the four Britons returned safely to Britain.

They arrived at Gatwick Airport and studiously resisted attempts at triumphalism made by the press. Waite paid tribute to 'my own Archbishop, without whom none of this would have happened and who has the grace and humility to stay in the background'.

The members of the first session of that year's General Synod in turn paid tribute to the courage and endeavour of Terry Waite. After prolonged applause the Archbishop expressed his 'gratitude for the prayers and support without which the mission could not have been brought to a successful conclusion'. This was a perspective lacking in the press, which were almost daily printing profiles of 'the Church of England's Dr Kissinger'.

Waite was preoccupied with planning the Archbishop's forthcoming visit to Australia. He was also in communication with the Reverend Frederick Wilson, Associate General Director of the Program Agency of the Presbyterian Church of the USA.

Fred Wilson was a colleague of the Reverend Benjamin Weir, the American Protestant missionary held hostage for nearly a year in Beirut. The Weir family and their associates had twice offered their own negotiator to the American administration. Both times they had been turned down for unexplained reasons.

Waite had been approached by them via Bob Lodwick, a Geneva-based American whom he knew through the World Council of Churches. Although he was already fully occupied and there was no obvious Anglican connection, in September 1984 he had told Wilson over the transatlantic telephone that, in Wilson's words, this was 'the kind of situation they could and would be involved in'.

Wilson had sent Waite briefing material on Benjamin Weir. Lodwick had then flown to London and met Waite at Lambeth. Now, after his success in Libya, Waite had agreed to meet Wilson in New York on his return from Australia.

The Synod had proceeded to its main business. This was the debate inspired by the Standing Committee report *The Nature of Christian Belief*, which was inevitably to be seen as a response to the furore over the pronouncements of the Bishop of Durham. Some years had passed since the Church of England had publicly examined its own conscience over matters of doctrine and the precedents were not promising.

But the present Bishop of Durham was no great exception. Bishop Hensley Henson (also of Durham), Bishop Barnes of Birmingham and the young William Temple had all inspired controversy with their views on the symbolic versus literal interpretations of certain key areas of doctrine. A report, *Doctrine in the Church of England*, produced in 1938 after seventeen years of investigation by a commission chaired by William Temple had reasserted the legitimacy of such diverse opinion. Temple became a doctrinally conservative Archbishop of Canterbury.

But, as Clifford Longley of the *Times* pointed out, until David Jenkins, no one since the Second World War who was publicly identified with a 'liberal' interpretation of the Virgin Birth and Resurrection had actually been made a bishop.

Longley went on:

*'Bishop Jenkins was saying something that many theologians had said many times before – and some of them would go a lot further. To him, Jesus's conception was a physical event, implying a human father; and the Resurrection was a "miracle" only in the sense that the disciples were given the faith to believe that Jesus was raised from the dead, implying that his physical body remained in the tomb. But he also said – and declared most solemnly in his own consecration service – that he believed in the Incarnation (that Jesus was God-made-Flesh) and in the Resurrection. Those two beliefs pervade his theological writings and lectures.'*

Longley gave as good a summary of this complex subject as was to be found anywhere:

*'His numerous critics do not think that is good enough, however. They say, in essence, that to divorce the doctrine of the Resurrection from its anchor in a historical event is to undermine it. In other words, Bishop Jenkins and theologians like him have redefined the Resurrection to mean something else. When he says he believes in it, he does not mean what the Church has always understood it to mean. Similarly with the Virgin Birth: if Jesus had a human father, the phrase "Son of God" must have a different meaning from that traditionally understood. Thus doubt is cast on the whole concept of Jesus's divinity.*

*Nothing in the Church's founding documents, whether the Creeds of the early centuries or the Thirty-Nine Articles of the sixteenth, explains exactly how the words Resurrection and Virgin Birth are to be understood. So theologians on either side can have a field-day. There is the common-sense approach: "Of course 'Virgin Birth' means what it says." There is the sophisticated view, influenced by modern philosophy and nineteenth century biblical criticism, that such stories in the Bible are there to express a religious truth about Jesus, not to describe historical events in detail. And there is a theological fashion, with its counterpart in every British bus queue, that just dismisses miracles as medieval fantasy.*

*'Both sides,'* Longley concluded, *'claim that their version is the one with most appeal. The liberals say modern man cannot swallow miracles and is repelled by a Christianity that relies on them. The conservatives say countless numbers of the simple faithful are bewildered and distressed to find their cherished beliefs swept aside by a bishop. And the public at large is simply confused.'*

The debate produced some familiar voices in some familiar positions.

Oswald Clark, Chairman of the House of Laity, rebuked the Bishop of Durham, though not by name: 'There is no doubt that people do want decisions and positive guidance, and not just words . . . This problem is not going to go away; and meaning cannot be divorced from publicly verified fact.'

The Bishop of London said that facts did not bring with them their own interpretation. 'It is we who must seek to understand how they should be interpreted.'

In an article in the *Mail on Sunday*, he quoted the Nicene Creed and wrote: 'Any bishop who says these words while in his heart allowing room for doubt, fudging or equivocation, should really be somewhere else.'

Dr Gareth Bennett said: 'Some academic theologians gave the impression that they can tell you the exact meaning of the Bible or make definitive judgements on traditional Christian doctrine. Do not believe them. There is nothing quite so dated as last generation's fashionable academic theology.'

David Holloway was Vicar of Jesmond in Newcastle and one of Bishop Jenkins' fiercest critics. He spoke of the 'cancer of false doctrine' and declared that they were living in a crisis time for the Church of England (a statement valid at any point in its history). He damned 'effete theological liberalism' as irrelevant to the thinking young; whether or not he was aware of the irony of regarding his own views as being relevant to the 'thinking' young was unclear.

The Archbishop of York, John Habgood, spoke with customary authority. There was nothing new in this debate, he told Synod, and by inference nothing to be so hysterical about.

'We are not a gnostic sect, playing with ideas,' he went on. 'We are witnesses to what God has done in history.

'The Virgin Birth is only one part of the historical anchorage, and a weak one at that. Those who do not believe it reject it not on account of their innate liberalness, but because of its inappropriateness to the doctrine of the Incarnation.

'I could argue that the Empty Tomb is lower down in the hierarchy of the Resurrection than the appearances of the disciples . . .'

The Archbishop of Canterbury would have agreed closely with Habgood, but also spoke as head of a Church whose integrity had been called into question. His task, as he saw it, was to reassert that integrity as Temple had done before him; without resorting to a denial of its basis in a living diversity rather than a dead conformity of thinking.

He also had to say something about Jenkins.

'I welcome this debate . . .' he began, 'the Church of God has a gospel to proclaim, a faith to affirm. Even though the entire course of Church history has been marked by controversies on issues great and small, the Church is still not a debating society but the people of

God, called to witness boldly to his goodness in creation, to his inestimable love in redemption . . . I think it right to begin in this way . . .'

He told them: 'A nerve has been touched and exposed with painful effect, but not for the first time,' he proclaimed the need for statements on particular points of doctrine, but such statements had to be made in the right way.

This brought him to the responsibilities of a bishop:

'First the bishop is the guardian of tradition. From the earliest times the bishop's essential, defining role has been that of teacher and expounder of God's word. The bishop's "cathedral" is a teaching chair, not a royal throne. Our canon says of diocesan bishops: "It appertains to his office to teach and uphold sound and wholesome doctrine, and to banish and drive away all erroneous and strange opinions". . .'

Jenkins, literally, took note. The Archbishop quoted the words of 'no stranger to this perilous path', the late John Robinson:

*'A bishop will be the more aware that his lightest word is liable to be taken up – and distorted – by the public media. The inordinate attention paid to what he says derives almost entirely from his office, and his utterances and actions will therefore appear, particularly outside the Church, but also to embarrassed faithful within, to commit many others than himself. This means he must exercise special prudence and imagination . . .*

*'A man of unimpeachable orthodoxy but uncertain integrity,'* the Archbishop concluded in Robinson's memorable words, *'is a far greater threat to Christian truth than the man of questionable orthodoxy but undeniable integrity.'*

This was a rebuke, but also a tribute to the integrity of the Bishop of Durham. As an assertion of his own authority at a time when it was needed, it was one of the most important addresses of the Archbishop of Canterbury's six years at Lambeth. No vote was taken. Instead, with his encouragement, a small and diverse group of bishops was assembled to look more closely into the matter.

The lessons of the Jenkins affair and the debate that followed had far wider implications than for the clergy of the Church of England. Crude invocations of 'the hungry sheep' made by evangelicals were not a constructive approach to the problem. What brought one person to the faith, to a particular 'knowledge' of God, was not what brought the next. A further problem was that the Church of England was a reflection of English society: a society in which the vast majority of people did not progress beyond what little they were taught of Christianity at school.

The philosophy had for too long been to keep them in ignorance, in the pews, and in awe of the man in the funny clothes. This did not work any more, and there was no point in pretending that it did. Fourteen hundred years after the arrival of St Augustine, the average Briton knew less about Christianity than Colonel Ghaddafi. But the British people still insisted that they had the right to know whether or not they would be reunited with their pets in heaven.

The Archbishop preached to a congregation of 2,000 people including the Queen and the Prince and Princess of Wales in St Paul's Cathedral on the 50th Anniversary of the King George V Jubilee Trust. He said they did not have to look as far as Ethiopia for social deprivation and hardship; they were here in the inner cities.

Some politicians predictably missed the point. Neil Hamilton, Conservative MP for Tatton, accused him of 'going over the top'. That very same day, the Archbishop was going to Number 10 Downing Street, where he and Terry Waite were entertained by the Prime Minister to lunch.

Shortly afterwards the Archbishop travelled to Newcastle, where he preached at an ecumenical service in the Cathedral Church of St Nicholas. He had been ordained priest here over thirty years earlier. During his visit he told a meeting: 'My father was a Scottish chief engineer in a refinery which is now a shell, my mother a hairdresser on a Cunard liner whose dock is now part of a desert wasteland. So you can appreciate that when I talk about cities I am in danger of wearing my heart on my sleeve.'

Ray Whitney, a junior government minister with responsibility for Social Security, launched a bizarre attack. The Archbishop, he said, was distorting the facts 'in a way which only the most extreme of political activists would dare'.

The furore over his role was fanned by the press and fuelled by the Jenkins affair and the Church and State debate. The Archbishop preached his Easter Sermon in Canterbury Cathedral. In speaking of the Resurrection he reaffirmed the simplicity, rather than the complexity, of gospel rather than theological 'truth'.

He and Waite departed shortly afterwards for a three-week visit to Australia. In Newcastle, New South Wales, the Archbishop met his long-lost aunt, Nancy Runcie's sister Isobel. In Sydney he met Australian bishops and clergy. In Canberra he spoke at the dawn service on ANZAC Day.

Back in London, at Westminster Abbey, he preached on the fortieth anniversary of VE-Day. This was one of his finest sermons.

'It is right that we should remember the pity of war,' he said. 'Today, in this place, it is fitting that we should remember the sorrows of the United Kingdom in particular – the lives lost or laid waste, the treasures obliterated.

'But it is also right to remember the good that can be set against the grief. Part of the Christian answer to the external riddle of evil is that great afflictions call forth great virtues, public and private . . .

'Some people question now whether the war was really necessary, and whether anything was achieved by the victory. I respect their freedom to make such a judgement, but I profoundly disagree with them. It was not a panacea for every ill. But the victory which closed down Belsen, Buchenwald and Auschwitz is in itself sufficient cause for thanksgiving . . .

'Every generation has its own problems to solve, and fresh forms of evil to resist.'


In New York, Terry Waite kept his appointment.

Waite was now at the height of his fame: a world figure in his own right who had brought great additional prominence to the Runcie primacy. At Lambeth visitors used to knock on Mary Cryer's door. 'Where's Terry's office?' they would ask. A sighting of him would send them into rhapsodies. Waite and the Archbishop were once walking in a London street when a builder called down from his scaffolding: 'Hey, Terry! Terry mate! Come up and have a cup of tea! and bring your friend with you!'

On 10 May 1985, Waite met Benjamin Weir's wife Carol and their son John in the offices of the Episcopal Church at 815 Second Avenue,

New York. He told them he worked from a humanitarian perspective and had no political point of view. He had to remain neutral in any mediation. Above all, he could not and would not represent the American government.

As well as the Weirs, Fred Wilson, Oscar McCloud and Alvin Puryear, all American church officials, were present. They showed Waite a letter dated that February from Benjamin Weir in Beirut. They repeated their request for his help, not just for Weir, but for the other Americans held hostage in Beirut: Father Martin Jenco, a Roman Catholic priest; Terry Anderson, the Beirut Bureau Chief of Associated Press; David Jacobsen, Director of the American University Hospital in Beirut; and Professor Thomas Sutherland, Dean of Agriculture at the American University.

Several days later Waite, the Weirs and their church associates met again, this time in the apartment of the Presiding Bishop of the Episcopal Church, John M. Allin. Waite was also introduced to a new figure. He was neither a priest nor a missionary, but he brought the zeal and urgency of both callings to his work for Robert McFarlane at the National Security Council. He had seen active service in Vietnam; he allowed it to be believed that he had had extensive special operations experience. He had met the Weirs only ten days earlier, but had shown an immediate interest in Benjamin Weir and the other hostages in the Lebanon.

With McFarlane's agreement he had offered himself as their contact with the State Department.

He told Carol Weir: 'I am a believer in the Lord Jesus Christ, and I have dedicated my life to him.'

His name was Lieutenant Colonel Oliver North.


In London the Archbishop deplored the waste of life in the Heysel stadium football disaster. He mourned the lack of 'reverence for life, reverence for other people . . . here we have a situation where other people are just rubbish,' he said, 'because they don't seem to matter.'

This was a time for public mourning, and for remembrance of other such occasions. At the service in St Paul's Cathedral to dedicate the Memorial to the South Atlantic Campaign four years earlier, he reminded his congregation:

'For those directly involved in the South Atlantic, and for those who through it suffered pain and loss, memories today will be many, fresh and sharp. I still think of the young wife of a marine, interviewed on television with her children as her husband's ship sailed from Portsmouth. "How do you feel to see him go?" she was asked. "It is his duty to fight," she said. "He is doing his job – he will be all right." He was among the first to be killed. It is primarily to those people and for those people I try to speak this morning.'

Terry Waite returned from New York and was awarded the £2,000 Templeton Award for his role in negotiating the release of the Britons held in Libya. Waite was not a rich man but he announced he would give half the money to his native village of Styal in Cheshire. The other half would go to a YMCA project in the Lebanon.

Waite's burgeoning interest in the Lebanon was one of many commitments he made without much consultation at Lambeth. The Archbishop remained as admiring of him as ever, but was also as dependent on him to pave the way for his numerous overseas visits. Waite was now designated his 'Secretary for Anglican Communion Affairs', an elevation from 'Assistant' although nobody quite seemed to know what it meant. This latest undertaking to help Americans held in Beirut seemed further than ever outside his official remit.

This was not necessarily a bad thing – after all as a hostage negotiator Waite had raised the profile of the Archbishop of Canterbury throughout and beyond the Anglican Communion – but for this reason and others, including the imminent possibility of reprisals against the Beirut hostages, the Archbishop invited Alvin Puryear, the Presbyterian associate of Benjamin Weir whom Waite had met in New York, to visit him at Lambeth.

The exact contents of their meeting were not broadcast. The Archbishop was willing to sanction if not actually encourage Waite's continued involvement with Churches beyond the Anglican Communion. In the minds of the Weir family there was no ambiguity whatsoever about the matter.

'Alvin made a quick trip to London,' Carol Weir later noted in her account of this period. 'Subsequently it was agreed that Terry Waite would work full-time for the release of the hostages.'

If this was agreed, it was not clear by whom, and what steps would be taken to cover for Waite in his official capacity as Secretary for Anglican Communion Affairs at Lambeth. This was, if not an outright contradiction, a difference of interpretation that was to lead rapidly to confusion; and, within eighteen months, to tragedy.

With some relief, after the momentous doctrinal debates of the first session, the second session of the Synod of 1985 passed uneventfully. The Bishops' Commission into Doctrine was under way, and was expected to produce a low-key report somewhat sooner than the seventeen years it had taken their predecessors. The Archbishop amiably reminded Synod that: 'Since the sixteenth century we have been an ecumenical movement in our own right.'

He travelled to Oxford, to deliver the inaugural address of the Vacation Term for Biblical Study at the University Church of St Mary the Virgin. St Mary the Virgin had been John Henry Newman's own church before he became a Roman Catholic. Peter Cornwell, Robert's vice-principal at Cuddesdon and Vicar of St Mary's for ten years, had recently announced his secession to Rome, a move which had left its mark on his colleagues in the Cell, Robert Runcie, Jim Thompson and Mark Santer.

Terry Waite visited Libyans detained in Britain and was to be seen coming to the aid of the Historic Churches Preservation Trust bicycle ride by riding a penny-farthing around the Outer Courtyard at Lambeth. He was also visited by Carol and John Weir, Fred Wilson and Alvin Puryear. He told them, although he could not say why, he thought Benjamin Weir would be among hostages released shortly.

Waite, Witheridge and the Archbishop were due to depart at the end of August on a three-week tour of North America and Canada. So was Lindy, whose inclusion provoked some salacious press speculation about why the Archbishop and Mrs Runcie normally spent so little time together. The gutter press had long tried to extend their lines into the Palace of Lambeth, and were prepared to bribe and suborn former employees to this end. But the source of these particular stories was closer to home, and all the more hurtful for that.

One woman employed at the Palace had befriended Lindy but

antagonised nearly everyone else. She was eventually encouraged to leave.

Inez Luckcraft had been away from Lambeth for over two years, and was surprised to be telephoned at her home in Dorset by reporters from a newspaper. They said they had been given stories about life at Lambeth by a former employee. They were wondering if Mrs Luckcraft might help them dish the dirt on Rosalind Runcie.

Mrs Luckcraft politely declined the invitation; the words 'thirty pieces of silver' may have crossed her mind. She then telephoned Eve Keatley, the Lambeth Palace Press Officer. Mrs Keatley in turn issued various warnings but the gutter press did not give up. In the *Star* Peter Tory quoted numerous unnamed 'friends' of the Archbishop and Mrs Runcie: 'Official separation' he declared, 'is probably out of the question.'

The following day Tory quoted Bishop Hook's denial that anything was amiss in such a way as to suggest the opposite. He then had another unnamed 'close source we have consulted' claim that 'the matter is vital for the church'. Lindy was appalled by these stories. Her reaction was uncomfortable, if appropriate; they made her physically sick.

James Runcie had been rehearsing a fashion show of which he was director when a *Sunday People* reporter approached him. Having issued a defence of his mother, he too was distressed when the *Sunday People* used his words out of context in what they termed 'a remarkable exclusive interview' with him.

A proposed book revealing 'life behind the scenes' at Lambeth did not appear. There would be other more unpleasant personal attacks on the Archbishop of Canterbury and his family. Lindy would learn that, however lonely she was, it did not always pay to trust people she thought were her friends. James Runcie would learn that even when he tried to deflect prurient interpretations of his forthcoming marriage to a divorcee with a child, it was better to say nothing; anything he said would be used with apparent impunity against him. Eve Keatley warned him that this was only the beginning. If the tabloids truly wanted to go after his father, she said, they would stop James' wife at the theatre where she worked; and his step-daughter on her way home from school.

*

It was from this atmosphere that Robert and Lindy Runcie travelled together in late August on the first leg of the Archbishop of Canterbury's three-week tour of North America and Canada. For the first two weeks she accompanied him, giving charity piano recitals along the way.

In Gander, Newfoundland, he spoke of how the Anglican Communion could reach farther and wider than the Commonwealth to make the world a better place. In Halifax, Nova Scotia, he preached on leadership in Church and State and called for a positive Anglican response to the recent ARCIC agreements. In Ottawa he had lunch with the Prime Minister, denied that the British government was considering the disestablishment of the Church of England, and advised his fellow-guests not to believe everything they read in the newspapers. In Saskatchewan he drove a tractor that towed a combine harvester which unloaded grain on to a truck driven by the local farmer's son. In Montreal he addressed the Canadian House of Bishops. In Anaheim, Los Angeles, he preached at the opening service of the General Convention of the Episcopal Church of America.

At the last of these engagements he ended on a personal note that yet conveyed to the assembled a sense of the indivisibility of the Anglican Communion. The Church of England, as he had said a year earlier in Nigeria, was but a part of this. Invoking the Lambeth Conference, to which many of them would be invited to travel, he brought them briefly to the Cathedral to which they would come in three years' time:

'When sometimes I stand in the silence and stillness of the great Cathedral at Canterbury, I reflect that so far from everything being at peace, I am surrounded by mighty forces. The high vaults are striving to push the walls outwards; the buttresses are trying to push them inwards; the aisle vaults are doing their best to push the nave columns inwards but are unable to move them under the weight of the triforium. The whole fabric is struggling to explode and come crashing down. Yet forces which could prove so disastrous and destructive are miraculously harnessed into a building of transcendent and indescribable beauty and harmony.

'Within the construction of our Church, within the building up of the body, there are today many countervailing forces which make for destruction and disintegration. But our faith and trust is in One who can take us and build us up into a rich and various solidarity and unity which may be used in his service and to his honour and glory in the years to come.'

In the middle of September 1985, the Islamic Jihad organisation released the Reverend Benjamin Weir from his sixteen-month captivity in Beirut. They told the missionary they wanted him to give a message to the American government to place pressure on Kuwait for the release of Moslem Arabs held after the bombings of embassies there. They also hoped he would convince the American public of the idea that their government should listen harder to their aims if the remaining hostages were to be freed.

Weir was reunited with his family at a military airfield in Norfolk, Virginia. Wilson and Puryear, his Presbyterian colleagues, were present; as were a clutch of CIA men; and Oliver North.

Weir called a press conference at the National Presbyterian Church Centre in New York. He invited Terry Waite to be there. Waite immediately flew out from London. Also present were former hostages, families and friends of those still held, and several hundred news reporters. Weir spoke at length of his own ordeal, of the others still held and of the need to keep the issue of the hostages alive. His last request was that they support the efforts of the man who had done so much to help other hostages, the Archbishop of Canterbury's 'special envoy', Terry Waite.

What neither Waite, nor the Weirs, nor their associates in the Presbyterian Church knew, was the truth behind the release of Benjamin Weir. This was at that time known only to a few people: Oliver North, Robert McFarlane, David Kimche, a diplomat and former agent of Mossad, the Israeli intelligence service, and Manuchar Ghorbanifar, an Iranian arms dealer.

These men were already embarked on a plan to supply missiles to Iran in exchange for the release of the American hostages by their Iranian-controlled captors in Beirut. The missiles were intended to help Iran continue its war against Saddam Hussein's Iraq, the power most feared by the other countries including Israel in the Middle East. The hostage they particularly wanted released was William Buckley, the CIA station chief in Beirut.

The first batch of missiles was secretly flown to Iran. McFarlane was offered the choice of which hostage should be freed. He chose Buckley. Ghorbanifar sent word that Buckley was 'too ill' to be moved. In fact he had already been tortured to death. The Reverend Benjamin Weir was freed instead.

North and his associates still hoped for the release of Buckley and others, but looked for a better cover under which to conduct their next arms-for-hostages deal. Terry Waite, only tangentially concerned with the release of Weir, was an Englishman rather than an American, unconnected with political and intelligence agencies, and willing and able to travel back and forth to liaise with hostage-takers in the Lebanon.

North offered him transport and logistical support. Waite already had the money; since his success in Libya a special Church of England fund had collected huge public donations to enable him to continue his good work. Waite was encouraged by North, and by the grateful Presbyterians. Now, as he had done so successfully in Iran and Libya, he agreed to take the central role in Lebanon.


The Archbishop was increasingly concerned with planning the Lambeth Conference, and his sermons and addresses reflected his preoccupation with the subject. Among the many issues that were likely to surface, and by no means the most important, was that of the ordination of women to the priesthood.

Wippell's, the clerical outfitters, had already demonstrated their readiness for the prospect of women deacons, raised by the Synod's recent vote to allow legislation to be brought forward for the ordination of women to the priesthood. In what the *Church Times* called a 'fetchingly illustrated leaflet' they unveiled their latest designs in 'Clergy Wear for Women'.

These included cassocks nipped at the waist in both 'Anglican' and 'Latin' style, and the 'old English' surplice with 'angel-wing' sleeves. Wippell's also advertised black clerical shirts with ample gussets. 'It's all a matter of contours,' added a spokesman for the firm.

But there were others to whom the clothing of 'the monstrous regiment' was cause for anything but celebration. Prominent among these was the Bishop of London, Graham Leonard, noted for his own fondness for vestments and episcopal adornment, but undisposed to the same for women. At a private conference at New College, Oxford, the academic home of Dr Gareth Bennett, Bishop Leonard addressed over one hundred clergy opposed to the ordination of women.

Unlike Bennett he was not a misogynist, and his views on the subject belied to some critics a caring pastoral nature. But like Bennett, this was a subject on which the Bishop and his followers would not be moved. 'It is commonly assumed,' he told the conference, 'by those who are determined to proceed with legislation that those who cannot accept it will either depart for other Churches or will in due course come to accept it. This is not the case.'

The Bishop denied suggestions that he was encouraging schism within the Church of England, or that he would be willing to lead a breakaway Church. But in his diocesan newsletter the following month he added that the consecration of a woman bishop

*'would be a very serious matter for the Anglican Communion. I would regard those who took part in such a consecration, and the bishops of that part of the Anglican Communion of which she was a member, as having departed from the apostolic episcopate . . .'*

If this sounded more like a letter from a Pope than a Bishop of London, there was a whiff of idolatry in the air. When Bishop Leonard had finished speaking at the conference, he was handed a glass of brandy; afterwards it was suggested that the unwashed glass should be kept as a relic of the occasion.

But if Leonard was in the minority of bishops in his views, the opponents of the ordination of women numbered several hundred among the male clergy. Among these in turn was Dr Gareth Bennett's friend and admirer Dr William Oddie, who had published a book entitled *What Will Happen to God?* This purported to explore the new Christian feminist theology in America and Britain.

Oddie's book exposed the anti-Christian nature of much radical American feminist theology. But his pre-existing thesis that a woman could not be a priest seemed to blinker his vision as much as the pagan harpies he damned so vehemently. Rosemary Hartill, the BBC Radio Religious Affairs Correspondent, herself no radical, politely wiped the sneer off his face:

*'The dangerous effect of this book is if it makes people imagine that the far shores of feminist theology are synonymous with the thinking of organisations like the Movement for the Ordination of Women. On the whole, MOW is so conservative a group, it is practically genteel. Most of its members are ordinary middle-of-the-road Anglicans who feel the Church is wasting marvellous resources in continuing to refuse to ordain women. Most of them have come to that view not through theory, but through knowing some of the women who feel called by God to the priesthood. These are not women who go off dancing in the moonlight in feminist covens, but women some of whom have already spent a lifetime quietly and faithfully serving the Church they know and love.'*

Dr Oddie, a part-time journalist as well as a priest in the Church of England, would not confine his attention to this matter. The Archbishop of Canterbury would also come to be among his targets. The Archbishop had other and more pressing matters in mind.

Among these were the third session of that year's General Synod and the forthcoming publication of the findings of his Commission on Urban Priority Areas. He was also increasingly involved in the latest hostage initiative of his Secretary for Anglican Affairs, Terry Waite.

Waite's undertaking to the Weirs and the American Presbyterian Church to attempt the release of other Westerners in the Lebanon had brought him into a political arena far more complicated than relations between Britain and Iran and Britain and Libya. America had stepped reluctantly into the role previously occupied by Britain as policeman of the Gulf. The result had been catastrophic for both the United States and the countries of the Middle East. It was essential that those Westerners who genuinely wished to act out of humanitarian rather than political motives were above all seen to be doing so.

Given that he was unaware of the potentially dangerous position in which he had already been placed by Oliver North, the need for the appearance as well as reality of integrity would have been uppermost in Waite's mind and indeed in that of the Archbishop. It was in this atmosphere that they received a visit from the Right Reverend Elia Khoury, Bishop in the Anglican Diocese of Jerusalem, early that autumn.

The Bishop's party included the Deputy Prime Minister of Jordan. Both were brave and distinguished men, and both were delegates of the official diplomatic wing of the Palestine Liberation Organisation. The British Foreign Secretary, Sir Geoffrey Howe, had already cancelled proposed talks with the two men after American pressure.

While Jewish groups protested about the visit and the *Daily Mirror* screamed that 'Runcie prays with PLO terror envoys', the Archbishop and Waite were receiving this delegation as legitimate members of the dialogue within the Anglican Communion. They were also sending a clear signal to the men behind the hostage-takers in Beirut.

Waite made one of his strongest public statements on the subject. In doing so he revealed a man of sterner stuff behind the expedient 'gentle giant' exterior. 'It is customary for the Archbishop to meet bishops who come here,' he said, 'and as is customary he prayed with him – for peace. Surely this is not an unreasonable thing to do?

'It is true that accusations have been made against the Bishop. He has always vigorously and strenuously denied them. The Israelis saw fit not to bring him to court but to deport him. He was never tried, never convicted; accusations have simply been made – and that is not good enough.

'He has assured me,' Waite went on, 'that he is against violence and terrorism from any source whatsoever. He has confirmed his personal support for a peaceful settlement in the Middle East, based on the relevant resolutions of the United Nations which mention the right of Israel to exist behind secure boundaries.

'The Bishop believes the settlement should acknowledge the right of the Palestinian people to exist on a secure basis also. He has said these things clearly and repeatedly. What more can he do?'

Three weeks later a letter was delivered by hand to Lambeth Palace. It was signed by the four Americans held hostage in Beirut. Four days later, Waite flew to the Lebanon.

In November 1985, the Archbishop celebrated the Inaugural Eucharist of the Fourth General Synod in Westminster Abbey in the presence of a congregation led by the Queen as Supreme Governor of the Church of England.

The Synod welcomed the report of the Crown Appointments Review Group and passed a motion to review the methods of appointing cathedral clergy. Dr Gareth Bennett spoke on the subject of suffragan bishops: 'a bright light', as Rosemary Hartill described his contribution, 'in a rather dim debate'.

The Archbishop of Canterbury welcomed the report. In his presidential address to the Synod he spoke at length of the state and nature of the Anglican Communion, of the forthcoming Lambeth Conference, the prospects for the Anglican-Roman Catholic International Commission (ARCIC) and other major issues of the Church of England and the Anglican Communion in the next five years.

He spoke of how he saw his own role in a world wider than the General Synod of the Church of England:

'Perhaps this is the moment to speak of how I understand my own role within the Anglican Communion. It is clear that the mass media would sometimes like to treat me as the Anglican equivalent of the Pope; they find it easier to concentrate their attention on a person rather than a committee, especially when that person lives in a sophisticated modern capital with a diplomatic network and efficient communications. There is, therefore, a constant demand for crisis management, for pronouncements from someone whom they can identify as an authority figure. I should like to assure you that I am aware of the dangers in this.'

At Lambeth, Eve Keatley could hear Waite's voice over the telephone in the Commodore Hotel. Beyond it she could also hear the gunfire of the rival militias, fighting for control of West Beirut.

Waite had been given a white bullet-proof vest which he wore; even as he ducked and ran for cover with the foreign press he always seemed to have a joke or a ready quote. He appeared exhilarated by the crazy high speed rides on which he was taken by heavily armed Shi'ite militiamen, to destinations which he always insisted on keeping secret. It was as if, in his innocence, he could not believe the excitement this unique position of trust had brought him.

The press loved him and likened him to a Scarlet Pimpernel, a modern-day miracle worker. Waite was a lone crusader, a popular hero, and this brave and private man was already beginning to tread the tightrope between hagiography and martyrdom. 'I think what I am doing is most important, don't you?' he would ask his colleagues

at Lambeth. 'It is important for the Archbishop, don't you think?' And
his overworked colleagues told him he was right, he was living proof
of the Christian response to the world. Privately, they wondered what
in heaven's name his latest mission had to do with Christianity or the
Archbishop of Canterbury.

Waite also seemed to be experiencing a kind of belated personal
liberation. He bought an open-topped MGB sports car and a peaked
cap, and posed in both for photographs in the Outer Courtyard at
Lambeth. His colleagues had only a vague idea of his contacts with
the Americans. He shuttled back and forth that winter, from Beirut
via London to Washington, to 'brief' Vice-President Bush on the
latest developments in the Lebanon; unaware that the Vice-President
and future President of the United States was party to the stratagems
of Robert McFarlane and Oliver North.

The Archbishop was also in regular contact with Waite; but he was
among those who were always pleasantly surprised to see him. 'Good
heavens, Terry,' he would say, 'there you are. Where have you been?'
The Archbishop was too busy to know, as a rule, more than vague
details of Waite's movements.

That December, while Waite was travelling between London, New
York and Beirut, the Archbishop was concerned with the publication
of one of the most important documents of his primacy. This was the
report of his Commission on Urban Priority Areas: the report called
*Faith In the City*.

The Archbishop's Commission had spent two years travelling the
cities of Britain. David Sheppard was Bishop of Liverpool, the city of
Toxteth, synonymous with riot and disorder. Wilfred Wood, Bishop
of Croydon, another member, was the Assistant General Secretary of
the National Union of Public Employees (NUPE).

There were more than a dozen members in all, men and women,
priests and laity, under the chairmanship of Sir Richard O'Brien. Yet
these three members, and one approving reference to Karl Marx in the
Report's theological section, were targeted in advance on the leakage
of the Report by certain government ministers through their outlets
in the press.

One result was that the 400 page-long *Faith In the City* sold out its
first print run of 7,500 copies and was immediately reprinted.

'Pure Marxist theology' was the reaction of one cabinet minister to part of the report.

In its early pages it contained the memorable words:

*'The city in human history is synonymous with civilisation; yet now we investigate it as a point of breakdown of Christian society.'*

'We have to report,' the Commission members said, 'that we have been deeply disturbed by what we have seen and heard.'

The Archbishop's Commission was equally critical of Church and State. The Urban Priority Areas were recognised, it said, yet

*'no adequate response is being made by Government, nation or Church. There is barely even widespread public discussion.'*

The Commission called for the establishment of a Church Urban Fund to underpin the Church's mission in these areas. The implication that a parallel initiative was needed, and was lacking, was embarrassing and painful to members of the Thatcher government.

But the conclusion of the Commission was neither negative nor self-congratulatory. The Church of England could not and should not do what it regarded was the job of the State. The Church of England could, however

*'by its example and its exertions proclaim the ethic of altruism against egotism, of community against self-seeking and of charity against greed'.*

The members of the Commission came to this conclusion:

*'Somewhere along the road which we have travelled in the past two years each of us has faced a personal challenge to our lives and lifestyles: a call to change our thinking and action in such a way as to help us to stand more closely alongside the risen Christ with those who are poor and powerless. We have found faith in the city.'*

The Archbishop listened to the mounting clamour and mounted a robust defence. 'This is a report,' he said, 'which raises questions not only about Church priorities, but about national, ethical and moral priorities, too. That does not make it Marxist in any sense of the term. It does not seem to me that the report or its conclusions can be categorised or slotted as left-wing or right-wing. It is a Christian critique with political implications.'

This was a remarkably restrained defence, however, given the irony of the situation. The leading priest of the Church of England, entrusted with the 'cure' or care of souls, was now having to defend his commitment to do so against the contempt of the State which had so entrusted him in the first place. Furthermore, he was being attacked by the very agencies of government which themselves purported to be concerned with poverty: the departments of social security and the environment.

In England, Church and State had not been mutually exclusive since the sixteenth century. Were those critics of the Church in government now saying that they were, or should be so?

The new edition of *Crockford's*, contained as usual an anonymous preface. The author in this case was probably David Edwards, Provost of Southwark:

*'Against the will of most of them,'* he said, *'the bishops have been made to sound like an Opposition.'*

He moved even-handedly through the issues of the past three years: the nature of marriage, the ordination of women, relations with other Churches, the doctrinal controversies of Jenkins and Cupitt.

The Pope's visit to Canterbury was 'a golden memory' for Anglicans, and there were many Roman Catholics who wished more progress of this kind had been made during this Pontificate:

*'At present,'* he wrote, *'the entire Roman Catholic Church is dominated by the personality of Pope John Paul II . . . The nature of his popularity is comparable with President Reagan's, although he is much more intelligent.'*

The Archbishop of Canterbury had more time than usual to read that Christmas; he was at Canterbury recovering from a hernia operation. The *Crockford's* Preface, besides being anonymous, was traditionally uncensored. As well as for his wit, the author was chosen for his honesty and lucidity, qualities required for any plausible assessment of the strengths and weaknesses of the Church of England. In that sense the anonymity of the author was irrelevant, and there was usually no secret as to his identity within the Church. It was all rather gentlemanly and churchy, but it was also a unique guide to the outsider interested in the Church of England, and possibly even in God. The Archbishop approved of that.

# RECESSIONAL

# 7

# *Turbulent Priests*

'In the Church of England things are not always what they seem to be.'
DR GARETH BENNETT, PREFACE TO *CROCKFORD'S* CLERICAL
DIRECTORY, 1987–88

THE Lambeth Palace administration continued to be run whenever the Archbishop was away by his Head of Staff, Bishop Gordon. As Research Officer Keith Cawdron had succeeded Andrew Acland, who had departed but would continue to work with Terry Waite. Wilfred Grenville-Grey was approaching retirement as Secretary for Public Affairs and Deputy Head of Staff. Grenville-Grey, Waite, Waite's secretary Stella Taylor, the Archbishop's Chaplain John Witheridge, the Secretary for Ecumenical Affairs Christopher Hill, Press Secretary Eve Keatley, Bursar Mary Cryer, Adviser for Deaconesses and Lay Workers Anne Tompson and the Archbishop's secretary Eleanor Phillips were the core of his personal staff, as he began his seventh year as Archbishop of Canterbury at Lambeth.

At the end of January he consecrated two pairs of new bishops in the cathedrals of Gloucester and Southwark, including his Cuddesdon student Nigel McCulloch, and David Wilcox, one of his successors as Principal of what was now Ripon College, Cuddesdon. Wilcox's successor as Principal was John Garton, also a Cuddesdon man of the Runcie era, who had served his title as curate with the Scots Guards and been a Chaplain to the Forces in Northern Ireland.

Ripon College, Cuddesdon, had changed a good deal since the amalgamation that resulted from the Runcie Report. But many of the decorative renovations remained from his time as Principal. Cuddesdon had a special personal significance for the Archbishop. When Garton became Principal the Archbishop had been sitting late in the Lords, but found time to write him a two-page letter on his appointment. He had built up ten years' worth of names there of future clergy for his diocese and his archiepiscopate. He treasured it as the one parish of which he had been vicar. He went back there whenever he could, and, however exhausted he was, he instantly relaxed. He wanted to be buried in Cuddeson, not Canterbury; in the churchyard of the small, simple church that stood in the middle of the village on the hill.

One change that would take place at Cuddesdon during his primacy was the admission of women. The day after the consecration in Gloucester, he received a letter at Lambeth from the Bishop of London on the subject. Leonard had recently been cited in the diocesan newsletter of the American Episcopalian Bishop John 'Jack' Spong of Newark.

*'I cherish a dream,'* Spong wrote, *'and entertain a hope that the diocese of Newark, which frequently by God's grace has been a leader in the Episcopal Church, might now be called to the vocation of providing the Anglican Communion with its first woman bishop.'*

As if this was not enough to alarm Leonard, Spong went on:

*'As the moment draws nearer when episcopacy will open to women, opponents are beginning to recycle all the arguments of the past and to make dire threats of chaos and schism. The Bishop of London, Graham Leonard, thinks so little of the Church decision-making processes that he threatens to encourage a division of the Church of England into two separate bodies if his point of view opposing women is not sustained.'*

Nor did Spong wish to leave out the Pope.

*'The discredited biblical argument,'* he added, *'continues to be heard from no less a person than Pope John Paul II.'*

This was bad news for Leonard and for the Archbishop of Canterbury, the leader of a Church of England in communion with the Episcopalians but concerned to maintain and improve relations with Rome. The

Archbishop was due to meet the Pope in Bombay in ten days' time. He had written in reply to the latter's own anxious letter about the ordination of women only that December. Now Leonard was making his own position uncomfortably clear.

'I would not be able to remain silent', he wrote to the Archbishop, 'if a woman bishop were consecrated uncanonically, and would feel bound to say that I could no longer be in communion with bishops who took part.'

This was the first of a series of letters from and encounters with Graham Leonard that year that was to culminate in Leonard making one of the most controversial episcopal visits in recent Church history. The issue on that occasion would not be the ordination of women, or their consecration as bishops; but the consequence would be similar to the case of David Jenkins: a public rebuke in the General Synod by the Archbishop of Canterbury.

The Archbishop spoke in the first session of Synod in the long debate on *Faith In the City* and the work of his Urban Priority Areas Commission. As he had done before Christmas, he made a robust and impassioned statement in its defence.

'I am delighted and grateful to receive their report,' he told the Synod. 'The report, I believe we can claim, is a Blue Book on the urban crisis of our times. A careful and expert diagnosis has been made, and the prognosis now requires a careful and sustained discussion and examination by us all.

'Not for a generation has the Church ventured to produce such a prophetic survey of a major issue.'

He welcomed government plans to invest in the inner cities. 'Such poverty of life,' he said, 'can surely never become acceptable to the largely affluent and industrial society that we have in Britain today.'

Sir John Stokes MP, a newcomer to the House of Laity and a Conservative backbencher, begged to differ. He revealed a rather different attitude. 'Many people living in these areas do not feel deprived,' he declared, 'they are certainly nothing like so poor as the cheerful Cockneys in my regiment during the last war.'

Sir John criticised *Faith In the City* for mentioning crime and vandalism, but not the riots, 'which were sinful', nor 'the sin sometimes involved in one-parent families'. People needed a standard to look up to, he said, and praised a recent statement on the virtues of self-help by the Chief Rabbi, of whom the Prime Minister also happened to be an admirer.

*Faith In the City* was a long and considered report requiring long and considered study. But, if the answers in it were sometimes naïve and aroused controversy, they were significant evidence that the right questions had been asked by its members.

The fact that it seemed to be writing out a prescription for the government may have indicated a degree of insensitivity on the part of its authors. *Faith In the City* certainly did nothing to dispel the notion that the Church of England had in the absence of an effective Opposition taken its place in the firing line. But, as the Archbishop had shown in his Coningsby Club address, this was sometimes the only honourable place for the Church of England to be. To some, *Faith In the City* had chosen soft targets and ignored the deeper causes of poverty in urban Britain. To others, the informal gathering of urban bishops, given shape by Eric James and encouraged by the Archbishop of Canterbury, had with its offspring the Church Urban Fund produced two of the greater achievements of the Church of England this century.

The Archbishop and Witheridge left for India, on yet another exhausting peregrination through the Anglican Communion. Everywhere they went, the Pope seemed to have been there before.

This became something of a joke; they entered Bombay just before the Pope was due to leave and were greeted by banners reading 'Welcome Papa'. But the timing was deliberate, so that the Archbishop and the Pope could meet at the end of the Pope's visit and the beginning of the Archbishop's tour.

After Accra in 1980 and Canterbury in 1982, this was their third meeting. In his confidential letter to the Pope the previous December, the Archbishop had made his position clear:

*'Lambeth Palace London SE1 7JU 11th December 1985*

*'YOUR HOLINESS*

*'The Churches of the Anglican Communion and the Roman Catholic Church are fully committed to the quest for full ecclesial unity. No one,*

*however, anticipates that the path towards unity will be without difficulties. One such difficulty, I fully recognise, is the difference of thinking and action about the ordination of women to the ministerial priesthood.*

*'The receipt of your letter of December last year on this question therefore prompted me to confidential consultation with the Primates of the autonomous provinces of the Anglican Communion throughout the world. They also judged your letter to be of great importance and by various means themselves sought the counsel of their own Provinces. Accordingly it is only now that I am able to make a substantive reply to your letter in the light of the responses I have received from the different parts of the Anglican Communion.*

*'Before all else, I want to thank Your Holiness for the constructive and frank character of your letter. The question of the admission of women to the ministerial priesthood is a divisive matter not only between the Churches but also within them. It is surely a sign of both the seriousness and the maturity of Anglican-Roman Catholic relations that we can exchange letters on a subject surrounded by controversy.'*

Since the departure of Richard Chartres, the Archbishop had leaned heavily on John Witheridge as sounding board for his statements. But the team which produced this letter was almost certainly the Archbishop and Christopher Hill:

*'I read your letter as an expression of that responsibility in pastoral care for the unity of all God's people which is part of the office of the Bishop of Rome. You may be certain that I received your letter in the same spirit of brotherly love with which it was sent and also intend this reply to reflect that "speaking the truth in love" of which your letter spoke.*

*'In this fraternal spirit I am bound to report that – although Anglican opinion is itself divided – those churches which have admitted women to priestly ministry have done so for serious doctrinal reasons. I have therefore felt an obligation to explain this more fully in a letter to His Eminence Cardinal Jan Willebrands, President of the Vatican Secretariat for Promoting Christian Unity, whose recent letter to the Co-Chairman of the Anglican-Roman Catholic International Commission now raises the discussion of the reconciliation of ministries to some prominence in the theological dialogue between our Churches. I fully realise what a serious*

*obstacle the actual admission of women to the priesthood appears to place in
the way of such a possibility.*

'*I would therefore propose to Your Holiness the urgent need for a joint
study of the question of the ordination of women to the ministerial priesthood,
especially in respect of its consequences for the mutual reconciliation of our
Churches and the recognition of their ministries. Indeed such a study
seems already implicit in the mandate of the Anglican-Roman Catholic
International Commission expressed in our Common Declaration at Canterbury of the 29th of May, 1982.*

'*Though the difficulty is grave, to face it together would, I suggest, give
real substance to the hope expressed at the end of your letter . . .'*

The Archbishop and the Pope were not able to make progress on the
subject of the ordination of women to the priesthood during their
forty-minute meeting in Bombay. But they did discuss a wide range
of subjects in a conversation which both hoped would keep alive the
warm personal relationship that underpinned the sometimes awkward
and procedurally cumbersome dialogues of ARCIC. The Pope also
extended an invitation to join him in a pilgrimage of peace at Assisi
later that year, which the Archbishop accepted.

In Delhi he met Prime Minister Rajiv Gandhi; in Calcutta he met
Mother Teresa and spoke of Indian Christianity at the Bishop's
House. In Madras he was greeted by a huge hoarding showing himself
instead of the Pope, and which read 'Welcome His Most Holiness
Archbishop of Canterbury'; he preached at the cathedral and he and
Lindy, who had joined him, were garlanded with flowers. In Vellore
he visited the Christian Medical College; in drought-stricken Bangalore he made a pre-prandial speech even longer than that made by his
hosts.

In fertile Kerala he addressed one hundred and fifty thousand people
at the ninety-second Maramon Convention of Mar Thoma Syrian
Christians, the spiritual legatees of St Thomas, the missionary who
first brought Christianity to India.

This was a far cry from the days of Robert Runcie, the Westcott
House chaplain who declined to contribute to *The Historic Episcopate
in the Fullness of the Church* on the grounds that he might be incrimi-
nated by his lack of theological qualifications to pronounce on the
Church of South India; and of Robert Runcie, the Principal of

Cuddesdon, who had torn up his Teape lectures on the aeroplane on the way home from Delhi.

In London he received another letter from Bishop Leonard. Leonard was becoming more and more public in his rejection of the validity of the consecration of women bishops. In the United States, where this event was likely to happen first, there were ninety-eight dioceses and two and a half million Anglicans/Episcopalians.

*'Some, like myself,'* Leonard wrote, *'would (I know) have to reconsider very carefully whether we would be able to be present at Lambeth in 1988 if women bishops were among those invited, since their very presence would indicate acceptance of them.'*

Leonard could cite bishops in Australia, the West Indies, Japan, South Africa and Scotland who supported him. But in doing so he was conveniently ignoring the fact that each of these disparate parts of the Anglican Communion was operating on a schedule according to its indigenous Christian history; a fact of which the Archbishop was aware and strongly respected. Leonard, by contrast, seemed to regard the Anglican Communion as some sort of appendage to the Church of England. He seemed in turn to see Lambeth as an appendage to Rome, and appeared unable to understand why the Archbishop of Canterbury did not share his point of view.

In Canterbury for Easter, in his sermon on Maundy Thursday at the Liturgy of the Blessing of the Oils, the Archbishop spoke of the healing ministry of the Church in the example of the hospital at Vellore. He called for an end to the territorialisation of the Christian ministry: 'We are not meant, it seems to me, to put a fence around fonts and altars with passport and tariff restrictions.'

In his Easter Day sermon he spoke of the 'quiet gladness' of Christians on that day. Ten days later, Bishop Leonard of London placed an advertisement in the *Church Times* and the *Church of England Newspaper*.

The advertisement invited bishops, priests, deacons, deaconesses, members of religious orders and lay people to add their names in confidence to a register of those who believed that the ordination of women to the priesthood would imperil the doctrinal basis of the Church of England. Replies were to be addressed to the Reverend Robert Gould of Windsor, Chaplain to the Sisters of the Community of St John the Baptist, Clewer, and a member of the Order of the Good Shepherd, a dispersed society of celibate priests and laymen.

At the same time, the Movement for the Ordination of Women were finalising plans for their own symbolic event to take place in Canterbury Cathedral with the permission of the Cathedral Chapter in a week's time. A huge congregation was expected from all over the world. The battle lines were being drawn.


The event organised by the Movement for the Ordination of Women took place over three days and began with a three-hour vigil of repentance by the Priests for Women's Ordination and a candlelit 'liturgy of hope' on the evening of the Friday. An American woman priest pronounced peace 'in the nature of an absolution'.

As the Archbishop had done with his small band of colleagues from St Albans shortly before his enthronement, the several hundred participants then processed holding candles through the darkened Cathedral, to the place of the martyrdom of St Thomas Becket, to the cloisters and the chapel of martyrs.

On the Saturday the congregation of two and a half thousand were joined by processions which had made their way to the Cathedral. They were welcomed by the Vice-Dean, John de Sausmarez, and the Secretary General of the Anglican Consultative Council, Sam Van Culin, responded to the greeting. The reading of the gospel, the preaching of the sermon and the administering of Communion were all performed by women; only the consecration of the bread and wine still had to be performed by a man, in this case the Vice-Dean of the Cathedral.

The Archbishop of York, the Primus of Scotland and the Primate of Canada sent messages of support. David Sheppard, Bishop of Liverpool, received Communion from Helena-Rose Houldcroft, a woman priested by Archbishop 'Ted' Scott from Qu'Appelle, Canada. At the end of the service the congregation burst into applause. Then at the final Eucharist of the weekend, a small group walked out in protest at the fact that a male priest, albeit a supporter, had to perform the service. But the event had been a success: solemn, celebratory and moving.

The Archbishop of Canterbury had declined the invitation to take part. He had invited a group of women to Lambeth Palace three days earlier. They were unimpressed by his refusal to make the ordination of women to the priesthood a high priority on the grounds that he wanted to hold together both the Anglican Communion and the Anglican and Roman Catholic Churches. Later he telephoned a message of support after the successful end of the ceremonies.

Given the present delicate climate of relations with the Pope (the contents of the Archbishop's letter to him were still unpublished), it could be argued that there was nothing else he could do. He had already signalled his acknowledgement of the need for a greater role for women in the ministry. He did not see any contradiction between his disinclination to make an outright statement of support, and the legitimacy of the case for women priests.

But these were ramifications which did not make good copy even for journalists who understood them. Susan Young had travelled with the Archbishop in India as a journalist for the *Church Times*. She knew him well and was one of the best religious affairs journalists of her time. In her newspaper she now gave a vivid and powerful description of the events of that weekend at Canterbury. But she could not resist a certain disingenuousness about the Archbishop of Canterbury's position:

*'And it was the cruel position in which a lonely man found himself placed over that service,'* she wrote, *'which most poignantly demonstrated how it feels to be a woman excluded from the priesthood.'*

Nobody 'excluded' the Archbishop of Canterbury from the proceedings, nor was he any the more or less lonely for not having taken part. If anything, these words demonstrated the triumphalist tendency which gave ammunition to Bishop Leonard and his supporters, and to which the Archbishop could not and would never subscribe, no matter what was at stake. Only three weeks later, the Bishop of London was on television, raising the spectre of schism.

'I'm not prepared to leave the Church of England wholly in the hands of the liberals,' he declared, wearing one of his most conspicuous pectoral crosses and looking for all the world like a Cardinal from the Vatican. 'From my point of view the whole question of the ordination of women raises some absolutely fundamental questions about the way God has spoken to us, the way the world is made; and I don't think we are free to discard these.'

He was asked if this was not the time for him to issue a 'clarion call'.

He denied that. 'It mustn't be the kind of call which says we are going out, we are going to isolate ourselves,' he said. 'It has got to be a call to the Church of England to come to its mind about what it actually stands for, what it believes, what its own formulae are. This is what I'm trying to do.'

But, he was asked, would he like to assume the leadership of a breakaway Church?

'If it's there, yes,' he replied, 'naturally, yes.'

Bishop Leonard was a valued member of the small group of bishops who produced the report on *The Nature of Christian Belief* commissioned by the Archbishop after the debates ignited by the Jenkins affair in Synod a year earlier. The Archbishop welcomed the conclusions of the report. The Bishop of Durham pronounced it 'disappointing'. Dr David Samuel of the Church Society found it 'ambiguous and inconclusive'. Tony Higton, Rector of Hawkwell, Chelmsford, member of the General Synod and founder of the evangelical Association for Biblical Witness to Our Nation, said the time allotted for discussion of the report at the next Synod was 'quite inadequate'.

The Archbishop also gave a press conference at Lambeth to release the texts of the letters between himself and the Pope, and to announce the continuation of talks aimed at better links with Rome under the auspices of the Anglican-Roman Catholic International Commission (ARCIC). The issue of the ordination of women to the priesthood, he said, was not an insuperable obstacle.

The second session of that year's Synod opened with a Eucharist in York Minster. It was 6 July 1986, the feast day of St Thomas More: 'a martyr for steadfast conviction,' said the Archbishop, 'if ever there was one.'

In his address to the General Synod that same day he described the report on *The Nature of Christian Belief* as 'a consensus document' and quoted the late Stephen Neill, Bishop of Tinevelli, South India. The passage was reminiscent of his own temperamental preference for not rocking the boat:

'What is notable in Anglican history is not that violent passions have sometimes been stirred up, but that in times of passion, the climate of equable and discriminating study has so soon been restored.

'We only debate,' he went on, 'what we care about,' and finished with a plea for unity in the form of a tribute to Anglicanism: 'Anglicanism lives dangerously because it tries to maximise that liberty for the individual without losing the central definition and coherence of belief and practice. This is the spirit in which the House has responded to this Synod, and we hope to have your critical solidarity in our effort to offer guidance to our Church in these things.'

Anglicanism continued to live dangerously. Neither the report nor the debates that ensued prevented polarisation on these questions of doctrine and other issues. The debate on the approval of the draft *Measure for Women Ordained Abroad* resulted in its defeat after insufficient majorities. The Synod continued to be a safe place in which to debate these dangerous issues. But elsewhere one particular Anglican was living increasingly dangerously in his own quest for liberty for the individual.

Terry Waite had already spent one perilous week in June in South Africa during the state of emergency. He was gathering information for the Archbishop to use during the debate at the General Synod which called for effective sanctions against South Africa. On 23 July he flew to Jordan, ostensibly to attend the first meeting of the International Board of the Jordan Hospital. In fact he was waiting for a telephone call from Oliver North.

Waite was still utterly unaware of the true motives behind North's interest in the plight of hostages in Beirut. He was as pleased as ever that he had managed to enlist North's support. Furthermore, North seemed willing to forgo any credit for his role in the matter. Now North was even offering Waite the credit for an imminent release that rightly belonged to him.

What Waite did not know was that North and his superior Robert McFarlane had been thrown into panic by the near-breakdown of their arms deals with the Iranians. They had decided that the only way to revive the scheme was to warn the Iranians that, unless another Westerner was released, they would not see another missile. Ghorbani-far, the arms dealer and middleman, had delivered the message. The Iranians wanted the missiles. The message came back that North could expect the release of another hostage.

North had telephoned the unsuspecting Waite in Jordan. He told him to go to Damascus. Here, on 26 July 1986, Waite met the missionary Father Martin Jenco, who had been blindfolded, bundled into the boot of a car and driven for three hours over the mountains south-east of Beirut to the Beka'a Valley, where he was dumped dazed but free beside the main Damascus highway.

Waite and Jenco travelled to Frankfurt and then to the American Hospital at Wiesbaden, where Jenco was debriefed by officials from the State Department hostage team. The latter too knew nothing of the arms deals, and were perplexed and suspicious when they learned that North was only a few miles away in Frankfurt. North was meeting Ghorbanifar, but this too remained secret. Father Jenco, meanwhile, telephoned the Archbishop of Canterbury and the Pope to thank them for the part played in securing his release by their two Churches.

On Wednesday 29 July, Father Jenco and Waite flew to Rome where Jenco had an audience with the Pope. On Friday 31 July, Father Jenco arrived to meet the Archbishop of Canterbury at Lambeth. The Pope and the Archbishop were given a confidential message by Jenco from his captors. Also present at Lambeth was the Reverend Benjamin Weir.

Weir, like Jenco, Waite, the Archbishop and the Pope for that matter, was still unaware that his release had been secured by the sale of weapons rather than through Christian diplomacy. As he later recalled:

'On the morning of 31 July 1986, in London, I opened the door to the office of the Archbishop of Canterbury. The Archbishop was talking with another man who had his back to me. He said to him quietly, "Father Martin, a friend is waiting to see you."

'Father Lawrence Martin Jenco turned around. It was five days after his release. We held each other at arm's length for a few seconds and then embraced. It was a tearful, joyous, emotional hug. He said to me, simply but repeatedly, "Peace."

*'I responded with feeling. "I'm deeply thankful that the Almighty has delivered you. Praise God."'*

Waite, the Archbishop, Weir and Jenco posed happily for photographs at Lambeth. Waite was exultant, but let it be known that 'for security reasons involving the safety and future of the other detainees' he was unable to comment about his activities in the last few days.

He said he was holding himself in readiness to go back to the Lebanon at any time.

'His Holiness the Pope and the Archbishop of Canterbury,' he announced the next day, 'would wish the captors to meet with me as soon as possible to help find a solution to the problem based on the tenets common to Islam and Christianity. It is our belief and firm hope that there can be a resolution based on religious grounds.'

In Washington, Oliver North was still digesting the unpleasant news Ghorbanifar had given him at their secret meeting in Frankfurt. Without consulting him, the Iranian middleman had agreed a new deal with Tehran. The deal was for a series of arms deliveries in exchange for the release of hostages, one by one. North had been appalled, but now believed that this was the only way forward. He deliberately fed to his superiors the notion that the remaining hostages would be killed if the deals were not carried out in this way.

In fact William Buckley's case had been unique, and there was no evidence that the lives of the other hostages, however grim, were similarly endangered. Unlike Buckley they were not CIA agents. But North's superiors, with the knowledge of Vice-President Bush and President Reagan, approved this course of action. The missile deliveries would continue on this basis. So too would the need for a suitable cover; and, as Waite himself kept saying, there were still several hostages held in the Lebanon.

The Archbishop, Witheridge, Waite and Lindy travelled to the United States shortly afterwards, to San Francisco for a conference for overseas bishops. The Archbishop addressed the conference. 'I am most grateful,' he said, 'to the Episcopal Church in the USA, and especially to the Presiding Bishop's Fund for World Relief, for all that they have done to assist me in my attempts to find a just solution to some of the Lebanon's problems.'

Another problem, over which in reality he had just as little jurisdiction, was the sudden interest the Bishop of London appeared to be taking in the American Episcopalian diocese of Oklahoma; and in particular the parish of St Michael's, Tulsa.

The parish priest, Father John C. Pasco, had been disciplined after a dispute over church property. A deeper dispute lay in his refusal to accept many of the Episcopalian Church's policies, including the ordination of women to the priesthood. In November 1984 he had written to Leonard appealing for help.

Leonard had been about to enter hospital for a serious operation and had simply sent his good wishes. Pasco had pressed for a statement that Leonard was in communion with him and what remained of his congregation. Leonard had not initially felt able to oblige. Nor had the Archbishop of Canterbury. When Pasco had written to him in September 1985, he received a reply from Terry Waite saying, correctly, that the Archbishop had no jurisdiction in the matter.

Pasco had been 'deposed' or expelled from the Episcopalian Church. In June 1986 Leonard had written saying he was in communion with him. Leonard's Suffragan Bishop of Fulham, John Klyberg, agreed to conduct confirmations in Tulsa.

A flood of letters protesting at this had reached the Bishop of Oklahoma, including many from English clergy. The bishops and clergy of the Episcopalian Church had made it clear for their part that they found Leonard's intervention in their internal affairs 'offensive in the extreme'. The Diocesan Administrator of Oklahoma, Father Charles Woltz, was 'puzzled by the Bishop of London, because he seems to be out of step with the Church of England, never mind the rest of the Anglican Communion'.

The Archbishop had a number of meetings to discuss the matter with the Presiding Bishop of the Episcopal Church of the United States, Edmund Lee Browning. The Archbishop hoped that Leonard would retreat from his embarrassing position; after all, Leonard had been incensed when a woman priest ordained by Bishop Spong in America had celebrated the Eucharist in the Deanery of his own Cathedral four years earlier. But Leonard did not see it that way.

Although his relations with the Archbishop were still amicable, they would come under increasing strain that summer.

Terry Waite too was feeling the strain that summer. He went on holiday to have a 'long, hard think' as he put it, about his future. He was making meaningful noises at Lambeth about the demands of his job and the lack of financial remuneration. He hinted that he had been approached with the prospect of highly-paid work in America. He had already agreed to undertake a lecture tour there in the spring of 1987.

He remained as mysterious as ever about the efforts he was making to free the hostages in the Lebanon. He would come into Mary Cryer's office, shut the door, and ask her to arrange insurance for him to travel to America and Geneva. 'Don't tell anyone,' he would say, 'I don't want anyone to know,' and he would laugh conspiratorially.

He was spending more and more time travelling on hostage business and less and less at his desk doing the job a Secretary for Anglican Communion Affairs was supposed to do. Even the Archbishop was beginning to be aware that there was a burgeoning conflict of interest. But he was loyal to Waite, and Waite was an awesomely stubborn man whose own loyalty was beyond question and whose work had been of inestimable value to Lambeth. Everybody loved Terry Waite; and, if it was sometimes necessary to humour him, ultimately it was impossible to dislike him.

The Archbishop, Waite and Witheridge travelled to South Africa early that September for the enthronement of the eleventh Archbishop of Cape Town, and the first black person to hold the post, Bishop Desmond Tutu. Sixteen years earlier Archbishop Michael Ramsey had described his meeting with President Vorster as 'the worst day of my life', and Vorster as 'the most totally rude man I had ever met'. Ramsey had had to pick his words during his visit to South Africa as a soldier picks his way through a minefield. On his way back he had visited Uganda, where one of his most valuable contacts was a young lay Christian worker named Terry Waite.

Sixteen years later, Waite, Witheridge and Archbishop Runcie rejoiced at the enthronement of South Africa's first black archbishop and despaired at the poverty and violence caused by the divisions in South African society. After Tutu's enthronement the Archbishop told a congregation of ten thousand at an open-air Eucharist: 'Here in South Africa an old order is dying. As we watch, we experience agony, doubt and uncertainty which surround death.'

He quoted, illegally, from the trial speech of Nelson Mandela, then incarcerated on Robben Island. Mandela spoke of having fought 'against white domination and against black domination'. The Archbishop described Archbishop Tutu as 'a man of love, vision and peace, whose valiant stand for Christ has brought such life and hope to South Africa, and far beyond'.

He visited Crossroads, the derelict and burnt-out squatter camp outside Cape Town, whose inhabitants had been evicted three months earlier. He stood by a barbed-wire entanglement erected by police to prevent families from returning to what was left of their homes. 'People often stand by the Berlin Wall,' he said, 'and say what a dreadful symbol this is in our modern world. Well, isn't this a symbol in our modern world which is shocking?'

He knew that what mattered was not just what he said, but the fact that the Archbishop of Canterbury said it. He was depressed and sickened by what he saw. On the eve of his departure he tried to telephone home. He was told that all the lines were busy.

He gave his name to the operator. The latter replied in a way that even the Archbishop could only describe later as 'gratuitous and offensive'. 'I'm sure,' the operator told him, 'all that trivia about Tutu can wait until your return.'


Before his departure for South Africa he had issued an invitation to the Bishop of London. Leonard arrived on 10 September 1986 and their meeting was one of the Archbishop's first appointments on his return to Lambeth.

The interview was civil but awkward. Did Leonard not see that, by suggesting his Suffragan Bishop go to Tulsa on 12 October to conduct confirmations for Father Pasco, he was himself appearing to assist a priest who had been deposed by the Episcopalian Church?

Leonard did not see that.

Did Leonard not see the implications of exercising his ministry as a bishop of the Church of England in a diocese of the USA without the approval of the bishop there?

Leonard did not appear to see them, but agreed to think about this. He also agreed to think about the propriety of his support for a parish that was out of kilter with its own Church; and about the responsibilities of being Bishop of London.

Leonard said he would think about all these things. The Archbishop said he would be obliged if Leonard did so sooner rather than later. He was being pressed on all sides to do something about this turbulent bishop.

In September the report *A Rural Strategy for the Church of England* was produced by the Synod's Standing Committee. It was proposed to enlarge the field of enquiry by establishing a commission under the Archbishops of Canterbury and York to study the role of the Church in rural areas. Although funds would not be forthcoming until the following year, 1987, this was the genesis of the Archbishops' Commission on Rural England (ACORE), the rural counterpart to *Faith In the City*.

Two days later the Archbishop of Canterbury received his reply from the Bishop of London.

*'I accept,'* wrote Leonard, *'that to ask the Bishop of Fulham to go [to Tulsa] would be open to misunderstandings and could be taken as an exercise of my jurisdiction as Bishop of London, though I did not see it in that light. I also think, on reflection, that it would be unfair to ask him to do so.'*

This was a relief. Then came the bombshell:

*'I propose to go myself . . .'*

The House of Bishops of the Episcopal Church of the United States of America was meeting in San Antonio, Texas. They were outraged. They issued an official demand that Leonard be corrected and disciplined. The Bishop of London was unrepentant; he was going to Tulsa. The Archbishop thought he was wrong and told him so. Even the Bishop of London's Examining Chaplain, Dr Gareth Bennett, said he did not believe Leonard had any precedents for taking such action. Hugh Montefiore was concerned to find precedents for showing that Leonard should not go, and set about consulting learned authorities for this purpose. He also called for a motion in the House of Bishops to discuss the matter.

Leonard defended his position, knowing that the so-called 'liberals' on whom he poured such scorn would not in all conscience feel able forcibly to prevent him from boarding the aircraft for Tulsa. The Archbishop himself would be suspected of weakness even by his friends in this respect. Leonard also ignored the fact that the Archbishop of Canterbury had repeatedly been criticised in the press for his own alleged 'liberalism', and had himself publicly rebuked the Bishop of Durham for 'liberal' tendencies. Instead, Leonard suggested that the 'liberals' were unfairly exempted from criticism.

He made one particularly revealing statement, in his anger, that suggested a less articulate but perhaps deeper yearning:

*'It always seems to be those who believe they must stand for traditional belief and morals who get criticised publicly. However that is the stuff of martyrdom and while we must not seek it, I suppose we must embrace it when it comes.'*

Few doubted the sincerity which made Bishop Graham Leonard feel he must answer what he saw as a pastoral call several thousand miles away in another country. But like many a real martyr before and after him, he may have lacked the wisdom to distinguish between the vice of seeking martyrdom, and the virtue of embracing it when it came.

The Archbishop preached on the eight hundredth anniversary of the enthronement of St Hugh in Lincoln Cathedral. The Bishop was his old friend and acting partner from Westcott House, Simon Phipps. Phipps was to retire that year and was succeeded by one of the Archbishop's first Cuddesdon ordinands and later Director of the St Albans Ministerial Training Scheme, Robert Hardy.

Phipps was aware that one of the Archbishop's qualities was his ability to endure without panicking the suffering and fatigue that went with the job. The question of the ordination of women and the potentially schismatic nature of this were genuinely agonising to the Archbishop; he was not acting the part. The Archbishop's stay only confirmed him in this opinion.

He had known Robert Runcie since before he was ordained, and the friendship would last after Robert was no longer Archbishop of Canterbury. After his own retirement Phipps wrote Robert a letter in which he told the following story.

Phipps was being driven home in Sussex by taxi. The driver had droned on in the usual desultory way, until he asked Phipps his occupation. Upon receiving the answer 'retired bishop' he immediately cheered up. He began talking about the Archbishop of Canterbury.

'I think he's bloody marvellous,' said the taxi driver.

Phipps did not disagree.

'Now, how about that Bishop of Durham?' the driver asked.

'He's an old and good friend of mine.'

'Oh, so you're a bloody radical too, are you?'

Phipps was delivered home, and thanked the driver. 'Don't worry about the Church of England,' he said, 'you and I are the majority.'

'Well, I wouldn't say the majority,' the driver replied, 'let's say we're the intelligentsia.'

Phipps was so enchanted, he nearly got back into the taxi and asked him to drive on again.


Joyce Bennett, a woman priest ordained in Hong Kong, celebrated Holy Communion in a room at Church House before the annual general meeting of the Movement for the Ordination of Women. The Bishop of Kingston and the Dean of St Paul's, Alan Webster, whose wife Margaret was MOW's retiring executive secretary, were present and were pleased to receive Communion with a hundred others. The Archbishop was not pleased, and announced that, since he was in America at the time, he had asked his Head of Staff Bishop Gordon to investigate the matter.

The Reykjavik summit talks failed between Ronald Reagan and Mikhail Gorbachev. The Archbishop and Cardinal Hume held a press conference at Lambeth Palace to announce their forthcoming journey to join the Pope at Assisi, and maintained that world peace would be encouraged in this way.

The Archbishop's relationship with his wife continued to be peaceful, but the tabloid press had not given up in their attempts to present a marketable version of life 'behind the scenes at Lambeth'.

Thomas Hodgekinson, the gatekeeper, had refused to succumb to their blandishments. They had more luck with Jim and Maureen Stringer, who had just retired as the Lambeth Palace gardeners. Armed with the gardeners' gossip, they decided to launch another offensive against the Runcies of Lambeth.

Lindy was proud of her achievements with the gardens and the Palace. A change had come over her since she had realised that her husband was there to stay for the foreseeable future. With Sir Hector Laing's moral and financial support, she and Laing and Mary Cryer had resurrected the Lambeth Fund and raised thousands of pounds. The results were visible in the renovations being carried out to the Palace and gardens.

Lindy had not only inherited the bursarial talents of her father, but also his robust irreverence for the clergy. Lambeth when she arrived, she said, was 'a tip'. She did not mean this as a hurtful reflection on the Coggans, who naturally took it as such. 'They hardly even entertained,' Lindy went on, 'they were a quiet, rather elderly couple, and when they did entertain they hired everything. Can you imagine the cost?'

The *News of the World* had had no hesitation in presenting the death of Lindy's friend Jeffrey Daniels as 'Archbishop's pal is killed by AIDS' earlier that year, while the Archbishop and Lindy were abroad in India. Now the *Star* had little difficulty in embellishing the Stringers' stories.

*'Lindy, the flirting Lady of Lambeth'*

became

*'The Crisis that is Rocking the Church of England'*

which became

*'THE QUEEN IN RUNCIE CRISIS'*
*'She is told of their bizarre marriage'*

which became

> *'Dr Runcie is under "tremendous pressure" to quit'*
> *'Many bishops are already said to be campaigning for Dr Runcie to resign'*

which became

> *'Racy Photos Man Denies Lindy Affair'*

and, enigmatically,

> *'Retirement age is now fixed at 70'*

which was shortly followed by

> *'RUNCIE: I STAY WITH MY WIFE'*

but also by

> *'Top Churchman says "The Star is right"*
> *'A senior member of the Church of England Synod confirmed the accuracy of our reports.*
> *'The lay member, who also has close contacts with the Government, said it was an "open secret" that Dr Runcie was facing wide-ranging problems.'*

It was a mystery, however, why a senior member of the Church of England Synod expected to find credibility in the pages of a gutter newspaper, behind which he chose to take the kind of anonymous refuge denied his victims.

Unlike him, the members of the House of Bishops of the General Synod were honest enough to put their names to their feelings. In an unprecedented display of outrage and loyalty, they issued a formal statement condemning 'the scurrilous and baseless attacks on the Archbishop and Mrs Runcie in the *Sun* and the *Star* newspapers'.

The Archbishop and his wife acknowledged this in their own statement. 'We have been a happily married couple for nearly thirty years,' they said, 'and we both look forward to our rewarding partnership continuing for the rest of our lives.'

The novelist A. N. Wilson was co-author of a recent book entitled *The Church in Crisis* and self-appointed preacher to the congregation of the young right. Wilson touched a more tender nerve writing for the middlebrow *Daily Mail*. Dr Runcie, he said, was 'not particularly clever' and 'not conspicuously holy': qualities which Wilson, who did not know the Archbishop, did not ascribe to anyone else. Seven years earlier, in the anonymous 'Lucifer' column in *Private Eye*, Wilson had described Runcie as a 'tenth-rater.' Runcie, said Wilson in the *Daily Mail*, was 'the Harold Wilson of the Church of England', a man who had 'sold himself as a successful politician . . . His punishment will be that he achieves his ambition. Whether or not he is forced into resignation as a result of all this tittle-tattle, he will certainly retire, when the time comes, under a cloud.'

These attacks on the Archbishop were discredited by their personal nature and lack of basis in fact. The Archbishop would not retire under a cloud. A. N. Wilson would declare he no longer believed in God, but still signed a book contract to write a Life of Christ. Lindy would successfully sue the *Star* for libel and spend the award on a statue for the Lambeth Palace gardens. But the taste of bile seemed to appeal to both the more cynical and the more naïve palates of the Church of England. This was the genesis of the unofficial tripartite offensive alliance – part Anglo-Catholic, part Conservative back-benchers, part popular press – that was to dog the Archbishop for the rest of his primacy. Not all of them would have welcomed the idea of the Bishop of London as Archbishop of Canterbury. But neither would the Bishop, nor would any of the factions, do anything to dispel the idea, however preposterous and constitutionally fallacious, in the four years to come.

The Archbishop flew to Assisi for the Day of Prayer for Peace led by Pope John Paul II. Two days later, on 29 October 1986, Leonard flew to Tulsa.

The Archbishop issued a statement: 'I regret that the Bishop of London, despite the strong objections of myself and of fellow bishops here and in the USA, still thinks it right to exercise sacramental or episcopal care to a congregation which will not accept the discipline of their diocesan bishop.'

The gathering at Assisi was attended not only by representatives of Christian Churches all over the world, but also by Moslems, Buddhists, Hindus, Shintoists, Jains, Jews, Sikhs, Zoroastrians, African animists and American Indians, the last augmenting their own contribution to prayers and sacred readings with the smoking of a peace pipe. The Pope rubbed shoulders with the Dalai Lama, Mother Teresa of Calcutta, the Archbishop of Canterbury and the Orthodox Archbishop Methodius, as well as his own cardinals and clergy.

Two choirs, one Franciscan and the other Greek Orthodox, sang throughout the day. The Bible was read in English, Swahili, Japanese, Russian and Arabic. The Pope described himself and each guest as a 'brother among brothers' and at the end of the day, as the Archbishop noted, had to look in the same way as everyone else for a seat on the bus.

The Archbishop thought he detected at Assisi that day what he afterwards described in an address on 'ARCIC and Authority' as 'a new style of Petrine ministry; an ARCIC primacy rather than a papal monarchy'. He also acknowledged that 'whether we like it or not, there is only one church, and one bishop, who could have effectively convoked such an ecumenical gathering'.

In the same address he had asserted the international and non-party-political aspects of events such as the day at Assisi. 'This has nothing to do with political sovereignty,' he said, 'it has everything to do with the universality of the Kingdom of God. My assistant, Terry Waite, who recently described himself as "a mote or beam always in the public eye", wins international attention and respect because he is perceived as someone not with the credentials of office or denomination but with the universal appeal of God's justice and Christ's compassion for the captive . . .'

Waite himself was en route for the Lebanon again, on the advice of Oliver North. Unknown to Waite, another consignment of five hundred missiles had just been delivered to Iran. North had accordingly informed Waite that there was a real possibility that Islamic Jihad were about to release another hostage.

Waite arrived in Beirut on Friday 31 October, 1986. One of the first things he did was telephone the Associated Press:

'I'm here,' he hinted heavily. 'Something might happen. Nothing hard yet, but it's moving.'

He had in reality no direct contact with the kidnappers at that moment. But he added: 'It appears to be moving. You keep an eye, just keep an eye. Bye-bye for now.'

The following day, North and his partner in conspiracy Dick Secord, were also in Beirut. The two clandestine warfare experts flew in by helicopter from Cyprus and landed in the US Embassy compound. After a brief conference with the American ambassador they took off again for Larnaca.

Waite himself visited Damascus that day and evening before returning to his hotel and waiting for the call. On the following day, Sunday 2 November, it came. Waite was taken to the embassy to meet David Jacobsen, the Director of the American University Hospital, who had just been released by Islamic Jihad after seventeen months in captivity.

Waite and Jacobsen were flown out of the city by US Navy helicopter to Cyprus. Another US embassy car took him and Jacobsen to a private Lear jet, and thence, like Jenco, to Wiesbaden. The journalists, alerted by Waite's call to the Associated Press, observed these comings and goings; they also observed the arrival of Oliver North, shortly afterwards. He too was driven off at high speed in a US embassy car. These scenes appeared on television all over the world. Bishop Dehqani-Tafti, still in exile in Basingstoke, shuddered when he saw the pictures linking the two men.

Two days later, the Iran-Contra story began to break. North, Secord, McFarlane, Poindexter and others had covertly been supplying arms to Iran in return for the release of hostages and funds for the Nicaraguan Contras. The news started in a small but well-connected Arabic magazine in Beirut, and spread like wildfire through the world's press.

By that time, Terry Waite had returned to London after his latest triumphant mission to the Lebanon. The Archbishop's special envoy had been in a state of shock; now he began uncharacteristically to distance himself from the press. He complained that the media attention was placing his own and the hostages' lives in danger. He still could not believe that he had allowed himself to be used in so comprehensive and damaging a way.

*

The Archbishop was more concerned at this time with limiting the damage caused by the Bishop of London's visit to Tulsa. At another private meeting between himself and Leonard at Lambeth Palace on 7 November, he told Leonard that however much he appreciated the latter's pastoral concern for a deposed priest and his congregation, he still believed he was wrong to fly in the face of overwhelming Episcopalian disapproval and conduct twenty-four confirmations.

After their meeting, Lambeth Palace issued a restrained press statement designed to calm the atmosphere. Leonard, however, took this as an opportunity to conduct a press conference of his own. 'I don't think I've been carpeted,' he said, and denied that the Lambeth Palace press statement actually ruled out the possibility of his making further trips to Tulsa. When asked what offence he had committed, he replied: 'I may have offended against the Club (I mean you don't rock the boat; you don't make a nuisance of yourself); but I have done nothing illegal or uncanonical. I think there is a difference between my action and that of women from overseas coming here and celebrating. I don't think I have interfered . . .'

The remarks about 'the Club' annoyed the Archbishop, who knew perfectly well that Leonard knew perfectly well that this was not the case. This was not playing the game of responsible criticism by the rules of the *Crockford's* Preface. This was simply an irresponsible, selfish and damaging way of presenting a complex matter to the press. At the third session of the General Synod that November the Archbishop tried to tell him so. 'Whatever their pastoral motives and however sincere they may have been,' he said, 'the actions taken have done damage to the trust in which that debate (about authority in the Anglican Communion) is going forward. I have spent much time in an attempt to limit the damage and to ensure that such actions are not repeated. I have done this without resorting to legal threats; and I appeal to my mandate to administer discipline with firmness but with mercy.'

He opposed the idea of an immediate debate on so serious a matter. But he took particular exception to the Bishop of London's remarks about 'boat rocking' and 'the Club'. In other matters, he said, such as the question of women and the episcopate, he doubted that the Bishop would have used such phrases.

The Tulsa affair, as it became known, petered out, leaving the differences between the Archbishop of Canterbury and the Bishop of London intact. The General Synod turned to other matters. The foundation of the Church Urban Fund, rising from the initiative of *Faith In the City*, was approved, and a board of trustees and members established.

The Archbishop then turned his attention to the recent activities of his secretary for Anglican Communion Affairs. At Lambeth Palace on 17 November, he and Waite met Benjamin Weir, Lawrence Jenco and David Jacobsen, the three freed hostages, and their friends and families. Their purpose ostensibly was to review the situation of the remaining hostages in the Lebanon.

The meeting was clouded by the growing public knowledge of the Iran-Contra affair. At the press conference at Lambeth that afternoon, it became clear that the main purpose of the meeting was to try to contain the potentially vast damage done by North's duplicity to the credibility of Terry Waite and the Archbishop of Canterbury.

The Archbishop went out of his way to stress what was, in comparison with the Iranian and Libyan hostage negotiations, a virtually non-existent Anglican connection which had not been cited in justification before. The Reverend Benjamin Weir, he said, had been connected with a theological seminary in Beirut in which Anglicans had a share, and 'thus his capture was of immediate and direct importance to us'.

He defended Waite's work on behalf of the hostages in the Lebanon and made no direct reference to the damaging revelations about Oliver North.

Waite too tried to distance himself from North and his associates, refusing even to confirm or deny that he had ever met him. This was unwise in retrospect, but an indication that he was still unwilling to accept that he too had been compromised. He conceded only that henceforth 'the task has been made immeasurably more difficult'. 'My experience over the years,' he said in a statement more of faith than fact, 'has taught me that in the Middle East, at the end of the day, there are no secrets. As a representative of the Church I would have nothing to do with any deal which seemed to me to breach the code to which I subscribe. Not only because I know that such actions would undoubtedly come to light one day, but, more importantly, they would destroy my independence and credibility. I feel obliged to say that in my conversations with the American administration they have always shown respect for my position and honoured that position . . .'

Two days later, on 19 November 1986, Colonel North and his superior Admiral Poindexter resigned. The British press continued to link Waite with North, and Waite and the Archbishop continued to try to play down the connection.

Their own communications were hampered by the fact that, on 23 November, the Archbishop fell six feet into an archaeological excavation at the Old Palace at Canterbury. He was rescued with two broken ribs and forced to cancel several days' engagements.

The extent of Waite's unwitting involvement with North had been as much of a surprise to the Archbishop as it had to John Witheridge, Mary Cryer, Eve Keatley, Stella Taylor and Waite's other close colleagues at Lambeth. As revelations of the extent of the Iran-Contra revelations grew, they began to come to terms with the uncomfortable truth which Waite found hardest of all to bear. But if they knew Waite too well, and regarded him too highly, to see him in anything other than a forgiving spirit, he himself seemed unable either to perceive this or take comfort from it himself.

These were difficult times at Lambeth. After a year in which the happiness of his marriage had been impugned and his schedule had been as exhausting as ever, the Archbishop was still convalescing from his accident. Eve Keatley was seriously ill and finding it difficult to cope with the demands of the media. John Witheridge had decided to leave and been offered the post of Conduct, or Chaplain, at Eton College, a position he would accept and take up the following September. Wilfred Grenville-Grey too was on the point of departure. Waite's own future at Lambeth was already in question before the Iran-Contra catastrophe, and the effects of this on his credibility as a lecturer in the United States the following spring must have weighed heavily on his mind. In this cold climate Waite alone clung to the belief that he could still salvage some good out of the disaster that had befallen him.

In doing so, he had both to confront certain realities and yet somehow retain the stubbornness to push them to one side of his mind. He knew what it was to speak late into the night on the telephone with anonymous guttural voices in Beirut's Shi'ite southern suburbs; to go out alone to rendezvous at street corners and petrol stations; to be blindfolded, placed in the back of a car and driven at high speed to an unknown destination; to plead for the lives of Westerners held by Islamic Jihad. He knew that Islamic Jihad already distrusted him after he had in their eyes failed to deliver on his pledge to secure clemency for their comrades held in Kuwait, a pledge the Kuwaitis had refused to help him honour. He knew what the response had been on his next visit. 'We are very unhappy at what you have done, Mr Waite,' their intermediaries had told him, 'your mission is over. You have forty-eight hours to leave Lebanon.' He knew that, if he had not left, the bearded young men who had kept watch on his apartment block would have taken him, as they had taken the block's previous occupier, Terry Anderson.

And yet, he had returned again to Beirut; he had seen the release of another hostage, David Jacobsen. Surely there had still been something in that of his doing? Surely the kidnappers still knew, deep down, that he was not a tool of the Americans? Surely they were not unreasonable men? Surely they did not want to keep the hostages for ever? And who else, surely, could they still trust and who had the knowledge and experience to negotiate with them?

He was advised, in no uncertain terms, not to go back.

He was advised not to go back by the British Foreign Office. He was advised not to back by John Gray, the British Ambassador to the Lebanon. He was advised not go back by the Archbishop of Canterbury. None of them had any physical or legal authority actually to prevent him from doing so.

In his weaker moments the strength and truth of their advice penetrated and terrified him. He told Mary Cryer he knew this was his most dangerous mission to date. He no longer laughed conspiratorially when he asked her to insure him. But he asked her to insure him all the same.

Waite continued to accept and carry out the public engagements which he could in all conscience only accept in the belief that he was worthy of being asked to do them. He accepted the Honorary Chairmanship of the Llangollen Eisteddfod; he agreed to switch on the Christmas lights in his own neighbourhood of Blackheath.

He wrote an article under the heading 'My Country Right or Wrong' for the *Sunday Telegraph Magazine*. He recalled the seasons of the spirit of his church-going youth, and lamented the passing of the old common prayer book. He deplored the lack of historical awareness in schools of the nation's heritage. He reasserted the traditional values of the ancient churches, the timeless countryside, the bucolic wisdom, of his native land:

*'It is too late to bring back that which has been lost for ever,'* he wrote, *'but it is not too late to recognise true value and worth. Yes, I love dear old Britain, with all its faults and foolishness. It's my home, my country.'*

The tragedy was that by this time there was only one place left where he could sustain these illusions. On 12 January 1987, unsanctioned by the British government, unsupported by American logistics and uninvited by Islamic Jihad, Terry Waite arrived back in Beirut.

# 8

# *The Good and the Grief*

WAITE arrived at Beirut Airport and was driven by his Druze bodyguard to the Riviera Hotel on the shattered seafront. As always, one of the first things he did was telephone the local press corps.

Most of the Westerners among them had been withdrawn by their bureau chiefs because of the increased risk of kidnapping. Waite told those left he was here on 'a most delicate mission' to attempt the release of the remaining hostages. He was acting, he told them, exclusively on behalf of the Church of England and the Archbishop of Canterbury.

Walid Jumblatt, the Lebanese Druze leader, had met him at the beginning of January in London en route from Washington, where his young son was receiving hospital treatment. Jumblatt had reluctantly agreed to guarantee Waite's safety in Beirut. He had insisted on one condition in particular. Waite must at all times stay within sight of his bodyguard.

Over the next few days, guarded by Jumblatt's militiamen, Waite shuttled in small, fast and heavily-armed convoys between the Riviera Hotel, Jumblatt's headquarters in the Chouf mountains south-east of Beirut, and meetings with other religious leaders. He also reopened contact, with Jumblatt's help, with the representatives of Islamic Jihad, whose hostages now also included the Englishman John McCarthy and the Irishman Brian Keenan. The link between Waite, Jumblatt and Islamic Jihad was a Shia doctor and gynaecologist at the American University Hospital, Dr Adnan Mroueh.

His contact with Lambeth, by contrast, was stretched to breaking point. Eve Keatley had great difficulty contacting him at the hotel although he managed to remain in touch, two or three times a day, with Lambeth. He would telephone without warning and speak to whoever was available: the Archbishop, Eve Keatley, Mary Cryer, the Lambeth telephonist.

As the days went by, the strain of his undertaking began to show. In a series of telephone conversations recorded by unknown agencies on his hotel telephone and later smuggled out of Beirut via Cyprus, Athens and Geneva, it became clear that in the looking-glass world of the Lebanon, he had moved the focus of responsibility for himself from Islamic Jihad, to the Church of England and the Archbishop of Canterbury in whose name he had said he was exclusively acting. But there was a terrible inverted logic about the way Waite came to see himself in these last days of freedom in Beirut.

'I've not heard a thing from my office. Honestly, I tell you one thing . . . you sit down here by yourself . . . you've no guidance from anybody.

'You have to make every decision for yourself. It's ludicrous in some ways, isn't it? I mean, I have nobody to share with . . . nobody to pick the 'phone up and answer any calls for me. Absolutely everything I do single-handed.

'Even getting myself onto the Tube for the airport . . . I was absolutely frantic trying to clear everything in the office. And then I had to leave myself sufficient time to walk with my cases to the Tube . . . It's incredible, isn't it? I tell you . . . they don't even pay me, for Christ's sake!'

He knew that the Archbishop had not encouraged his return here, but was publicly unable to acknowledge the fact. Even this became twisted under the pressure of his present position:

'Crikey! If HE ever 'phones me up, that WILL be news, won't it!'

Unknown to him the Archbishop and the Foreign Office were doing everything they could to make him heed the warnings issued before his return to Beirut. The day after he had arrived, an arrest had been made in connection with the terrorist hijacking of a TWA airliner to Beirut two years earlier. This arrest, and the fact that Kuwait had just reiterated, contrary to Waite's expectations, that they would show no clemency to prisoners held there, including the cousin of an Islamic Jihad leader, placed Waite in even greater danger.

Such was their sense of urgency that the Foreign Office resorted to a crude code which they hoped would alert the man with whom they had been unable to prearrange a safe transmission of information. Frank Gallagher, the British Consul in Beirut, managed to get through to Waite at the Riviera.

'Hello, good afternoon. Is that Terry Waite speaking?'

'Speaking.'

'Good afternoon to you. I've got a little message which I've got to pass on to you. It's a message from London.'

Waite said nothing, as Gallagher went on:

'I want to be quite discreet and introduce myself in guarded terms . . . *Loquerisne linguam Latinam?*

'Yes, I understand.'

'*Sum Consulus Britannicus.*'

'Uh, huh . . . right.'

'*Nomen meum est Frank Gallagher.*'

'Uh, huh.'

'*Atque sum Consulus in Beiruta.*'

Gallagher may have reached the limits of his Latin, or decided he could relax a little:

'The message is like this,' he said. 'Mr Waite may be aware that a Mr Hamadei was arrested in West Germany earlier this week, suspected of being one of those involved in the TWA hijacking of 1985. This could have a bearing on the security of Western interests in Lebanon.

'Mr Waite will no doubt have this in mind in attending to his own security arrangements. It's just that those concerned are quite concerned obviously because they don't wish in any way to cut across anything you are doing, but they are concerned that that message should reach you.'

'OK,' Waite told him. 'Thank you very much.'

'If you should want to get in touch with me,' Gallagher persisted, 'I dare say you would know how to. All the very best, Mr Waite. Best wishes. Bye Bye.'

'Bye bye,' said Waite.


Dr Mroueh, the supposed link between Waite and the kidnappers, continued to hold out the possibility of his meeting some of the hostages. On 19 January, however, a week after his arrival, Waite announced that he had gone as far as he could with this round of negotiations. He was leaving Beirut for the time being.

The Druze told him they were unable to escort him safely to the airport until they had agreed a truce over a separate matter in which they were in dispute with Shia militiamen. There was little evidence to suggest that the dispute would not have been resolved, or that some other means would not have been found of transporting Waite safely out of the Lebanon. The Druze maintained their insistence that they could guarantee his safety only on the terms he and Jumblatt had agreed in London.

But, instead of waiting for the truce and then leaving as he had announced, Waite responded to one more call from Dr Mroue. Mroue produced a man he claimed was a representative of the kidnappers. At the Riviera Hotel the man told Waite that two American hostages, Terry Anderson and Thomas Sutherland, wanted to see him.

Waite asked the man for proof of his credentials. The man replied by picking up a magazine from the table and saying he would return with a Polaroid photograph of one of the hostages holding the magazine. An hour later he returned with a photograph. Anderson was holding the magazine to his chest.

Waite agreed to meet Dr Mroueh at the latter's house the following day. He reportedly acquired a leather jacket and pair of dark glasses; he also asked his Druze bodyguards to buy three suitcases in different colours and deliver them to his room. These were not in evidence later.

He made an agitated telephone call to arrange transport to the rendezvous. 'I want your man to drop me somewhere and then just leave,' he said.

The Druze were most unhappy at this. But he insisted.

'My job is full of adventures,' he told them, 'I have to do this.' He repeated his demand that they should not follow him: 'My life depends on it,' he told them

Then, in a gesture that puzzled them, he took off his watch and waved it about, saying: 'Look, no battery. Nothing they can think is a bug.'

Waite was driven away from the Riviera Hotel on 20 January 1987, to the rendezvous with the man he hoped would take him to the hostages he knew were held only a tantalisingly short distance away.

As instructed, the Druze took him to the house of Dr Mroueh and drove away. The doctor was at home. Shortly afterwards he was called away on an urgent errand to deliver a baby.

He reportedly left Waite with instructions to stay there and not to go anywhere without him. He would be back as soon as possible, he said, adding that he would leave the gate and front door unlocked. They were still unlocked when the doctor returned an hour later.

At Lambeth there was consternation long before the speculation began publicly about whether or not he had been kidnapped. They knew as soon as he stopped telephoning that something terrible had happened.

'It won't be days,' Eve Keatley told her colleague Mary Cryer, 'it will be months.'

In the Lebanon his Druze bodyguards searched frantically for him even though he had broken the terms of their agreement. Waite was reputedly seen in a three-car convoy speeding through the Beka'a Valley; he was safe under house arrest at a militia headquarters; he was being held prisoner in the southern suburbs of Beirut. In Beirut all these things were simultaneously possible because there was no way of confirming or denying the truth of any of them.

A week after his telephone calls stopped, the calls began to increase from the press. The Archbishop and Eve Keatley had no answer except reassuring hopes for his safety. John Lyttle, who had succeeded Wilfred Grenville-Grey as the Archbishop's Secretary for Public Affairs and Deputy Head of Staff and had not yet met Waite, was deputed to deal with the inquiries about Waite and co-ordinate Lambeth's part in the search for him; in the desperate humour that sustained them, he became known as the 'Waite-watcher'. Canon Roger Symon would also be quietly brought in for the duration of what they hoped and prayed would be Waite's brief absence. As 'Acting Secretary for Anglican Communion Affairs' he would still be in the position three years later.

The Archbishop himself was in a state of disbelief about the disappearance of his most wayward and celebrated associate. Waite had been honest to him about the opposition of the Foreign Office to his journey, but he had been equally convincing about the efficiency of the protection Jumblatt had offered him.

He had seemed so authoritative, so knowledgeable about the

Byzantine complexities of Beirut and the Lebanon, an area about which the Archbishop knew little and with which he had had no contact since his own brief stay there twenty-five years earlier. Now, as information trickled in, it seemed Waite had apparently rid himself of that protection for fear of returning empty-handed to Britain.

By early February, two weeks after Waite's last sighting, the press were openly describing him as having been kidnapped. The Archbishop was having to make repeated statements to the effect that he had been unable to dissuade him from going. The Archbishop wrote to Ali Akbar Hashemi Rafsanjani, Speaker of the Iranian Parliament, appealing for assistance. He met President Gemayel of the Lebanon in London who promised to do what little he could to help. He continued to reassert Waite's political neutrality and to call for his release.

At Canterbury Cathedral, he asked for prayers for Waite to be said at Evensong. In London the House of Bishops prayed for Waite and his family. In Blackheath prayers were said daily for him at the local Church Army headquarters. At Downing Street the Prime Minister expressed the hope that: 'We hope that we will soon have him back.' At Westminster an all-party group of MPs declared that he should be awarded the Nobel Peace Prize. In the Chouf mountains of the Lebanon, the Druze leader Walid Jumblatt offered himself as a hostage in Waite's place, a proposition which was unlikely to be accepted.

Waite himself, in a letter he left behind at Lambeth before he set off on his journey to the Lebanon, said that if he was taken hostage he wanted no life endangered, no money paid and no prisoners traded for him in exchange.

In Synod, five weeks after his disappearance, they remembered Waite. The Archbishop thanked them. He also paid tribute to Hugh Montefiore, who was to retire shortly as Bishop of Birmingham.

'My knowledge of him goes back forty years, and during that time he has been in a permanent state of enthusiasm,' he said, and recalled the late Bishop Gore, turning halfway across Lambeth Bridge to shake his fist at Lambeth Palace. 'Bishop Montefiore,' he said, 'stands in a great tradition!'

The Archbishop had to try to place Waite to one side of his mind in continuing to meet his own commitments, a difficult task at the best of times and an impossible one in the present circumstances. The ordination of women, as he had told the representatives of MOW at Lambeth Palace, had never been high on his list of priorities. Now it was higher than ever on other people's, and as Archbishop of Canterbury he was prepared to welcome that.

At the General Synod he opened the debate by declaring that no Church which had ordained women had regretted doing so. He did not differ from the conclusion of the Bishops' Report, that there was no way forward in parallel or competing episcopates:

'I, for one, do not intend to preside over the abolition of diocesan episcopacy and the parochial system as the Church of England has known it from the time of my predecessor, Archbishop Theodore of Tarsus [the seventh Archbishop of Canterbury],' he observed. 'I do not want the Church of England to slide into a kind of episcopal congregationalism. This would certainly be to betray our Catholic and Anglican heritage.'

He stressed that actual implementation of these measures, in the form of legislation, was still several years away.

'It's therefore a little early,' he continued amid laughter, 'to be taking the tarpaulins off the lifeboats, or even signalling to other shipping to stand by to take on board some of the passengers.'

John Gummer MP declared that a Church of England with women priests would 'no longer be the Church into which I was born, which I love and in which I hope I shall stay until I die'. His remarks failed to impress many in spite of the fact that he spoke as the son of a clergyman and Chairman of the Conservative Party.

The Bishop of London had issued a number of public statements before the debate which irritated John Habgood, Hugh Montefiore and the Archbishop of Canterbury. During the debate itself a strangely low-key Leonard continued to prophesy that the ordination of women to the priesthood would open the door to interpretation of Scripture as the justification for doubtful decisions of Church policy. He would continue to deny that he was encouraging schism by his views; and he also denied that seventy women whom he ordained to the diaconate shortly afterwards were on the first step to the priesthood.

He was supported by the Bishop of Chichester, who was supported by Dr Margaret Hewitt, a redoubtable lay member and National

Co-ordinator of Women Against the Ordination of Women, whose skill in debate was matched by the size and style of her hats.

Canon Brian Brindley failed in his attempt to introduce two amendments which would have delayed the next step towards legislation. David Edwards, Provost of Southwark, was in favour and could not understand all the murmurings about opposition to women's ordination leading to an 'exodus' from the Church of England. 'We keep learning about this exodus,' he said. 'I was born in Egypt and I don't understand you. Why do you believe that out there is a promised land where you could serve God better? It is the wilderness!'

Dr Gareth Bennett praised the Bishops' Report as 'Eirenic' (unflustered and conciliatory) but said that proposals for the ordination of women to the priesthood carried 'a fearful cost . . . I am convinced,' he added, 'that you cannot ordain women as priests unless you also ordain them as bishops,' and there were many who agreed with him in this, albeit disagreeing in their conclusions.

The motion approving the next step towards the ordination of women to the priesthood was passed emphatically in all three houses and there was rejoicing among supporters of it everywhere. Dr Bennett himself was much concerned with a report of his own that spring; he had just been asked by Derek Pattinson, Secretary General of the General Synod, and James Shelley, Secretary General of the Church Commissioners, to follow in the footsteps of David Edwards and others as author of the Preface to the next edition of *Crockford's* Clerical Directory.

Pattinson and Shelley were by no means of the same opinions as David Edwards, John Habgood or Robert Runcie. Pattinson and Shelley were looking for a rather different interpretation of the state of the Church of England. Gareth Bennett, they felt, was the perfect man for the job. He was a distinguished Church historian and an elegant prose stylist. He was a lucid and economical speaker in the General Synod. He was strongly opposed to the ordination of women and a passionate preacher on what he saw as the enduring values of the Oxford Movement. He had a small but devoted circle of admirers in Oxford, and in Bishop Leonard and others a number of influential sympathisers in the higher regions of the Church.

But Gareth Bennett was also distanced from the Church and the society in which it tried to function to a degree which was remarkable even by the standards of academic life. He had given up the relatively undemanding job of Chaplain of New College and his teaching load could hardly have been described as onerous. He had little or no contact with non-academics in the form of pastoral duties. He was a don who had not published a book for nearly twelve years.

Yet he had shown increasing disappointment at what he saw was his passing over for other, far more substantial appointments. These included the Bishopric of Durham, and, more recently, the Regius Professorship of Ecclesiastical History at Oxford, a post which was frozen but for which he believed himself admirably suited.

In his meetings with the Archbishop in Oxford he had hinted heavily at the idea of preferment. He rarely dined in college these days, to the relief of some of his colleagues. In his diary he wrote: 'The nights have been rather long since Mother died.' Since her death six years earlier, he had lived alone in a semi-detached house in Moody Road, Marston, with his pet cat.

This, then, was the man to whom Pattinson and Shelley had entrusted the authorship of the influential, uncensored and anonymous guide to the present state of the Church of England. Bennett was delighted to have been asked and immediately set to work.


The Archbishop, looking strained, posed for his photograph in *The Times*. He had just given a long interview to Bernard Levin on the decline of personal morality and the unreliability of absolute standards, during which he had revealed his own diminished liberalism on subjects like homosexuality and abortion:

'You have clearly moved, as you described it,' Levin remarked, 'but why? What was it that sowed the doubts?'

'I think that I am less of a rationalist than I was,' the Archbishop replied. 'I am less of a pragmatic rationalist, and that's because it's important that moral attitudes should fit not into the logic of thinking which will be the same for a humanist or a believer, but somehow that will fit adequately into my vision of God's love for us.

'Salvation comes from outside,' he went on, 'and I believe that we can be responsible. We can be responsible and we can respond; and that enables me to escape from this dilemma, this moral dilemma, of being either "stiff" or "woolly".'

He deplored what Cardinal Hume had described as the most distressing thing about the modern world: 'the loss of truth'. 'That makes me sad,' he said, 'and when we've been talking about sex and debt and violence and drugs and so on, I think that the loss of truth has had an insidious effect; the need to entertain or to excite or to encourage at all costs has had a serious effect on attitudes, that people seem to me to get away with concocted simplicities, to such a degree that it seeps into the atmosphere, that it is more important to entertain or to comfort people than to tell them the truth. I think that's a moral area that needs to be explored.'

Levin had one last question.

'You made the distinction,' he said, 'between the stiff and the woolly; they are both pejorative terms, and I see exactly why you argued a criticism of both of them. But if you had to fall into one or other of the camps, which would it be?'

'Stiff with myself, woolly with others,' the Archbishop replied. 'Jesus never encouraged us to be soft with ourselves, and when I look at myself it's a tough judgement I must make. But when I think of the other sheep that have gone astray, it's the parable of the Good Shepherd that guides my thoughts.'

In Oxford, Dr Bennett was well advanced on his report. He was working to a deadline of the end of May. But, as the weeks passed, the deadline was extended. There was so much to say, about the Church of England, about the Anglican Communion; and about the Archbishop of Canterbury.

'One may well feel great sympathy,' he wrote, 'for the man whose office gives him responsibility for guiding the affairs both of the Anglican Communion and the Church of England. Robert Runcie has been Archbishop of Canterbury since 1980 and has already established himself as a notable holder of the primacy . . .'

He acknowledged the Archbishop's intelligence, personal warmth, capacity for hard work; his talent for listening, his witty speeches, his willingness to travel to remote parts of the world.

Then came the first thrust of the knife.

*'His influence is now probably at its height. It would therefore be good to be assured that he actually knew what he was doing,'* Bennett went on, *'and had a clear basis for his policies other than taking the line of least resistance on each issue.'*

Then the first twist.

*'He has a major disadvantage,'* Bennett went on, *'in not having been trained as a theologian, and though he makes extensive use of academics as advisers and speechwriters'* (these included, from time to time, Dr Gareth Bennett), *'his own position is often unclear. He has the disadvantage of the intelligent pragmatist: the desire to put off all questions until someone else makes a decision. One recalls a lapidary phrase of Mr Frank Field that the Archbishop is usually to be found nailing his colours to the fence . . .'*

Having twisted the knife once, he had no desire yet to stand back and admire his handiwork.

*'His effective background is the elitist liberalism of Westcott House in the immediate post-war years and this he shares with Dr John Habgood, the Archbishop of York. In particular it gives him a distaste for those who are so unstylish as to inhabit the clerical ghettoes of Evangelicalism and Anglo-Catholicism, and he certainly tends to underestimate their influence in the spiritual life and mission of the Church.'*

Bennett, like Robert Runcie, had himself attended Westcott House. Unlike him, he had not spent ten years running Cuddesdon Theological College. He went on:

*'His clear preference is for men of liberal disposition with a moderately Catholic style which is not taken to the point of having firm principles. If in addition they have a good appearance and are articulate over the media, he is prepared to overlook a certain theological deficiency. Dr Runcie and his closest associates are men who have nothing to prevent them following what they think is the wish of the majority of the moment . . .'*

There was more, much more, in this vein. In his house in the Oxford suburbs Gareth Bennett must have worked long and late into the nights. More than occasionally he must have allowed himself a donnish chuckle at the fine phraseology, the subtle irony, the soundless movement of the internal logic of his work. Occasionally he must have congratulated himself on giving a sophisticated intellectual gloss to the vitriol that had poured forth from certain quarters against his subject in recent years.

This was the arena he knew best, where an audience held captive at High Table and a knowing nod afterwards in the Fellows' Parlour signalled another reputation made, remade or broken. Never in his most restless and disturbed dreams can he have seen beyond the bounds of his lonely, bitter, clever little world; to the pain he would cause in others, to the damage he would inflict on his own reputation, and to the catastrophe he would bring upon himself.


The Archbishop was in Oxford that spring for a six-week sabbatical at All Souls', with which his office traditionally had an association. A framed copy of the college's Founder's Prayer hung outside his chapel at Lambeth.

This was the kind of environment in which a former don felt at home and where like Cuddesdon he could relax. He was due to travel abroad again shortly, to Singapore for the seventh conference of the Anglican Consultative Council. After the events of the last few months a sabbatical was more than usually welcome. This was the environment in which he received a telephone call from a man named John Entwistle.

Entwistle said he was an import-export agent who had done business in the Lebanon. He had contacts there, he added, who might help locate and free Terry Waite.

The Archbishop asked for his telephone number and telephoned John Lyttle, his new Secretary for Public Affairs at Lambeth. Lyttle was still fully occupied with handling the case of the colleague whom he had never met. The Archbishop repeated the conversation he had just had with Entwistle, and asked Lyttle to arrange to meet the man. It was with this meeting and the predicament of Waite in their minds that the Archbishop and Lyttle met at All Souls' early that March.

Lyttle had arranged a rendezvous with Entwistle to take place on his way back from Oxford to London. They met in Pangbourne, in an attic flat above the stable block belonging to Entwistle's business partner Charles Armstrong. Armstrong was a bloodstock agent.

Lyttle was suspicious from the start. But such was the desperation over Waite at Lambeth that he and the Archbishop had agreed not to neglect any avenue of action that might lead to his recovery. Nor did they necessarily have to breach the terms of Waite's last letter asking that no money be paid to free him. Any funds disbursed could safely be described as travel expenses.

Entwistle told Lyttle a good deal about their contacts in Lebanon. He also told him he had served a prison sentence for a fraud committed against the Fife water board. Lyttle continued to be suspicious. But he also felt he had to continue to listen, and agreed to arrange a further meeting with Entwistle and Armstrong at Lambeth. He and the Archbishop agreed it would be wrong at this stage to inform Waite's family about any attempt they might make to free him in this way.

At Lambeth, the domestic effects of Waite's absence were creating as many difficulties as the emotional shock of his disappearance. His lecture tour of the United States had to be cancelled. His desk and paperwork revealed a jumble of bewildering and sometimes disturbing correspondence. As official enquiries into his disappearance and whereabouts began, the Palace insurance records revealed the extent and frequency of his secretive trips to America and Geneva. He had also agreed to a request from a church in Japan for the loan of certain Lambeth treasures for an exhibition there; Mary Cryer and the Archbishop would travel there with them later that year.

This was the ultimate test of 'the man from everywhere', which many thought the Archbishop would fail. After all, what possible connection could the Archbishop produce with Japan for his hosts?

But they were of little faith. 'My mother,' the Archbishop told them, 'was a hairdresser on Cunard liners, and she visited Japan . . .'

Stella Taylor, Waite's long-serving secretary, had to write hundreds of letters about him to people all over the world. Among these were the committee of the Llangollen Eisteddfod, which Waite had agreed to chair. She had received a second letter from them, which she read out at a staff meeting.

In view of the unfortunate circumstances, they said, and given the possibility that Mr Waite might not be back in time for the Eisteddfod, would the Archbishop consider 'standing in' for him?

The Archbishop was not present at the meeting. Except for Mrs Taylor, everyone else around the table burst into laughter.

This was not meant unkindly, but there was a streak of insensitivity, even cruelty, in the structure of the administration at Lambeth. As time went by and Waite did not return, Stella Taylor was no longer invited to staff meetings. She became an increasingly marginal and lonely figure, after the disappearance of the man for whom she had worked devotedly for several years. 'Can you tell me?' she would say to anyone she met there. 'Is there any news?'

Bishop Gordon's was a robustly businesslike style; unlike Ross Hook, he was perhaps less attuned to the finer sensibilities of women members of staff whose devotion to duty was out of all proportion to their salaries and job descriptions. Like Inez Luckcraft before her, Stella Taylor was eventually ordained deacon, and two years later she left Lambeth. Like Inez Luckcraft, too, she remained loyal and discreet about the public man whom she had served so long.


Mark Santer, Robert Runcie's chaplain at Cuddesdon and colleague in the Cell, succeeded Hugh Montefiore as Bishop of Birmingham. Some said Santer had been preferred over Robert's other chaplain at Cuddesdon and colleague in the Cell, 'Bishop Jim' Thompson of Stepney. The Prime Minister was rumoured, perhaps erroneously, to have made the second choice of Santer, on the grounds that the Tory Church-supportes believed he was not as 'left wing' as Thompson, the first candidate.

The Archbishop's sabbatical was over. On 15 April 1987 he preached a powerful and compassionate sermon at the memorial service for the victims of the Zeebrugge ferry disaster in Canterbury Cathedral.

'Faith,' he said, 'is not hoping the worst won't happen. It's knowing there is no tragedy which cannot be redeemed.

'These things we shall remember again on Good Friday. On Saturday, on the night before Easter Day, we shall light the Easter fire in Canterbury. A large single candle is lit from it and carried into the Cathedral. With the shadows of the vast vaulted roof above us, it seems such a little, vulnerable thing – and yet it is there, making its way through the darkness, and, as other candles are lit from it, a pool of light and hope begins to spread. Such is our faith and hope in the risen Christ.'

This was one of his finest displays of public leadership. He had to address that rare and most difficult combination, of public shock and private grief at a particularly terrible human tragedy which no one could ignore; a challenge to which he rose in the knowledge that only he in his position would be expected to do so. He created a moment of catharsis to match the strength of the catastrophe which had embraced the drowned and the saved, the believer and the sceptic alike.

'Those who died at Zeebrugge,' he said, 'did not die deserted by God, abandoned by him in an alien element, far away from his care and love. Though for a few who died their graves should be the sea bed, nevertheless they are as truly in God's loving hands as if their bodies lay in the most gracious of country churchyards. There also his right hand shall hold them in death as in life.'


On Easter Day he included a tribute to his missing Secretary for Anglican Affairs in his sermon at Canterbury. He was unable to give fresh news of Waite, or disclose the latest initiative that had begun with the telephone calls to him at All Souls' two months earlier.

Entwistle and Armstrong had had a number of meetings with John Lyttle at Lambeth. Lyttle had remained as suspicious as ever. But he knew that almost anything was possible when it came to dealing with the Lebanon. The two men insisted that they had the contacts to set Waite free, and possibly other hostages. In the absence of any other hard information, and after consulting both Scotland Yard and the Foreign Office, Lyttle had agreed to a plan.

Thus it was that John Lyttle and Mary Cryer had found themselves crossing the Thames and going to the bank. Here they withdrew £10,000 in used notes from a Lambeth Palace account. They then went back over the river to Lambeth Palace, where Entwistle and Armstrong were waiting. Lyttle handed over the money. Entwistle and Armstrong gave him a receipt. These two men, a convicted fraudster and a bloodstock agent, had just been entrusted with funds to finance the latest bid to free Terry Waite from his nightmare in the Lebanon.

The Archbishop travelled to the seventh conference of the Anglican Consultative Council in Singapore. In his opening sermon at St Andrew's Cathedral on Coleman Street, he made a blunt appeal.

'We shall be talking about unity,' he said. 'How do we proclaim the Gospel of reconciliation to all nations in a world divided into North and South, East and West, by poverty or politics, while the Christian Churches remain themselves divided and we Anglicans squabble over the ordination of women?'

In his opening address to the conference, he reminded the audience of how Terry Waite's work had begun, as a response of one Anglican to others, and while stressing that 'Terry's work has always been built on a Christian and humanitarian basis', further requests were 'difficult to refuse'.

He told them:

'When we think about staff-work my mind naturally turns to the colourful and couragous member of my own staff who has been such a character at the two ACC meetings we have attended together. We have all been praying for him in the last two months: and I know that Council members are anxious about him. I cannot give you any hard news about Terry Waite at the moment, but that does not mean that we are doing nothing. Every rumour from Beirut and elsewhere is being followed up, every story checked, every political and religious contact used. But for the moment we still wait.'

Shortly after the Archbishop spoke these words, Charles Armstrong flew to Cyprus.

Armstrong had told John Lyttle that he would be meeting people there who had contacts with the kidnappers of Terry Waite. Armstrong was going out first to 'soften them up'. Lyttle was to follow him two days later.

The two men were booked into the Ledra Hotel in Nicosia. But, when Lyttle arrived, he was surprised to find Armstrong there but no sign of the mysterious men from the Lebanon. Armstrong mumbled something about them having 'been and gone' and said that they had 'got cold feet'. Lyttle's suspicions were even more aroused.

Lyttle and Armstrong returned to Britain and Lyttle communicated his doubts to the Archbishop and his colleagues at Lambeth. Eventually, in the absence of what the Archbishop in Singapore had called 'hard news', they decided to give Armstrong and Entwistle one last chance.

Eve Keatley was now having to deny persistent reports that Waite was dead. The Archbishop had said prayers for him at Lambeth Palace on Waite's forty-eighth birthday. All over Britain, and throughout the countries of the Anglican Communion, people were doing the same. There was nothing else they could do.

The two men, Armstrong and Entwistle, were given a further £2,000 in cash. This was for a second trip to Cyprus, to prove whether or not they could really locate and release Terry Waite.

The second session of that year's General Synod debated such subjects as homelessness, freemasonry and the report of the Church of England Doctrine Commission reassuringly entitled *We Believe in God*.

Four advertising agencies were asked to help in an imaginary relaunch of the 'lacklustre' image of the Church of England. They all agreed that 'the brand was losing its exposure at a near-catastrophic rate'. One of them suggested a picture of Terry Waite, with the following caption: 'He can't make it to church this Sunday. What's your excuse?'

At Lambeth a single candle burned for him on the altar of the chapel. Six months had passed since his diappearance and there was still no reliable word about whether he was alive or dead. Stella Taylor continued to reply to the hundreds of letters about him. His office overlooking the Outer Courtyard had been taken over by Roger Symon. The Archbishop could only issue another thinly disguised plea in the form of an official statement:

*'Six months seems a very long time – for Terry Waite's family, for all of us at Lambeth Palace with whom he worked, and of course for Terry Waite himself. It has been six months of silence, in which we have heard nothing whatsoever of a definite kind, but in which there have been countless rumours and false reports which have added to the pain of those who are waiting.*

*'We will continue to use every legitimate means open to us to bring about the release of Terry Waite and other hostages, most of whom have been held for even longer than six months. Terry's mission was a wholly humanitarian*

*one; but, like other innocent people caught up in the Lebanese tragedy, he is a victim of the savagery and confusion brought about by rival warring factions.*

'*We will pray for Terry Waite particularly because it is six months since he disappeared. But, in doing so, we will also pray for the safe return of all the other hostages of many other nationalities, and for the people of Lebanon who have suffered so long from these tragic conflicts.*'

Armstrong and Entwistle had so far been paid £12,000 in cash from one of the Lambeth Palace bank accounts. Armstrong had made a further trip to Cyprus which produced no new information. Shortly afterwards, John Lyttle was in America. There he met Brian Jenkins, a terrorism expert.

Jenkins warned him to beware of conmen. Only the previous year, he said, two men had approached him saying they had information that would lead to the release of Father Martin Jenco. The American Catholic Relief Service had even gone so far as to earmark $100,000 for them before it realised they would not be able to deliver. Fortunately it had withdrawn the money in time and the men had not received a cent. Their names were Charles Armstrong and John Entwistle.

The Archbishop, in Lyttle's words, was 'not very pleased.' Armstrong was probably an innocent dupe, but there was little doubt of his partner's criminal tendencies. Less than a year later Entwistle would be back in jail for Customs offences, and Waite would still be missing in the Lebanon. Lyttle tried hard, and temporarily succeeded, in preventing the embarrassing story from leaking. But internally the damage was done, and compounded the near-mortal blow Waite's disappearance had dealt to Lambeth. Meanwhile in that same month of July, in Oxford, Dr Gareth Bennett had finished writing his anonymous Preface to *Crockford's* Clerical Directory.

John Witheridge left the Chaplaincy of Lambeth for Eton. The Archbishop gave him a farewell party in the Guard Room and made a characteristically witty speech.

The tradition, as had been the case with Richard Chartres, was that the outgoing person would reply in similar velvet tones. But, although

Witheridge remained an admirer of the Archbishop, he also had a few trenchant things to say about life at Lambeth. In the eyes of some present it was fortunate that the tension generated by Witheridge's oration was to some extent relieved by his small son, who spent most of it hopping round the room on one leg.

Witheridge was succeeded by Graham James, a Cornishman who has arrived as a curate in the St Albans diocese in the last year of Bishop Runcie. James had gone on to be Senior Secretary of the Advisory Council for the Church's Ministry. Like Witheridge he was married to a nurse and had young children with whom he took up residence in a courtyard cottage at Lambeth.

As Chartres had done, Witheridge advised his successor to maintain his outside contacts during his time as Archbishop's Chaplain. Having initially placed Robert Runcie on a pedestal, Witheridge had found life as his 'lightning conductor' a demanding and emotionally draining experience. He knew that the Archbishop depended on him to the extent that he would never have encouraged him to leave. If he was going to move on, like Chartres, he would have to take the initiative himself. After three years, and with only four years to go before the Archbishop himself was due to retire, the time had come to do just that.

Witheridge remained on good terms with Robert Runcie, and when a little volume of essays was published in the latter's honour he contributed a sensitive and deeply-felt description of what he saw was the impossibility of the Archbishop's job. He gave the photograph of the Archbishop, the Pope and himself pride of place on his mantelpiece at Eton. But he also kept a shrewd cartoon of the Archbishop looking at his most harassed, hanging over the downstairs lavatory.


The Archbishop appealed with John Habgood of York, in a letter read from the pulpit of every church in England, for £18 million. Raised over a two-year period this would make the Church Urban Fund a reality and not just an idea suggested in *Faith In the City*.

He applauded Cardinal Hume's call for Roman Catholics to enter into full communion with other churches. Hume made this call at the Swanwick ecumenical conference, which the Archbishop attended and described as 'a historic meeting'. Cardinal Hume also said he was 'totally confused' as to what form such a new ecumenical body might take.

The Archbishop declined to comment on the suggestion made by one interviewer that there might have been some sort of 'dirty tricks' campaign against him. Given the tabloid press smears against his family, the vitriol of some Conservative MPs and the behaviour of a few of his bishops, perhaps the interviewer had a point.

'Mmm,' he said, 'I'd rather not speculate. I try to keep a sense of humour. I am able to cope with hostility, and I hope I've learnt from criticism – in a creative way rather than becoming thick-skinned. I wouldn't say I've always succeeded.'

He set off on a ten-day tour of Hungary and Egypt with Graham James and Roger Symon. He broadcast conspicuously on the frequency of Moslem-Christian understanding and reconciliation; as ever, he thought of Terry Waite.

The American bishops sent their wishes for Waite's deliverance. John Lyttle interrupted his holiday in Cyprus to travel to Syria and the Lebanon. The Syrians, it was felt, held the key to unlocking the Lebanese conundrum. But the British government seemed bent on making political capital out of severing diplomatic relations with them, at the Western hostages' expense.

The Archbishop preached at Hungerford, where seven weeks earlier a crazed inadequate had run amok with an automatic rifle.

Hungerford, he said, was 'typical of England as we like to think of it. A small country town, long in history, rich in community, beautiful in its surroundings.' He mourned with the whole land 'that such a place should, on a summer afternoon, erupt in gunfire and terror, blood and death'.

He addressed himself, as he had done after Zeebrugge, directly to the bereaved and to the nature of bereavement.

'If, in spite of your loss and suffering, a spark of faith remains in you; if, in spite of everything, you still believe in a good and loving God from whose embrace no gun, no bloodshed, nothing in this world or beyond it can ever separate a single one of his people from him; if, trusting in him, you can still hold fast to the hope of everlasting life which overcomes the tragedy of death – if such faith and hope and trust are still shedding a little light on your dark road, then do not let that light be for you alone.

'Do not hide it from those others walking that same road. Let your light so shine – quietly, gently, steadily – that it may give light to others who sit in darkness and in the shadow of death and so guide the feet of all into the way of peace.'

While Lyttle was in the Middle East the Archbishop travelled to South Korea for five days to visit the three dioceses of which he was Metropolitan: Seoul, Taejon and Pusan. In his absence a great storm struck England; and not since the burning of York Minster had there been such speculation about the devastation of Church property in the form of churches, vicarages and churchyards. Some pointed out that the Synod was shortly due to debate sexual morality. A private member's motion, as it was called, had been tabled by Tony Higton, Rector of Hawkwell, Chelmsford, and founder of Action for Biblical Witness to our Nation.

The motion, in the earthly form of Higton and his one hundred and sixty-seven signatories, wanted the Synod to affirm the following: that sexual intercourse should take place only between men and women who were married to each other; that fornication, adultery and homosexual acts were sinful in all circumstances; and that Christian leaders should be exemplary in all spheres of morality, including sexual morality, 'as a condition of being appointed to or remaining in office'.

The Prime Minister herself was reported as supporting the Higton proposals. In an interview with *Woman's Own* magazine she let slip that she had only just become aware of the Church of England's loss of moral authority over the nation. The *Daily Mail* made her comments a front-page story, resuscitating the legend of the Runcie-Thatcher quarrel that had begun with the Falklands service.

By this time the Synod had received a counter-reactive 'wrecking' amendment from Malcolm Johnson, Rector of St Botolph's, Aldgate.

Johnson stood firm for homosexuals against the Southend Savonarola and asked the Synod to affirm the following: the essentials of the Biblical message, that human love was a reflection of divine love, and should be characterised by the permanency and commitment of relationships. Johnson's amendment also called for the education of young people and parents in the dangers, spiritual and physical, of sexual promiscuity 'whether heterosexual or homosexual' and urged 'the provision of counsel and absolution for those troubled by guilt or sin in any aspect of their human relationships'.

All this was unwelcome news for the Archbishop, whose own view was that the more thankful society should be for a great blessing like marriage, the less it should use it as a stick with which to beat the unfortunate. He privately deplored the Higton point of view; not least because it encouraged the likes of his former Hitchin curate, Richard Kirker.

Higton, claimed Kirker, was the leader of a Conservative Evangelical campaign which had presented the Lesbian and Gay Christian Movement as a 'pornography-peddling subversive organisation which is undermining the Church'.

'Is the Lesbian and Gay Christian Movement a Christian organisation?' Higton had asked, anticipating an answer in the negative. 'Of course we are' came the reply from Kirker. 'The Lesbian and Gay Christian Movement is made up of practising Christians who believe that God's love is for homosexuals no less than for heterosexuals.'

The Archbishop had spoken to prolonged applause in Synod about AIDS the day before Higton's motion was debated. On the following day he was on more difficult ground, having to acknowledge the fact that homosexual acts were condemned in the biblical and Christian tradition while rejecting Higton's call to help homosexual Christians to 'see the error of their ways'. He profoundly disagreed with Higton's assertion that 'the nation is waiting for a positive response to this motion'. 'There is a danger,' he said, 'that we shall treat this whole matter as a choice between two lobbies. Lobbies do not like having to face up to complexities. Lobbies have their place, but the Church of England cannot be taken over by them. There is no escape from the need for reasoned, persistent, patient work on the issues. The attempt to short-cut proper Christian work, leading to carefully prepared defensible statements which hold true to our tradition, is foolish.

'Nothing will be solved,' he went on the more applause, 'by the Church of England being railroaded down this or that lobby route.

'The danger of driving people out is that it will have the effect of undermining the serious pastoral practice of discipline. There is an urgent need to undermine ghetto experiences, and expose people to the full life of pastoral discipline by the Church. The irony is that it is only when we allow people to be more open and honest about themselves that we can respond with serious pastoral care and effective discipline.'

Both Higton's motion and Johnson's amendment were rejected. Into the breach stepped the Bishop of Chester, Michael Baughen.

His motion, as finally passed, called for the Synod to affirm that the biblical and traditional teaching on chastity and fidelity was a response to God's love; that sexual intercourse was an act of total commitment which belonged properly within marriage; that fornication and adultery were sins to be met with repentance and compassion; that 'homosexual genital acts' also 'fell short of this ideal'; and that Christians should be exemplary in all spheres of morality, with Christian leaders particularly being required to demonstrate 'holiness of life'.

As the 'dull echo of a liberal consensus' this may have been an exemplary performance. As an attempt to legislate for the unlegislatable, its reductive description of 'genital acts' was crude in the extreme. 'What ever happened,' as one bishop said later, 'to tenderness?' But the General Synod of the Church of England, although it occupied a good deal of the Archbishop of Canterbury's time, was not responsible for forming his own views on the matter.

The tabloid press drew its own conclusions:

*Pulpit Poofs Can Stay*

declared the *Sun*, while

*Holy Homos Escape Ban*

read another headline; and

*Church Votes to Keep Gay Vicars*

trumpeted a third.

Gerald Priestland, former BBC Religious Affairs Correspondent, wrote in his diary:

'What annoys me – as it did back in February when the synod debated women priests – is the synodical devotion to chasing cuckoos. This is not an important subject, and the church is not primarily a society for the virtuous, anyway. Where would it be without its gay vicars – or its fornicators and adulterers, I dare say? All the bishops I know devote a good deal of time to monitoring the morals of their clergy and it is simply not true that the country is being debauched by dog-collared sodomites. To put it pompously: I don't think this is the sort of thing that needs to be discussed in public. It's bad manners. You keep your nose out of my private life and I'll keep my nose out of yours.'

Bernard Levin, who had interviewed the Archbishop earlier that year, was also fascinated by the General Synod's ability to absorb issues which it could not possibly solve and could only exacerbate; a view shared by the Archbishop. As Levin put it in the *Times*:

'I emerged with a wondering but intense admiration for this amazing body. The Church of England, facing for once a real problem, predictably and inevitably fudged it. But in the very act of fudging, it spoke with tongues. It will be denounced from within and without its ranks, for both cowardice and brutality; but the result was a victory for all the best qualities of this country. The Church is as puzzled, worried and uncertain as the rest of us; but in a strange way, it gave us all a lead, if only to be telling us that to be puzzled, worried and uncertain is the lot of all thinking people, and it is no shame to confess as such.'

But there were appetites on which the Synod was qualified to pass judgement. One of its last motions was the following:

'This Synod expresses its thanks to Mr and Mrs Spagnoli and the staff of the Vitello Doro Restaurant for their service to its members and staff over the years, and trusts that they are able to continue their services to the Synod in a new location.'

There were no abstentions.

*

If the Prime Minister had inferred some disapproval of the Church of England by her reported support for Higton, she did not communicate this at a private meeting held at Chequers between herself, the Archbishop, and the Bishops of Durham, St Albans, Liverpool, Chester, Oxford, Peterborough and London that November.

Mrs Thatcher was keen to secure from this diverse group a consensus of opinion from the bench. How best could the Church of England play its part in the moral revolution she was keen to bring about? This was an amicable and friendly occasion. Because the meeting was kept secret at the time, it was also subjected to reinterpretation in the press: the *Daily Mail* had her berating her bishops for not doing more to stop the AIDS epidemic. Words like 'Prime Minister', 'AIDS' and 'Archbishop of Canterbury' were enough for any popular newspaper to construct a story without due regard to what other words had appeared between them. But there were some who should have known better:

*Junior Agriculture Minister John Gummer, who also attacked Church leaders in a hard-hitting speech about Britain's "condom culture", said yesterday: "Mrs Thatcher has a way of knowing what ordinary people are saying."'*

After proposing this radical notion, Gummer had gone on:

*'I was not at the lunch. But I know there is very real disillusion in the country that the bishops are not giving the lead many of us expect.'*

Gummer would never quite understand why some of his fellow members of both Parliament and the General Synod of the Church of England would not take him as seriously as he felt he deserved.

The storm was now imminent that Pattinson and Shelley had secretly and inadvertently unleashed eight months earlier. In the middle of November, as was the custom, the Archbishop received an advance copy of the latest edition of *Crockford's* Clerical Directory.

The author had not restricted himself to attacks on the Archbishop's lack of theological qualifications and 'liberal elitist' tendencies. He had wielded his knife the more frequently and more savagely as he went on; indeed, the Archbishop could not recall a *Crockford's* Preface in living memory so comprehensively dominated by personal aggression.

Bennett, who was among those the Archbishop immediately suspected of being the author, had gone on to accuse him and John Habgood of packing the bishops' bench with some kind of liberal mafia:

*'With the arrival of Dr Runcie and Dr Habgood at Canterbury and York there were in the two archbishoprics men who shared the same basic outlook and worked closely together to create a new kind of episcopate. The result has been a virtual exclusion of Anglo-Catholics from episcopal office and a serious under-representation of Evangelicals.'*

Apart from the Bishop of London, whom he would place in a special category, Bennett appeared to have a point. Of the prominent Anglo-Catholics on the bishops' bench, Eric Kemp of Chichester had been elected during Coggan's primacy, as had Peter Ball of Lewes. John Baker of Salisbury, David Lunn of Sheffield and Michael Ball of Jarrow had all been elected during the earliest years of the Runcie primacy. The Evangelicals were still few enough to be conspicuous, like the new Bishop-elect of Bath and Wells, George Carey.

But there were reasons for these circumstances which Bennett chose conveniently to ignore. In the case of the Evangelicals, the renaissance in this area was simply too young to have produced many candidates for the episcopate. When it did, they would be men of obvious ability, such as George Carey. In ten years' time, the bench would be full of them; in twenty years' time the heirs to Gareth Bennett would be squealing about the 'Evangelical elitism' of the 1980s and 1990s.

In the case of the Anglo-Catholics on the bench, precisely the opposite was true. They were fewer and older, it was true, but this was because the conspicuous, if not the fundamental, characteristics of Anglo-Catholicism had changed; it was the difference between Cuddesdon in the 1950s under Edward Knapp-Fisher and Cuddesdon in the 1960s under Robert Runcie. The theory and practice of theological education had evolved, and, instead of debating the pros and cons of this fact, Bennett omitted it from his argument altogether.

Many of the men Bennett, for the purposes of his argument, would have described as Anglo-Catholic, Evangelical or Liberal, would have taken deep offence at such a description. A supposed 'Liberal' like Bishop Jim Thompson of Stepney in reality regarded himself as nothing other than a Catholic, trained in a prayerful and disciplined Catholic tradition; and trained, moreover, under the direction of that supposed 'Liberal elitist' Robert Runcie. But Bennett was not concerned with this kind of fact; the function of contrary evidence, it seemed, was to obscure his view of the target:

*'One thing cannot be doubted: the personal connection of so many appointed with the Archbishop of Canterbury . . .'*

He went on to describe what sounded more like a KGB conspiracy than a *curriculum vitae*:

*'A brief biographical study will reveal the remarkable manner in which the careers of so many bishops have crossed the career of Dr Runcie: as students or colleagues at Westcott House and Cuddesdon, as incumbents or suffragans in the dioceses of St Albans or Canterbury, or as persons working in religious broadcasting at a time when he was chairman of the Central Religious Advisory Committee of the BBC and the IBA. There is indeed no more fertile recruiting ground for the new establishment than Broadcasting House. Though one may accept that an archbishop should have an influence on appointments, it is clearly unacceptable that so many are the protégés of one man and reflect his own ecclesiastical outlook. Those who speak so glibly of the Crown Appointments Commission as designed to allow "the Church" to have a decisive voice in appointments should ask themselves some pertinent questions as to whose voice the commission does actually represent.'*

Bennett also ignored the fact that the third and fourth most senior bishops in the Church of England, who were quoted in public almost as often and usually more controversially than the Archbishop of Canterbury, had both been elected during his primacy and in both cases had little or nothing in common with him. These were the Bishop of London, Graham Leonard, and the Bishop of Durham, David Jenkins.

Jenkins was dismissed with a venom that shocked even his critics:

*'They have indeed been considerably irritated by the pastoral insensitivity and intemperate partisanship of Bishop David Jenkins of Durham, and many of them have come to see that the appointment of a man of such imprecision of mind and expression under the guise of being a theologian was a minor Anglican disaster.'*

Apart from the fact that this was a gross exaggeration, the verdict on Jenkins' intellectual abilities was, quite simply, a deliberate and downright lie.

Bishop Leonard on the other hand was implicitly forgiven for his trip to Tulsa: 'It is not necessary here,' Bennett said, in a Preface which was otherwise conspicuously judgemental, 'to go into the rights and wrongs of that particular case.' Incredibly, and in spite of the frequent opposition to Leonard in all three Houses of the Synod and among many church-going inhabitants of Leonard's diocese, Bennett now cast Leonard of London as the man of the middle way:

*'Most exposed of all is Dr Graham Leonard, the Bishop of London, whom the Press love to portray as the Archbishop Lefebvre of the Anglican Communion. He has not always been particularly adroit in the presentation of his case and he has a predilection for popish ecclesiastical outfits but all this should not obscure the simple fact that his ideas on faith and order place him securely in the mainstream of Anglicanism . . .'*

. . . A stream which appeared to have shrunk on Bennett's map, to one smaller than the tiniest tributary of the Isis.

The preface was long as was the custom, and Bennett touched on many subjects. The Anglican Communion, the American Episcopal Church, relations with Rome, the General Synod, the Crown Appointments Commission, *Faith In the City*, the Church Urban Fund and the rural ministry were all mentioned and he said much about these things that was true and had to be said. But what ultimately endured in his Preface was the size, and yet, in its deeply personal nature, the smallness, of his attack on the Archbishop of Canterbury.

The Archbishop saw nothing new in the contents, but he was surprised and hurt at the tone. What wounded him and offended those who knew him, was the implication that he had no principles, and no knowledge of where he was going. Those who knew him, including

Bennett, knew that the first implication was a deep untruth. The second implication was more complicated, and over issues such as the ordination of women the Archbishop had lacked a decisiveness he might have called glib but others might have called a political necessity. But there were many more areas in both the Church of England and the Anglican Communion where his leadership had been clear and his courage conspicuous.

He and those who knew him also realised that he needed to be loved, but that he was, deep inside, a tougher man than he appeared.

On 29 November, two weeks after he had received his advance copy, the Archbishop preached at Pusey House, Oxford. Among those who took Communion from him was Dr Gareth Bennett.

Afterwards the two men attended a reception but contrary to later reports there was no contact between them. The Archbishop still suspected Bennett of the *Crockford's* authorship.

The *Crockford's* Clerical Directory was published four days later on 3 December 1987. In the serious press it caused extensive comment; in the popular press it provided a sensation. Even the *Sun* felt obliged to produce its rarely-sighted 'Religious Affairs Correspondent'; although he disappeared equally suddenly and mysteriously a few days later.

It seemed that all the unasked and unanswered questions, as well as the over-simplifications, half-truths and downright lies, had been condensed in one essay that characterised many of the more melodramatic stories about the Church of England in the previous few years. The hunt began, first as a gentlemanly guessing-game and then, in an unprecedented fashion, as a fully-blown investigation by rival newspapers, to establish the identity of its author.

Many of Gareth Bennett's contemporaries in the Church of England had long known both him and Robert Runcie. Simon Barrington-Ward, the Bishop of Coventry, was one. But while approving Runcie's ascent he had detected a sad decline in Bennett, the man he had known and loved at Westcott. When he read the Preface he was confirmed in his worst fears. 'This is clever,' he said to himself, 'but it's sick.'

Others were less forgiving in their reactions. The Bishop of Peterborough, William Westwood, described it as 'a sour piece of anonymous malice'.

John Taylor, Bishop of St Albans, said: 'This is a cowardly and disgraceful attack by a writer who has abused the privilege of anonymity.'

David Edwards, Provost of Southwark and himself a past *Crockford's* author, said: 'It represents a conservative backlash by someone who thinks the ordination of women is the last straw.'

John Habgood, Archbishop of York, said it was 'cowardly, sour and vicious'. It was, he added tellingly, the outburst of 'a disappointed cleric'. Habgood would later be accused by that remark of adding fuel to the media fire that would consume the disappointed cleric in question. David Holloway, Vicar of Jesmond said: 'Er, no, I think you'd be wrong, actually. I'm not the author. I think you'll find it very hard to discover who he is. Who told you it was me?'

Many were unsure as to the author's identity, but believed Derek Pattinson had upheld the tradition of uncensored anonymity to allow himself to neglect the responsibilities of an editor confronted with an irresponsibly offensive piece of writing.

Pattinson himself began to be described in the manner of a figure at the centre of a Byzantine plot. Names began to be mentioned as those of the possible author, most without much conviction. The one name mentioned with increasing conviction, however, was that of Gareth Bennett.

'It's anonymous and they will never know for certain that I wrote it,' he told his friend Philip Ursell, Principal of Pusey House, who had read several drafts of the Preface in manuscript.

'Are you sure you want to say all this?' Ursell had asked him.

'Yes, I do,' Bennett had replied. 'It may do some good.'

On another occasion he told Ursell breezily: 'It's amazing what a chap can do from his little semi-detached house in Oxford.'

Privately he was already close to despair.

*'My God, what a mess,'* he wrote in his diary on 3 December, publication day, *'basically my own fault.*

*I shall be lucky to weather this business through without disaster and some kind of public exposure. The more I think about it, the more I know how bloody foolish I have been.'*

Not everyone shared his opinion. That same morning of 3 December the Bishop of London had telephoned him, apparently ignorant of the fact of Bennett's authorship. During their conversation Leonard spoke of the Preface and expressed his pleasure at reading it. Bennett's relief was temporarily so great that he was nearly tempted to tell Leonard that he was the author.

On the same day, the Archbishop of Canterbury consecrated George Carey as Bishop of Bath and Wells in Southwark Cathedral. He sat up most of that night at Lambeth with the newspapers and his Head of Staff, Bishop Gordon, trying to pin down the identity of the author.

On Friday 4 December, the day the popular press began their calls for the Archbishop to resign, the telephone rang again in Bennett's house in Oxford. Bennett picked up the receiver.

There could have been no mistaking the Archbishop's distinctive voice, had it indeed been him and had these been normal circumstances. But these were abnormal circumstances and such was Bennett's state of mind that all voices were beginning to merge into one: the voice of the man whom he had attacked and whom he had first met nearly forty years earlier. Bennett listened in silence. The voice spoke again, and there was a different sound. Bennett had replaced the receiver.

The last days of Bennett's life unfolded like a classical tragedy. Hubris was swiftly followed by nemesis, and a chorus of lamentations.

Other telephone callers, from the press, had been more persistent. On that Friday afternoon of 4 December Bennett arrived in the New College porter's lodge.

'I'm being persecuted,' he told a colleague, oblivious of the irony 'I'm getting away from it all. Block all my calls.'

He drove to Cambridge with the Dean of New College, John Cowan, Stuart Dunnan, the Librarian of Pusey House, and Philip Ursell. Bennett and Cowan were to attend a feast at King's while Dunnan and Ursell went to a similar occasion at Emmanuel. Only Ursell knew that Bennett had written the Preface.

The two men worked their way through the Parma ham and the figs, the sole, the pheasant, the pear pudding and the fine claret. The following morning, Saturday 5 December, Bennett enjoyed a healthy breakfast.

The tabloid newspapers had been full of calls for the resignation of the Archbishop of Canterbury. Wild rumours abounded in their accounts of his ineptitude, his lack of principles, his inability to see where he was going. Hugh Montefiore and Richard Harries of Oxford had leapt to the Archbishop's defence. Bennett rarely read anything other than the *Daily Telegraph*. He was accordingly disturbed to be handed a copy of the *Daily Mail*. His name had already been mentioned briefly in the press. Now his photograph was attached to a major story.

Bennett was in a state of extreme agitation. 'I don't know if I can take much more of this,' he told Ursell. 'It's getting pretty close and pretty nasty.'

They drove back to Oxford and on the way he seemed to recover some of his good humour. He dropped off his three passengers and drove on to Moody Road. He said he had to feed his cat.


There was a letter on the doormat. It was from Derek Pattinson:

'*Gary,*' it read, '*I think you should see this for yourself.*'

Attached was a letter from the *Daily Mail*. It offered Bennett £10,000, to be donated to a charity of his choice, if he publicly revealed himself to be the author of the *Crockford's* Preface.

Bennett put the letter in his pocket. Shortly afterwards he went out of the house to the local hardware shop and purchased a hosepipe and a connector. He returned to his house and drove his car into the garage, a place he never normally kept it. He went into the house and put his case down at the foot of the stairs. He had two or three large drinks.

Later it would be alleged by some of Bennett's Oxford friends that what finally pushed him over the precipice was the death of his much-loved cat. This seems a psychologically implausible and unlikely interpretation. What is far more likely is that Bennett engineered its demise himself.

Aware that he would be unable to look after it, and given that it was in some ways an extension of himself, such was the loneliness of the life he led, he fed it a poisonous or toxic agent which would have been easily to hand in the kitchen. It would be found dead there, surrounded by excrement, two days later. By killing his much-loved cat, too, he had shut the door behind himself.

Bennett went back into the garage and attached the hosepipe to the exhaust of the car. He pushed it through the gap in the rear window, closing the latter so that the minimum of oxygen and the maximum of carbon monoxide would be able to pass through it. Then he closed the doors and started the engine for his last journey.

Cowan and a neighbour found him two days later. Ursell immediately telephoned the Archbishop of Canterbury.

There was a long silence.

'I was sure he wrote it,' the Archbishop told him.

There was nothing more to say. Now they had to set about preparing a statement for the following morning, when the news of the suicide of Dr Gareth Bennett would have to be announced to the press.

The *Crockford's* Affair, as it inevitably became known, was over, but the controversy it generated continued within and beyond the Church of England. Bennett's funeral, at New College on 15 December, was a masterpiece of Anglo-Catholic mourning, transforming him from a suicide into a martyr. The Bishops of London, Chichester and Winchester officiated. Derek Pattinson, the man who had commissioned the Preface, read the lesson. Bennett's friend Geoffrey Rowell gave the funeral address. The Archbishop of Canterbury did not attend, but sent Bishop Gordon as his representative. The hearse drove out of the college quadrangle, a wreath of red carnations on the coffin. On the unsigned, anonymous, uncensored card, it said: 'A man who spoke the truth.'

A small but potent cult grew up around the life and death of Dr Bennett with a literature to match. Chief among its proponents was Dr William Oddie, who would vigorously defend Dr Bennett's point of view. Three years later Oddie became a Roman Catholic.

But what were the greater consequences of the *Crockford's* tragedy in the longer term? Bennett was not destroyed by the Church or the press but by his own hand. In writing the Preface and ending his life in the way he did, he also destroyed the long and honourable tradition of the *Crockford's* Preface and any proper appraisal of his academic reputation. His interpretation was that of a sad and misguided man who had been encouraged to believe he was speaking for a generation. Ultimately it said little of depth and was unlikely to stand the test of time.

Neither the *Crockford's* Preface, nor the funeral that followed, was a fitting memorial to him. There were too many contradictions in the conspiratorial interpretation of the Runcie primacy. As the *Church Times* asked: 'If such a conspiracy is going on, why has it failed to appoint a less critical Preface-writer?'

The Archbishop himself had said in his Coningsby Club address three years earlier: 'I think the weaknesses of the Church can be exaggerated by those with a romantic view of its past or ignorance of its present life.' Bennett was culpable in both categories. He had neglected in his hunt for weaknesses the daily witness and weekly worship which many including the Archbishop saw as the true strengths of Anglicanism and the Church of England.

Derek Pattinson would be criticised but officially exonerated for the tragedy. For Bennett such forgiveness came too late. Perhaps both men, and Bennett's supporters, should have borne in mind the words of Robert Runcie's predecessor William Temple. To admit acrimony in theological discussion was more fundamentally heretical than any erroneous opinions upheld or condemned in the course of discussion.

But to admit heterodoxy in some quarters was plainly just too much to stomach. In Bennett's case this had led to his mounting an unChristian attack on a man he knew well and did not actually dislike, resulting in his own suicide and a funeral in the form of a Requiem Mass in Latin. Truly, as he himself had written only ten months earlier in the one part of the Preface that would surely stand the test of time:

*'In the Church of England things are not always what they seem to be.'*

In January 1988, six months before the Lambeth Conference was due to begin, the Archbishop travelled to Ireland to address its precursor, a conference of young Anglicans invited from all over the world by the Anglican Consultative Council.

He flew to the United States, to New York and San Francisco, to deliver a series of lectures later published in simplified form under the title *Authority in Crisis? An Anglican Response*. In some quarters these were also seen as a response to the Fulton lecture on *The Tyranny of Subjectivism* delivered by Bishop Leonard the previous year in Missouri.

In these lectures he dealt with the question of authority in what he saw was a changed historical context:

'This situation which confronts us in 1988 is very different. Now we must speak, not only of the crisis in authority, but also of its comeback. Throughout the world, and in a variety of different cultures, in the Islamic East as well as the Christian West, there is a sharp reassertion of what are held to be "old" values. Economic liberalism seems to be paving the way for moral conservatism and theological liberalism seems to be giving way to unrestricted fundamentalism. The New Right seems here to stay.'

He did not, however, see this kind of insular authoritarianism as the solution, so much as the problem, in the 1980s. 'We seem to be discovering that individualism is simply not enough,' he went on. '. . . We wake to the truth that interdependence is not the wild ideal of dreamers, but simply the way things are.'

This historical and political self-awareness was a hint of how he planned to approach the forthcoming Lambeth Conference. He did not underestimate the degree to which the other Churches and countries of the Anglican Communion depended for their focus on Lambeth and the Archbishop of Canterbury.

He had no illusions, however, about the limits of even his own authority as leader of an autonomous Anglican province, an authority which might have to be reduced by the need to find a common supra-provincial body to manage the worldwide Anglican Communion.

He quoted a surprising source.

'So, we are beginning to hear calls for a strengthening of the structures of world Anglicanism. Exploration began at the meeting of the Anglican Consultative Council in Singapore in April last year . . .

'It was the late and lamented Dr Gareth Bennett, the author of the recent unhappy *Crockford's* Preface, who surprisingly became a champion of a reconstituted Consultative Council. In a passage he clearly felt very deeply about – more deeply perhaps than his supposed attack on myself – he wrote:

*"It seems probable that there will have to be some self-denying ordinance by which the provinces agree that certain matters shall not be decided locally but only after a common mind has been established among the Churches. Finding a constitution for a new kind of Council will not be easy, but it is perhaps not to much to say that the future of Anglicanism as a world Christian community depends on its being achieved."*[5]

So be it, however, if at the 1988 Lambeth Conference, the focus of the autonomous provinces of the Anglican Communion happened on that particular occasion to be synonymous with his own particular authority.

He still faced the prospect of leading the Conference without his original Secretary for Anglican Communion affairs. At Christmas and in the new year he had continued to appeal for news about Terry Waite.

On the first anniversary of Waite's disappearance John Lyttle confirmed that initiatives to find him had not ceased. The kidnap and ransom firm Control Risks had offered their services, a proposition which was considered and eventually declined. The press had recently learned of and given wide publicity to the Armstrong and Entwistle débâcle; now it made capital out of what they called 'ambulance chasing' on behalf of the company. In fact the chairman of Control Risks, Tim Royle, was a prominent lay member of the General Synod of the Church of England. The press also targeted Waite's wife Frances on the first anniversary of her husband's disappearance. Invited to Lambeth Palace out of moral support on the occasion, she was understandably overwrought. Lindy took her for a quiet walk in the gardens. On their return indoors, Lindy suggested they deserved a drink. Frances Waite agreed, but the popular press had it otherwise. Their stories the next day had the callous Lindy Runcie carousing at Lambeth, while Terry Waite languished in prison in the Lebanon.

Prayers were said and vigils kept across the countries of the Anglican Communion to mark the loss of Waite and the plight of the hostages in the Lebanon. Roger Symon continued to do Waite's job in his 'Acting' capacity. More middle-ranking staff were taken on and there was a further diminution of the personal atmosphere that had character-ised the early days of Waite's tenure at Lambeth.

One of the more difficult decisions since his disappearance had concerned the war zone insurance cover that was taken out whenever Waite, the Archbishop, his Chaplain or Christopher Hill travelled in the less stable areas of the Anglican Communion. In the case of Waite's visits to Beirut this had meant premiums of £25 a day. These had run into many thousands of pounds since his disappearance. The insurance cover was reluctantly and quietly withdrawn, and the money put to the purpose of funding the search for his present whereabouts; still presumed to be somewhere in the Lebanon.

At the first session of that year's Synod the *Crockford's* Preface was inevitably on the agenda. Members voted against a motion brought by David Edwards that the tradition of the anonymous Preface be ended.

Lay members passed a motion requesting that the House of Bishops issue a clear policy statement on such aspects of sexual morality as homosexuality and lesbianism. The Archbishop repeated that actively homosexual clergy could expect to be disciplined in spite of the reluctance of the House of Bishops to vote in Synod to this effect.

His reasoning was that this was a matter for individual bishops; and, implicitly, that this was too important a matter either to be subjected to the polarising effects of a vote or to the 'dull echo of a liberal consensus'. Just as his former Hitchin curate Richard Kirker was fond of saying 'you can't tie a knot in it', so the Archbishop was saying that the General Synod of the Church of England could only tie itself in knots over it. The Archbishop, the Synod and Kirker would all persist in their points of view.

In mid-February the Archbishop, Graham James and Roger Symon departed on an official visit to Northern and Western Australia (the bishopric of the latter he had been offered nearly fifteen years earlier). In Perth he preached at a Eucharist attended by 8,000 people and was greeted by demonstrators bearing banners reading 'Jesus was a feminist too'. In the diocese of the Northern Territory he visited six Aboriginal parishes, five of them staffed by Aboriginal priests.

He also sent a message of support from Australia to Desmond Tutu, under threat of detention and possible assassination in South Africa. In the context of Aboriginal rights and the general turbulence of the Australian Church as it grappled with the ordination of women priests, his visit was regarded as a great success in its attempt to communicate the theme of breaking, sharing and healing that he proclaimed on his arrival. After his departure, his tour was described as 'a treasured visit from a family friend' in one Australian Anglican newspaper.

Sir John Ford, KCMG, MC, former lay administrator of Guildford Cathedral, nailed a copy of his book *Honest to Christ* to the gate of Lambeth Palace. His publisher said he was 'doing a Martin Luther'.

Sir John was much concerned that, at the forthcoming Lambeth Conference, the bishops address themselves as he had done to the clear need for a statement of belief, rather than wishy-washy liberalism. 'If they can't get a grip on that, their leadership isn't worth anything,' he revealed, 'and this is what my book is about – a question of leadership. I have written in the direct language of the laity. I regard myself as a perfectly normal layman,' he went on, 'frustrated because you can never get through to them. And I think I speak for vast numbers of lay people who feel as I do.'

Asked for his opinion of the recent effort of a carefully-selected working party of bishops to produce such a statement, he replied: 'Lousy!'


The Archbishop visited his predecessor, Michael Ramsey.

Lord and Lady Ramsey were now living in St John's Home in Oxford. Ramsey was near death but his interest in Church affairs was very much alive. The Archbishop prayed for him and gave him his blessing. Ramsey died of pneumonia nine days later. The Archbishop invited Lady Ramsey to stay with him at the Old Palace in Canterbury for the funeral service.

He continued his own packed schedule. He visited Wakefield for three days to mark the centenary of the diocese. In Westminster Abbey he preached on the inauguration of the Church Urban Fund; in Eltham he lectured at the annual Gallipoli memorial service; in Caistor he spoke at the third National Evangelical Celebration.

In Canterbury he gave the funeral address for Michael Ramsey. The Cathedral was crowded with people from all over the world, witness to Ramsey's stature as one of the greatest Church leaders of the century. The Archbishop described Ramsey's fortitude after the failure of the scheme for unity with the Methodists and his achievement in cementing relations with Rome. Ramsey wore the ring Pope Paul VI had given him until the day of his death; afterwards Lady Ramsey gave it to the Archbishop, who intended to give it to his successor.

He answered the question that would ultimately be asked in his own case, of the nature and origin of the bond between the man and the office:

'If we ask what was his outstanding characteristic we may say it was his sense of the reality and nearness of God. A sense that he conveyed by all that he was, as much as by all that he said. An unselfconscious awareness of God. It was that which we saw and loved in him. It was that which won the respect even of those who disagreed with him. It was that which drew the seeker and won the spontaneous affection of children and strangers.

'Some of us can recall how we felt it twenty-seven years ago in Canterbury Cathedral as he gave out his enthronement text: *"There went with him a band of men whose hearts God had touched"* (1 Sam. 10:26). We recall perhaps the lift of his voice, the lilt of the words themselves, the unforgettable refrain, the searching invitation:

*"'Help one another, serve one another, for the times are urgent and the days are evil. Help one another, serve one another as from this hundredth ceremony at St Augustine's throne there goes a band whose hearts God has touched."'*

A month later he preached at the one thousandth anniversary of the death of St Dunstan, Abbot of Glastonbury and, for twenty-eight years, Archbishop of Canterbury. Pilgrims had walked from Glastonbury and travelled from St Dunstan's churches in the United States, South Africa, New Guinea and Malaysia.

He travelled to the Soviet Union again, this time to attend celebrations of the millennium of Christianity there. Like several hundred representatives of other Churches and religions, he was a guest of Patriarch Pimen, Archbishop Kyril and the Metropolitan Filaret of Minsk.

At Lambeth, the latest initiative was under way to find the whereabouts of Terry Waite, Brian Keenan and John McCarthy.

After long and secret negotiations with representatives of the Speaker of the Iranian Parliament, John Lyttle and a team of four MPs were dispatched to Tehran. The first signs were encouraging in spite of the anxiety of the Foreign Office, which was still labouring under the fruitless government policy of 'not doing deals with terrorists'.

Then this initiative too, was, literally, shot down; an American warship in the Gulf fired on and destroyed an Iranian civil airliner, killing every man, woman and child on board. The spectre of Waite's association with America was strong in many Iranian minds. The Archbishop of Canterbury issued a rapid and conspicuous statement of condolence; but the prospect receded, if it had been nearer, of the release of Waite or any other hostage.

The Archbishop spoke in the second session of that year's General Synod. At issue again was the ordination of women to the priesthood. A group of diverse bishops had produced a report. As ever, legislation proceeded too slowly for supporters of the motion and too swiftly for its opponents.

The Bishop of Durham made a well-reasoned and spiritually per-ceptive speech that met with prolonged applause. The Archbishop demonstrated how on two different days he believed he had to be two different people and correspondingly, of course, he was in two minds about the matter.

On Monday the Archbishop spoke for Robert Runcie. 'I find objections to women's ordination on the grounds of priesthood and the representation of Christ unconvincing,' he declared. 'Nor do I find myself in sympathy with arguments against the ordination of women on grounds of headship and the exercise of authority.

'So,' he went on, 'I have come to the judgement that the ordination of women to the priesthood would actually be an enlargement of the Catholic priesthood, an opening up of priesthood, rather than its overturning.'

On Tuesday he spoke for the Archbishop of Canterbury.

'I must also confess,' he declared, 'to feelings of despondency on reading this juridical machinery for the separation of the proponents and the antagonists.

'Do the proposals not in effect mean that parishes and whole dioceses by sole declaration of their bishop may become no-go areas? I do not believe this is what the bishops intended in our report.

'We should have impaired communion,' he went on, 'between the dioceses of the Church of England. You will understand why this is a potential nightmare for an Archbishop who, as Metropolitan, has a duty of fostering unity, not only within his own diocese and also within the ecclesiastical province.

'As Archbishop of Canterbury I will continue to recognise the ordination of women in other provinces. I will further the ministry of women as we have it, and rejoice that women deacons are winning so much acceptance in parishes . . .

'If the measure is passed, I will work hard at amendments, but I cannot honestly subscribe to legislation which would endanger the episcopal and pastoral character of the Church of England as we know it.'

He quoted William Temple on another occasion:

*'I am quite ready to face disestablishment if it be God's will. But I dread with all my soul what may come if the Church of England breaks in two.'*

The Archbishop of York and many in the three Houses of the Synod disagreed with him. It was impossible to avoid division over this issue; and difficult to avoid the conclusion that the sooner they settled it by passing the necessary legislation the better. Unlike the issue of homosexuality, this was something that could be decided by Synod. The motion was narrowly carried. The process, with agonising slowness, creaked and rumbled on.

Later it would be claimed that, had the 1988 Lambeth Conference not come when it had and gone as it did, Robert Runcie would have shortly afterwards retired as Archbishop of Canterbury. This claim was without substance.

Eight years into his primacy and still three years from compulsory retirement, he had, however, experienced even by the standards of modern archbishops an unparalleled siege of his tenure at Canterbury and Lambeth. The politically-motivated attacks on him in the press had been made on a man unprotected by the authority accorded to the Queen, the Prime Minister or the Pope. A prominent factor in these attacks had been a misunderstanding of the nature and extent of his authority. The extent of a more sinister Anglo-Catholic involvement would long be suspected and never be disproven.

The attacks on his family in the gutter press were no more than an unpleasant by-product, a toxic waste produced for cruder appetites than those for which the 'quality' press liked to think they were catering. But they left their scars on their victims. Equally misleading was the way Lindy was now presented as having undergone some sort of miraculous rehabilitation. The woman who had posed dreamily on top of her piano had now become that most wholesome of figures, the Englishwoman in her garden. The press had been encouraged to discover the transformation she had wrought in this respect at Lambeth. Lindy, it seemed, had finally adopted the right kind of supine posture traditionally preferred of clergy wives in the Church of England.

The *Crockford's* Preface had left him outwardly bloodied but inwardly unbowed. The attacks on Cuddesdon had hurt more than those on himself. He told John Garton on one of his visits: 'Well, you know, one carries on regardless although people don't realise this.' He was a very tough man, but he had very nearly had enough.

But the biggest blow of all had been the loss of Terry Waite. A single candle had burned day and night for him in the chapel since shortly after his disappearance. Not a day passed when the Archbishop did not pray for him and experience what he knew was an excessive degree of guilt at not having done what nobody else had managed to do: stop Waite going back to the Lebanon.

This then, and the success or failure of the Lambeth Conference, were questions it was still perhaps in his gift to answer. The refusal to bow to the more malevolent calls for his departure, the hope of Waite's return and the goal of the success of Lambeth '88, were what made him carry on.


The omens were not all promising. Activisits and reactivists had made noises suggesting they might consider hijacking the platform on numerous issues. The previous Lambeth Conference in 1978 had been a mixed affair, although by no means the disaster described by Gareth Bennett.

Donald Coggan's personal style had been a mixture of the severe and the conspicuously unobtrusive. Like Coggan, the Archbishop had determined to make Canterbury the focus of his conference. He had travelled in his longer primacy far more extensively in the Anglican Communion. He knew at first hand many of the personalities and problems of the five hundred and twenty-five bishops expected to be in attendance. Unlike Coggan, he was instinctively at home in the centre of the stage.

Of his own expectations, he was cautious. 'It isn't a question of us coming together in order to decide particular things,' he told Susan Young, 'or simply to look at our own structures. It is to give substance to the word "Communion".'

He took the line taken by Michael Ramsey, who had presided benignly over the Lambeth Conference of 1968:

*'There is such a thing as Anglican theology and it is sorely needed at the present day. But because it is neither a system nor a confession . . . but a method, a use and a direction, it cannot be defined or even perceived as a "thing in itself", and it may elude the eyes of those who ask "What is it?" and "Where is it?" It has been proved, and will be proved again, by its fruits and its works.'*

Trevor Beeson, the Dean of Winchester, had summed up Lambeth '78 for *American Christian Century*:

*'General conferences involving large numbers of people are always more interesting and significant for those who attend them than for those who read and write about them.'*

The five hundred and twenty-five bishops, their wives, and several hundred consultants, staff and members of the media, arrived in the few days preceding Saturday 16 July 1988. The Archbishop formally welcomed them that evening in the gymnasium of the University of Kent. He did so in English, French, Spanish, Japanese and Swahili.

He mentioned 'one member of my personal staff' and asked them to remember Terry Waite. He concluded:

'There is often confusion about the actual power and position of the Archbishop of Canterbury.

'I asked a friend who is a Rabbi what he thought the change had been in the position of the Archbishop. He told me this story. There was once a troublesome cat who made a great noise chasing the lady cats of the neighbourhood and disturbed everyone's peace and quiet. Eventually the owner had it neutered. When friends asked "did it work?" he answered: "Well, he's still making a lot of noise, but it's now only in an advisory capacity."'

On Sunday 17 July they processed in their splendour for the Inaugural Eucharist in Canterbury Cathedral. The Archbishop led the Primates, accompanied by the Chaplain to the Conference, Bishop Alastair Haggart, and the Assistant Chaplain, Mother Janet of the Whitby Sisters. The Venerable Yong Ping Chung of Malaysia, Chairman of the Anglican Consultative Council, read the ministry of the Word, and the Gospel was read by the Bishop of Ecuador. The Archbishop preached the sermon.

'As you enter this Cathedral,' he said, 'your eye is caught by its massive pillars. In their strength they seem to stand on their own feet, symbols of strong foundations and sturdy independence. Yet their strength is an illusion. Look up and you see the pillars converting into arches, which are upheld, not by independence, but through inter-dependence. "An arch," wrote Leonardo da Vinci, "is nothing else than a strength caused by two weaknesses; for the arch in buildings is made up of two segments of a circle, and each of these segments, being in itself very weak, desires to fall and as one withstands the downfall of the other, the two weaknesses are converted into a single strength."

'As we come here we do well to remember that human weakness and our dependence on each other are not things to overcome but gifts to offer to God as He works out His purpose in the world . . .'

He called upon the members of the Conference not to confuse affluence for richness of spirit and to live bravely enough to learn by their mistakes. They should not overestimate the power of a Lambeth Conference to flatten 'the walls of our particular Jerichos' but nor should they underestimate it. They should see the Anglican Communion 'in the range of God's purpose' as 'a small ship sailing on a wide, a very wide ocean'.

'We must guide that ship as best we can,' he concluded, 'but in the end its destination and that of our Communion will not be determined by our skill and diligence as navigators, but by the power of that all-sustaining, all-embracing, ever-flowing and ever-gracious purpose of God in this His beloved world.'

The next day he officially opened the Lambeth Conference of 1988. His long address was the keynote of the Conference, perhaps his primacy. It was entitled *The Nature of the Unity We Seek*.

He paid tribute to the power of the dispersed authority of Anglicanism in its survival from the dead political structures of colony and empire. He reasserted the validity of the Lambeth Conference in its long tradition. But it had to keep changing if it was to keep up; and the pace of change was never hotter than in the question of unity.

'Let me put it in starkly simple terms: do we really want unity within the Anglican Communion? Is our world-wide family of Christians worth bonding together? Or is our paramount concern the preservation or promotion of that particular expression of Anglicanism which has developed within the culture of our own province? Would it not be easier and more realistic to work towards more exclusively European, or North American, or African, or Pacific forms of Anglicanism? Yes, it might. Cultural adaptation would be easier. Mission would be easier. Local ecumenism would be easier. Do we actually need a world-wide communion?

'I believe we do, because Anglicans believe in the one holy catholic and apostolic church of the creed. I believe we do, because we live in one world created and redeemed by God. I believe we do, because it is only by being in communion together that diversity and difference have value. Without relationship difference divides.

'That is why I have called the present Lambeth Conference. That is why I have visited many of the provinces of the Anglican Communion in solidarity with both your joys and your sufferings. I have tried to be a personal and visible presence of the whole Anglican family in places like the Province of Southern Africa, where solidarity between the world-wide Church and particular Christians is a gospel imperative if ever there was one.

'So I believe we still need the Anglican Communion. But we have reached the stage in the growth of the Communion where we must begin to make radical choices, or growth will imperceptibly turn to decay. I believe the choice between independence and interdependence, already set before us as a communion in embryo twenty-five years ago, is quite simply the choice between unity or gradual fragmentation. It would be a gentle, even genteel, fragmentation – that much of Englishness still remains – and it would not be instant. As I have said, the Communion is not about to disappear tomorrow. But decisive choice is before us. Do we want the Anglican Communion? And if we do, what are we going to do about it?'

At the end of his speech he returned to his seat on the platform. As he did so, the entire Conference rose to its feet and burst into long and loud applause. The Archbishop had opened the Conference. In doing so, he had given of himself 'in a way', as one distinguished observer put it, 'which would mark him out in history'.

The first formal Lambeth Wives' Conference opened nearby at St Edmund's Church of England School. Lindy began the proceedings by saying: 'I do not believe it when I read that numbers are declining in the Church. There is a silent majority in the Church which believes in what's going on and does not start picking holes in everything.'

The Wives' Conference was attended by over four hundred women from seventy-four countries. They included six doctors, sixty-two teachers, thirty nurses, four professional musicians, two journalists, an architect and a beauty consultant. One bishop was heard to remark that it would be 'more interesting' than the Conference he was attending. The agenda was no longer restricted to issues traditionally associated with the wives of the clergy. Although there were workshops on 'Flower Arranging', 'Pottery' and 'Music in Worship', the workshop which attracted the most, with more than sixty members, was simply entitled 'Stress'.

The Conference dealt with dozens of motions and produced resolutions on issues as diverse as the ordination of women to the priesthood, ARCIC, evangelisation, dogma, the Iran-Iraq war, Northern Ireland, interfaith dialogue and many others. As diverse were the personalities of the debaters and there was greater strength in them than in many of the official resolutions. Bishop Jack Spong of Newark was pressed as to how he had managed to achieve a consensus that enabled him to vote with his arch-adversary the Bishop of London. He eventually conceded: 'We did it by not addressing any of the really significant issues.' Bishop Pwaisiho of Malaita, Melanesia, said that the ordination of women to the priesthood was 'heartbreaking for Third World Churches . . . if women's priesthood comes as a result of the movement for women's liberation, it is satanic'. The Reverend Nan Peete, a black woman Episcopalian priest who was a consultant to the Conference, won long applause simply by describing her own experiences as a woman already active in the ministry as rector of an Anglo-Catholic parish in Indianapolis.

More restrained applause greeted Bishop Leonard on the same subject. When asked at a press conference afterwards whether or not Nan Peete was a priest, he retorted: 'I don't think that is a fair question. I am not prepared to say that she is,' he went on, 'and I am not prepared to say she is not.'

The Conference cricket match between the Archbishop of Canterbury's XI and the Diocese of Canterbury XI was a wash-out. The Archbishop acted as umpire, but the short duration of play meant that he was saved from having to make any controversial decisions. The guest team won the toss and put the diocesan team in to bat.

Sheila McClachlan, a deacon and chaplain at the University of Kent, was no match for the Archbishop's star bowler Bishop Michael Nazir Ali, the Secretary General of the Church Missionary Society. Nazir Ali, an Oxford blue, bowled her out for a duck and took three more wickets before rain stopped play. The result was a draw.

The bishops and their wives travelled to London for the Lambeth Conference Service in St Paul's Cathedral. This was followed by Lambeth Palace Day and lunch for fifteen hundred people in the gardens, whose reconstruction and renaissance had been achieved by the Lambeth Fund, by Sir Hector Laing and most of all by Lindy. Some Anglo-Catholic bishops dispersed on an outing to Walsingham; others on a day trip to Boulogne.

On 7 August the Conference ended as it had begun, with a service in Canterbury Cathedral. The address was given by the Presiding Bishop of the Episcopal Church of America, Edmund Browning. The

Archbishop led the bishops out of the Cathedral, followed first by his Acting Secretary for Anglican Affairs, Roger Symon. That afternoon a specially chartered episcopal express with the bishops and their wives on board pulled out of Canterbury West station. The Archbishop and his wife waved goodbye.

In his last speech, the Archbishop had quoted the sermon he had heard preached in Cambridge by Martin Niemoller over thirty years earlier. He also said: 'The first Lambeth Conference lasted four days; the second, in 1878, lasted four weeks. If succeeding Lambeth Conferences had lengthened at the same rate they would now last over ten years, and there would be no need for us to go home at all.'

In many cases they went home with the same picture in mind. On the second Sunday of the Conference the Dean, John Simpson, and Chapter had held open house at the Cathedral and the Cathedral Precincts. That night the members of the Conference had said Compline in the darkened Quire. Above them, a single beam of light had shone on St Augustine's chair.

After the train had gone, in came the hundreds of letters, many containing the same impression. This one light was the abiding image, the strongest memory, taken back to disparate dioceses around the world.

# 9

# *Life After Lambeth*

IN LATE July, 1988, Bishop Brown of Cyprus and the Gulf returned from a mission to the Lebanon. He said he was optimistic about the release of Terry Waite.

Archbishop Penman of Melbourne had visited Iran en route to the Lambeth Conference; he too was optimistic. He would not be surprised, he said, if Waite and the other hostages were home for Christmas.

Bishop Brown visited the Archbishop at Lambeth Palace, as did a senior Iranian foreign ministry official. According to a French press source the Western hostages had been split up. Waite was being held in a Hizbollah barracks north of Beirut at Baalbek. As ever there was no hard information, a seemingly worthless currency in the Lebanon.

The Archbishop was preoccupied with the Episcopal Church of America's choice of its next Suffragan Bishop of Massachusetts. Barbara Harris was black, female and a divorcee; she had been PR officer for the Sun Oil Company. She also had considerable pastoral and theological credentials. But her appointment seemed to have been made simply to offend some Anglo-Catholics.

In Britain Bishops Leonard and Kemp made the usual noises. The Archbishop reminded them of the resolution of the Lambeth Conference to urge respect between different provinces, and that he had just established the Eames Commission, under the Archbishop of Armagh, on women and the episcopate.

Bishop Leonard was to spend much time and energy that autumn trying to prevent the American priest Suzanne Fageol from celebrating the Eucharist in his diocese. He said she had breached the laws of the Church. She replied that the restrictions applied in Britain only to the diocese of Ripon, where she was an honorary member of a Leeds parish church. But she promised to give the Bishop of London's letters her full and considered attention.

The latest attempts to ascertain Waite's whereabouts would again be clouded by outside interference. The latest freelancer to muddy the pool was the notorious self-styled 'mercenary' John Banks.

In 1969 Banks had been dishonourably discharged from the 2nd Battalion the Parachute Regiment, and his activities since then had seemed designed to discredit the British freelance security profession. He had been responsible for recruiting the doomed strike force of 'Colonel Callan' which conducted operations in Angola. This had not affected his ability to bounce back and make money out of more bungled operations. He was plausible, ruthless and flexible when it came to the difference between fact and fiction. He was ideally equipped to participate in the affairs of the Lebanon.

Banks contacted Lambeth Palace in October 1988 and hinted heavily that he was in a position to succeed where Control Risks had not proceeded. John Lyttle wasted no time in advising him of Lambeth's utter lack of interest in his project. Unknown to Lyttle and the Archbishop, Banks had already seen an operation he had assembled to release an American hostage in Beirut blow up in his face when his men mutinied in Cyprus. He had neglected to tell them the true purpose of their mission. His backers wished to speak to him about their £1 million investment. His approach to Lambeth had been an attempt to give his project renewed credibility. Instead his interference damaged the latest legitimate attempts to negotiate with the hostage-takers in the Lebanon.

The Archbishop preached on the Feast of All Saints at All Saints', Margaret Street, London, synonymous with British Anglo-Catholicism. His theme again was the nature of unity, and the means to a better understanding of the same.

'A sense of proportion,' he said, 'has often meant that holiness and humour have kissed each other. I remember,' the 'man from everywhere', went on, 'worshipping in All Saints' Church in 1945 on the evening of VJ Day, which was also the Feast of the Assumption. One might have pondered whether our victory in the Far East or the taking of Our Lady into heavenly glory would take precedence. Instead, I heard Cyril Tomkinson [the Vicar] begin his sermon with the words,

"Today is the birthday of Napoleon III." A sense of proportion is a great gift . . .'

In Lambeth Palace Chapel he addressed a service to mark its restoration. Archbishop Laud's screen had survived the bomb damage done during the Second World War and was replaced where it had once been when Laud had said his prayers before being taken down the Thames to the Tower of London and eventual execution. Leonard Rosoman had painted a series of representations of early Christianty and English history on the ceiling. The stalls had been re-ordered so that there was a place for each Primate of the Anglican Communion. The Archbishop spoke of the role of the chapel as a place of devotion: 'In a holy place the power of sacred association penetrates deeply into human hearts. Coming into this place you do not enter silence simply, for silence can be dead. You move rather into stillness – coming through the screen you must let the mystery of stillness disclose itself. Movement, life, can be gathered into stillness; that is the difference between silence and the poet's stillness.'

The election of Bishop Harris in America continued to have its effects on the Church of England. At the third session of that year's Synod the Archbishop said that Anglican priests, male or female, who were ordained by a woman bishop would not be permitted to minister in the Church of England for the time being. He stressed, however, that this was a legal position which could change if the Church of England decided to ordain women priests or consecrate them bishops.

This was a complex legal issue. As he also pointed out, if the Church of England permitted priests ordained by a woman to officiate, it would involve 'the theological absurdity of being able to recognise and accept the ministry of male priests or deacons, but not the ministry of the woman bishop who ordained them'.

The legal position meant that the Church of England could still be in communion with a Church, some of whose ministers it did not recognise. This was of paramount importance to him. Unlike some of Barbara Harris' opponents, as long as he was Archbishop of Canterbury he would not now or ever call for the withdrawal from the Anglican Communion of the Episcopal Church of the United States of America.

In London that November he made Kristallnacht memorial addresses at the Friends Meeting House and West London Synagogue to remember the night of Nazi terror fifty years earlier. As he had done a year before, he received his advance copy of *Crockford's* Clerical Directory.

After the advertisements, there was a brief introduction:

### 'A Departure from Tradition'

*'Crockford has long included a Preface in which an anonymous writer expressed a wholly independent view of Anglican affairs. However, as the Press Release of May 1988 stated, a review of this traditional practice was undertaken in response to the unprecedented events which followed the publication of the ninetieth edition in December 1987.*

*'We concluded,'* said the anonymous author on behalf of the Church Commissioners, *'that an anonymous Preface was no longer a viable option, and, after considering the full range of theoretical possibilities, were unable to identify a satisfactory alternative arrangement. The present edition, therefore, does not include a Preface.'*

The *Mail on Sunday*, in its role as voice of the Church of England, published its own version:

### CHURCH IN TURMOIL

*'The most serious split in the history of the Church of England loomed last night when more than 1,500 clergy publicly declared their opposition to women priests.*

*'They have taken the extraordinary step of collectively publishing their names in an "open list" saying that they will not accept the ordination of women.'*

In fact, there was nothing extraordinary about this step or the list in question. Names had been openly canvassed in the religious press for some time and the list had been deliberately leaked to the paper.

*'Some have threatened to leave the church if it happens. But most say they will stay and fight from within . . .'*

*'Details of the list, revealed exclusively in the* Mail on Sunday, *will stun the Archbishop of Canterbury – because of both the number and seniority of those who are prepared to risk their careers and their livelihoods by going public . . .'*

In fact, the list came as no surprise to the Archbishop of Canterbury, who was personally acquainted with the views of many of its signatories. Nor was the size of it a surprise to him. Nor, as long as he was Archbishop of Canterbury, was there a risk to the careers and livelihoods of those who had signed it.

This last notion was a piece of malevolent disingenuousness. Now it was faithfully delivered by the *Mail on Sunday,* to a nation for which it purported to speak, and thus for whose ignorance of religious matters it could claim a major responsibility. Deprived of the *Crockford's* Preface, those responsible had at last found a mouthpiece to match their worth; at least it gave a more topical meaning to the title of the newspaper.

The Archbishop began the round of Christmas addresses: to the Soviet Union on the BBC Russian Service after his recent memorable visit; to his congregation, on Christmas Day from the pulpit of Canterbury Cathedral; and to the nation, at midnight, in a New Year broadcast. He asked for prayers for the hostages in the Lebanon. He spoke of recent tragedies; of the earthquake in Armenia, of the rail crash in Clapham, of the terrorist outrage in the air over Lockerbie. As he had done after the Zeebrugge ferry disaster and the killings in Hungerford, he tried to articulate the feelings of the nation and the bereaved.

He also made a broadcast for the BBC Radio Programme *Desert Island Discs.* He spoke of his father and of Betty Cooke, the girl for whom his adolescent crush had led him instead to the arms of the Church. He made a number of selectively discreet revelations.

Inez Luckcraft, now Scott, was listening. What struck her was not the fact that one of his favourite records was *Diamonds* by Fats Waller. What she noticed was how he spoke of Kath, his elder sister.

In all the years Mrs Luckcraft had known him, he had never spoken of Kath as he did now. Her influence in his entering the Church of

England had been profound. Kath had died a few months earlier. Through the invisible medium of the radio, and with the help of a skilled interviewer, Sue Lawley, he was at last able to express the depth of his own feelings.

By January 1989 John Fenwick had joined Christopher Hill at Lambeth as Assistant Secretary for Ecumenical Affairs. Roger Symon continued as Acting Secretary for Anglican Communion Affairs in the absence of Terry Waite.

The second anniversary of Waite's disappearance came and went; like the first it was marked by prayers and vigils in many parts of the country.

In London, the Archbishop joined Waite's wife and brothers in a service at All Souls', Langham Place. There was still no firm positive or negative news; the prospect of there being any again receded with the publication of Salman Rushdie's novel *The Satanic Verses*, which caused widespread offence in the Moslem world and resulted in a *fatwa* or pronouncement, in this case of the death sentence against the author.

In the Lebanon, the British Ambassador Allan Ramsay made regular trips from East Beirut into West Beirut in the search for information about the missing Westerners. Walid Jumblatt, the Druze leader whose men had protected Waite until he dismissed them, appealed for his release on Lebanese television. 'I don't think Mr Waite was a big spy,' he said.

In Synod that February the Archbishop called for the recruitment of younger ordinands to the ministry. He criticised what he called 'the cult of experience' and said it was 'in danger of becoming an idol'.

The impression was too often given, he said, that the best ordination candidates were people 'who have had long stretches of secular employment, been on a trek to the Himalayas, and, if possible, known what it was to sleep rough or be down and out. And so the frequent admonition is "Come back later when you've knocked around a bit" – and then you discover that the average age in the colleges is about thirty-five.

'Say it too often,' he went on, 'and you will soon ensure we have no clergy in their twenties at all. And, secondly, you collude with the idea that the priest or deacon leads some cloistered, sheltered life.'

There was applause, and cries of 'Hear, hear'.

He concluded: 'More raw experience of life,' he concluded, 'is often available as a priest on a council estate or in a city suburb than in many a secular job. We need young priests who will grow to maturity as priests. We do not need only mature people who take on priesthood later in life.'

Barbara Harris, who had come late to the priesthood, was consecrated Suffragan Bishop of Massachusetts. In opposition to the rumours put about by traditionalists that she was the figurehead of an ultra-feminist conspiracy, the occasion was attended and supported by a wide range of Episcopalian worshippers and clergy.

The Pope did not approve, and wrote a letter to the Archbishop of Canterbury. This further complicated the difficult labours of ARCIC to close the gap between their two Churches.

The *Mail on Sunday*, fed by the usual sources, carried the huge headline 'CRISIS AS THE POPE BLAMES RUNCIE'. The paper neglected to mention the fact that the Pope had also sent the Archbishop an affectionate Easter letter.

The Anglican Co-Chairman of ARCIC was the Archbishop's Cuddesdon student and colleague in the Cell, Mark Santer. The Archbishop and Santer were due to travel to the Vatican in September. Their trip was now portrayed as a hasty attempt to postpone the inevitable breakdown of communications between Rome and Lambeth.

The Archbishop and Santer were nonetheless hoping that the Pope would come to a better understanding of the difficulties facing an Archbishop of Canterbury, who, without possessing a papal kind of authority, sought to achieve unity among the Anglican Communion. The distress caused to the Pope by the consecration of a divorced woman bishop was a price the Archbishop was personally forced to pay.

In both his Easter sermon and his Easter letter to the Orthodox and Protestant Churches he reiterated the truth of 'the miracle of the Resurrection' and said 'the relevance of this credal truth is as great as ever'. The Bishop of Durham gave his own familiar version in an interview recorded for Easter on Tyne Tees Television. As usual the press gave him disproportionate prominence and as usual he seemed surprised that they had done so.

He said he was optimistic in the long term. '. . . because I believe so strongly in the Resurrection. I'm a bit browned off at the moment,' he went on disarmingly. '(I'm getting a bit old!) by the way in which so-called religious people seem to turn inwards and have arguments about things other people don't bother about. Or you get people laying down the law,' he concluded, 'in alarming ways that could seem to put people off.'

In London the Archbishop attended a speech given at the Guildhall by President Gorbachev. The vicar of the adjoining church of St Lawrence Jewry was his Cuddesdon ordinand David Burgess.

Burgess observed the Archbishop's obvious fatigue and suggested that at least he could sit quietly and let his own thoughts develop at such a gathering. The Archbishop appreciated the sentiment but did not appear convinced. Later that day he and Gorbachev spoke at Windsor Castle through an interpreter.

In Cyprus two weeks later he was among the delegates at the Anglican Communion Primates Conference. They welcomed the Eames Commission report on the unity of Anglicanism in the context of women in the episcopate. He reassured them of his confidence in his forthcoming visit to Rome. He had assembled his team: Mark Santer, the ACC Secretary-General Sam Van Culin, and Joseph Adetiloye, Archbishop of Nigeria, as one who, in the Archbishop's words, 'does not come from the Anglo-Saxon world'.

Less than a week later, on 31 May 1989, he joined Terry Waite's wife and brother for a moment of remembrance in Lambeth Palace Chapel on Waite's fiftieth birthday. Two and a half years had now passed since his disappearance in Beirut. That same day the Archbishop flew to Africa with Graham James and Roger Symon.

This was the beginning of a two-week tour of the Anglican Province of Central Africa: Botswana, Zimbabwe, Zambia and Malawi. The province had a long history of missionary endeavour and gruesome martyrdom. The four very different countries were united by a movable Archbishop of Central Africa.

In Botswana he was welcomed by his host Archbishop Khotso Makhulu. He preached in Holy Cross Cathedral, Gabarone, and at huge outdoor gatherings in Malawi. In Zimbabwe he visited the shrine of the murdered African catechist Bernard Mizeki. In Zambia he preached at more outdoor gatherings, was honoured by the march-past of the Chingola Boys Brigade and inspected the great Nchanga Open Copper Pit.

In America, Bishop Leonard led a Church of England contingent at the traditionalist 'alternative' Synod at Fort Worth, Texas. Nine members of the Church of England House of Bishops and twenty-five per cent of the membership of the General Synod in all had signed a message supporting the gathering.

*'We welcome,'* the message read, *'the initiative taken by the ECM to convene a special synod of bishops, clergy and laity. We share your concern at the continual erosion of the authority of Scripture and of the doctrinal and moral standards which are founded on it . . .'*

But the talk in Fort Worth was not of schism. The consecration of Bishop Harris, however unpleasant to them, was a reality. Instead, the phrase they used was 'alternative episcopal oversight'. The American Evangelical and Catholic Mission wanted to find a way of remaining in the Episcopal Church of America.

The second session of that year's General Synod was treated to a rare sight by Mrs Jill Dann, former Mayoress of Chippenham and the Evangelical lay member for Bristol.

Mrs Dann was to be seen solemnly passing round photocopies of the *News of the World*. Her target, like the newspaper's, was the Chairman of the General Synod Business Sub-Committee and Vicar of Holy Trinity, Reading, Brian Brindley.

Canon Brindley had been the victim of an unfortunately graphic article about homosexuality within the Church of England. To the *News of the World* he had just been the peg for another prurient story about a gay vicar. He was harmless, if flamboyantly indiscreet. But Mrs Dann was made of sterner stuff. To her and David Holloway, Vicar of Jesmond, this was one 'pulpit poof' who definitely could not stay. Brindley resigned two months later.

The Archbishop had been loyal over the years to individual homosexual clergy. He had not personally defined their identities according to their sexual preferences and did not encourage them to do the same. He had not been well disposed towards the homosexuality lobby, to the displeasure of the General Secretary of the Lesbian and Gay Christian Movement, Richard Kirker.

The Archbishop's attitude to homosexuality as an issue was similar to his attitide to evangelism. The loudest voices represented not the courageous voicing of uncomfortable truths, but the trumpeting of comfortable certainties. There was no coincidence in the fact that the Evangelicals were dominant among those who hounded the homo-sexual clergy. To many, however, Synod would have been a duller and less representative a place, without the right of each to temper the worst excesses of the other.

Mary Cryer left Lambeth Palace after seven years as Second Secretary, Palace Secretary and Bursar. She had worked closely with Lindy and the Lambeth Fund and written the guide to the Palace of Lambeth. She had co-ordinated the opening of Lambeth to the public. She had hoped to stay on until the Archbishop retired.

Bishop Gordon had seen no reason why she should stay beyond the age of sixty. She was a Justice of the Peace and presumably had plenty to occupy herself. As in the case of Stella Taylor, his businesslike attitude left a bitter taste. To Mary Cryer too, Lambeth could be a cruel place: 'No need,' the Bishop had told her when she suggested she should stay on.

She refused to appeal to the Archbishop. In any case she assumed his Head of Staff would mention it to him. She was hurt.

The Archbishop gave her a party in the Guard Room. She realised that she had to let go. She would eventually be replaced by four people, none of whom was given proper training. She wrote to the Archbishop, thanking him for the party.

She added that she was sorry that he had not felt able to allow her to see him out. But they were old friends, and they did not need to explain anything to each other.

He came into her office. He had no idea, he said, that she felt this way. They left it at that, and she left with her memories.

That summer the Archbishop travelled north to Northumberland to visit Brother Harold, a hermit.

The Archbishop was an admirer and a supporter of the religious life, which he suspected formed a secret energy source within the Church of England. He hosted a party for members of religious orders that month at Lambeth. Sister Jane of the Sisters of the Love of God was a friend of long-standing. Mother Janet of Whitby had been an invaluable pillar of the Lambeth Conference.

Brother Harold had spent the last eighteen years labouring to make his dream come true on the high moors of this sparsely populated part of the country. He had finished building with his own hands the latest additional cells of Shepherd's Law, his hermitage. Brother Harold and Brother Jean-Claude, a French Franciscan, served at the Eucharist celebrated by the Archbishop of Canterbury. The local Roman Catholic and United Reformed clergy also took part.

The Archbishop gave the address. He shared Brother Harold's hope that people would come to live here and his belief that their lives would be enriched in the process. The new cells were also an extension of Anglican religious life.

Brother Harold agreed with him. He was the very model of a modern hermit, used to travelling about the Northumberland moors by miniature four-wheel-drive vehicle. He knew that even a hermit had to move with the times. But he was a little dismayed when the Archbishop of Canterbury, the star of the Lambeth Conference, turned up accompanied by what seemed like half the world's press. Perhaps he had built just too public a hermitage extension after all.


The Archbishops' Commission on Rural England passed the half-way mark in its researches, established to do for rural areas what had been done for urban life by *Faith In the City*. The Commission was headed by the former Agriculture Minister Lord Prior and the Bishop of Norwich.

The Archbishop had given his support to the 'Canterbury Festival of Faith and the Environment'. The festival began on 15 September 1989 with the arrival of three groups of pilgrims, led by an Anglican, a Hindu and a Baha'i.

John Simpson, Dean of Canterbury, took the service of welcome which was attended by the Archbishop of York. Exhibitions and displays were mounted in the Cathedral Precincts by members of different faiths and different environmental groups. On the Sunday morning the Archbishop of Canterbury preached at the Alternative Service Book Rite 'A' Eucharist, which was attended by representatives of other Christian denominations.

There was never any question of inter-faith worship. But this was not enough for Tony Higton, Rector of Hawkwell, founder of Action for Biblical Witness to our Nation, and self-styled Grand Inquisitor of the Church of England.

Higton regarded the Festival as 'encouraging people to come to God other than through Jesus' and instructed his supporters accordingly.

He told them to write in protest to the Archbishop and Dean of Canterbury.

*'Don't refer to Action for Biblical Witness to our Nation,'* he told them, *'people take less notice of what they see as organised protest.'*

Higton did not actually bother to contact the organisers of the Festival, presumably on the grounds that, as in the case of Gareth Bennett, first-hand research might cause him to doubt instead of worshipping at the altar of bigotry. He wrote to his supporters:

*'We could see the following: worship of other gods and idols, earth worship, pagan meditation, inter-faith worship, occult practices from mediums, witches, and the like; recruiting campaigns for other religions, sects and cults.'*

So unsound was the fundamentalist argument that Higton eventually had to resort to the declaration that he had been banned from the Cathedral Precincts. This too was untrue. But in Higton's world no further proof was needed that he was right than if an argument could be produced in opposition to him.

The Archbishop visited the Vatican with his team including Christopher Hill and Mark Santer.

Santer had been Peter Walker's successor as Principal of Westcott House and was now Hugh Montefiore's successor as Bishop of Birmingham. He had risen fast in the Church of England. Like the Archbishop he had served on the Anglican-Orthodox Joint Doctrinal

Commission. At forty-five he had been elected Suffragan Bishop of Kensington. He was Co-Chairman of ARCIC. He was capable and ambitious; perhaps a little too conspicuously so. Some pointed to the fact that he had only four years' parish experience, all of which he had spent as curate at Cuddesdon under Robert Runcie. Others believed he would one day follow Robert Runcie to Canterbury. Now they went together to Rome.

The visit was beset from the start, after remarks made by the Archbishop in an interview with *Il Regno* magazine. He called for the acceptance of the 'universal primacy' of the Pope, coupled with reconciliation between Roman Catholics and Anglicans. This was little more than diplomacy aimed at his host, and the conditions for reconciliation as he knew were particularly difficult since they included the ordination of women. The press chose to concentrate on the first half of his statement, and there were immediate counterblasts from Protestants in Britain. The same people now dusted off their placards and their slogans who had shouted him down in Liverpool seven years earlier.

The Archbishop and his party lodged in the English College at Rome. The Pope gave a party of welcome for him in the Vatican gardens. The Archbishop said a few words in reply.

'I am reminded of the brilliant Roman Catholic theologian and preacher Ronald Knox,' he told the Pope and assembled cardinals, 'he hated foreign travel. When asked why he hadn't visited Rome, he replied: "As I'm a poor sailor, I've no desire to visit the engine room."'

On the second day of his visit their talks began in earnest and he became only the second Archbishop of Canterbury to attend a Papal Mass since Henry VIII broke with Rome in 1534. He saw love letters from Henry VIII to Anne Boleyn in the Vatican archives. At the church of San Gregorio he addressed the congregation in the name of the unity he sought. 'Could not all Christians,' he said, 'come to reconsider the kind of primacy the Bishop of Rome exercised within the early Church, a "presiding in love" for the sake of unity of the Churches in the diversity of their missions?'

He acknowledged the differences between Rome and Canterbury, just as the Pope had acknowledged the fact that neither he nor the Archbishop of Canterbury had any jurisdiction over the autonomous provinces of the Anglican Communion.

The Archbishop and the Pope met five times to pray and talk. Their personal relationship remained a warm one. The Pope had become a more autocratic figure over the years since they had first met, to the dismay of many members of his own Church. In a Common Declaration signed by the two men they repeated the need for closer links between the two Churches. The Archbishop's visit to Rome had kept open the dialogue. The Pope had developed a better understanding of the nature of Anglicanism. The Roman Catholic Church had conceded that it had been slow to respond to the latest work of ARCIC. The Archbishop and his party left Rome in good heart. He arrived back at Heathrow Airport to a Protestant demonstration, and another manufactured political controversy.

This concerned remarks he had made in a recently published interview with *Director* magazine. These were taken out of context and promoted under such headlines as 'Runcie Hits at Maggie' and 'Thatcher's "nation of Pharisees"'. The widespread impression given was that the Archbishop who seemed so fond of the Pope had hardened his treasonous and unsound views on the Prime Minister and her government.

The interview had of course taken no such line. 'The tensions which you speak of,' he had said, 'between Church and Government are never as evident to me as they seem to be to the popular press. Relationships between Lambeth Palace and Government departments are friendly and co-operative. My own meetings with Mrs Thatcher and her ministers do not betray the sort of suspicion which is often spoken of.'

This was the key passage:

'One of the challenges sometimes presented to the churches – and particularly to the Church of England – comes from the section of our political and commercial leadership which says, "We have made the people wealthy; it's the Church's job to make them good." That is not the Church's view of its task. It wants to make people godly. Godliness and goodness are not the same thing.

'Jesus reserved his most astringent criticism for the Pharisees. We tend to think that the Pharisees were unscrupulous, double-dealing, untrustworthy. That was not the case. Most of them led lives of exemplary moral rectitude. That did not cause them to escape the sharp edge of Jesus' tongue. He disliked their self-righteousness and their judgmental attitudes.

'Those are the real dangers in our society today. I sense that they are both increasing. The successful are always tempted to regard their success as a sort of blessing or reward for righteousness. This can lead to judgements being made about the unsuccessful, the unemployed, the poor and the unintelligent which are both uncharitable and untrue.

'I'm thinking of the sort of attitude that suggests that the unemployed do too little to help themselves, that if only you have determination and drive you can get on in the world. Those attitudes lead people to be dismissive of the value of their fellow human beings. Those attitudes create barriers between us and God.'

15 October 1989 was declared the thousandth day of the presumed captivity of Terry Waite. There was no firm news to add to the persistent rumours that he was alive somewhere in the Lebanon. There was even confusion as to exactly when the thousandth day fell.

No new initiatives had been taken and circumstances continued to militate against them. As the depth of the Iran-Contra conspiracy was revealed the scale of Oliver North's cynicism became clear. Reliable American intelligence sources suggested that North had even tried to encourage Waite to visit Tripoli in order to ensure that Colonel Ghaddafi would be in residence on the night of the American bombing raid in April 1986. North, whom President Reagan would call to his face 'a national hero', would escape serious indictment and be a free man long before any hard news was known of Terry Waite.

The other hostages such as the journalist John McCarthy and the teacher Brian Keenan were comparative innocents, caught in the crossfire. What hope was there for Waite, whose release, if it were even possible, was set back by every Israeli kidnapping in the Lebanon, every shift of power in Tehran? Archbishop Penman of Melbourne, who knew the Lebanon well and had interceded on his behalf in Tehran, had died suddenly a week earlier. The controversy over Salman Rushdie's novel *The Satanic Verses* did little to engender trust in Westerners in the eyes of militant Islam. All the Archbishop could do was pray.

*

One thousand, one hundred priests opposed to the ordination of women to the priesthood gathered in a 'Cost of Conscience' rally led by the Bishop of London. At Church House, Westminster, they pledged themselves to 'fight' the ordination of women to the priesthood 'both now and after any enactment of legislation'. The Eames Commission on communion and women in the episcopate held its third meeting, and pronounced itself 'much encouraged by continuing positive response to their report'.

The Archbishop conferred with the Commission and then welcomed the Principal of Ripon College, Cuddesdon. John Garton was at Lambeth to discuss the college's £1 million appeal to build new accommodation for married ordinands.

Approximately one third of the students were now married. Much had changed since the Archbishop's years as Principal, when married ordinands lived in unheated cottages and their wives kept a key to the Bishop of Oxford's bathroom. The Archbishop was exhausted and busy, but spoke with freshness about Cuddesdon and what it meant to him. The appeal would prosper and he would preside over the opening of the new building.

In Synod that November of 1989, he reported on his visit to the Pope. The ordination of women and divorcees was high on the agenda. A group of women celebrated the Eucharist during their vigil outside the gates of Lambeth Palace. The *News of the World*, Mrs Dann's unlikely ally, celebrated in its own way:

*'We probe the big religious issues of today'*

it declared. The verdict, like the print, was black and white:

*'PETTICOAT PRIESTS GET YOUR BLESSING'*
*'But you don't want to pray with a gay'*

The Osborne Report on homosexuality and the Church of England, quietly and carefully compiled over the previous two years, came up with its own findings. These were eminently sensible, with such suggestions as a coherent policy towards homosexual clergymen and some form of service to bless relationships between members of the same sex anxious to proclaim their Christianity. Yet such was his anxiety about the way it would be interpreted in some quarters that the Archbishop asked his bishops not to make public statements about the report for the time being. This was neither a report that could be contained, nor a policy that could be sustained for long, and he was much preoccupied with developing a strategy before the inevitable leaks.

He was also busy with a series of addresses: to the Senior Evangelical Clergy Conference (he told them how the Festival of Faith and the Environment at Canterbury had taught him about the New Age movement); to the Prison Reform Trust at the English Speaking Union (he was advised in this by Graham Howes, the Trinity Hall don who had become his permanent part-time sociology adviser); and the Cardinal Heenan Memorial Lecture at Heythrop College, London (his theme was Rome and the 'winter of ecumenism'). He did not underestimate the barriers to closer union between Rome and the Anglican Communion. In New Zealand, as if on cue, Penelope Jamieson, a forty-seven-year-old Englishwoman, was elected the seventh Bishop of Dunedin.

In Canterbury on Christmas Day 1989, the Archbishop lit a candle for Romania, a country he knew well and had frequently visited. As had been the case the preceding Christmas, his address was necessarily concerned with human suffering. 'We thought it was all in the past,' he said, 'the suffering and deaths of dissidents who never compromised. In the blood of Romania the price is writ large in the present. Truly it has been said you cannot have the faith of the crib without the cross.'

Over Christmas there was a series of telephone calls between him and John Garton at Cuddesdon. The Archbishop had agreed to conduct the funerals of Bert Turner, the retired gardener there, and his sister. The arrangements were made and the service in the little church was a great and simple occasion. By then, although he would not announce it for another three months, he had come to a decision about his own future.

Stephen Platten, a Cuddesdon man from the post-Runcie era and organiser of *Surrexit '89*, a celebration of faith by hundreds of people from many dioceses which had taken place in Portsmouth, succeeded Christopher Hill as the Archbishop's Secretary for Ecumenical Affairs.

The Archbishop had leaned heavily on Hill for help during his visits to Rome and the 1988 Lambeth Conference. Eve Keatley too had decided to retire through illness. With Terry Waite still missing on the third anniversary of his disappearance, the Archbishop had lost three of the key figures in his staff of the past nine years.

In January 1990 he departed on another round of overseas visits, to Ethiopia, Pakistan and Bangladesh. In Addis Ababa he preached to the Anglican congregation and addressed the sixth UN Economic Commission for Africa. At Bahir he visited Ura Kidanemihret, a sixteenth-century monastery on the Zeghi peninsula. In Eritrea he visited shelters for the homeless and food distribution centres. In Lahore he spoke at a college prize-giving and laid the foundation stone of a new church in Islamabad. He became briefly involved in a local squabble over the Church of Pakistan's ownership and management of vast tracts of the country. In Dacca he attended a Church of Bangladesh service in a Roman Catholic church and toured rural areas. He met President Mengistu, Benazir Bhutto and President Ershad.

He returned to London in time for the Osborne Report to be leaked and the contents widely publicised. The Episcopal Church in America was already tying itself in knots over the homosexuality issue. Bishop Spong of Newark had recently priested Robert Williams, an openly practising homosexual, in a ceremony which included Williams' male partner. The Bishop of the Rio Grande was up in arms. Elsewhere an article appeared claiming that Bishop Spong had violated Church teaching; the author was Kendall S. Harmon, adviser on human sexuality to the Bishop of South Carolina.

Six weeks later Bishop Spong too concluded that he had made a mistake. Robert Williams had helped him reach this conclusion.

At a Detroit symposium on 'gay' marriages, Williams had declared: 'Monogamy is as unnatural as celibacy. If people want to try, OK, but the fact is people are not monogamous. It is crazy to hold up this ideal and pretend it is what we're doing and we're not.'

Having disposed of the traditional concept of Christian marriage, Williams had then turned his attention to Mother Teresa of Calcutta. He told one questioner that she would be 'better off' if she had had sex. Williams was shortly afterwards invited to depart from his ministry.

In London, the Archbishop tried to defuse the row over the Osborne

Report by inviting a small group of bishops to spend at least two years compiling their own conservative corrective. He was due to retire at the latest by 2 October 1991, his seventieth birthday. This was one particularly difficult and dangerous issue he might legitimately feel entitled to bequeath to his successor.

The first session of the Synod of 1990 was dominated by questions of human sexuality and theological doctrine. A private member's bill was debated affirming a literal belief in the Virgin Birth and the Resurrection. The mover said she was speaking for 'the ordinary man and woman in the pew'. The Archbishop of York described as 'crass' the original wording of the motion.

Tony Higton thought that subscription to the wording of the motion should be made a prerequisite for the holding and retaining of office in the Church of England. He also believed that 'if there are a million homosexuals in the country today, that is partly the fault of the church'. He saw fellow-travellers everywhere: 'I am sad to see,' he wrote, 'that the *Church Times* has become a vehicle for homosexual propaganda.'

David Holloway, who had been in the forefront in the campaign to expel Canon Brindley, made a request for an emergency motion. He said a man of conservative beliefs should be the next tenant of Lambeth. Would the Synod report back at its next meeting in July, on how to ensure that the next Archbishop of Canterbury could 'affirm the Apostolic faith . . . including the uniqueness and finality of Jesus Christ, together with the virginal conception and empty tomb, and can uphold basic Christian sexual morality as taught in the Scriptures and the clear tradition of the Church?'

The Archbishop of Canterbury, a man of conservative beliefs if not in the primitive sense meant by Holloway, said he would consider the request.

He declined either to disown or endorse the Osborne Report. 'The advice we have received,' he said, 'is simply advice.'

He praised the work of the Church Urban Fund and illustrated the fallacy of the criticism that it did not support evangelism. It did not support evangelism, of course, in the sense implicit in the criticism.

Derek Pattinson, Secretary General of the General Synod, had announced his own forthcoming retirement. He looked forward to a brief period in South Africa for the Society for Promoting Christian Knowledge, founded in 1698 and the Church of England's oldest missionary organisation. After that, and in spite of the Archbishop of Canterbury's recent call for younger ordinands, he intended to train for the priesthood.

As 'Mr Synod', he had been synonymous for seventeen years with the permanent civil service of the Church of England. He was a devout man given to conspiratorially-phrased asides, and yet far less of a power broker than he was painted. Pattinson had emerged from the *Crockford's* disaster exonerated and unrepentant. 'It is not something I have always wanted to do,' he said, 'it has come out of doing this job. And the Gary Bennett affair did not weaken it, but rather made it stronger.'

Pattinson was not the only man of conservative Anglo-Catholic inclinations to announce his retirement that spring. The Bishop of London, Graham Leonard, was due to retire on grounds of age by May 1991. The Archbishop, to whom Leonard had been something of a trial, was determined not to allow Leonard's retirement to affect the preferment prospects of his own successor.

On Saturday 24 March 1990, he travelled from Lambeth to Canterbury with Lindy and Rebecca. The following day was the tenth anniversary of his enthronement. He chose this occasion to make his announcement. His own retirement, he said, would take place on 31 January 1991. This was only eight months earlier than the date set by his age; hardly 'early', as it was described in some newspapers.

The press gave far more coverage to his retirement than they had done to that of his predecessor. There was an urgent quality to the Runcie years which had caught the imagination of the public and the mind-managers of Fleet Street. They concocted their headlines, and warm tributes began to arrive from religious leaders all over the world.

The Archbishop posed for photographs, looking immensely relieved. 'It has been rather fashionable recently,' he said, 'to say "I am going in order that I can see more of my family." There is an element of truth in that. I am going to do the washing up.

'I want to unclutter my life,' he said, 'and live a peaceful existence. I will take up my interest in Greek history, and lecture again on

Hellenic cruises. And I hope to spend some time watching cricket.

'I might even still keep an eye on some twenty black pigs which I have looked after for a group of handicapped children.'

In the opinion of seventy-seven archdeacons canvassed, 'No comment' was the reply in twenty-four cases to the question of who could follow Robert Runcie as Archbishop of Canterbury. The Archbishop of York, John Habgood, came next with twenty-three votes. The bookmakers also contemplated the future.

Ron Pollard of Ladbroke's offered odds of 2 to 1 against Robin Eames, Archbishop of Armagh; 5 to 1 against Richard Harries of Oxford; 6 to 1 against David Sheppard of Liverpool, and 8 to 1 against both Mark Santer of Birmingham and John Taylor of St Albans. The Archbishop of York led the second group of runners in his book at 12 to 1, neck and neck at the same odds with the episcopal newcomer and dark horse, the Bishop of Bath and Wells, George Carey. William Westwood of Peterborough was 16 to 1; Colin James of Winchester, Michael Baughen of Chester, John Waine of Chelmsford, Keith Sutton of Lichfield and Michael Adie of Guildford could safely be included as also-rans. Asked how much money the firm could expect to take, Mr Pollard replied: 'A lot more than what we take on the Pope.'

The debate accelerated in the press. In the *Independent on Sunday*, Peter Stanford and Simon Lee wrote:

*'The first leaders of the Christian church were the Twelve Apostles. None of them would be likely to be made a bishop today. They did not go to the right universities; they would not have been impressive on television; they were ordinary men.'*

They went on:

*'If the matter were left entirely to the clergy and laity, then the favourite to succeed Dr Runcie would be one of the handful of the bishops from the evangelical wing of the Church of England. Why? Because some 80 per cent of church-goers come from that tradition – variously entitled low church, evangelical or Protestant – which dislikes the regalia and the pomp and circumstance of their high church, or Anglo-Catholic, fellows. Most able candidates in these evangelical quarters are the Bishop of Bath and Wells,*

*George Carey, and the Bishop of Chester, Michael Baughen. Neither,'* they concluded, *'stands any real hope of success . . .'*

The job was increasingly linked with the name of his close colleague, John Habgood of York. The Archbishop kept his own counsel about his preference. He was only one individual in a process dominated by the Crown Appointments Commission. He exerted no more pull over the appointment than Coggan had done over his election, or Ramsey had over Coggan's.

In his last Easter sermon at Canterbury, he too referred to the first disciples:

'I said at the beginning of this, my last Easter sermon as your Archbishop, that the Risen Christ offers a meaning to the world and the gift of a personal faith. In Him we find a new sense of security. That is not the same as safety. A believer in Jesus Christ is still exposed to hazards of conscience and doubts of mind. Yet faith brings a sense of being secure in the hands of One who loves us and cares for us. It is always those who have an inner sense of security who are most free to take risks.

'In Him we find a new sort of power . . .'

Three weeks later on 7 May, the Archbishop's former Chaplain John Witheridge wrote at length in *The Times*. His theme was the nature of the demands placed on one man by the office. His article was entitled: 'An impossible job for one man?'

He quoted the disbelieving reactions to their workloads of Arch-bishops down the years:

*'One measure of Dr Runcie's achievement as Archbishop of Canterbury has been his determination to devote himself to all aspects of his office. To do so he has had to enlarge his staff at Lambeth and Canterbury, and to delegate perhaps more than his predecessors.'*

Witheridge was writing from deeply-felt personal experience:

*'These may be sensible developments. But what is not excusable is the immense and unrelenting pressure of work that a man as scrupulously conscientious as Dr Runcie has felt himself bound to shoulder. Frankly, another man of*

*his age, but not blessed with his admirable constitution, might not have survived.*

*'Before the Church gets down to names it must look again, responsibly and practically, at the office. It must ask itself "What should we expect of the Archbishop of Canterbury?" Only then will it be qualified to ask "Who best can fulfil our expectations?" '*

In this valedictory atmosphere the Archbishop was still fulfilling engagements arranged months earlier. He had just returned from a visit to Washington and would shortly depart with Lindy for an extended tour of South America. Between the two, he appealed to the British government to open negotiations with Iran over the Western hostages in the Lebanon.

Two Americans had been released within eight days of each other. Waite's disappearance had been the nadir of his primacy. The thought of Waite's continued absence, and the prospect of his own departure from Lambeth without news of the man who had done so much to establish him there, was almost too much to bear.

The question of the Archbishop's successor assumed ever larger and more ludicrous proportions. The *Church Times* was surprised to be telephoned by Ladbroke's. 'According to William Hill, the Bishop of St Albans has gone down from 14 to 1 to 4 to 1,' they said. 'Is there something we should know?'

William Hill suspended their book after further heavy betting that Robert Runcie's successor at St Albans would also succeed him at Lambeth. The Bishop himself, John Taylor, issued a brief denial. 'I am not,' he said, 'a horse.'

Mrs Taylor was even more literal in her interpretation. 'He does not want the job,' she said, 'and I am not at all keen either.'

The Archbishop of York remained in first place in most people's books. Habgood's intellectual ability meant that he was routinely referred to even by the likes of Hugh Montefiore as 'the best brain on the bench'.

But others placed a lower premium on intellectual prowess. They wanted a man at Lambeth capable of uttering frequent black and white declarations of literal truth with the maximum of visible conviction.

They deplored what they saw as the refusal of the present Archbishop of Canterbury to do so. In the Archbishop of York, who had played such a strong role in supporting the Bishop of Durham, they saw a 'liberal' of an even greyer hue. 'ABH' became their rallying cry . . . 'Anyone but Habgood'.

Their cry was met with growing support in the form of the alliance of the Anglican Evangelical Assembly, the evangelical Church Society, the Anglo-Catholic Church Union, and the Agriculture Minister and General Synod member John Gummer.

Gummer had long disliked Habgood and the feeling was mutual. In a letter to the *Daily Telegraph* the Archbishop of York had described Gummer as 'foolish' in his attempts to 'enlist God' in his crusade against vegetarianism. He wondered if the Agriculture Minister's understanding of Scripture did not leave something to be desired.

But the alliance against Habgood was beginning to gain the upper hand. Intensive lobbying was taking place of the advisers and members of the Crown Appointments Commission under Viscount Caldecote. As the late Dr Bennett had pointed out, there were few Anglo-Catholic bishops left on the bench. The future, and the present, belonged to the Evangelical bishops, although there were still only a few of these and some had already made plain their dislike of the idea of going to Canterbury. As the lobbying and speculation grew, the dangers of this situation became plain. Of the few acceptable men, one had to be chosen, and chosen soon.


The *Church Times* was not only providing the bookmakers with an expert consultancy service for only thirty pence a week. Anyone could read the series of profiles entitled 'The Successors': the men likely to follow Robert Runcie to Canterbury.

Some of these were more likely than others. Some were unknown quantities. Three months after the Archbishop's retirement announcement, the 15 June issue carried a profile by Mrs Jill Dann of the Bishop of Bath and Wells, George Carey.

George Carey had been consecrated by the Archbishop only two and a half years earlier. He had been Principal of Trinity College, Bristol and a vicar in Durham. He was an Evangelical with Charismatic inclinations. He had had extensive pastoral and teaching experience.

He favoured the ordination of women to the priesthood and said as much. He was something of a missionary in his own country. He was physically tough and a workaholic, like the Archbishop of Canterbury. Like the Archbishop of Canterbury, he came from a comparatively humble background, only much more so.

Mrs Dann was now a well-known and powerful figure in the General Synod of the Church of England. She had seen off Canon Brindley and was firmly associated with the desire for a man capable of voicing definite ideas at Lambeth. She was more sophisticated than Tony Higton. Her opinions were less easily disputed (she was a barrister) and they carried more weight.

*In the world's eyes,' she wrote, 'he is very much a self-made man. George would, I think, prefer to be called a God-made man – and still in the making. To quote him: "I did not encounter living Christianity until I was 17 when, through my brother of 13, I went along to the local Anglican church, found the worship appallingly boring but the fellowship and preaching riveting. There I found Christ, or should I say, he found me." '*

Mrs Dann went on:

*'More of the man and his pilgrimage can be learned from the many books he has written – on Christology, the Church, ministry, humanity and God. Even today he taps out a daily 2,000 words on his Amstrad (between 6.15 and 7 in the morning!). He contributes to numerous journals. All this flows from the depth of his experience and understanding and draws on the breadth of his own reading and study of scripture. At the same time he keeps his feet in the real world . . . He actually knows about football . . . an effective leader in a whole series of Church of England establishments without ever becoming an establishment man . . . George Carey is a man of the late 20th century . . .'*

The following day it was announced that the Archbishop had been made a life peer in the Queen's Birthday Honours List. Derek Pattinson was knighted. Sir Derek was shortly to take up the position of curate to David Skeoch, at St Gabriel's, Pimlico. Skeoch had been Graham Leonard's Domestic Chaplain, both in Truro and London. The Bishop of London himself would ordain Pattinson deacon the following spring.

The Archbishop also had ordination on his mind. He opened the new wing of Ripon College, Cuddesdon. 'Ripon College, Cuddesdon,' he said, 'is a college with a great tradition from the past and a clear vision for the future. The Church needs clergy who are leaders inspired with the vision of God and the love of Christ, equipped to engage with the realities of their own day. That is what the college aims to produce.'

Cuddesdon still needed more than half the money required to pay for the new wing. The Archbishop suggested that people would be better off giving money to the appeal than betting on his successor.

Two women were priested in Belfast in the Church of Ireland, the first women priests in the United Kingdom. But as the law stood there could still be no legal Eucharist in the Church of England celebrated by a woman.

In the second session of that year's Synod at York, a strong defence of the Archbishop was made by Mark Santer. He pointed to the confusion over who was in charge of the Church: the Standing Committee of the General Synod, or the House of Bishops? The Synod, he said, showed 'mistrust and downright hostility towards the episcopate and the Archbishop of Canterbury'.

The Archbishop took a lighter line. He suggested the General Synod meet twice and not three times a year, and at the universities of Canterbury and York instead of Church House, Westminster. Church House, he said, should be used for more 'representative' gatherings.

Canterbury was nearer to Europe than York, he said; and futhermore it was warmer. 'I know this case will be demolished,' he concluded, 'but I would like it to go on record that in this debate I made it, because one day it will surely happen, and I will be credited.'

The Synod concluded with tributes by the Archbishop and others to Sir Derek Pattinson. The official speeches were interrupted by an *ad hoc* choir led by Canon Bruce Grainer. They sang a variant of the song from *The Pirates of Penzance*, each verse ending with the words: 'He was the very model of a Secretary General.'

\*

At Lambeth Palace the Archbishop hosted the annual dinner of the Nikaean Club, founded in 1925 on the 1600th anniversary of the Council of Nikaea, which existed to offer hospitality on his behalf to Christians from other Churches.

Drinks were served in the State Drawing Room. The Archbishop and Lindy circulated among the one hundred and fifty people present. As ever a small notice asked guests not to place objects on 'Mrs Runcie's precious piano'.

Dinner was served in the Guard Room, hung with the portraits of his predecessors. The Secretary of the Club made a speech and presented him with a Georgian skewer. The Archbishop brandished this as if it might have been of more use earlier in his primacy. Lindy was presented with a plant, which the Secretary claimed to have been looking after and which she claimed was dead.

The Archbishop replied in a characteristic speech in which moments of high seriousness were interspersed with remarks and anecdotes in his usual vein.

'My wife has actually been to Nikaea,' he said, 'which is more than most of you lot have done.'

There was some disagreement between husband and wife, however, about whether or not she had attended a Nikaean Dinner before. Like most of their disagreements, it was distinctly audible. The Archbishop ended it with an equally audible aside.

'Never mind,' he told her, and the entire audience, 'we won't argue now.'

He welcomed the guest speaker from Wales with a 'man from everywhere' story.

He was being driven back from Wales suffering from an eye infection which he could eventually bear no longer. He asked his driver to stop in Carmarthen.

He got out of the car and went into a chemist.

'You're Dr Runcie, then?' said the woman behind the counter.

The Archbishop had confirmed that he was.

'I'll just telephone my husband, then,' she said, 'and the vicar.'

The Archbishop had eventually left with the largest bottle of Optrex in Carmarthen. Two weeks later he bumped into the Speaker of the House of Commons in the Palace of Westminster.

George Thomas was a Welshman from Tonypandy.

'I hear you had a bit of trouble in Carmarthen, Archbishop,' were his opening words.'

'Now this illustrates three things about the Welsh,' the Archbishop told his audience. 'One, their generosity of spirit; two, their friendliness, and three, their excellent communications.'

The Welsh guest spoke after him, an unenviable task.

Afterwards, Lindy sold items of Wedgwood china at the top of the main staircase in aid of the Lambeth Fund. A pair of green wellington boots stood at the bottom of the steps. The guests, fortified by fine wines, summer pudding, loin of lamb and vichyssoise, walked in the floodlit gardens before departing into the night.


He was in Cardiff ten days later, addressing the eighth conference of the Anglican Consultative Council; the last time he would do so. It was here that he heard the news of who was to be his successor.

He immediately issued a statement.

*'George Carey is a teacher and theologian,'* he said, *'particularly qualified to lead the Church in a decade of evangelism. He commands respect and affection among us all in the House of Bishops.'*

Privately, like many others, he was surprised. He said he welcomed 'this imaginative appointment'.

Others were more explicit in their reactions. Donald Reeves was a Cuddesdon man from the Runcie years and Vicar of St James's, Piccadilly. 'The idea that we are now into something quite different which will save the Church of England from collapse is rubbish,' he said. 'The Archbishop is a very marginal figure. What goes on in parishes is what counts. I shall be pleased if he is as good as Dr Runcie has been.'

Another liberal theologian said of Carey: 'Catholic spirituality, green issues, charismatic movement, a bit of this and a bit of that. He's beginning to sound like Runcie already.'

The Lesbian and Gay Christian Movement, in the form of Richard Kirker, was dismayed at the appointment. Bishop Carey, he said, was 'plainly hostile' to homosexuals; he was 'homophobic'. Kirker called for an early meeting.

Dr Carey's own Suffragan Bishop of Taunton was Nigel McCulloch, another Cuddesdon man of the Runcie era who had been one of Lindy's waiters and washers-up. He said the appointment was 'visionary'.

The Cost of Conscience movement opposed the ordination of women and did not entirely like what it saw. 'We might have got an archbishop who would say: "It depends what you mean by resurrection", said a spokesman. 'From that point of view it's a plus.'

The Church Society was fundamentally gloomy. 'We feel that Dr Carey represents the liberal wing of the Evangelicals,' said its director, 'he is not at all the person we hoped would appear. There are a number of things, especially his championing of ARCIC. We feel that the clear leadership we had hoped for will not be forthcoming.'

Bishop Carey himself wisely departed on a family holiday, and then on a diocesan trip to the Holy Land. He and his party stayed in Bethlehem, now the symbol of the bitter conflict between Jew and Moslem. As the present Archbishop had found, it was a fitting place of reflection for an Archbishop of Canterbury.

Launcelot Fleming, Robert Runcie's friend and predecessor at Trinity Hall, Cambridge, died at the age of eighty-three. The Archbishop's own wedding had been conducted by Fleming, but his voice was giving him increasing trouble and there was the likelihood of surgery. He was unable to attend Fleming's memorial service. Instead of a formal address, he contributed a brief obituary:

*'When I was a Tutor at Trinity Hall,'* he wrote, *'we kept among admission candidates a category known as Launcelot's lambs. These were young people he had met on railway trains or football touchlines or playing squash. We knew they would be admirable characters, for Launcelot was a discerning man. Our task was to discover whether they also had the ability to pass examinations.'*

The number and style of the tributes to him that continued to come in gave a ghostly flavour to his last months at Lambeth. The planning was underway for the return to St Albans, and the house reputedly filled with Lindy's pianos. The Archbishop liked to paint his future self as a typical retired figure, tottering out from under his wife's feet and along to the shops to fetch the newspapers.

In reality there would also be a large number of his books in their new, compact premises. He had been forced ruthlessly to prune his library. There were other works at Lambeth he was happy to leave behind.

These included three hundred volumes of the mental health of King George III, ruler of England from 1760 to 1820. The King suffered from mental illness induced by porphyria, and three successive Archbishops, Frederick Cornwallis, John Moore and Charles Manners-Sutton had been afflicted with daily bulletins as was their historic right.'

The three men had also stamped their own character on the archiepiscopate. Cornwallis was a man of liberal views whose wife's lively character brought her vilification in the press. Moore was a self-made man who had been tutor to the son of the Duke of Marlborough. Manners-Sutton was a High Churchman who presided over a revival in the Church of England after a period of excessive dominance by the Evangelicals.

Robert Runcie, their successor, had not committed himself to any significant retirement role beyond that of honorary assistant bishop in the diocese of St Albans where he had once been Bishop. Invited to assist at the confirmation of James' step-daughter, he said he would rather be one of the congregation. He had, however, committed himself to a further cruise lecture. This was a refreshing prospect.

But what still gave his last few months a sense of urgency was the fate of Terry Waite. With the Archbishop's retirement, Waite would not officially cease to be Secretary for Anglican Affairs, but his connection would inevitably be diminished with Lambeth. The new Archbishop had neither the same relationship nor the same sense of personal responsibility for him. Waite was still missing, presumed a prisoner; now the Archbishop was about to be set free.

He continued to broadcast with Waite in mind on every available frequency. He stressed the need for calm in his advice to Anglicans trapped by the Iraqi invasion of Kuwait and the increased tension in the Arabian Gulf. He condemned Israeli killings in Jerusalem of Arab civilians. He welcomed the release of Brian Keenan after over four years of captivity in the Lebanon. Keenan believed he had heard

Waite, ill but alive; what he said in private helped revive the Archbishop's own fading optimism. The candle still burned at Lambeth.

The Archbishops' Commission on Rural Areas, *Faith In the Countryside*, was published to mixed reviews. He attended the Churches Together in England inaugural service in Southwark Roman Catholic Cathedral, at which John Habgood gave the address. The Archbishop was losing his voice. He preached at the service to mark the 50th anniversary of the Battle of Britain in St Paul's Cathedral. Ten days later he travelled again to South Korea on the last major overseas visit of his primacy. This was to celebrate the centenary of the Anglican Church there; he crossed the Imjin River into the demilitarised zone; he preached at a memorial High Mass in the Olympic gymnasium in Seoul and Lindy gave a charity piano recital at the Sejong Cultural Centre.

In Turkey, in the hills above Ephesus, another familiar figure was on the third day of his latest Swan Hellenic lecture cruise.

'As the sun sets over the Aegean,' he intoned, 'let us listen to the susurration of the leaves, one of the healing properties of ancient holy places.'

The Reverend Professor Richard Chartres was clearly enjoying himself.


On 15 October 1990, the Archbishop hosted a reunion of the Third Battalion Scots Guards at Lambeth. Sir Hector Laing, Lord Whitelaw, Lord Cathcart and Peter Balfour were among the many in attendance. The men who had first rejected him and then accepted him as 'Killer Runcie' had been a quiet support network throughout the years. Five days later he went into hospital for an operation on his vocal cords. For a while he was unable to speak above a whisper.

In the last session of the Synod that year, he welcomed the Queen as the only member of the platform who had survived in the same role from the first inauguration twenty years ago. He described to her the new Synod, whose House of Clergy now contained twenty-five women deacons, fourteen black members and many members under sixty. 'When you find Synod members looking younger all the time,' he added, 'you know retirement beckons.'

The Queen paid tribute to his eleven years in office; to his work in the Anglican Communion; to *Faith In the City*; to *Faith In the Countryside*; and to the Church Urban Fund. 'I am sure,' she said, 'that Synod in the next five years will display that unity, even in diversity, which is one of the Church's most enduring characteristics.'

In his presidential address he spoke on the prospect of war in the Gulf, and on the Church of England in the Decade of Evangelism. This was a reiteration of all he believed, as a priest, a principal, a bishop, and an archbishop; and as an Anglican.

'We are equipped to face the complexity of our situation,' he said, 'because we are not a church of hard edges. In our history, God has worked to keep our borders open. Confronted by the wistful, the half-believing and the seeking, we know what it is to minister to those who relate to the faith of Christ in unexpected ways . . .

'We can speak only because God himself has first spoken. We do not have to sell his gospel, but welcome others to share it. St Paul reminded the Romans, "Welcome one another, therefore, as Christ has welcomed you, for the glory of God" (Romans 15.7). That is a little summary of the heart of Christian doctrine and ethics. Unless the good news that we preach in a decade of evangelism is founded upon God's welcome for people who are not worthy, there is little point in sorting out problems about authority, giving a moral lead to the nation, or even having a decade of evangelism at all.'

They gave him a standing ovation and he went on his way. He would go of his own accord, unlike the Prime Minister, Margaret Thatcher, who resigned a week later.

The imminence of retirement put a new spring in his step. He sent his last message to the Anglican Communion. He preached his last Christmas sermon from Canterbury. He conferred his last honorary degrees. He consecrated his last new bishops in St Paul's Cathedral. He presided over his last Synod. On 31 January 1991, he retired as 102nd Archbishop of Canterbury. He returned to the house in St Albans. Apart from the things he wanted to leave behind, the one thing he most wanted to take with him had to remain at Lambeth. A single candle burned night and day in the Crypt of the Palace. Eleven days earlier, the fourth anniversary of the disappearance of Terry Waite had passed.

*

The fortunes of the Archbishops of Canterbury have been long and sometimes lethally linked to the Establishment of the Church of England.

By comparison with Archbishop Cranmer, who walked in the Crypt with Anne Boleyn and was burned at the stake; with Archbishop Laud, who did much to restore Lambeth Palace but died on the scaffold; and with Archbishop Sancroft, who was exiled to the country, Robert Runcie had escaped lightly. But in modern times these fortunes were never more mixed, than in the case of the 102nd Archbishop of Canterbury and Primate of All England.

The story of the life and times of Robert Runcie was the story of seventy years compressed into a single decade. Those seventy years were the span of his life, and that of the country of which he was called to be spiritual leader. The 1980s were remarkable years for Runcie, for the Church of England, and for the society in which that Church existed. The aberration of the Falklands War, the long duel between Westminster and Lambeth, the pronouncements of the Bishop of Durham, the victories and vicissitudes of Terry Waite, the suicide of Gareth Bennett, the contortions of his critics and the attacks on his family, brought the Archbishop of Canterbury and the Church of England to the forefront of public awareness as never before in living memory.

He extended the range of the archiepiscopate in a way that his successor would find difficult if not impossible to follow. His ability to communicate was conspicuous in his many journeys in the Anglican Communion. His liberalism was founded in scholarship and not in ignorance: '*Solemnly intoning "The Bible Says" or "The Church teaches" is no substitute for hard thinking*,' he had written twenty-five years earlier in his Cuddesdon newsletter. His lightness of touch was rooted in a faith deep enough to survive and flourish in the intervening and increasingly demanding years.

The choice of his successor would perhaps provide less fertile ground for the biographer. But the issues raised in the extraordinary Runcie decade would not go away. Questions of faith and spiritual values transformed nations and societies across the world in the 1980s. They underpinned popular movements and even revolutions in the Soviet Union, the Middle East, Eastern Europe, South America and Southern Africa. Even in Europe and the West, a reaction began to be felt to environmental issues and the Pharisaical side of government. But, in Britain, the Church of England remained to many an introverted and eccentric institution, obsessed with its own salvation rather than that of the society it was expected to serve and lead.

To those who believed the Anglican Communion was a chimera, Runcie paid it too much attention at the expense of the Church of England. To those in the Anglican Communion who believed that the only future for the Church of England lay as one of many members, he was hamstrung by the introverted and parochial behaviour of his more conservative diocesans.

To those who wanted closer relations with Rome, he condoned too much freethinking in his diocesans and paid too little attention to the Pope. To those who saw the salvation of the Church of England in Evangelical absolutism, he also condoned too much freethinking in his diocesans but paid too much attention to the Pope. To those who feared too much Papal authority, he paid too much attention to the Pope. To many he paid too little attention to the ordination of a great many patient and devout women.

To all these believers and more, he paid a great deal of attention, and, during the eleven years of his leadership, a high personal price.

*'In our Church in our time,'* wrote David Edwards the Church historian and his former chaplain at Westcott, *'a leader has greatness thrust upon him by the Church which values and loves him as a father-in-God. By doing an almost impossible job as well as any of the modern Archbishops, Robert Runcie has been made great.'*

The choice of the evangelical George Carey as his successor was symbolic of the cyclical priorities of the Church of England. Apart from down-grading the importance of relations with Rome, with a possible fourteen years at Lambeth, his successor would be likely to attend the next Lambeth Conference. He would also be likely only to be one of many overseas visitors. Given the personality of Robert Runcie, and the character of his primacy, in the difficult times to come there would be many who would look back on the Runcie years as a golden era.

*

To his personal staff, and those who knew him and therefore knew his worth, Robert Runcie could be a source of both concern and dismay. He was a man who said 'Yes' too readily to too many relatively minor obligations, and 'Yes' or 'No' too slowly in matters of greater ecclesiastical importance. There was an irony in his losing his voice in his last months at Lambeth. After leaving Lambeth, he would slowly but surely come to terms with the fact that he no longer had to say 'Yes' to so many obligations. He no longer had to consider so many issues on behalf of the Church that he lost his own voice in the process. He would find his voice again.

He had a deep relationship with the cyclical duties and devotions of the Church of England: to Christmas Day; to Easter; to his weekends at Canterbury. He had a strong devotion to the daily service at Lambeth; and to the convening of the Cell; to the guardsmanlike prayer life he had led, from Matins to Compline, since Westcott.

He would rediscover the priest, the ordinand, in himself. This was the figure who had sustained him through the Principalship of Cuddesdon, the Bishopric of St Albans, and the Archbishopric of Canterbury. Beneath the uncertainty, the tendency to go this way and that, there was, deep down, a creativity with which he had sometimes lost touch.

He had acknowledged the importance of this creativity in his address at the service of thanksgiving for the restoration of Lambeth Chapel.

'There is a design here to convey to others,' he had said, 'even to the casual visitor. The meaning of a place where that most hidden movement of all movements, the movement of the human heart towards God, has been made day in and day out, year in and year out; where the Eucharist has been celebrated and the Offices said. The decoration of the ceiling is not primarily to be studied as a series of pictures. It is part of the creation of an atmosphere; but it does disclose an inner mystery.'

'The thing I miss most,' he said in the last months of his primacy, 'is having enough time to pray.'

In his obituary of Launcelot Fleming, he had written a rough draft of his own memorial:

*His quiet integrity and understated wisdom were of a peculiarly English kind, though he was the first to call himself a Scot. His mixture of holiness and humanity made him one of the lights of the Church of England in our day.'*

But, to the believer, there was always the prospect of another life beyond the biographer's final full stop.

*January 1991*

# Acknowledgements

All the interpretations and opinions expressed in this biography are the responsibility of the author.

The author would nonetheless like to thank the Archbishop of Canterbury for his tolerance and trust during the research and writing of this book.

The author would also like to thank:

Andrew Acland; Jim Alldred; The Reverend John Andrew; The Anglican Consultative Council; Bishop Simon Barrington-Ward; The Reverend Anthony Bird; George Brock; The Reverend David Burgess; Audrey and Leslie Carey; The Church of England Record Centre; The *Church Times*, especially Yolande Clarke, Glyn Paflin, Betty Saunders and Fania Stoney; Provost Nicholas Coulton; Mary Cryer; Bishop Hassan Dehqani-Tafti; The Episcopal Church Centre in New York; Canon John Garton; Bishop Richard Hare; Rosemary Hartill; Canon Christopher Hill; Bishop Ross Hook; Canon Eric James; The Reverend David Johnson; Eve Keatley; Bishop Edward Knapp-Fisher; Sir Hector Laing; Vickie Macnair; Bishop Nigel McCulloch; Canon Tony Meakin; Bishop Hugh Montefiore; Canon Michael Moore; Bishop Simon Phipps; Jonathan Prichard; Mary Jean Pritchard; James Runcie; Charles Saumarez-Smith; Canon Jeremy Saville; The Reverend Inez Scott; Bishop Michael Scott-Joynt; Dasha Shenkman; Dean John Simpson; Christopher Sinclair-Stevenson; Edda Tasiemka; Bishop Jim Thompson; Olivia Timbs; Bishop Tony Tremlett; Bishop Peter Walker; Dean Alan Webster; The Reverend Doctor Lionel Wickham; The Reverend John Witheridge; Noel Wylie.

I am indebted to the following books:

*One Light For One World*; *The Unity We Seek*; and *Authority in Crisis?* by Robert Runcie; *Runcie: the Making of an Archbishop* by Margaret Duggan; *To the Church of England* by Gareth Bennett; *In Perspective* by Rosemary

Hartill; *Honest to God* by John Robinson; *Lambeth Palace* by Mary Cryer; *The Unquiet Suitcase* by Gerald Priestland; *Hostage Bound, Hostage Free* by Ben and Carol Weir; *Church at the Crossroads: Lambeth '88* by Michael Marshall; *A Life of Bishop John A.T. Robinson* by Eric James; *Michael Ramsey: A Life* by Owen Chadwick; *Michael Ramsey: A Portrait* by Michael De-la-Noye; *Crockford's* Clerical Directory; *Graham Leonard: Bishop of London* by John S. Peart-Binns; *Pity the Nation* by Robert Fisk.

I am also indebted to *The Director* magazine; to Times Newspapers Ltd. for permission to quote from articles by Clifford Longley and Bernard Levin; and to the following picture sources:

P.1 *Church Times* / Mike Waterman; *Church Times* / The Press Agency (Yorkshire) Ltd.

P.2 *Church Times* / PA; © *Daily Telegraph plc* / Ewan Macnaughton Associates; Times Newspapers Ltd.

P3. *Church Times* / PA.

P.4 *Yorkshire Post*; *Church Times* / John Bristow; Times Newspapers Ltd. / Popperphoto.

P.5 Times Newspapers Ltd. and AP.

P.6 Times Newspapers Ltd.; Colin Davey / Camera Press; *Church Times* / Universal Pictorial Press.

P.7 John Manning / Times Newspapers Ltd.; *Church Times* / PA.

P.8 Martin Argles / The *Guardian*; Roger Taylor.

# Index

NOTE: Ranks, titles and appointments are generally the latest mentioned in the text

*Historic Episcopate in the Fullness of the Church*, *see* Carey, Kenneth

Hodgekinson, Thomas, 248

Hollerton (Guardsman tank gunner), 15–16

Holloway, David, 208, 287, 314, 324

*Homosexual Relations* (report), 113, 137

homosexuals and homsexuality: ordination of, 105; and morality, 278–80, 294; Brindley and, 314; Osborne Report on, 321–3; in USA, 323

*Honest to God Debate*, 58, 64

Hong Kong, 147

Hook, Ross, Bishop of Bradford: as RR's Chief of Staff, 134–5, 139, 146, 179, 271; and Dehqani-Tafti, 138; and Prince of Wales' visit, 140; military experience, 155; and RR's overwork, 163; retires, 204; and press attacks on Runcies, 215

Hook, Ruth, 135, 204

Houldcroft, Helena-Rose, 236

Houlden, Leslie, 71

Howard, (Dame) Christian, 112, 198

Howe, Sir Geoffrey, 115–16, 221

Howe, Bishop John, 107

Howes, Graham, 322

Hudson, Noel Baring, Bishop of Newcastle, 26–9, 32

Hume, Cardinal Basil, Archbishop of Westminster: welcomes RR's election to Primacy, 112; at RR's enthronement, 117; at royal wedding, 141; and Pope's visit, 152; and Falklands service, 156–7; visits Pope in Assisi, 247; on loss of truth, 267; calls for Roman Catholic communion with others, 276

Hungary, 277

Hungerford, 277

*Independent on Sunday*, 326

India, 232, 234

Inglis, Angus, 6, 8, 18, 20, 24, 28, 43

Inglis, Kathleen (*née* Runcie; RR's sister): childhood, 3–4; influence on RR, 4–6, 8, 311; engagement and marriage, 6; during war, 8; and RR's ordination, 18; relations with RR, 24, 28; at RR's wedding, 43; and RR's career, 48; death, 310–11

Iran: hostages in, 131, 135–8; arms for hostages deal with USA, 217–18, 239–41, 251–2; Contra affair, 253–4, 320; Lyttle visits, 297; *see also* Dehqani-Tafti, Hassan Barnabe

Iraq, 217–18

Ireland, 140, 291

Islamic Jihad organisation, 217, 251–2, 255, 257–9

Istanbul, 95–6, 105–6

JACKSON, Jill, 79

Jacobsen, David, 212, 252, 254, 256

James, Clive, 142

James, Colin, Bishop of Winchester, 326

James, Eric: at Cambridge, 42; at St Albans, 82–3, 110; at St Albans centenary celebrations, 96; and RR's candidacy for Canterbury, 110–11, 118–19; and Falklands service, 157; and John Robinson, 173; forms Commission on Urban Priority Areas, 173, 232

James, Graham, 276, 277, 294, 313

Jamieson, Penelope, Bishop of Dunedin, 322

Jane, Sister, 2, 316

Janet, Mother, 301, 316

Japan, 270

Jean-Claude, Brother, 316

Jenco, Father Martin, 212, 240–1, 254, 275

Jenkins, Brian, 275

Jenkins, David, Bishop of Durham: teaches at Cuddesdon, 51;